*Essentials of*

**GREEK AND ROMAN**

CLASSICS

*A Guide to the Humanities*

*Essentials of*

# GREEK AND ROMAN

# CLASSICS

*A Guide to the Humanities*

BY

## MEYER REINHOLD, Ph.D.

*Professor of Classical Studies,*
*Boston University*
*Professor Emeritus of Classical Studies,*
*University of Missouri, Columbia*

## REVISED

*Barron's Educational Series, Inc.*

NEW YORK • LONDON • TORONTO • SYDNEY

# PREFACE

◙

The Greek and Roman Classics in translation are today explored and discussed by more students and adults in a single year than studied them in the original languages during the entire nineteenth century combined. This fact constitutes a virtual renascence of the Classics; and this is due to their relevance to the human condition and their ability to stimulate fundamental thinking on basic problems and values. The greatest masterpieces of Greece and Rome are an established part of the curriculum of many American colleges, whether they are read in "Great Books", "Humanities", "Classical Civilization", or "Comparative Literature" courses.

The two foremost peoples of the ancient world, who, together with the Hebrews, have influenced us most, contributed an imposing share to the great literary Classics of the Western World. In the one semester which is usually allotted to the Greek and Roman Classics in translation it is feasible to explore only a selected number of works. No excuse need be made for not including in this companion to the Classics works interesting principally for their literary form and style or for their subsequent influence on later literatures, or which duplicate modes of thinking and behavior encountered in earlier writings. Thus such works as the orations of Demosthenes and Cicero, Cicero's popularizations of Greek philosophy, the comedies of Menander, Plautus and Terence, Livy's history of Rome, for example, have been omitted. It should be emphasized that this guide is not intended for courses in the histories of Greek and Roman literature which interest those who specialize in the field.

The aim of this book has been to analyze masterpieces of thought and literary art which bear a close relation to basic humanistic values, and to relate them to the concrete historical and cultural environments from which they emerged. Each major period is therefore introduced by a concise survey of its most significant historical and cultural developments. Detailed analyses have been made in most cases of complete works, in some of typical parts only.

The pervasive use by Greek and Roman writers of plots taken from, and references to, Classical mythology requires of the reader some acquaintance with this subject. The appendix on Mythology is not intended as a survey of the entire field — a vast one — but provides essential mythological information in summary form for understanding works analyzed in this volume. Similarly the Glossary contains brief explanations of all important names and terms that appear in this book. The bibliographical appendix is designed to guide students in further study of specific authors and Greek and Roman culture.

Brooklyn, N. Y.                                    MEYER REINHOLD
January, 1971

# CONTENTS

# CONTENTS

## CHAPTER ONE

# INTRODUCTION TO EARLY GREECE

◻

## AEGEAN AREA

I.  Hellas, principal center of Greek civilization, a peninsula in S.E. Europe, about 45,000 sq. miles in area (approximately the size of Maine).

A.  Mountain ranges and peaks cover about 80% of Hellas. The mountains of Hellas afforded natural protection against invasion, but at the same time impeded travel and communication by land. Mt. Olympus (ca. 10,000 ft.), in N.E. Thessaly, is the highest peak; in the center of Hellas stands Mt. Parnassus (ca. 8,000 ft.), another important peak.

B.  Almost all of the numerous valleys and plains of Greece open out on the eastern side. "Greece faces east."

C.  Rivers of Hellas are non-navigable, acting as obstacles to communication.

D.  Important regions of Hellas.
   1.  Thessaly, Northern Hellas
   2.  Phocis, Central Hellas (principal city, Delphi)
   3.  Boeotia, S.E. of Phocis (principal city, Thebes)
   4.  Attica, S.E. of Boeotia (principal city, Athens)
   5.  Isthmus of Corinth, west of Attica, connecting Central Hellas with the Peloponnesus to the south (principal city, Corinth)
   6.  Peloponnesus, Southern Hellas, shaped like a maple leaf or hand. Most important subdivision, Lacedaemonia (Laconia), with its principal city of Sparta. Other important cities of

Peloponnesus: Mycenae, in the northeast; Olympia, in the west central part.

E. The sea is a dominant aspect of Greek life. The coastline, especially on the eastern seaboard, possesses numerous bays, gulfs, inlets, promontories. The most important seas travelled by the Greeks were the Aegean, between Hellas and Asia Minor, the Euxine (Black Sea), and the Mediterranean.

II. The Cyclades Islands, a complex of the numerous islands (ca. 500) in the Aegean Sea, served as a natural bridge of stepping-stones to the Asiatic continent.

III. Crete, large island south of the Cyclades, with its principal early city of Cnossus in the north central part. Cradle of European culture, the stepping-stone to Egypt.

IV. Coast of Asia Minor (Anatolia).

A. Same intricate coastline as Eastern Hellas.

B. Regions: Aeolis, northern coast; Ionia, central; Doris, southwestern.

C. Hellespont (Dardanelles), important strategic strait, separating Europe from Asia, leading northeast from the Aegean, along the northeastern coast of Asia Minor. Ilium (Troy) was ca. 3 miles from the mouth of the Hellespont.

## EFFECTS OF GEOGRAPHY

I. Smallness of states, evolving into the numerous city-states of the Greek world.

II. Disunity, isolationism, fierce local patriotism, mutual jealousy, constant warfare.

III. Cultural variety.

IV. Ease of communication by sea with the East, making possible the absorption of the cultural achievements of the Orient.

V. Crete, Aegean islands, and Hellas the first parts of Europe to be civilized.

## AEGEAN CIVILIZATION (ca. 3000-1100 B.C.)

I. Pre-Hellenic Bronze Age culture of the Aegean area. Population of Mediterranean stock. The existence of this civilization is suggested in Greek legends, but was definitely proved by the pioneering archaeological discoveries, beginning in 1870, of Heinrich Schliemann, who excavated Mycenae, Tiryns, and Troy, and of Sir Arthur Evans at Cnossus in Crete.

II. Cretan-Minoan Supremacy (acme ca. 1800-1400 B.C.). Crete, at a strategic spot almost equidistant from three continents, was the first maritime power in the world, and controlled a large part of the Aegean complex. It was the forerunner of Greece, possessing the first important European art. Its power was destroyed and its capital, with the famous palace of "Minos," sacked probably by invaders from the North.

III. Migrations of Peoples (ca. 2000-1000 B.C.). Gradual infiltration into the Aegean area of northerners, coming probably from Central Europe, speaking an Indo-European language. (Principal branches of Indo-European: Sanskrit, Armenian, Albanian, Greek, Latin, Celtic, Persian, Germanic, Slavic.) They intermingled with the earlier inhabitants, adopted their culture, and ultimately became dominant.

IV. Mycenaean Supremacy (acme ca. 1400-1100 B.C.). Aegean culture modified by the northern invaders. Petty kingdoms in a loose Achaean confederacy, the most powerful overlord at Mycenae in the Peloponnesus, supplanted the Cretan Empire. Rulers lived in heavily-walled fortress palaces on low hills, the nuclei of the later Greek city-states. The latter part of this period known in Greek tradition as the "Heroic Age." Waves of migrations spread eastward across the Hellespont and the Aegean Sea to the coast of Asia Minor, the Achaean-Aeolians occupying the N.W. seaboard, the Ionians the central coast, and ultimately the Dorians the S.W. part. One incident in this movement was the siege and destruction of Troy in the 12th Cent. B.C. by Achaean invaders.

V. Dorian Invasion (ca. 1100-1000 B.C.). In the 13th and 12th Cents. B.C. major upheavals, accompanied by great wars and population shifts, occurred. The climax was the violent, destructive invasion of the last of the northern migrants, the Dorians. Equipped with superior weapons made of iron, they delivered the death blow to the Aegean Civilization.

## GREEK PEOPLE (HELLENES) AND LANGUAGE

I.  Linguistic study, archaeology, and anthropology have proved that the Hellenes of classical times were a mixed people, composed of the following elements:

A.  Primitive inhabitants, the so-called "Pelasgians" (Helladics)

B.  Aegeo-Cretans of Mediterranean stock

C.  Northern Indo-Europeans

II.  Principal divisions of Hellenes in classical times were:

A.  Ionians

B.  Aeolians

C.  Dorians

III.  The Hellenes spoke different dialects of a hybrid language, possessing an Indo-European substratum and elements derived from pre-Hellenic languages. The Greek language was an exceptionally rich medium of expression, melodious, flexible, with many vowel sounds, no harsh gutturals, and an enormous vocabulary. The principal dialects were Aeolic, the rugged Doric, the soft and graceful Ionic, and its offshoot Attic, which added energy and dignity to Ionic.

## BEGINNINGS OF HELLENIC CIVILIZATION
## (1000-750 B.C.)

The coming of the Dorians ushered in the Iron Age. At the same time, the havoc created by the upheavals of the 11th Cent. B.C. brought about a Dark Age, characterized by sharp cultural decline, depopulation, and highly unstable political, economic, and social conditions. With the gradual subsiding of the great wars of settlement and the migratory movements there emerged slowly the main elements of a new, Hellenic culture. Though some form of writing had been in use in the Aegean for many centuries, between 1000 and 800 B.C. the Greeks acquired from the North Semitic Phoenicians a very important new writing tool, an alphabetical form of writing, to which they added vowel sounds, and which they were amongst the first to employ in producing works of literature.

## LATE MYCENAEAN-EARLY HELLENIC SOCIETY (ca. 13th-8th Cents. B.C.)

I.  Social organization in transition from tribal institutions, based on kinship ties of a large group acknowledging a common ancestor and common chieftain, and on collective ownership of clan property, to small family unit and private property.

II.  Economic life based on agriculture, stock-breeding, plunder, and piracy. Labor performed by property owners themselves, hired men, and slaves. Slavery mostly of mild domestic variety; slaves few, mostly female war captives.

III.  Ruling class of nobles, comparable to feudal barons. Their principal activities were war, agriculture, grazing, hunting, attending banquets at which minstrels entertained. Hospitality was traditional and generous.

IV.  Government—small kingdoms.

A.  King (Basileus) hereditary ruler, military leader, judge, possessing also religious duties; unlike Oriental monarchs, his power was limited. He was *primus inter pares,* first among equals.

B.  Council (Boule) of chiefs; aristocratic elders who advised king.

C.  Assembly (Agora) of fighting freemen; vote yes or no on matters presented to them, especially war and peace; no right of debate. (Present here are the germs of the future political institutions of the Western world—limited power of executive, division of powers, popular vote, consent of the governed).

V.  Family life, of patriarchal type, with close family ties. Women of higher class possessed more respected position and greater freedom than those of similar status in classical times.

**5**

## CHAPTER TWO

# HOMER

◙

## HOMER (ca. 900-800 B.C.)

I.   Western literature may be said to begin with Homer. There are no remains of earlier literature, though there undoubtedly was a mass of "floating" literature long before him, especially epic lays composed and handed down orally by court minstrels.

II.   Homer lived on the Ionian coast of Asia Minor, the birthplace of literature, most likely in Smyrna or Chios, a generation or two after the reigns of the biblical kings David and Solomon. There is a persistent tradition in antiquity that Homer was blind.

III.   Author of the epic poems *Iliad* and *Odyssey,* the world's greatest epics.

## HOMERIC QUESTION

I.   In antiquity it was universally accepted that the *Iliad* and the *Odyssey* were written by Homer, with the exception of some later Greek critics at Alexandria who believed that another author wrote the *Odyssey.*

II.   At the time of the French Revolution the interest in folk poetry, and the idealization of primitive society led to the belief that early epics were not the work of single geniuses but communal creations of a people. The Homeric Question was launched by F. A. Wolf in 1795, with his *Prolegomena ad Homerum* (Introduction to Homer). In the 19th Cent. Wolf and his successors were dominant. Bringing to bear on the two epics the pulverization method of German Higher Criticism, noting the time interval (ca. 300 years) between Homer and the Trojan War, observing inconsistencies and contradictions in tne stories, differences in customs, style, religion, and language in various parts of the two epics, these scholars argued variously that the *Iliad* and *Odyssey* were written by different authors, that the poems consisted of earlier independent poems gathered and unified by a later poet or by a commission of scholars, or that each poem had an original genuine Homeric nucleus to which later additions were made.

III.  Modern archaeology, linguistic study, and literary criticism have convinced most scholars that the *Iliad* and the *Odyssey* are the work of a single consummate genius, who employed a traditional style, language and meter, and borrowed from a common pool of traditional material.  There are post-Homeric interpolations in the poems, but essentially the civilization presented, the style, plot construction, and character treatment show unity.  "Everything fits into the theory of a single Homer: the civilization, the language, the gods, the outlines, the marks of genius; and all these are supported by the unanimous verdict of the best poets and the greatest critics of twenty-five hundred years.  The evidence for the unity of the Iliad and the Odyssey is so strong that we should be compelled to postulate a single Homer even if ancient Greece had believed in many."*

## EPIC POETRY

I.  Epic derived from Greek words "epos," meaning word, saying, speech.  Distinguishes recited verse from sung poetry (lyric) and acted poetry (drama).

II.  An epic poem is a long narrative poem, written in a dignified style on a majestic theme, relating the exploits of a national hero at the beginnings of a people's legendary past.

III.  Epics like the *Iliad,* the *Odyssey, Beowulf,* the *Niebelungenlied,* the *Song of Roland,* and the *Cid* are called Popular Epics

---

*Scott, J. A., *The Unity of Homer* (Berkeley, 1921), p. 269.

or Folk Epics, to distinguish them from later learned and subtle epics, like Vergil's *Aeneid,* Milton's *Paradise Lost,* and Dante's *Divine Comedy.* The essential difference between the two types is, however, that the former were composd for and recited to a listening audience, the latter written to be read by learned people. Homer is a sophisticated literary artist.

## METER

Dactylic Hexameter. Six feet to the verse, the first five feet being either a dactyl ($-\ \smile\ \smile$) or a spondee ($-\ -$), the last always a spondee (or a variation). Thus the maximum number of syllables to the line is 17, the minimum 12. However, Greek meter depends not on accent but quantity, the long syllable taking twice as much time to say as the short. Cf. Longfellow, *Evangeline:* "This is the forest primeval, the murmuring pines and the hemlocks."

# ILIAD

## BACKGROUND OF THE ILIAD

I.   The siege of Troy is an historical event, an incident in the migrations of the Achaeans (see pp. 2–3). According to Greek tradition, the city fell in 1184 B.C. Some of the characters are undoubtedly historical personages, but the stories of the Greek expedition against Troy are a mass of legend handed down and embellished by centuries of oral transmission.

II.   At the marriage of Peleus and the sea-divinity Thetis all the gods were invited but Eris (Discord). Angered, she threw a golden apple among the guests inscribed "for the fairest." Unwilling to decide among his wife and daughters, Hera, Athena, and Aphrodite, Zeus appointed as judge of the beauty contest Paris, a Trojan prince, son of King Priam. To influence his decision, Hera offered him wealth and power, Athena military glory, and Aphrodite the most beautiful woman in the world. Paris awarded the apple to Aphrodite (Judgment of Paris). The most beautiful woman was Helen, but she was already married to Menelaus, King of Sparta. Aided by Aphrodite, Paris journeyed to Sparta, was hospitably entertained by Menelaus, and shortly after ran off with Helen to Troy.

Helen had had numerous suitors before her marriage to Menelaus, and they all had taken an oath to fight, if necessary, to preserve her marriage to the suitor she chose. Thus was organized the great expedition against Troy to recover Helen and take vengeance on the Trojans. It was led by Agamemnon, King of Mycenae, the elder brother of Menelaus. Odysseus, King of Ithaca, who was happily married to Penelope, the mother of his infant son, Telemachus, attempted to evade military service by feigning insanity. When his ruse was exposed, Odysseus set out disguised as a merchant to find Achilles, King of Phthia and Hellas in Thessaly. Thetis, knowing that, although her son Achilles was invulnerable except in his heel, he would die if he went to Troy, dressed him as a girl and sent him to live with the daughters of a king. When Odysseus arrived at Achilles' hiding place, he displayed to the daughters of the king a collection of feminine clothing. But he also included a sword. The girls examined the clothing, but Achilles fondled the sword, and thus Odysseus forced him to join the expedition.

The Achaean fleet assembled at Aulis, in Boeotia. Here, while hunting, Agamemnon slew a stag sacred to Artemis. The winds ceased blowing, and the expedition was becalmed. Calchas, the soothsayer, was summoned, and he declared that the winds would not blow again until Agamemnon sacrificed his eldest daughter, Iphigenia, to Artemis. On the pretense that Iphigenia was to be married to Achilles, Agamemnon sent for his daughter and sacrificed her. For this cruel act Agamemnon's wife, Clytemnestra, never forgave him.

For nine years the Achaeans besieged Troy, but without success, living off the country. The *Iliad* begins at a point sometime in the tenth year of the war.

9

## TROY (ILIUM)

Royal fortress, ca. 3 miles from mouth of Hellespont, controlling traffic between Europe and Asia, and between the Aegean and Black Seas. On a hill (modern Hissarlik, meaning Castle Hill), discovered by Schliemann, one of the nine cities excavated by him on this hill.

## OTHER IMPORTANT PLACES

Achaea. Homeric name for Greece

Argos. The city Argos, or the region Argolis, or the Peloponnesus, or all of Greece

Hellas. Part of kingdom of Achilles in Thessaly

Ida. Mountain near Troy

Lacedaemon (Laconia). Kingdom of Menelaus

Lycia. Region in Asia Minor from which come principal allies of Trojans

Mycenae. Home of Agamemnon

Olympus. Mountain in N.E. Thessaly, supposed home of the gods

Phthia. Part of kingdom of Achilles in Thessaly

Pylus. Home of Nestor

Sparta. Home of Menelaus

## PEOPLES

Greeks are called by Homer Achaeans, Argives, Danaans

Myrmidons. Achilles' soldiers

Trojans. Inhabitants of Ilium

Lycians. Principal allies of Trojans

## PRINCIPAL CHARACTERS ON ACHAEAN SIDE

Achilles. Son of Peleus (Pelides), and Thetis; King of Phthia and Hellas in N.E. Greece (Thessaly)

Agamemnon. Son of Atreus (Atrides); King of Mycenae

Ajax. Son of Telamon, from Salamis; first cousin of Achilles; great physical prowess, but lacking in brains (Shakespeare: "beef-witted Ajax"); mightiest and handsomest of the Achaeans after Achilles

Antilochus. Son of Nestor; close friend of Achilles

Briseis. Beloved war captive of Achilles

Diomedes. Son of Tydeus (Tydides); King of Argos; youngest and one of the mightiest of Greek chieftains

Idomeneus. Grandson of Minos; Cretan ally of Achaeans

Menelaus. Son of Atreus (Atrides); King of Sparta; husband of Helen; younger brother of Agamemnon

Nestor. Son of Neleus (Nelides); aged King of Pylus

Odysseus. Son of Laertes (Laertides); King of Ithaca

Patroclus. Son of Menoetius; closest friend of Achilles

## PRINCIPAL CHARACTERS ON TROJAN SIDE

Aeneas. Son-in-law of Priam; son of Aphrodite and Anchises; second to Hector in military prowess

Andromache. Wife of Hector

Astyanax. Infant son of Hector and Andromache

Glaucus. Grandson of Bellerophon; Trojan ally from Lycia

Hector. Eldest son of Priam; greatest of Trojan heroes

Hecuba. Wife of Priam

Helen. Daughter of Leda and Zeus; wife of Paris, former wife of Menelaus

Pandarus. Son of Lycaon; Trojan ally from Lycia

Paris (Alexander). Son of Priam; husband of Helen

Priam. Son of Laomedon; aged King of Troy

Sarpedon. Son of Zeus; Trojan ally from Lycia

## GODS*

| Achaean Side | Trojan Side | Other Divinities |
|---|---|---|
| Athena | Aphrodite | Demeter |
| Hephaestus | Apollo | Dionysus |
| Hera | Artemis | Hades |
| Poseidon | Ares | Hermes |
| Thetis | Zeus (at times) | Iris |
| | | Persephone |

*See pp. 329-331.

*Chronology of the Iliad*

(47 days in the tenth year of the Trojan War)

## SUMMARY OF THE ILIAD (II)

**Book I.**

A. Invocation to the Muse; statement of the central theme of the work; the wrath of Achilles against Agamemnon, and the disastrous consequences of this quarrel to the Achaeans.

B. Agamemnon summarily repulses Chryses, priest of Apollo, who comes to him to ransom his captive daughter, Chryseis, Agamemnon's war booty. Chryses prays to Apollo for revenge; the god sends a devastating plague amongst the Achaean forces. After nine days of plague, Achilles summons an assembly of the entire army. Calchas, the soothsayer, hesitates to reveal the reason for Apollo's anger. After Achilles promises him protection, Calchas places the blame on Agamemnon, and asserts that the plague will not end until the girl is returned to her father and a sacrifice made to Apollo. Agamemnon, angry, offers to relinquish the girl, but he demands in compensation another girl of equal merit to replace Chryseis immediately. A quarrel develops between Agamemnon and Achilles, who feels that Agamemnon is putting his personal pride before the welfare of the army. In passing, Agamemnon threatens to seize Achilles' war captive, Briseis. Achilles' anger mounts because he has been fighting at Troy for the sake of Agamemnon and his brother, Menelaus. Further, though he does most of the fighting, Achilles' shares of the booty is less than Agamemnon's. He finally threatens to return to his kingdom with his troops. Undaunted, Agamemnon, acting with insolence and pride, announces that he has decided to seize Briseis, merely to demonstrate his authority. The sensitive and impulsive Achilles is about to kill Agamemnon, when the goddess Athena convinces him not to use violence, and promises recompense. Achilles petulantly swears a mighty oath that he will not fight any longer.

C. Old Nestor attempts fruitlessly to reconcile the quarreling leaders. The assembly is dissolved, and Agamemnon sends Odysseus to return Chryseis to her father and perform the necessary sacrifices. Meanwhile, Agamemnon dispatches his heralds to fetch Briseis from Achilles' tent. Reluctantly relinquishing the damsel, Briseis, Achilles prays to his mother Thetis, the sea-goddess. When she appears, he asks her to request of Zeus that he exact vengeance on all the Achaeans by making the Trojans victorious. Thetis, bewailing his coming early death and his present dishonor, promises to approach Zeus, and urges him to continue in his refusal to join in the battle. Meanwhile, Odysseus fulfills his mission to Chryses, and the plague ends. Achilles sulks in his tent (for the next fifteen days).

D. Twelve days later, Thetis rises to Mt. Olympus. Zeus grants her request that he make the Trojans victorious. Hera, who sides with the Achaeans against the Trojans, suspecting Thetis purpose, quarrels with Zeus. He threatens her, but their son, Hephaestus, intervenes. Laughter unquenchable, feasting, and music complete the day of the gods. Book I ends on a calm note—Zeus and Hera sleeping together peacefully.

## Book II.

A. Zeus, in partial fulfillment of his promise to Thetis, sends Agamemnon a deceptive dream which urges him to muster his troops, for he will take Troy immediately. In the morning Agamemnon summons the Achaeans to assembly. In preparation, a meeting of the council of chiefs is held. Here it is agreed to test the morale of the troops by urging that they abandon the fight and return home. Agamemnon addresses the assembly in this vein, reminding them of their homes and families. The effect is electric; the common soldiers rush to the ships prepared to depart. But Athena intervenes, and Odysseus successfully restores discipline and obedience to Agamemnon. Thersites, a common soldier, seizes the floor and harangues the multitude, attacking Agamemnon for his greed and urging return home. He is rebuked and beaten into silence by Odysseus. The army is reinspired by Odysseus, who reminds them of Calchas' prophecy that they would win the war in the tenth year. Nestor voices approval, and the assembly is dissolved, all agreed to fight on.

B. Catalogue of the Ships. Agamemnon sends heralds to summon the Achaeans to battle. The Muses are invoked for assistance in listing the Achaean troops who came to Troy, together with the names of their captains. Achilles and his men, the Myrmidons, abstain from battle.

C. Catalogue of the Trojans and their Allies. Hector orders the Trojans and their allies to muster for battle.

**Book III.**

A. The Trojans and Achaeans march towards each other. A proposal is made by Hector and Paris that the issue of the war be decided by a single combat between Menelaus and Paris, acting as champions for their peoples, the winner to keep Helen and her property. Paris then shrinks from meeting Menelaus, but, chided by Hector, agrees.

B. Helen appears at the tower of the main gates of Troy to see the armies. She points out the great Greek heroes to Priam and the other Trojan elders. Priam is summoned to give his word, as an oath is taken on both sides to abide by the outcome of the duel.

C. Menelaus is victorious, but Aphrodite rescues Paris from certain death, and removes him miraculously to his chamber. Aphrodite then brings the reluctant Helen to Paris. Agamemnon claims victory for Menelaus, and demands Helen.

**14**

**Book IV.**

A. The goddesses Hera and Athena quarrel with Zeus over the fate of Troy, and it is decided that the truce be broken. Pandarus, a Lycian ally of the Trojans, is egged on by Athena to shoot an arrow at Menelaus, who is slightly wounded.

B. The truce being thus suddenly broken, despite the sacred oaths, a grand battle begins. Vowing war to the end, Agamemnon reviews the army, encouraging his captains, especially Idomeneus, the two Ajaxes, Nestor, Odysseus, and Diomedes. The Achaean and Trojan armies clash on the plain before Troy, and many are killed on both sides.

**Book V.**

Inspired by Athena, Diomedes performs remarkable feats of valor during the heated battle, almost single-handedly routing the Trojans, and slaying many of them. He slays Pandarus, who has wounded him with an arrow. He also wounds Pandarus' battle-companion, Aeneas, but the latter is miraculously rescued by his divine mother, Aphrodite. In anger Diomedes even wounds Aphrodite, but Aeneas is then rescued by Apollo. Finally, even Ares, who is assisting the Trojans, is wounded by Diomedes.

**Book VI.**

A. As the battle swirls back and forth across the plain, many Trojans are slain by Ajax, Diomedes, and Menelaus. They are pushed back to Troy. Priam's son, Helenus, a soothsayer, urges Hector and Aeneas to prepare a strong defense and advises Hector to instruct the women of Troy to offer prayers, honors, and sacrifices to Athena.

B. Diomedes meets Glaucus, son of Hippolochus, a Lycian ally of the Trojans, on the field of battle. Diomedes admires his valor, and inquires who he is. Glaucus then relates the story of his ancestors, of Achaean origin, in particular of Bellerophon, who in his wanderings slew the Chimaera and performed many other feats. Diomedes reveals that his own grandfather had once enter-

**15**

tained Bellerophon and that, therefore, he and Glaucus are guest-friends. Gladly they agree not to fight each other. Instead, they exchange armor, Glaucus exchanging his golden armor for Diomedes' bronze equipment.

C. Meanwhile, Hector enters Priam's palace and is greeted by his mother Hecuba, who offers him the refreshment of wine. He rejects her motherly ministrations, and advises her to gather the old women of Troy to pray and sacrifice to Athena to save the city from Diomedes. The prayers, however, are unavailing.

D. Hector then goes to Paris' palace, where he finds Paris toying with his armor in the company of Helen. Hector rebukes his brother for his lack of responsibility to the city. Paris lightly excuses himself, and promises to join the battle in good time. Helen sadly tells Hector of her unhappiness over Paris' irresponsible character.

E. Hector, then, not finding his wife, Andromache, and their son, Scamandrius (Astyanax), at his own palace, goes out to bid farewell to them. He meets Andromache at the Scaean Gates, and a tender scene ensues. She weeps, reminds him what will happen to her and the child if he dies, since he is both father, mother and husband to her, and begs him to avoid combat. Hector lovingly explains why he must fight: duty calls. Moreover, he has always been reputed for his courage. Yet, his greatest concern is for her fate, if Troy should fall. He would rather die fighting before she is led into captivity. Then, Hector reaches for his infant son, Astyanax. But the child cries, frightened by his terrifying plumed helmet. Laughingly, he removes his helmet, fondles his son, and prays that he too may become a great warrior, even more famous than himself. He finally takes leave of his adoring wife by consoling her with the thought that he will not die unless it is so fated. Andromache returns weeping to her home.

F. Paris, after lingering in his palace, finally runs out gallantly, and meets Hector, who rebukes him again for his light-heartedness and lack of a sense of responsibility.

**Book VII.**

A. Hector and Paris re-enter the battle. Hector, divinely inspired, challenges one of the Achaeans to single combat. Menelaus offers to be the Achaean champion, but is dissuaded because of Hector's superior might. Nestor rebukes the Achaeans for their hesitancy, and soon nine volunteers arise. Ajax, the son of Telamon, is chosen by lot. The duel between Ajax and Hector is furious but inconclusive. They exchange gifts, and both sides retire.

B. Then, an assembly of the Trojans is held inside Troy. In a stormy meeting it is proposed that Helen be returned to Menelaus. Paris indignantly rejects this, but offers to return Helen's wealth and additional property to Menelaus. The following day, Paris' offer is reported to the Achaeans, but it is forthwith rejected. However, a truce for burning of the dead is agreed upon. The Achaeans also spend that day constructing a wall and a ditch to protect their ships beached on the shore.

**Book VIII.**

A. The next day Zeus summons an assembly of the gods on Mt. Olympus, and instructs them all to cease intervening on either side. He himself speeds to Mt. Ida near Troy, and when the battle resumes, he begins to fulfill his promise to Thetis that he would give the Trojans victory over the Achaeans.

B. The morale of the Achaeans declines, and in the ensuing battles the tide of battle turns. Even Diomedes retreats. The Achaeans rally, but are again repulsed. The attempt of Hera and Athena to aid the faltering Achaeans is summarily halted by Zeus. At the end of the day's fighting the Trojans bivouac on the plain before the Greek ships.

**Book IX.**

A. The Achaeans are panic stricken. That night Agamemnon summons an assembly of the soldiers, and weeping unashamedly before them, admits defeat and proposes flight to

Greece. When Diomedes rebukes Agamemnon for cowardice, and urges that they fight on, the army approves. Agamemnon then calls a meeting of the council of chiefs, at which he admits that he was in the wrong in angering Achilles, and offers to make amends to Achilles, in order to induce him to return to battle. The compensation for the insult is to consist of the immediate return of Briseis, unsullied, 7 tripods, 12 caldrons, 10 talents of gold, 12 horses, and 7 beautiful women of Lesbos. In addition, when they capture Troy, a shipload of gold and bronze and 20 beautiful Trojan women, and when they return, one of his daughters in marriage together with 7 cities as a dowry.

B. An embassy consisting of Phoenix, Ajax, and Odysseus is dispatched to Achilles' tent to communicate the offer. They find Achilles singing of the deeds of heroes, watched by Patroclus. Odysseus describes the plight of the Achaeans to Achilles, begs him to assist them, urges him to suppress his pride, and reports the gifts offered by Agamemnon. Achilles remains adamant, arguing that he was insulted instead of honored for his previous efforts, that Agamemnon received the greatest part of the captured booty, that he feels as injured with respect to the seizure of Briseis as Agamemnon and Menelaus do because of Paris' abduction of Helen. He contemptuously refuses reconciliation, and, moreover, announces that he will sail for his kingdom the next day. It is honor not material possessions that he prizes, for he has been told by his mother, Thetis, that he has a choice of two fates: either to die young fighting at Troy but win undying fame; or to return home and live a long but undistinguished life.

C. Phoenix, Achilles' old retainer, in a long-winded speech, reminds him of his own unhappy past, and how he came to be his foster-father. He urges him to curb his pride and high spirit, and accept Agamemnon's gifts. Rejecting Phoenix's plea, Achilles bids him remain and return to Greece with him.

D. Finally, Ajax, realizing the uselessness of further advances to Achilles, rebukes him for his pride, stubbornness, and neglect of his comrades' welfare. Phoenix remains with Achilles, while Ajax and Odysseus return to report the failure of their mission.

## Book X.

Agamemnon, unable to sleep because of anxiety, rouses other chieftains for the purpose of strengthening the sentry watches. At a meeting of the council of chiefs, Diomedes and Odysseus volunteer for dangerous reconnaissance duty. Meanwhile, at a meeting of the Trojan council, Dolon had volunteered for the same task. He is captured by Diomedes and Odysseus, and under a false promise of security, reveals Trojan military secrets. Then he is promptly murdered by them. The two Achaean leaders next enter the Trojan encampment, slay some men, and steal the horses of Rhesus, King of the Thracians.

## Book XI.

In the morning, the Achaean army, encouraged, advances and meets the Trojans. After initial successes of mighty prowess, Agamemnon is wounded and retires. The tide of battle turns again, and Hector comes to the fore. Diomedes and Odysseus, among others, are also wounded. At this point, for the first time since the swearing of his oath, Achilles begins to show an interest in the military situation. He sends Patroclus to Nestor to enquire who has been wounded. Nestor, in his usual long-winded, reminiscing fashion, bewails Achilles' hard-heartedness and selfish pride. He urges Patroclus to influence Achilles to permit him to disguise himself in Achilles' armor and lead the Myrmidons back into battle.

## Book XII.

The Trojans and their allies descend from their chariots, array themselves in five columns, and assault the walls, aided by Zeus. The Achaeans regroup their forces, and offer stout resistance, but Hector breaches a gate with a huge stone. The Trojans swarm beyond the wall.

**Book XIII.**

Their first line of defense having been taken, the Achaeans retreat to their ships beached along the shore. Poseidon, disguised as Calchas, intervenes on the side of the Achaeans, and spurs them on to resist. The Trojans, led by Hector, advance to the ships, but are held at bay by the valor of Idomeneus and Ajax, the son of Telamon.

**Book XIV.**

A. Agamemnon again counsels flight from Troy, but he is rebuked by Odysseus and Diomedes.

B. Hera, armed with a love charm secured deceitfully from Aphrodite, sets out to distract Zeus' attention on Mt. Ida. She is successful, and while Zeus sleeps in her arms, Poseidon increases his aid to the Achaeans.

C. Wounded as they are, Diomedes, Odysseus, and Agamemnon return to battle. Hector is stunned by a stone hurled by Ajax, son of Telamon, and the Trojans retreat from the Achaean camp.

**Book XV.**

Zeus awakens, realizes Hera's motive, and summons Iris, who is sent to order Poseidon to abandon his intervention on the side of the Achaeans. Zeus also dispatches Apollo to revive Hector. Supported by Apollo, the Trojans attack again and regain their lost ground. Advancing up to the ships on the shore, the Trojans begin to hurl fire into the Achaean ships.

**Book XVI.**

A. Patroclus, alarmed, persuades Achilles to permit him, attired in his own armor for the purpose of frightening the Trojans, to lead the Myrmidons. But Achilles commands him to return after he has driven the Trojans away from the ships.

B. When Hector sets fire to a ship, Achilles urges Patroclus to hasten. At the arrival of Patroclus, the Trojans are driven back. Patroclus performs mighty deeds of valor, culminating in the slaying of Sarpedon. The tide of battle has been turned, but disobeying Achilles' orders, Patroclus pursues the retreating Trojans up to the walls of Troy. Apollo himself thrusts Patroclus off the walls of the city. In the ensuing sharp fighting, Patroclus is stunned by Apollo, and finally slain by Hector.

**Book XVII.**

A fierce struggle ensues over possession of Patroclus' body. Hector strips him of Achilles' armor and dons it himself. The Achaeans, however, succeed in recovering the body of Patroclus and retreat to the camp, under heavy pressure from the Trojans.

**Book XVIII.**

A. The news of Patroclus' death leaves Achilles prostrate with grief. It is even feared that he may commit suicide. When his mother, Thetis, comes to comfort him, she warns him that he is fated to die soon after Hector. Achilles now renounces his wrath against Agamemnon, and Thetis promises to secure for him a new suit of armor from Hephaestus.

B. The body of Patroclus being endangered by the Trojans, Achilles appears outside the wall and frightens the Trojans away with his war-cry. The Trojans bivouac on the plain that night, while the Achaeans lament for Patroclus. Achilles vows that he will slay Hector before the funeral of Patroclus is held.

C. At Thetis' behest, Hephaestus makes new armor for Achilles, including an artistically wrought shield decorated with varied urban and rural scenes of war and peace.

**Book XIX.**

A. The next morning Thetis brings Achilles his new armor. An assembly is summoned and Achilles publicly renounces his anger against Agamemnon, who apologizes for his conduct in seizing Briseis on the grounds that his judgment was blinded by Ate, the goddess of infatuation. The offer of gifts to Achilles is re-

**21**

newed, and when the latter lightly discounts the need for this gesture, Odysseus convinces him that it is necessary, despite his eagerness to get down to the business of fighting, for him to accept the recompense in order that the reconciliation may be formally effected. Briseis returns unsullied to Achilles' tent.

B. There is renewed mourning for Patroclus. Achilles dons his armor and prepares for battle. As he is about to set out, one of his horses miraculously prophesies his coming death.

## Book XX.

A. Zeus summons the gods to council, and grants them permission to engage in the battle as they will. The gods descend to earth, and the battle is resumed.

B. Achilles, victoriously leading the Achaeans, is opposed by Aeneas, who is spurred on by Apollo. Aeneas is rescued from certain death by Poseidon, because it is fated that he and his descendants will rule the Trojans. Hector, too, is temporarily rescued from Achilles by Apollo. The Trojans retreat, mercilessly and irresistibly pursued by Achilles.

## Book XXI.

A. The Trojans, in full retreat, are slaughtered at the river Xanthus. The river, however, angered at Achilles' bloodthirstiness, suddenly rises against him with its waters. He is rescued from drowning by Hephaestus, who checks the water with fire.

B. The gods, some siding with the Trojans, some with the Achaeans, now openly clash with each other.

C. Achilles pursues the routed Trojans toward the walls of the city. Apollo, disguised as a Trojan, causes Achilles to pursue him away from the city, long enough to permit the Trojans to escape inside the walls.

## Book XXII.

A. Apollo reveals his deception to Achilles, who returns at once to the walls to find Hector all alone outside the gates, ready to face him. Despite the plea of Priam and Hecuba that he not risk the encounter, Hector remains to fight. But when Achilles approaches he loses courage and flees. Achilles pursues him three times around the walls of Troy, aided by Apollo.

B. The scales of fate in Zeus' hands reveal Hector's doom. Athena, disguised as his brother, Deiphobus, deceitfully urges Hector to stand and fight, promising him aid. Achilles contemptuously rejects Hector's proposal of a mutual agreement to return the body of the loser to his people for burial. The duel begins. Athena aids Achilles by returning to him the sprear he had cast, and Hector discovers that he is alone. He makes a desperate charge at Achilles with his sword, and is mortally wounded. His dying request for decent burial is again brutally rejected by Achilles.

C. Achilles strips him of his armor, and other Achaeans run up to gaze on the body of Hector and to wound it. In full view of the Trojans on the walls, Achilles brutally ties Hector's feet to his chariot and drags his body back in the dust to the Achaean camp.

D. Priam and Hecuba lament. But Andromache, unsuspecting, prepares for Hector's homecoming. When she discovers the truth, she faints. Upon being revived, she mournfully bewails her own fate and that of her fatherless son, Astyanax.

## Book XXIII.

A. Achilles and the Myrmidons renew their mourning for Patroclus, and preparations are made for his funeral. Achilles, overcome with grief, finally sleeps. During the night, the soul of Patroclus comes to him and begs for speedy burial, so that his soul may reach its resting place in Hades.

B. The following day, the funeral of Patroclus is held in great splendor. The funeral pyre is heaped up with slaughtered animals of various kinds. Then Achilles massacres twelve Trojan war prisoners on the pyre as a sacrifice to Patroclus.

**23**

C. Then next day, varied athletic contests are held in Patroclus' honor, with prizes offered by Achilles: chariot-racing, boxing, wrestling, foot-races, javelin-throwing.

### Book XXIV.

A. Achilles cannot sleep, grieving for Patroclus. Whenever his anger overmasters him, he drags the body of Hector, tied to his chariot, in the dust around the grave of Patroclus.

B. Nine days later on Mt. Olympus the gods quarrel over the body of Hector, which has been miraculously preserved by them. Iris is dispatched by Zeus to summon Thetis, whom he sends to order Achilles to permit the body to be ransomed. Achilles consents. Meanwhile, Iris is also sent by Zeus to bid Priam to go to Achilles' tent at night to ransom the body.

C. The old king of Troy sets out in a wagon, loaded with a rich ransom, on the dangerous mission, against Hecuba's wishes. Zeus orders Hermes to guide the old man safely to Achilles' tent. Disguised as a Myrmidon, he conducts Priam to Achilles. Priam is kindly received by Achilles, and when he explains his mission, they both weep, Achilles for his own father and his friend Patroclus, Priam for his son Hector. Achilles accepts the ransom, and orders the body of Hector to be prepared. They eat together, and a bed is provided for Priam. Achilles, moreover, generously grants Priam a truce of eleven days for the funeral of Hector.

D. Hermes conducts Priam safely back to Troy before dawn. Mourning for the dead Hector begins. Laments are pronounced by Andromache, Hecuba, and lastly by Helen. The *Iliad* ends with a brief account of the burning and burial of Hector's body.

## THE ODYSSEY

### BACKGROUND OF THE ODYSSEY

After the death of Hector, Achilles was treacherously killed by a poisoned arrow shot in his heel by Paris. A contest ensued between Odysseus and Ajax over the armor of Achilles. When it was awarded to Odysseus, Ajax became insane and committed suicide.

Shortly after, Paris was killed. Then, at Odysseus' suggestion, the Greeks built a wooden horse, which was filled with volunteers and left outside Troy. The Achaeans sailed away, pretending to have given up the struggle, but their ships waited nearby. The Trojans, disregarding the warning of their priest, Laocoön, dragged the horse into the city. That night the Greeks broke out of the horse, the fleet returned, and the city was doomed.

After the sack of the city, the surviving Greek heroes returned to their homes. Odysseus left Troy with 12 ships and about 600 men, but his sufferings began at once, for he had angered Athena by stealing her sacred image (the Palladium) from Troy. Later he incurred the anger of Poseidon, and his men that of Helios. Meanwhile, a long time before Odysseus' homecoming, about 100 suitors among the aristocrats of his kingdom had assembled at his palace insisting that his wife Penelope choose one of them as her husband, so that Ithaca might have a king. Faithful to Odysseus, though despairing of his return, Penelope devised a plan for putting off the necessity of making a choice. She announced that she first would weave a funeral shroud for her aged father-in-law, Laertes. But each night she unravelled the day's weaving. The suitors spent the time feasting in Odysseus' banqueting hall, carousing and wasting his property, mocking Odysseus' helpless young son, Telemachus. The *Odyssey* begins at a point sometime in the 10th year of Odysseus' wanderings, the 20th of his absence from Ithaca.

## PRINCIPAL PLACES

Ithaca. Exact location disputed, probably modern Thiaki; small island off west central coast of Hellas; home of Odysseus.

Ogygia. Island in Mediterranean, home of the nymph Calypso.

Scheria. Island in Mediterranean, home of the Phaeacians.

## PRINCIPAL CHARACTERS

Alcinous. King of Phaeacians, husband of Arete, father of Nausicaa

Antinous. Leading suitor of Penelope

Arete. Queen of Phaeacians, wife of Alcinous, mother of Nausicaa

Calypso. Nymph, daughter of Atlas
Circe. Enchantress, goddess, daughter of Helios
Eumaeus. Faithful swineherd of Odysseus
Eurycleia. Faithful old nurse of Odysseus
Eurymachus. Leading suitor of Penelope
Helen. Wife of Menelaus, King of Sparta
Laertes. Aged father of Odysseus
Melanthius. Traitorous goatherd of Odysseus
Menelaus. King of Sparta; husband of Helen
Nausicaa. Young daughter of Alcinous and Arete
Nestor. Aged King of Pylus
Odysseus. King of Ithaca, son of Laertes and Anticleia
Penelope. Wife of Odysseus
Phaeacians. People ruled by Alcinous on island of Scheria
Polyphemus. One-eyed cannibalistic giant
Teiresias. Blind soothsayer of Thebes
Telemachus. Young son of Odysseus and Penelope

### Chronology of the Odyssey

(41 days in the tenth year of Odysseus' wanderings)

| | |
|---|---|
| Book I | 1 day |
| Book II | 1 day |
| Books III-IV | 4 days |
| Book V | 25 days |
| Books VI-VII | 1 day |
| Books VIII-XII | 1 day |
| Books XIII-XIV | 2 days |
| Books XV-XVI | 3 days |
| Books XVII-XIX | 1 day |
| Books XX-XXIII | 1 day |
| Book XXIV | 1 day |

## SUMMARY OF THE ODYSSEY

**Book I.**

A. Invocation to the Muse; the central theme of the *Odys-*

*sey:* the wanderings, and the trials and tribulations of Odysseus after the fall of Troy.

B. The gods meet on Mt. Olympus during the absence of Poseidon, who has been persecuting Odysseus for many years. Athena requests that Hermes be sent to bid the goddess Calypso to permit Odysseus to leave her island. She herself prepares to descend to Ithaca to rouse Telemachus to action, so that he may be more respected. She proposes to encourage him to take a firm stand against the suitors of his mother Penelope, and to go in search of news of his father.

C. Athena appears to Telemachus, disguised as Mentes, a friend of Odysseus from Taphos. Telemachus entertains her graciously in the feasting hall, apart from the rowdy suitors, and complains of their behavior, their wasting of his property, and he bewails his father's fate. She predicts Odysseus' early return, and outlines a plan of action for him, urging him to behave like a man.

D. Penelope descends when she hears the minstrel, Phemius, singing of the return of the Achaeans from Troy, and weeps. Telemachus begins to assert himself.

**Book II.**

A. Telemachus summons an assembly, the first held on the island since Odysseus' departure twenty years ago, and, complaining bitterly of the suitors' waste of his property, demands that they leave the palace. Antinous and Eurymachus, speaking in behalf of the suitors, arrogantly refuse, and demand that Penelope choose one of them at once as her husband.

B. In answer to his prayers, Athena appears to Telemachus in the shape of Mentor, another friend of Odysseus. She arranges transportation for him by ship, and together they leave Ithaca secretly for Pylus and Sparta in search of news of Odysseus.

**Book III.**

A. The next morning the ship arrives at Pylus on the mainland. After they have been welcomed hospitably by King Nestor,

27

Telemachus inquires about news of his father. In a long-winded speech Nestor tells of the homecoming of the Achaean heroes from Troy, but he lacks knowledge of the whereabouts of Odysseus. Athena disappears.

B. The next day, after sacrificing to Athena, Nestor dispatches Telemachus by chariot, together with his son, Peisistratus, to consult Menelaus in Sparta.

## Book IV.

A. They arrive in two days at the palace of Menelaus in Sparta, and are hospitably entertained by him and Helen. They reminisce and weep over the Achaean heroes.

B. The following morning, Menelaus relates to Telemachus in detail the story of the wanderings, homecomings and fates of the Achaean leaders, told to him by Proteus, the old man of the sea, who had revealed that Odysseus was being held captive on an island by the nymph Calypso.

C. Meanwhile, in Ithaca, the suitors discover Telemachus' absence, and instigated by Antinous, plot an ambush to kill Telemachus. Penelope is prostrated at discovering the plot, but, helpless as she is, she is reassured by a dream sent by Athena.

## Book V.

A. The following day, at a meeting of the council of the gods, Athene repeats her request that Odysseus be permitted to return. Zeus then sends Hermes to Calypso's beautiful island to instruct her to release Odysseus.

B. Odysseus is discovered constantly weeping at the shore, yearning for his home. Calypso reveals to him the decision of Zeus, but she makes a final fruitless attempt to keep him with her by offering him immortality. Five days later, after constructing a raft with Calypso's aid, he sets sail for home. After seventeen days at sea he sights land, but at that moment Poseidon spies him, and rouses a terrible storm which wrecks the raft.

C. Odysseus despairingly bewails his lot, fearing death by

drowning. But he is pitied by the sea-divinity Ino, who gives him a magic veil which buoys him up. After two days of swimming, he lands with difficulty, aided by Athena, on the shore of the island of Scheria, the home of the Phaeacians. He kisses the earth, and, being naked and exhausted, falls asleep on a bed of leaves underneath some bushes.

## Book VI.

A. During the night Athena appears in a dream to the princess Nausicaa, daughter of Alcinous, King of the Phaeacians. She informs her that her marriage day is near, and urges her to go in the morning to the mouth of the river to wash the family clothing.

B. The next day Nausicaa and her hand-maidens are lovingly dispatched by her parents, and go a-washing. While they wait for the clothes to dry, they play at ball. Odysseus, awakened by their excited shouting, comes out, covering his nakedness with a branch of leaves. All the girls run in horror, but Nausicaa. Odysseus, in a glib speech, praises her beauty, hopes she will marry soon, and begs for assistance. She provides him with clothing and food. After he bathes the seabrine from his body and dresses, Athena makes him appear unusually handsome. Nausicaa is not unimpressed.

C. Nausicaa conducts him to the outskirts of the town, and informs him that modesty forbids her to be seen within the city in the presence of a strange man. She gives him explicit instruction how to find the palace of Alcinous, and advises him first to approach her mother as a suppliant.

## Book VII.

Odysseus, guided and made invisible by Athena, enters the palace of Alcinous, and approaches Queen Arete, the mother of Nausicaa, with a prayer for assistance in completing his homeward journey. Arete and Alcinous welcome the stranger, and grant his request for assistance. He relates to the king and queen how he had been on Calypso's island for seven years, how he had been shipwrecked, and rescued by Nausicaa. Alcinous, impressed, renews his offer of a swift ship.

## Book VIII.

A. The following day Alcinous proclaims athletic contests and a feast in honor of the stranger. When Odysseus is tactlessly taunted and challenged by a young Phaeacian, he wins their respect, amazing them by a tremendous throw of a discus.

B. The blind minstrel, Demodocus, then sings a song about how Ares and Aphrodite were detected in their adulterous love by her husband, Hephaestus.

C. The Phaeacians bestow many precious gifts upon the stranger. Nausicaa asks Odysseus not to forget her after he leaves Scheria. When they have feasted at a banquet in his honor at the palace, Odysseus asks the blind bard, Demodocus, to sing of the Trojan horse and the fall of Troy. Alcinous notes Odysseus weeping, and enquires his name.

## Book IX.

For the first time since his arrival among the Phaeacians, Odysseus reveals his identity. Then he embarks on the long story of his three years of adventures and wanderings after the fall of Troy up to the point where he was shipwrecked on the island of Calypso.

### ODYSSEUS' STORY

A. Odysseus and the Ithacans sailed from Troy in twelve ships. First they made a raid for booty upon the Cicones in Thrace, but were routed with some losses.

B. They reached the southern Peloponnesus, but a storm drove them south to the land of the Lotus-eaters (probably N. Africa). Some of his men ate the lotus, were afflicted with amnesia, and desired to remain. They had to be carried to the ships by force.

C. Thence they came to the land of the Cyclopes (probably somewhere in the western Mediterranean), a strange tribe of barbaric, cave-dwelling, one-eyed giants. Odysseus reconnoitered with his own shipmates. With twelve men and a skin filled with wine, Odysseus entered the cave of the Cyclops, Polyphemus. When Polyphemus arrived with his flocks, he imprisoned Odysseus and his men by closing the mouth of the cave with a huge rock which they could not move. Then he proceeded to kill and devour two of the men for each meal. In the Cyclops' absence, Odysseus devised a scheme. He sharpened a huge stake to a point, and then succeeded in making the Cyclops drunk. When Polyphemus, taking a liking to him, asked him his name he replied that it was "Noman." While the Cyclops was in a drunken sleep, they burned out his eye with the heated point of the stake. Polyphemus bellowed for aid from his fellow-Cyclopes, but when he said that "Noman" had blinded him, they departed. At dawn the blinded Cyclops tried to catch Odysseus and the surviving men, but they escaped by clinging to the bellies of the animals as they left the cave. But, as their ship departed, Odysseus could not resist the temptation to taunt the Cyclops, and boasted that his true name was Odysseus. Polyphemus then prayed to his father, Poseidon, to avenge him by keeping Odysseus from his home.

## Book X.

D. Then they reached the island of Aeolus, the god of the winds, who gave him a bag containing all the winds but the one necessary to blow him home. They actually sighted Ithaca, but his men stealthily opened the bag, expecting to find treasure, and the winds drove them far off their course.

E. They came next to the land of the Laestrygonians, giant cannibals who unceremoniously devoured all his men, except Odysseus and his crew.

F. With his last ship Odysseus then came to the island Aeaea, the home of the goddess Circe. He dispatched half of his crew to reconnoiter. Circe welcomed them, drugged them, and transformed them into swine. Rushing to the rescue, Odysseus was met by Hermes who provided him with the magic herb *moly*. Equipped with this charm, he overpowered Circe, and compelled her to restore his men to human shape. Becoming Circe's lover, Odysseus remained with his men in Circe's palace for a full year. When he decided to leave, Circe informed him that he must visit Hades to consult the Theban prophet Teiresias about his future. Provided with explicit directions, he departed, leaving behind, unburied, the body of Elpenor, the youngest of his men, who accidentally lost his life just before they sailed.

## Book XI.

G. Following Circe's directions, he sailed to the end of the world (Atlantic Ocean), and reached the entrance to Hades.

1. Making the proper sacrifices, Odysseus evoked the spirits of the dead. Elpenor's soul was already in Hades, and implored him to return to Circe's island to give decent burial to his body, so that his soul might rest. Odysseus promised.

2. Odysseus then permitted the soul of the Theban soothsayer, Teiresias, to drink the blood of the sacrificial victims. Teiresias then told him much of his future.

3. The soul of his mother, Anticleia, whom he had left alive in Ithaca, next appeared, and related to him how she had died of a broken heart, waiting for his return.

4. A procession of famous women of the past then paraded before him, including Antiope, Alcmene, Jocasta, Leda, Phaedra, and Ariadne. (At this point Odysseus stops his narrative to the Phaeacians, mindful of the lateness of the hour, but Alcinous bids him to tell the rest of the story.)

5. The appearance of the soul of Agamemnon moved Odysseus to tears. Agamemnon told him of his unhappy death, together with that of Cassandra, at the hands of his wife, Clytemnestra, and her lover, Aegisthus. He expressed distrust of all women, and warned Odysseus against his wife, Penelope, as faithful as she was.

a. Achilles' soul next spoke to him, expressing sorrow over being dead though famous, and wished he were alive again, even if he were exceedingly poor. Odysseus told him of the bravery of his son at the fall of Troy.

b. The soul of Ajax, the son of Telamon, who had committed suicide when Odysseus was awarded the armor of Achilles, refused to talk to Odysseus.

c. In this parade of famous men of the past Odysseus saw also Minos, Orion, Tantalus, Sisyphus, and Heracles.

## Book XII.

H. Odysseus returned to Circe's island to bury Elpenor. Here he received new instructions from Circe how to evade future difficulties.

I. Odysseus listened unharmed to the alluring song of the two Sirens, mermaids who lured sailors to shipwreck, by having himself lashed to the mast and stopping his men's ears with wax.

J. Next they made the perilous passage through the narrow strait between the monster Scylla and the whirlpool Charybdis, losing six men to Scylla.

K. Finally, they landed on an island where lived the sacred cattle of Helios Hyperion (the sun). Odysseus warned his men of dire consequences if they killed the cattle. Here they were becalmed for a long time, and when provisions were exhausted, his men slew and ate some of the cattle. Eventually, they left the island, but the ship was soon destroyed by a thunderbolt of Zeus in punishment for the slaying of the sacred cattle of the sun. Odysseus, the only survivor, was shipwrecked on the island of Ogygia, where Calypso kept him for seven years.

### THE END OF ODYSSEUS' STORY

## Book XIII.

A. Next day Odysseus, laden with gifts, is taken by the Phaeacians in one of their swift ships to Ithaca. After a day's sail he is landed asleep on the island of Ithaca. Upon returning, the Phaeacian ship is turned into stone in the harbor of Scheria by the angry Poseidon.

B. Odysseus awakens, but does not recognize the land. Athena appears, tells him where he is, advises him how to destroy the suitors, and finally transforms him into an old beggar.

## Book XIV.

Odysseus goes to the hut of Eumaeus, his swineherd, who receives him hospitably. From Eumaeus he hears details about the behavior of his suitors. Odysseus predicts the coming of Odysseus, but conceals his own identity, telling a long fictitious tale about himself.

## Book XV.

A. Athena appears to Telemachus at Sparta in a dream, bids him to return at once to Ithaca, and warns him of the ambush of the suitors. The next day, bearing gifts of Menelaus, Telemachus, together with Nestor's son, makes the two-day journey to Pylus, whence Telemachus takes ship for home. Meanwhile Eumaeus and Odysseus exchange stories.

B. The next day Telemachus arrives safely, evading the wooers in ambush, and goes directly to Eumaeus' hut.

## Book XVI.

A. Telemachus and Eumaeus talk about conditions in Ithaca, and Telemachus bids Eumaeus go to Penelope to inform her of his safe return.

B. Athena then restores Odysseus to his true appearance, and he makes himself known to his son. Together they plot vengeance against the 108 suitors, agreeing to conceal Odysseus' identity from all.

C. The suitors are dismayed at the failure of their plot to kill Telemachus. Penelope rebukes them for their attempt.

## Book XVII.

A. The following day, Telemachus returns to the palace, is

welcomed by Penelope, and tells her of what he heard at Pylus and Sparta.

B. Odysseus, again transformed into an old beggar, together with Eumaeus goes to the city. Melanthius, the goatherd of Odysseus, meets them on the way, and insults and kicks Odysseus.

C. As they enter the courtyard of the palace, Odysseus is recognized by his hunting dog, Argus, who makes a feeble attempt to greet him and then dies.

D. As Odysseus, playing his part, begs from the suitors, Antinous strikes him with a footstool.

## Book XVIII.

A. Another beggar reviles Odysseus as a competitor, and Antinous forces them to fight. Seeking to avoid suspicion, Odysseus strikes the beggar very gently, but breaks his jaw.

B. Penelope, made more beautiful than ever before by Athena, appears in the hall, and evokes the admiration of all.

C. Odysseus rebukes one of Penelope's hand-maidens for her shameless behavior with the suitors. Eurymachus throws a stool at Odysseus for his insolence.

## Book XIX.

A. When the suitors leave the feasting hall, Odysseus and Telemachus remove all the arms.

B. Penelope appears, and she and Odysseus converse. He invents a story about himself, reveals some accurate knowledge of Odysseus, and predicts his speedy return. She is deeply moved by his talk. As Eurycleia, his old nurse, washes his feet, she recognizes on his thigh a scar he had once received while hunting. He barely succeeds in preventing her from revealing his identity.

C. Penelope tells Odysseus that she has decided to ordain a shooting contest the following day, and that she will marry the suitor who can string Odysseus' bow and shoot an arrow through twelve axe-heads placed in a row.

## Book XX.

The gods and good omens join in giving heart to Odysseus and Penelope. The next morning, the suitors assemble, and Odysseus further notes those among his own people who are faithful and those who are unfaithful to him. One of the wooers, Ctesippos, jeeringly throws him a bone, and is rebuked by Telemachus. A soothsayer foretells the coming destruction of the suitors. They laugh at him.

## Book XXI.

A. Penelope brings out Odysseus' bow, and proposes the shooting contest. The axes are set in order. Telemachus playfully tries to string the bow. Preparations are made for the trials.

B. Odysseus meanwhile reveals his identity to his two faithful herdsmen, Eumaeus and Philoetius. They arrange to trap the suitors in the hall by closing all doors.

C. Each of the suitors in order tries to string the bow. All fail, even their leaders Antinous and Eurymachus. Odysseus asks to be permitted to try. There is considerable opposition to this on the grounds of impropriety, but finally Odysseus obtains the bow, strings it easily, and shoots an arrow through the axes.

## Book XXII.

A. With that, Telemachus arms himself and stands beside his father. Odysseus strips off his rags and first kills Antinous with an arrow. When Eurymachus discovers who the stranger really is, he seeks to lay all the blame for the behavior of the suitors on the dead Antinous. Odysseus slays him too.

B. The trapped suitors resist, but are slain one by one by Odysseus with the aid of Telemachus, Eumaeus, Philoetius, and Athena. Melanthius, the faithless goatherd, who has been aiding the suitors with weapons, is caught by the two herdsmen and bound with ropes. Odysseus spares none but the minstrel, Phemius, and the herald, Medon.

C. The nurse Eurycleia is then asked to single out the hand-maidens of Penelope who have fraternized with the suitors. These twelve girls are forced to carry out the dead and clean the feasting hall. Then they are all hanged, and Melanthius is horribly mutilated and killed. The hall is then purified by fumigation.

## Book XXIII.

A. Penelope is informed of what has happened, but after twenty years of waiting, finds it difficult to believe that the ragged stranger is Odysseus. Telemachus rebukes her as hard-hearted because of her doubt.

B. While a pretense of dancing and feasting is kept up to deceive the townsmen, particularly the relatives of the dead suitors, Odysseus and Penelope converse. When Odysseus mentions the secret in the construction of their bridal-bed, she is finally convinced. After a tender greeting, they retire, telling each other of their sufferings and adventures far into the night. Athena holds back the dawn.

C. But before dawn Odysseus, Telemachus, and the two herdsmen head out to the country to the house of Odysseus' father, Laertes.

## Book XXIV.

A. Hermes meanwhile conducts the souls of the dead suitors to Hades, where they are greeted by Achilles, Patroclus, Antilochus, Ajax, and Agamemnon. Agamemnon envies Odysseus for his faithful wife.

B. Odysseus arrives at the house of his aged father. After he has revealed himself to Laertes in a touching scene, they prepare to defend themselves from the expected retaliation of the relatives of the suitors.

C. Meanwhile, the relatives have discovered the slaughter, bury the suitors, and then arm to attack Odysseus. The two sides have begun the struggle, when suddenly at the intervention of Athena and a warning thunderbolt of Zeus, peace is restored.

## ÏLIAD VS. ODYSSEY

Though both epics have the same style, language and meter, and the similarities are far greater than dissimilarities, the following differences may be noted in the *Odyssey*:

I. Greater evidence in *Odyssey* of private property, increased importance of the individual, use of iron;

II. Decreased power of kings, rising importance of nobles;

III. Religion more spiritual; gods no longer in violent conflict;

IV. *Odyssey* technically superior to *Iliad;* greater unity of plot;

V. Characters not so majestic; *Odyssey* emphasizes cunning, *Iliad* military prowess;

VI. Greater use of abstractions.

## STYLE AND TECHNIQUE OF HOMERIC EPICS

I. Epics begin with invocation to the Muse

II. The story begins *in medias res*. Homer assumes that audience is familiar with the traditional story. He begins at a moment of crisis, gradually drawing in background material, and employing the "flashback" technique.

III. Use of supernatural; gods mingle with human beings and intervene in their affairs.

IV. Stock epithets; traditional formulaic phrases, which help listening audience visualize material better, conserve attention of listener, help the memory, and lessen burden of composition: e.g., loud-sounding sea, wine-dark sea, rosy-fingered dawn, deep-soiled Phthia, white-armed Andromache, swift-footed Achilles, long-haired Achaeans, winged words.

V. Repetitions, of epithets, phrases, incidents. About ⅓ of *Iliad* and *Odyssey* is repetitious in whole or part. This device lessens the labor of the poet, helps audience anticipate what is to come, like recurrent phrases and themes in music, thus arousing pleasure in rehearing what is familiar. It helps to reinforce and make emphatic material for a listening audience, and, morever, since the poems were never recited in their entirety at one occasion, repetitions are necessary to refresh memory and would be less noticed.

VI.  Similes, lengthy, taken from nature, animal life, everyday life. Element of lyric in Homer, taken from common experience of listeners.

VII.  Epic question, answered immediately by the poet.

VIII.  Speeches. About ½ of *Iliad,* more of *Odyssey* consists of lengthy speeches. Rapid dialogue sequences would be difficult for the minstrel to recite and confusing to the listening audience.

IX.  Catalogues of names.

X.  Objectivity. No author's comments; Homer is impersonal and reserved. This forces the audience to contribute to the story, thus sustaining attention.

XI.  Conventional literary language, mostly Ionic with Aeolic elements; artificial traditional language.

XII.  Balanced contrast, in plot, scenes, phrases, characters.

XIII.  Matthew Arnold: "Homer is rapid, plain in thought, plain in diction, and noble."

## HOMER'S HUMANISM

I.  The greatness of Homer lies not only in his consummate artistry in style and plot construction, but, above all, in his knowledge and portrayal of human personality and behavior.

II.  He touches on almost all basic human emotions and motives.

III.  He created about 40 great characters of universal scope.

A.  His characters are individualized up to a certain point.

B.  Their personalities are not described by Homer, but must be deduced by the reader from their actions and words.

C.  His characters are living human beings, portrayed with the fine qualities, limitations and contradictions of real people.

D.  He has a broad human understanding, exhibiting sympathy for the suffering Trojans, though the common man is largely disregarded, especially in the *Iliad.*

E. He expresses the dignity and joy of life, but also its tragedy and sadness, especially the inevitability of death.

## RELIGION IN HOMER

I. There are many gods of human shape and with human attributes, who devote their time to feasting, intrigue, and love. There is little of an ethical nature in his religion; the essence of the gods is power.

II. Human beings obtain benefits from the gods by prayer and sacrifices.

III. Fate and the gods are not in conflict; there is little distinction between them.

IV. The future is revealed by omens, dreams, oracles, and soothsayers.

V. Cremation of dead is uniform; burial is a religious duty. The soul is supposed to have a mere shadowy existence in Hades, though the concept of punishment for evil exists.

## ETHICAL CODE IN HOMER

I. *Aidos* (shame), sense of honor which deters people from breaking the unwritten laws of the clan.

II. *Nemesis,* indignation of public opinion against those who break the unwritten laws.

III. Hospitality to strangers is obligatory.

IV. Revenge for wrongdoing is undertaken by the family.

V. Desire for personal glory (*kudos*) is the principal drive.

## CHAPTER THREE

# HISTORY AND SOCIETY
## 750-500 B.C.

▣

## ARISTOCRATIC GOVERNMENT

I.   By the 8th Cent. B.C. the nobles had everywhere super-seded the power of the clan-kings.

II.   The growth of the power of this hereditary nobility was the result of the disintegration of the tribal organization, the crystallization of the family system, and the increase in private property in land. The landed estates of the nobles were the source of their power.

## POLIS (CITY-STATE)

I.   By the 8th Cent. there emerged the most characteristic feature of Greek society, the city-state (*polis*), the autonomous city of the Greek world. At the height of Greek civilization there were hundreds of such self-governing states. Some of the famous ones were: Athens, Sparta, Thebes, Miletus, Ephesus, Corinth, Argos, Sicyon, Olympia, Delphi, Megara.

II.   This development took place by the fusion of villages, acknowledging a single political center which controlled the surrounding territory.

III.   Officials were elected, normally for one-year terms, at first by the nobility from among their own numbers, later by greater numbers of citizens with extension of the vote.

IV.   Citizenship was jealously guarded, being restricted to descendants of citizens.

**41**

## COLONIZATION MOVEMENT (750-550 B.C.)

I. In this period the Greeks in the Aegean area planted colonies, which became independent city-states, from the straits of Gibraltar to the shores of the Black Sea. They colonized especially Sicily and Southern Italy (called by the Italians Magna Graecia). Some famous Greek colonies were Massilia (Marseilles), Neapolis (Naples), Syracuse, Byzantium (Istanbul), Tarentum, Sybaris, Croton, Naucratis, Cyrene.

II. The causes of the Age of Colonization were varied: overpopulation, economic distress as the result of changes in agriculture, political upheavals.

III. The results of these developments were: spread of Greek culture, growth of commerce and manufacture and wealth of non-aristocratic classes of population, sharper class divisions, intellectual awakening, especially in Ionia (Ionian Renaissance).

## AGE OF TYRANTS

I. Growing opposition to the power of the nobles resulted in the 6th Cent. B.C. in the rise of tyrants in many city-states. These were unconstitutional rulers who overthrew the aristocrats with the support of coalitions of non-aristocratic classes. They were as a whole progressive rulers, who, though often ruthless, extended democratic rights, and were patrons of the arts and literature. Some of the famous tyrants were Thrasybulus of Miletus, Polycrates of Samos, Cleisthenes of Sicyon, Peisistratus of Athens, Cypselus of Corinth, Periander of Corinth.

II. The Tyrants were ultimately overthrown by revolutions, and the city-states were transformed into oligarchies (rule by few, resulting from merger of aristocrats with wealthy commoners) or democracies (rule by all citizens).

## GENERAL RESULTS

I. Growth of individualism and interest in the present.

II. Sharp class divisions and political unrest.

III. Period of rapid change, independent thought and action.

CHAPTER FOUR

# GREEK LYRIC POETRY

## 750-450 B.C.

### LYRIC POEM

A short poem, set to music, reflecting the personal emotion and thought of the author.

### LYRIC VS. EPIC

| *Epic* | *Lyric* |
|---|---|
| 1. long | 1. short |
| 2. recited | 2. sung |
| 3. objective narrative | 3. personal and introspective |
| 4. dactylic hexameter | 4. variety of meters |
| 5. looks back to past | 5. emphasis on present |

### ELEGIAC POETRY

I. Not regarded by Greeks as pure lyric, because it was written to the accompaniment of the flute *(aulos),* a reed instrument, while lyric as such was accompanied by the lyre.

II. Metrical form: elegiac couplet—dactylic hexameter alternating with syncopated dactylic pentameter.

III. Elegy, largely reflective, was used for military themes, banquet, songs, political thought, dedications on monuments, epitaphs on tombstones, love.

### IAMBIC POETRY

I. Employs the basic rhythm of everyday speech, the iamb (◡—), the most popular verse being the iambic trimeter.

II. Recited, not sung, and used for satire and lampoons of individuals.

## TYPICAL ELEGIAC AND IAMBIC POETS
## ARCHILOCHUS OF PAROS (ca. 650 B.C.)

I.    Soldier-poet, life filled with misfortune and unhappiness.

II.   Next to Homer, greatest Ionic poet.

III.  Earliest elegiac poems, earliest and greatest iambic verses.

IV.  First poet to reveal self, first poet of satire and hate.

V.    Style: violent, passionate, graceful, cynical, bitter, melancholy, sincere.

*Typical Poems of Archilochus*

1. Cynically and nonchalantly, he tells how he fled from battle, discarding his shield. Better to throw away one's arms than be killed.

2. Life is hard, but there is a cycle of ups and downs. Don't exult in victory, or despair in defeat; don't rejoice too much in pleasure, or grieve too much in trouble. Learn to take things as they come.

## TYRTAEUS OF SPARTA (ca. 650 B.C.)

I.    Martial elegies, war songs for Spartan army.

II.   Appeals to courage, pride, and sense of duty to city-state; grim attitude toward war.

III.  Style: sincere, direct.

*Typical Poem of Tyrtaeus*

It is noble to die for one's country. Flight from battle means exile and the shameful life of a beggar for self and family. It is disgraceful for the young to desert the old on the battlefield. The ideal youth, in all his beauty, dies nobly in battle. Bite your lip and stand firm.

## SOLON OF ATHENS (ca. 640-559 B.C.)

I.    Athenian aristocrat, statesman, legislator, one of the seven wise men of Greece, first Athenian poet.

II.  Martial and didactic poems expressing political and ethical opinions.

III.  Style: serious, dignified, though he was not a great poet.

*Typical Poem of Solon*

His philosophy of life. Prayer to the Muses for assistance in obtaining for him the good things of life. Unjustly obtained wealth and arrogance are punished. Be content with what the gods give. There is personal responsibility for human suffering. For people do wrong by wanting too much out of pride *(hybris),* and are afflicted by infatuation *(ate).* The wrath of Zeus *(Nemesis)* is visited upon such people personally; if not, their innocent descendants will pay the penalty. Men have varying ambitions and occupy themselves in various ways in life. But all is illusory, for we are at the mercy of fate. All is uncertain in life. We must limit our desires for wealth, otherwise retribution will come. The ways of the gods are inscrutable.

## MELIC POETRY (pure lyric)

I.  Written to be sung to the accompaniment of the seven-stringed lyre. Ode means song.

II.  Great variety of metrical schemes.

III.  Two distinct types of lyric poetry.

A.  Monodic lyric: sung by poet to friends; origin in folk-song; poet composes words and music.

B.  Choral lyric: sung and danced by chorus on religious and social occasions; poet composes words, music, and dance steps; many types of choral lyrics, e.g., hymn, dirge, marriage-song *(epithalamion),* victory song *(epinicion),* hymn to Dionysus *(dithyramb).*

IV.  Alexandrian canon of lyric poets: Pindar, Bacchylides, Sappho, Anacreon, Stesichorus, Simonides, Ibycus, Alcaeus, Alcman.

## TYPICAL MONODIC LYRIC POETS
## ALCMAN OF SPARTA (ca. 630 B.C.)

1.  Came to Sparta from Sardis in Lydia.

II.  Wrote mostly choral lyrics, but also monodic.

*Typical poems of Alcman*

1.  He wishes that he were carefree as the kingfisher on the wing, so that he could join the maidens in their dance, but age forbids.

2.  All nature is asleep at night.

## ALCAEUS OF LESBOS (ca. 600 B.C.)

I.  Aristocratic landowner, man of action, soldier in struggle against tyrants of his city-state, Mytilene. Exiled, but returned after amnesty.

II.  Poems of war, politics, love, and wine. First known poet of pleasure of wine.

III.  Created Alcaic stanza.

IV.  Style: masculine force, simplicity, directness, seriousness, passion, hate, grace.

*Typical Poems of Alcaeus*

1.  Ship of State. There is internal dissension, and the ship of state, tossed by clashing winds and tides, is endangered. A new wave strikes, adding to the distress. Courage, unity, and action are needed. A brighter future lies ahead.

2.  Wine is the anodyne of sorrow. Forget the raw weather. Grieving will not help. All is cured by wine.

3.  Prepare yourself for the banquet with wreaths of parsley.

4.  Why wait for night to drink? Wine is the gift of Dionysus to banish man's cares. Mix each measure of wine with two of water, and keep the beakers full.

5.  Quench your thirst with wine, now that the Dog Days are here. All nature sings in the summer heat. Girls are overcome with desire, but the men do not respond in the oppressive heat.

6.  On my suffering gray head pour perfume in preparation for the banquet.

7.  Drink, for when once death comes, there is no return

from Hades. Sisyphus thought he could escape, but was forced to return, and was assigned great punishment. Enjoy the present moment, while you are young. Do not hope for immortality.

## SAPPHO OF LESBOS (ca. 590 B.C.)

I.  Aristocrat of Mytilene, exiled; myth that she committed suicide by leaping off the Leucadian cliff because of unrequited love.

II.  First and greatest woman poet, "the poetess," "the tenth Muse."

III.  Leader of club of aristocratic girls devoted to Aphrodite and the Muses. Preparation for marriage was important aim of club.

IV.  Wrote mostly on subject of love (greatest epithalamia of antiquity). About 5 per cent of her work has survived.

V.  Created Sapphic stanza.

VI.  Style: consummate artistry, perfect taste, simple, direct, sincere, and frank, sensitive, intense passion, spontaneity, dignity.

*Typical Poems of Sappho*

1.  She prays to Aphrodite, for she is suffering from unrequited love. She begs her to help her now, as before, to win the girl to her love.

2.  She expresses her overwhelming love for one of her girls on the occasion of the girl's marriage. Her affection consumes her entire body and leaves her almost lifeless.

3.  The flooding light of the moon.

4.  A gentle stream entrances her.

5.  She who knows nothing of beauty will be without fame both in life and in death.

6.  Weave garlands for thy head, maiden, for Aphrodite and the Graces show favor to those who wear them.

7.  I loved you, Atthis, a long time ago; you were young and not ripe for marriage.

8.  A girl on leaving her weeps unashamedly at the sorrow

of parting. Sappho bids her farewell, and asks that she not forget their love, reminding her of her activities in the school.

9. She muses sadly over the absence of Atthis, her favorite, who now lives in Lydia, excelling the women there in beauty. Her longing grows as she remembers her.

10. The sudden onslaught of love causes her to tremble with passion.

11. She would not exchange her daughter, Cleis, for all the world.

12. The melancholy loneliness of Sappho at night.

13. The love-sick girl cannot tend to her weaving.

14. The nightingale, the harbinger of spring.

15. The bride's maidenhood is gone forever; the bride-groom is tall and straight.

16. The young bride is like the sweet red apple on the topmost bough, difficult to pluck; or like a wild hyacinth flower.

17. All come home at eventide.

## ANACREON OF TEOS (ca. 563-478 B.C.)

I. Court poet, travelled much.

II. Wrote on love, wine, and song. Characterized especially by pursuit of pleasure, dislike of war, sophistication, wit, irony, grace, dignity, polish, no deep emotion.

*Typical Poems of Anacreon*

1. Eros (Cupid) summons him to love. A beautiful Lesbian girl attracts him, but his hair is white, and her fancy turns to another.

2. His white hair and missing teeth reveal his old age. There is little time left to enjoy life. Hence he sighs at the thought of death. For Hades is a dismal place, from which there is no return.

3. O Thracian lass, don't think to flee from me. I know how to master you, as a horseman breaks the frisky colt.

## SIMONIDES OF CEOS (556-467 B.C.)

I. Many-sided genius; wrote choral lyrics, monodies, and

unsurpassed elegiacs to commemorate the dead; professional poet.

II. Style: delicate pathos without sentimentality, grace, elegance, sophistication, dignity, simplicity, and exquisite perfection of epitaphs.

*Typical Poems of Simonides*

1. Personal worth, not birth, is the true meaning of goodness and nobility. The old aristocratic ideal of nobility, inherited wealth, physical and mental excellence, is an impossible one, for man is not personally responsible for these. Further, these qualities are not permanent; they are due to circumstance of birth, and changed circumstance may remove them. The test of goodness is nobility of behavior, conscious choice of one's own free will of right actions. Not physical, mental, or material endowment, but ethical conduct is the key to true nobility. Excellence is not hereditary; anyone can achieve it, but it must be combined with civic virtue and conscious effort.

2. Danae and her infant son, Perseus, are adrift in a wooden chest. Tearfully she fondles the child, and with exquisite pathos marvels how the child sleeps peacefully, and prays to Zeus for aid.

3. Virtue dwells on a lofty peak guarded by nymphs. The climb to her is a laborious one.

4. (Epitaph for the Athenians who died in 506 B.C. fighting in Euboea.) To the Athenians who died in Euboea their countrymen have erected this monument. Though youth is precious, they gave their lives, and did not flee from the stormy battle.

5. (Epitaph for the Spartans who died in 480 B.C. fighting the Persians at Thermopylae.) They died far from their home in obedience to orders.

## ANONYMOUS POEMS

1. (Swallow Song, sung at Rhodes in Spring by children.) Welcome, swallow, harbinger of Spring. Give us gifts of food and wine. If you don't, we'll carry off the door, or lintel, or your wife.

**49**

If you do, give generously. Let the swallow in. We are not old beggars, but children.

2. (Attic drinking song, commemorating the murder of the tyrant Hipparchus in 514 B.C. by Harmodius and Aristogeiton.) The sword is wreathed with myrtle, as when Harmodius and Aristogeiton slew the tyrant and liberated Athens. You have not died, Harmodius and Aristogeiton, but have gone to the Isles of the Blest to join the heroes Achilles and Diomedes. You will always be famous, because you slew the tyrant and liberated Athens.

## TYPICAL CHORAL LYRIC POET
## PINDAR OF THEBES (ca. 522-448 B.C.)

I.   Greatest Greek lyric poet; professional writer.

II.   Famous especially for *epinicia,* commemorating athletic victors in the Olympic, Pythian, Nemean, and Isthmian games.

III.  Pindaric Ode.

A. Unit of three stanzas: strophe, antistrophe, epode. Strophes and antistrophes have same metrical pattern and music, divided among the two halves of the chorus. Epodes performed by entire chorus, have same meter and music throughout poem.

B. Contents of ode: prelude, personal observations on victor; myth of gods or heroes; epilogue, moral maxims and personal observations.

IV.   Conservative, aristocratic point of view; glorification of hereditary nobility; profoundly religious.

V.   Style: "the scholar's poet," majesty, grand, obscure and difficult, dazzling imagination, brilliant metaphor, swift transitions and associations, orchestral effect.

*Typical Poem of Pindar*

*First Olympian Ode* (Pindar's masterpiece)

(Honoring victory of the horse of Hiero, tyrant of Syracuse, in 476 B.C. at Olympia.)

Strophe I.  Water is the best of elements, gold the most precious form of wealth, fire at night is the brightest blaze, the sun the warmest heavenly body. So the Olympic games surpass all other contests. The games inspire minstrels to sing the praises of Hiero.

Antistrophe I. Hail to great Hiero, as the chorus sings in his honor. Hail to his horse Pherenikos (Victor), who won the race at Olympia.

Epode I. The horse brought fame to Hiero. His victory occurred in the land once ruled by Pelops, a favorite of the gods. About Pelops false legends are told, beautiful in form.

Strophe II. I shall speak reverently, and tell another myth of Pelops, son of Tantalus.

Antistrophe II. Poseidon took Pelops to Olympus to be cup-bearer of the gods. It is not true that he was fed to the gods by his father.

Epode II. It is irreverent to call the gods cannibals. Tantalus was a favorite of the gods, but his prosperity brought pride, and he was punished by Zeus.

Strophe III. Tantalus received eternal punishment for stealing nectar and ambrosia from the gods. In addition, Pelops, his son, was banished back to earth.

Antistrophe III. Near Olympia he sought a bride, Hippodameia, and asked aid of Poseidon.

Epode III. It was a dangerous wooing, for Hippodameia's father, Oenomaus, sought to slay each suitor in a chariot race. But Poseidon aided Pelops.

Strophe IV. Thus Pelops won Hippodameia. And in the Peloponnesus he now lies buried, greatly honored, where he won his victory at Olympia.

Antistrophe IV. Here too great Hiero won his victory, he too a favorite of the gods. An even greater victory with the four-horse chariot is in store for him.

Epode IV. King Hiero is at the summit of his fortune. May he be supreme as long as he lives, as may the poet too be foremost among Greek writers.

## PASTORAL (BUCOLIC) POETRY

Short poem, lyric in nature, dealing with the lives and loves of shepherds. (A creation of the Hellenistic Period.) (See pp. 245-248).

## THEOCRITUS OF SYRACUSE (ca. 270 B.C.)

I.  Father of pastoral poetry; greatest poet of Alexandrian period (see p. 246).

II. Wrote *Idyls* (little pictures).

    A. Pastoral poems, rustic life in Sicily

    B. Mimes, dramatic dialogues reflecting city life

III. Style: combination of artificiality and sophistication with realism, spontaneity and freshness; love of nature and country; emphasis on love; dramatic skill.

*Typical Idyls of Theocritus*

    *Idyl I* The Death of Daphnis

Thyrsis, a shepherd, meets a goatherd. He asks the goatherd to play his pipes, but the latter instead requests Thyrsis to sing the Song of Daphnis, offering him a reward, especially an ivy-wood bowl beautifully carved with rustic scenes. Thyrsis sings of the ideal shepherd, Daphnis, who boasted of his imperishable love for his bride, the nymph Nais. But Aphrodite caused him to fall in love with another girl, and desperately resisting his new passion he slowly died. Hermes and shepherds came to aid him, but to no avail. When Aphrodite came to mock him, he reviled her. Wild animals and the flocks lamented for him. He called on Pan to pipe at his passing, prayed that nature be turned topsy-turvy, and died. Aphrodite regretted her action, but it was too late. Thyrsis, having ended the song, receives his rewards.

    *Idyl II* The Sorceress (a mime)

Simaetha is lovesick for Delphis, her lover, who deserted her. With the aid of her maid, Thestylis, she tries to regain his love with magic spells and incantations, recalling all the while the progress of her love and how her uncontrollable passion for Delphis led her to give herself to him. Her regrets and passion, her love and hate are inextricably enmeshed. She dismisses her maid, and in the calm night addresses the moon, rehearsing the details of her love affair unashamedly, how she first met Delphis, how she pined for him, how he came at her summoning, how he spoke deceitful words of love, and how he finally deserted her for another. She tells of her magic spells to win him back or punish him, and bids farewell to the moon.

*Idyl XI*   Polyphemus, the Cyclops, in Love

The physician Nicias being in love, Theocritus tells him how even the monstrous Cyclops Polyphemus eased his love-pangs for the sea-nymph Galatea by singing. Sitting on a hilltop overlooking the sea, Polyphemus sings to Galatea of his love. He tells how he fell in love with her, recognizes his ugliness, recounts his assets, and promises her happiness and true love. But his humbleness finally changes to pride, and he boasts that he is attractive to other girls.

*Idyl XV*   The Syracusan Women (a mime)

Two Syracusan women, Gorgo and Praxinoe, are in Alexandria. Gorgo comes to Praxinoe's home, and after chatting about the crowds of the big city, the stupidity of their husbands, their new clothing, they set out to the palace of King Ptolemy to see the procession in honor of Adonis. They move with difficulty through the crowds, arrive at the palace, admire the decorations and the image of Adonis lying on a couch. A singer then sings the Psalm of Adonis, telling of the love of Aphrodite for Adonis, and of his annual death and resurrection. Gorgo and Praxinoe express admiration for the singer and hasten home to prepare dinner for their husbands.

## CHAPTER FIVE

# HISTORY AND SOCIETY
## 500-400 B.C.

◎

## SPARTA (LACEDAEMON)

I.   Descendants of Dorian invaders; gradual conquest of S. Peloponnesus; by 500 B.C. leader of Peloponnesian League, loose confederacy of most free city-states of Peloponnesus under Spartan hegemony.

II.   Economic and Social System

    A.   Conservative agricultural community.

    B.   Highly militarized, authoritarian state; individualism suppressed.

    C.   All citizens (Spartiates) leisure-class landowners; soldiers most of their lives; education state-controlled, emphasized physical training and military courage; small minority of population; lived in barracks.

    D.   Helots, inferior producing class supporting soldier-citizens; majority of population; serfs paying fixed rent to landowners.

    E.   Perioeci (dwellers around), above helots in status; commerce and manufacture in their hands.

III.   Political Organization

    A.   Two kings, figureheads; Council (aristocratic families); Assembly (all citizens over 30); Ephors (real rulers; 5 elected annually by Assembly).

    B.   Political policy of supporting conservative oligarchies in other states.

IV.  Spartan women; greater freedom than in most Greek cities; physical training for breeding future soldiers.

## ATHENS

I.  Ionians; early population more homogeneous than at Sparta; by 700 B.C. entire peninsula of Attica organized as city-state with Athens as political center.

II.  By 7th Cent. B.C. aristocratic government supersedes monarchy, with Council (Areopagus) of nobles supreme; executives (9 archons) elected annually from aristocratic class.

III.  Economic, political and social unrest leads to repressive measures by aristocrats and threats of revolution.

IV.  Solon, moderate aristocrat, sole archon in 594 B.C., introduces broad reform program to mitigate economic, social, and political ferment; extension of vote in Popular Assembly to lowest class of population, first step toward democracy.

V.  Tyranny of Peisistratus and his sons, Hippias and Hipparchus (560-510 B.C.).

A.  Great cultural progress of Athens.

B.  Murder of Hipparchus by Harmodius and Aristogeiton, who were lynched; repressive tyranny of Hippias, followed by revolution.

VI.  Cleisthenes' reforms (508 B.C.)—first democratic government in world history.

A.  Full political equality of all citizens; Popular Assembly supreme, chief law-making body.

B.  Vote by place of residence, not in accordance with wealth or tribal association; election of civil executives (archons) and board of 10 generals by all citizens.

## PERSIAN WARS

I.  Conquest of Ionian Greeks by Lydian Empire under King Croesus; overthrow of Croesus by Cyrus, founder of Persian Empire; annexation of Anatolia by Persians; harsh treatment of Greek subjects by Persian King Darius (521-486 B.C.); Ionian revolt, supported by Athens and Eretria; suppression of revolt (494 B.C.) by Persians.

II. Persian invasion of Greece, under leadership of Datis and Artaphernes (490 B.C.); defeat of Persians at Marathon (26 miles N.E. of Athens) by small army of Athenians, led by Miltiades.

III. Development of Athens as sea-power under influence of Themistocles; Congress of Corinth (481 B.C.)—many Greek cities agree on united opposition to Persia.

IV. Persian invasion of Greece, under leadership of King Xerxes (Ahasuerus of Old Testament) in 480 B.C.; large amphibious operation; main body of Persian troops crosses Hellespont, marches through Thrace, Macedonia, Thessaly; heroic, but futile, stand of Greek army, led by Leonidas and his 300 Spartans, at the Pass of Thermopylae; evacuation of Athenians to Salamis; brilliant naval victory of Greeks, led by Themistocles, in Bay of Salamis (480 B.C.); smashing defeat of Persian by combined Greek forces at Plataea in Boeotia (479 B.C.); retreat of Persians; liberation of Ionia.

## DELIAN LEAGUE (477 B.C.)

I. Many eastern city-states join in a confederacy, under Athenian leadership, for defense against Persia.

II. Ships and money contributed by members; executive headquarters and treasury on Island of Delos.

III. Athens uses force to prevent secession from league.

## ATHENIAN EMPIRE (454 B.C.)

Athens transfers treasury of Delian League to Athens; members of league lose their freedom; pay tribute to Athens.

## GOLDEN AGE OF PERICLES (461-429 B.C.)

I. Pericles, elected chief general numerous times, leader of Popular Assembly, unofficial ruler of democratic Athens.

II. Athenian imperialism based on naval power, strongest in world.

III. Wealth of Athenian government from tribute exacted from cities of Empire, and from heavy taxation of rich; money used to beautify the city (buildings of Acropolis, especially the Parthenon), and to extend Athenian democracy.

IV. Athens a great commercial center.

## ATHENIAN DEMOCRACY

I. Limited to citizens, who comprised small number (10 per cent of population, ca. 40,000); women, foreigners (metics), slaves excluded.

II. Direct democracy; all important measures passed by majority vote in mass meetings of citizens; executive, legislative, judicial functions directly controlled by entire citizen body.

III. Only Board of Generals elected; all other officials chosen by lot; principle of rotation in office.

IV. Citizens paid for all services to community: office holding, jury service, attendance in Assembly, later even for attendance at theater.

## WOMEN

I. Principal occupation, housework.

II. Upper class women segregated and secluded.

III. Marriages arranged by parents, with dowry as important consideration.

IV. Divorce easy for men by return of dowry, almost impossible for women.

## ATHENIAN EDUCATION

I. Almost universal primary education in private schools for citizens from age of 6 to 14; basic aim—sound mind in sound body as preparation for good citizenship.

II. Principal subjects: reading, writing, arithmetic, literature, music, gymnastics.

III. Ephebic Oath, pledging devotion to the welfare of the city, taken on becoming citizen at age of 18.

IV. State-controlled military training from 18 to 20 years of age.

## SOPHISTS (IN ATHENS)

I.  Teachers of wisdom, professors of higher education; private teachers; high fees, foreigners.

II.  Famous Sophists: Protagoras of Abdera, Gorgias of Leontini, Evenus of Paros, Prodicus of Ceos, Hippias of Elis, Thrasymachus of Chalcedon.

III.  Their teaching in great demand because of need for training for civic life in democratic Athens (speaking in Assembly, law courts), growth of individualism, and highly competitive Athenian life.

IV.  Humanistic interest in place of man in universe and society; main emphasis of teaching—training for success (political, financial) in social life through public speaking; clever methods of argumentation, without regard for truth, on both sides of a question.

V.  Developed rhetoric and artistic prose.

VI.  Principal ideas of Sophists

A.  Opposed to traditional morality and religion; scepticism, agnosticism, rationalism.

B.  Opposed to absolute standards of conduct; all knowledge subjective; relativity in ethics. ("Man is the measure of all things.")

C.  Theory of state and society: individuals and classes are in constant opposition; life is constant struggle for superiority and power by all; justice is not absolute but the imposed will of the stronger ("Might makes right"); individual self-interest the dominant drive of all (Law of Nature); laws and customs are man-made, subject to constant change.

VII.  Famous statements of Sophists

A.  Protagoras: "Man is the measure of all things"; "With

regard to the gods it is impossible to determine whether they exist or what they are like."

B. Gorgias: "Nothing exists; if it exists it cannot be known by man; if it can be known it cannot be expressed."

C. Hippias: "Religion is a man-made device for enforcing morality through fear"; "Laws are the conventions of an older generation."

## PELOPONNESIAN WAR (431-404 B.C.)

I.      Basic cause: rival imperialism of Athens and Sparta.

II.      Athenian naval power pitted against infantry forces of Sparta and her allies.

III.      Plague at Athens (430–429 B.C.); death of Pericles.

IV.      Peace of Nicias (421 B.C.) soon broken.

V.      Melos brutally forced into Athenian Empire in 416 B.C.

VI.      Disaster of Athenian naval expedition sent to conquer Sicily (415-413 B.C.), due to bad leadership; failure of siege of Syracuse and loss of all forces in Sicily.

VII.      Chaotic political conditions in Athens; final loss of entire Athenian navy.

VIII.     Surrender of Athens (404 B.C.); loss of Athenian Empire and military power.

## CHAPTER SIX

# THE DRAMA: TRAGEDY

◻

## ORIGIN

Dithyramb, choral lyric in honor of Dionysus, god of wine, performed in circular dancing-place *(orchestra)* by chorus of men dressed in goatskins (hence the term *tragoedia*—goat-song). They represented satyrs, companions of Dionysus. A story about Dionysus was improvised by the leader of the chorus.

## THESPIS OF ATHENS (ca. 535 B.C.)

Father of the drama. Created first actor *(hypokrites),* who performed in intervals between dancing of chorus in dithyramb, taking several parts and conversing at times with the leader of the chorus.

## FURTHER DEVELOPMENT OF TRAGEDY

I.    New myths, other than those about Dionysus, were introduced, thus changing the nature of the chorus from satyrs to a group appropriate to the individual story.

II.    A second actor was added by Aeschylus.

III.    A third actor was added by Sophocles, and the number of the chorus was fixed at 15.

IV.    The part assigned to the chorus was gradually reduced, the dialogue of the actors becoming increasingly more important. The drama thus contained alternating dialogue (iambic trimeter) and choral odes.

## STRUCTURE OF TRAGEDY

I.    Prologue:  first act.

II.    Parodos: entrance of chorus.

III.   Episodes: acts.

IV.   Stasima: choral odes.

V.    Exodos: action after last stasimon.

## TETRALOGY

Plays were produced in groups of four, called a tetralogy whose parts were:

I.    Trilogy—three plays, at first on one unified theme, later on separate subjects.

II.   Satyr Play—somewhat lighter, dealing with Dionysus, so that the association with the origin of the drama as part of the worship of the god of wine would not be forgotten.

## FUNCTIONS OF THE CHORUS

I.    Beauty of poetry and dancing.

II.   Mood and central themes of the drama, interprets events.

III.   Relieves tension.

IV.   Often converses with and gives advice to characters.

V.    Gives background of preceding events.

## PRODUCTION OF PLAYS

I.    Produced by the state as function of state religion in public theater, principally at the celebration known as the Great Dionysia in the early spring.

II.   Three playwrights produce tetralogies.

III.   Prizes awarded by jury, chosen by lot, to winning poet, star actor (protagonist), and wealthy sponsor of play (choregus).

IV.   Actors, all men, play several parts, wear masks, wigs, and cothurnus (buskin), shoe with high sole which gives added dignity to actor.

V.    Admission free or at nominal fee.

## TYPICAL GREEK THEATER

I.    *Theatron*—where audience sits, on hollowed-out hillside, in open air; seats of honor for public officials and priests, especially priest of Dionysus; seating capacity of Theater of Dionysus at Athens ca. 17,000.

II.  *Orchestra*—dancing place of chorus; actors performed in orchestra in front of *proscenium*; there was apparently no stage in

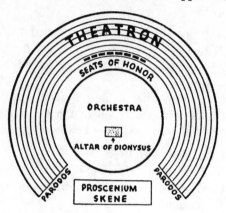

the Greek theater of classical times; sacrifices were performed at the altar of Dionysus before the plays.

III.  *Skene*—dressing rooms for actors; the *proscenium* is the façade of the skene building. The *proscenium* is the scenery of the play; it usually represents the front of a palace or temple, and has three doorways.

IV.  *Parodos*—point of entry and exit of the chorus.

V.  There is no curtain.

VI.  *Deus ex machina*—technical device, consisting of metal crane, on top of skene building, from which is suspended dummy representing a god. It is employed largely by Euripides to give a miraculous conclusion to a tragedy. The god appears as if from on high and unravels all the unsolved problems of the play.

## DIFFERENCES BETWEEN GREEK AND MODERN DRAMA

I.  Greek drama religious ceremony; community art in public theater.

II.     Poetic drama; musical tragedy, like Wagner's operas.

III.    Subjects from mythology.

IV.    Outlines of plot known in advance by audience; little suspense; main interest in dramatic irony, and religious and ethical instruction.

V.     Each play short (longest extant 1700 lines, shortest 900 lines).

VI.    No violent action before audience; scenes of horror "off-stage," reported to audience, usually by messenger.

VII.   Unity of action—entire drama subordinated to one single action, no sub-plots; unity of place (no change of scenery) and unity of time (maximum of 1 day) not always adhered to.

VIII. No intermissions—alternation of dialogue and choral dances.

IX.    Economy of roles—maximum of 3 actors, who may take several parts.

X.     Performed in open-air theater, during daytime, twice a year.

XI.    Tragedies produced in groups of four (tetralogy).

## CHAPTER SEVEN

# ÆSCHYLUS

◨

## AESCHYLUS OF ATHENS (525-455 B.C.)

I.   The real creator of the drama.

II.  Added second actor, increased dialogue, reduced importance of chorus.

III. Wrote ca. 90 plays.

IV.  Soldier at battles of Marathon and Salamis; died in Sicily.

## EXTANT PLAYS

*The Persians*
*The Seven against Thebes*
*The Suppliants*
*Prometheus Bound*
*Agamemnon*
*Choephoroe* (*Libation Bearers*)
*Eumenides*

## PROMETHEUS BOUND

### BACKGROUND

The Titans had long ruled the universe. Their king, Cronus (Saturn), had six children, the oldest of the later Olympian gods. Led by Zeus, the gods revolted against Cronus' tyranny and overthrew him. In their war with the gods the Titans were deserted by the opportunist Oceanus, and by Prometheus (Forethought), who aided Zeus because he represented intelligence warring against brute force. All the defeated Titans were consigned to Tartarus, except Cronus, who was banished to the West, and Atlas, who was compelled to support the heavens on his shoulders.

The new ruler of the universe, Zeus, now himself became despotic. Prometheus created man, and stood forth as the benefactor and champion of men, defending them and aiding them in the advance toward civilization. As men grew evil, Zeus decided to destroy them. But Prometheus persisted in defending them and championing their cause. Finally, defying the decrees of Zeus, he stole for men forbidden fire to better their life.

## CHARACTERS
Power, servant of Zeus
Force, another servant of Zeus
Hephaestus, smith of the gods
Prometheus, a Titan
Oceanus, another Titan
Io, one of the loves of Zeus
Hermes, messenger of Zeus
Chorus: daughters of Oceanus

## SUMMARY
*Prologue* (lines 1-127)

Power and Force drag in Prometheus. Zeus has ordered Hephaestus to bind Prometheus to a rock in a desolate gorge in Scythia for giving fire to mankind. Hephaestus is reluctant to bind his relative and friend, pities him, but fears disobeying Zeus. As Power ruthlessly directs him, Hephaestus shackles the silent Prometheus to the rock. Left alone, Prometheus bewails his lot, with mingled pain, apprehension, and defiance.

*Parodos* (lines 128-192)

The Chorus of sweet and compassionate Oceanids enters, expresses sympathy for his sufferings, and distress at Zeus' tyranny. Prometheus hints at a secret he alone knows which endangers Zeus' rule. He defiantly asserts that he will not reveal the secret until

Zeus softens and removes his bonds. (Secret: if Zeus consum-
mates his love for Thetis, their son will overthrow him.)

*First Episode* (lines 193-396)

At the bidding of the Chorus, Prometheus tells how he aided
Zeus against the Titans, how Zeus became tyrannical once he assumed power, how Prometheus prevented him from destroying
mankind and gave them fire, and how Zeus punished him. Oceanus
enters on a winged horse. He expresses friendship for Prometheus,
counsels him to submit to the new tyrant, to cease his defiance,
and to take thought for his own welfare. He offers to intercede
with Zeus to secure his release. Prometheus, ever altruistic, cautions him of the danger to himself. Zeus has caused others to
suffer, too. Oceanus, rebuked, loses his temper and leaves.

*First Stasimon* (lines 397-435)

The Chorus bewails the sufferings of Prometheus in the East and
of his brother Atlas in the West.

*Second Episode* (lines 436-525)

Prometheus recounts the advance of human civilization and the
varied inventions and discoveries he bestowed upon mankind. He
declares that Fate has ordained that he will ultimately be released,
and he hints again at his secret.

*Second Stasimon* (lines 526-560)

The Chorus pities Prometheus, but expresses reverence for Zeus,
emphasizes the limitations of man, and counsels moderation.

*Third Episode* (lines 561-886)

Io, transformed into a heifer, enters pursued by the ghost of
Argus in a stinging insect. She raves over her sufferings because
of Zeus' love for her. When she hears of Prometheus' sufferings at
Zeus' hands, she relates the story of her sorrows, how Zeus fell in
love with her, how she was driven out to wander by her father, how
she was turned into a heifer pursued first by the 100-eyed Argus,
the creation of Hera, and, after the slaying of Argus by Hermes,
by a stinging fly urged on by Argus' ghost. Prometheus then
prophesies her future wanderings over Europe, Asia, and Africa.

He tells her, too, that she will finally find rest and be turned into a woman in Egypt, and that a descendant of Io will release him (Hercules). He hints again at his secret. She leaves in frenzy to continue her wandering.

*Third Stasimon* (lines 887-907)

The Chorus prays that they may never be wooed by the superior gods, as was Io. Marriage between equals is best.

*Exodos* (lines 908-1093)

As Prometheus utters renewed defiance against Zeus and predicts his overthrow, Hermes arrives and demands to know the secret affecting Zeus. Prometheus insults Hermes as Zeus' lackey, and defiantly refuses to tell. Hermes warns him of new punishments, especially how the eagle of Zeus will come down to devour his liver daily. As Prometheus hurls defiance against Zeus, a furious storm breaks, the rock is struck by lightning, and earth opens up and Prometheus sinks out of sight.

## INTERPRETATION

Interpretation is difficult because play was part of *Prometheus Trilogy,* of which the other two plays are lost:

1. *Prometheus Bound*
2. *Prometheus Unbound*
3. *Prometheus the Fire-bringer*

I.    Conflict of wills between two leading characters, Prometheus and Zeus, both of whom are guilty of lack of moderation.

II.    Conflict between necessity for authority and for progress and enlightenment of humanity; between rebellious reform and harsh tyranny; between reason and brute force.

III.    After 30,000 years of suffering for both Zeus and Prometheus, they are reconciled: Zeus learns mercy and justice, Prometheus respect for authority; compromise between brute force and wisdom.

IV.    Purification of popular religion, from crude anthropomorphism toward ethical monotheism: Zeus evolves into humane god combining stern justice with mercy, omnipotence with omniscience.

V.    The tragic pattern of life: suffering is inevitable, it must be endured, even the innocent suffer, but there is personal responsibility for sin; the remedy is moderation; wisdom comes from suffering.

VI.    There are good and evil in divinities, but faith in Zeus must be maintained, despite the sufferings of life.

VII.    Authority must be humane and wise to be respected, reformers must be patient and slow and respect such authority. Man must subordinate himself to the good state, as to benevolent divinities.

# ORESTES TRILOGY

## ORESTEIA (only extant Greek trilogy)
I.    *Agamemnon*
II.    *Choephoroe* (*Libation Bearers*)
III.    *Eumenides*

## BACKGROUND

King Atreus (son of Pelops, grandson of Tantalus), after a quarrel with his brother, Thyestes, slew two of the latter's children and fed their flesh to him. Upon discovering what had happened, Thyestes contrived to kill Atreus, whose sons Agamemnon and Menelaus fled. Agamemnon and his wife Clytemnestra, had four children, Orestes, Electra, Iphigenia, and Chrysothemis. Before sailing for Troy as commander of the Greek forces Agamemnon cruelly sacrificed Iphigenia (see p. 9). Clytemnestra never forgave him for this. During his ten-year absence, she secretly became the mistress of Aegisthus, a son of Thyestes. In order to facilitate her amours with Aegisthus, she sent her son Orestes away to live with a king in Phocis. With Aegisthus she plots the murder of Agamemnon.

# AGAMEMNON

## CHARACTERS

Watchman
Clytemnestra, wife of Agamemnon
Herald
Agamemnon
Cassandra, prophetess daughter of Priam, captive of Agamemnon
Aegisthus, son of Thyestes, lover of Clytemnestra
Chorus of elders

## SUMMARY

*Prologue* (lines 1-39)

It is night. A watchman is seen on the roof of the palace of Agamemnon. He has been posted there by Clytemnestra, and has been watching many months for the signal fire which is to proclaim the fall of Troy. He suddenly sees the beacon and hails it with joy. But at the same time he expresses a sense of fear and foreboding.

*Parodos and First Stasimon* (lines 40-269)

The Chorus enters. Ten years have passed since Menelaus and Agamemnon set sail with a thousand ships to avenge the abduction of Helen by Paris of Troy. The men of the Chorus were too old to join the expedition to Troy. Clytemnestra has come out of the palace, and they see her praying at an altar. The Chorus relates the omen seen before the war, of two eagles killing a hare and her unborn young. The soothsayer Calchas predicted the destruction of Troy by the two sons of Atreus. Calchas prayed to Artemis and Apollo, and gloomily predicted future woe. The Chorus prays to almighty and benevolent Zeus, who punishes men for their sins, but teaches them wisdom through suffering. Proudly and confidently, Agamemnon gathered his forces at Aulis. But Artemis caused the winds to cease blowing because Agamemnon slew a sacred animal. When Calchas ordered him to sacrifice Iphigenia in order to appease Artemis, he hesitated to slay his child. But his ambition to be a great conqueror overmastered his fatherly love, and he consented. Iphigenia was sacrificed, despite her heart-rending pleas. Justice is inevitable, and from suffering comes wisdom.

*First Episode* (lines 270-366)

Clytemnestra proclaims the fall of Troy, and relates in detail how the signal was speedily flashed by beacon fires from mountain to mountain. She depicts the probable suffering of the Trojans, and meaningfully suggests that the homecoming of the victorious heroes is fraught with peril.

*Second Stasimon* (lines 367-480)

Zeus has punished Troy for the sin of Paris. Pride leads to inevitable downfall. Great prosperity is harmful. Sin is always punished, and often involves whole cities. So Paris sinned and was punished for stealing Helen. Predictions of woe for Troy were made at the time. Prophetic dreams of death and destruction came to Agamemnon, visions of funeral urns of dead Greeks, and the anger of their relatives. The gods note all who commit bloodshed and punish them. Too much fame is dangerous.

*Second Episode* (lines 481-685)

Several days have elapsed. The Chorus cautiously doubts Clytemnestra's story of the beacon fire announcing the fall of Troy. A herald arrives, overjoyed at being home after ten years overseas, and announces the imminent arrival of Agamemnon. The Chorus intimates there were difficulties at home during the army's absence, and the herald details the sufferings of the army. Clytemnestra appears and deceitfully proclaims her fidelity to and love for Agamemnon. The herald relates how Menelaus was diverted by a storm and that he will not arrive with Agamemnon.

*Third Stasimon* (lines 686-773)

Helen brought misery to the Greeks and the Trojans. The Trojans welcomed her with joyous song, but later their tune was changed. An oxherd reared a lion's cub, but the grown lion became a beast of prey. So Helen brought woe to Troy. Good fortune is said to bring disaster to men; but only when it comes from evil deeds. Pride and arrogance bring retribution and justice. Humility is safest.

*Third Episode* (lines 774-965)

The conquering hero Agamemnon arrives in a chariot, followed by Cassandra. The Chorus greets him with tempered joy. Agamemnon gives thanks to the gods for his victory and return, and declares he will reorganize the state. Clytemnestra unashamedly declares her love to Agamemnon. Of her own accord she informs him that Orestes has been sent away for safekeeping. Then she urges him, prompting his pride, to walk into the palace on a purple carpet she has had spread out for him. Agamemnon greets his wife coldly, expresses fear of tempting the gods with pride. When she insists, he is easily swayed, and, removing his shoes, he enters the palace on the purple carpet. Before doing so, he commits his concubine Cassandra to Clytemnestra's care.

*Fourth Stasimon* (lines 966-1018)

The Chorus has gloomy forebodings despite the joyful home-coming of the army.

*Fourth Episode* (lines 1019-1410)

Clytemnestra reappears from the palace, and orders Cassandra within. Cassandra does not answer or move until Clytemnestra re-enters the palace. Then in a frenzied mood, inspired by Apollo, she raves prophetically of her own sad fate, paints the past horrible crimes of the House of Atreus, the coming murders of Agamemnon and herself, and tells how Agamemnon is to be murdered. The Chorus does not believe her predictions of Agamemnon's death. She continues to rave, mingling the past crimes with predictions of the future, including the coming vengeance by Orestes for the murders of Agamemnon and herself. She recoils as she is about to enter the palace, but finally, submitting to her fate, she goes in stoically and with resignation.

Agamemnon's death cry is heard. There is consternation in the Chorus. Clytemnestra now appears in her true colors, holding a bloody axe in her hands. She triumphantly announces how she murdered her husband and Cassandra.

*Exodos* (lines 1411-1673)

Clytemnestra vehemently states her reasons for killing Agamemnon—his sacrifice of Iphigenia, her love for Aegisthus, Agamemnon's infidelity with Cassandra and other women, and the family curse which mastered her. The Chorus predict that murder will be punished. Aegisthus enters with his bodyguard and gloats over the death of Agamemnon, admitting his share in plotting the murder, and his association with Clytemnestra. He declares he will become joint ruler with Clytemnestra. The Chorus hopes for vengeance by Orestes. Clytemnestra and Aegisthus assert that they will establish a severe rule over the kingdom.

# CHOEPHOROE

## BACKGROUND

Several years have elapsed. Orestes returns with his friend Plyades. He has been ordered by Apollo to avenge his father's death.

## CHARACTERS

Orestes, son of Agamemnon and Clytemnestra
Pylades, Orestes' friend
Electra, Orestes' sister
Nurse
Clytemnestra, wife of Aegisthus
Servant
Aegisthus, husband of Clytemnestra
Chorus of maidens

## SUMMARY

*Prologue* (lines 1-21)

Orestes, in disguise, enters with Pylades. He lays a lock of his hair on Agamemnon's tomb. They hear a cry of woe from the palace. As they retire, the Chorus enters sorrowfully with Electra.

They have been ordered to make offerings at Agamemnon's tomb by Clytemnestra who has had bad dreams.

*Parodos* (lines 22-82)

The Chorus wails. Agamemnon's soul is angry. Clytemnestra cannot sleep. They have been sent to placate his soul. But murder must be avenged; justice is inescapable. Such a sin cannot be purged away.

*First Episode* (lines 83-304)

Confused and sad, the young innocent Electra does not want to pray to help her mother. Urged by the Chorus, she prays for Orestes' return and vengeance. As the Chorus laments over Agamemnon, Electra discovers the lock of hair on the tomb. She recognizes it as like her own hair, and surmises that Orestes has returned. Then her surmise is confirmed by his footprints which she recognizes as resembling her own. Orestes comes forward, and the long-parted pair embrace. After praying to Zeus for protection, Orestes relates how he was ordered by the oracle of Apollo to take unfailing vengeance upon his mother and Aegisthus.

*First Stasimon* (lines 305-476)

Kneeling at the grave of Agamemnon, the Chorus, Orestes, and Electra chant, lamenting Agamemnon, exchanging thoughts on his greatness and his murder, and swearing vengeance. At the end Orestes' resolution is fixed, and Electra has become a changed person, savage for revenge.

*Second Episode* (lines 477-582)

Strengthened in determination by this mystic communion at Agamemnon's grave, they pray for guidance and help. The Chorus tells Orestes of Clytemnestra's terrifying dreams. His determination is reinforced. Then he tells his plans for the murder of Clytemnestra and Aegisthus.

*Second Stasimon* (lines 583-648)

The monsters of the earth are many, but woman's passion causes her to commit horrible crimes, as witness Clytemnestra's sins. Justice will triumph.

*Third Episode* (lines 649-778)

Orestes and Pylades, disguised, knock on the palace door, asking for hospitality. Clytemnestra appears, accompanied by Electra, and welcomes them. Orestes asserts that he has come as a messenger from Phocis to announce Orestes' death. Clytemnestra is elated, but conceals her emotions. She immediately sends Orestes' sorrowing old nurse to summon Aegisthus to hear the news. The Chorus suggests to the nurse that she tell Aegisthus to come without his bodyguard.

*Third Stasimon* (lines 779-836)

The Chorus prays for the success of Orestes' plans, and that he may slay them as Perseus slew the Gorgon. No mercy for Clytemnestra and Aegisthus.

*Fourth Episode* (lines 837-933)

Aegisthus arrives, expressing doubt as to Orestes' death, and enters the palace. His death-cry is soon heard. A servant informs Clytemnestra of his death. When Orestes and Pylades appear, she begs for mercy. Orestes hesitates, but Pylades reminds him of Apollo's stern order. He becomes pitiless, and drags his mother into the palace to slay her by Aegisthus' side.

*Fourth Stasimon* (934-970)

Justice has triumphed. There will be deliverance from evil with time.

*Exodos* (971-1074)

The doors of the palace open, and the bodies of Aegisthus and Clytemnestra are seen on a couch covered with the robe Agamemnon wore at the time of his death. Orestes displays the corpses, and justifies the murders. As he begins to lose his mind, he declares it was Apollo who compelled him to this act. At the onset of his madness he sees the Furies as they begin to haunt and pursue him.

# EUMENIDES

**BACKGROUND**

The mad Orestes flees for protection to the Temple of Apollo at Delphi pursued relentlessly by the Furies stirred up by the murder of his mother.

## CHARACTERS

Priestess of Apollo
Apollo
Orestes
Ghost of Clytemnestra
Athena
12 Citizens of Athens
Chorus of Furies (horrible divinities who pursue murderers)

## SUMMARY

*Prologue* (lines 1-63)

The priestess of Apollo, standing before his temple at Delphi, prays to the various divinities associated with the shrine. She enters the temple, but quickly recoils in terror. For she has seen within the blood-stained Orestes at the altar and the Furies sleeping around him.

*First Episode* (lines 64-142)

The interior of the temple is disclosed. Apollo promises never to desert Orestes. He reviles the Furies as evil forces of darkness, and instructs Orestes to go to Athens to seek assistance of Athena for deliverance. As Hermes guides Orestes away, the ghost of Clytemnestra appears and rebukes the Furies for their inaction. They slowly awake.

*First Stasimon* (lines 143-178)

The Chorus bewails Orestes' escape. They rebuke Apollo scornfully, and promise that Orestes will not evade them.

*Second Episode* (lines 179-243)

Apollo drives out the Furies from his temple. They defend their pursuit of Orestes, cautioning him that he is defending a guilty matricide. Apollo replies that Clytemnestra deserved death because she slew her husband. The Chorus pledges unrelenting pursuit. Apollo aid for Orestes.

The scene changes to Athens. Orestes is seen clinging to the statue of Athena in front of her temple. He prays for deliverance.
*Parodos* (lines 244-275)

The Chorus of Furies enters hunting Orestes. They catch sight of him and swear vengeance.
*Second Episode* (lines 276-306)

Orestes again prays to Athena for divine assistance. He claims that he has atoned for his crime and has been purified. The Chorus proclaims that there is no help.
*Second Stasimon* (lines 307-395)

The Furies relate their function to avenge unpunished murders. They complain about Apollo's interference in their duties which have been assigned to them by Fate. They are powers of darkness and punish the guilty, even after death. They are implacable, bring the proud low, and are feared by all men.
*Third Episode* (lines 396-489)

Athena enters, coming from afar. She questions the Chorus and learns that Orestes slew his mother. Orestes pleads that he has been purified, and that he murdered Clytemnestra at Apollo's command. Since there is some justice on both sides, Athena will have the case tried before a group of judges.
*Third Stasimon* (lines 490-565)

Orestes must not be acquitted, for this will give license to new crimes. Justice will be at an end, and crime will triumph. There must be some authority in society which men fear. Lack of moderation and insolence are evil. Those who do evil shall perish and be utterly lost.
*Fourth Episode* (lines 566-776)

Athena enters accompanied by 12 Athenian citizens who are to be the jury. Apollo is attorney for Orestes, the Furies his prosecutors. Orestes confesses the murder of his mother under orders from Apollo. The latter speaks in Orestes' defense, urging that his command to Orestes had the sanction of Zeus. They argue as to which is the more serious crime—murder of husband by wife or mother by son. Athena as judge charges the jury. The vote is a tie. Athena then casts the deciding vote for acquittal of Orestes. He thanks Athena and leaves joyfully, proclaiming undying friendship between his people and the Athenians.

*Fourth Stasimon* (lines 777-792)

The Chorus of Furies bemoans the rising power of the younger gods, and how they themselves are dishonored. They threaten dire consequences to Athens.

*Fifth Episode* (lines 793-915)

Athena tries to soothe their wrath, arguing that Zeus and his justice have prevailed, and pledging them a new home and high honor in Athens. She pleads with them persistently until they finally relent and accept the new honors offered them.

*Exodos* (lines 916-1047)

The Chorus, softened, prays for varied blessings for Athens and the people, while Athena recounts their future benevolent functions. A procession of Athenians, led by Athena, with joyous chants escorts the Furies, renamed Eumenides (Kindly Ones) to their new home in a cave in Athens.

## INTERPRETATION OF THE ORESTES TRILOGY

I.    The inevitability of punishment ("the doer must suffer") is the supreme law of justice.

II.   Prosperity leads to the sin of hybris and inevitable retribution through Nemesis. Moderation is best.

III.  Evil breeds evil, one crime begets another through the family curse, and the innocent suffer with the guilty.

IV.   Suffering teaches people wisdom.

V.    The old tribal law of the vendetta and blood-feud ("an eye for an eye, a tooth for a tooth") must give way to legal procedures and a distinction between premeditated and involuntary murder.

VI.   Brute force and vengeance must be reconciled with wisdom and mercy.

VII. There is ultimate forgiveness through a benevolent Zeus. There is goodness in divine forces, as the gods of light (Zeus, Apollo, Athena) gradually become supreme over the forces of darkness (Furies).

VIII. But Fate is not absolute, and there is personal responsibility for self-willed evil.

## TECHNIQUE AND STYLE OF AESCHYLUS

I.    Trilogies on unified themes.

II.   Simplicity of plots; action static.

III.  Stark grandeur of characters who undergo little or no development. Their tragic suffering is not basically the result of character but sin, and they seem to march inevitably to their doom.

IV.   Majestic grandeur and exalted sublimity of imagination and style, though sometimes obscure and bombastic.

## BASIS IDEAS OF AESCHYLUS

I.    A religious thinker; deals with profound moral and religious problems.

II.   Purification of primitive religion; evolution of gods and law from primitive concepts of force and vengeance toward ethical monotheism; the ultimate goodness of divinities.

III.  There is retribution and personal responsibility for sin.

IV.   Excessive pride and self-will are punished; the cure is moderation.

V.    The pattern of life is basically tragic, but wisdom comes from suffering.

VI.   Man has limitations, and must subordinate himself to wise authority both in the state and among the gods.

## CHAPTER EIGHT

# SOPHOCLES

**SOPHOCLES OF ATHENS (ca. 497-405 B.C.)**
I.   Most successful Greek dramatist.
II.  Wrote ca. 125 plays.
III. Added 3rd actor; increased dialogue; decreased importance of chorus; invented scene painting.
IV.  Made each play of trilogy an organic unit; plays in trilogy no longer deal with unified theme.

**EXTANT PLAYS**
*Oedipus Rex*
*Philoctetes*
*Women of Trachis*
*Electra*
*Oedipus at Colonus*
*Antigone*
*Ajax*

## OEDIPUS REX

**BACKGROUND**
Laius and Jocasta, king and queen of Thebes, were warned by an oracle at Delphi that a son to be born would kill his father, Laius, and marry his mother, Jocasta. When the child was born, it was given to a shepherd to be killed. This shepherd first pierced

**79**

the child's feet, but pitying the baby, he gave it to another shepherd from Corinth. The child was then adopted by Polibus and Merope, king and queen of Corinth, who named him Oedipus ("Swollen-foot"). When Oedipus reached man's estate, he learned from the oracle that he was fated to kill his father and marry his mother. He left Delphi, determined never to return to Corinth, in order to avoid his horrible fate. On his journey his chariot was blocked by another chariot at a spot where three roads met. In an argument over the right of way, the hot-headed Oedipus lost his temper and killed the rider. It was his father Laius. Soon after, he reached Thebes, which was plagued by the Sphinx. She asked all as they entered and left the city a riddle, and killed all who could not answer it. When Oedipus quickly answered the riddle, the Sphinx destroyed herself, and Oedipus was hailed as the savior of the city. Shortly after the news of Laius' death was received, Oedipus was proclaimed king of Thebes and married Laius' widow, his own mother Jocasta. They had four children, Antigone, Ismene, Eteocles, and Polynices. After he has ruled for many years admired for his wisdom and ability, a plague suddenly strikes the city.

## CHARACTERS
Oedipus, King of Thebes
Priest
Creon, Oedipus' uncle, Jocasta's brother
Teiresias, blind soothsayer
Jocasta, Queen of Thebes
Messenger from Corinth
Shepherd
2nd Messenger
Chorus of Theban Elders

## SUMMARY
*Prologue* (lines 1-150)

Oedipus enters from his palace and hears from the priest details about the plague which is devastating Thebes. In the name of the people the priest begs Oedipus to aid them now as he did when he rid the city of the Sphinx. Oedipus consoles them, and declares that he has sent Creon to consult the oracle of Apollo at Delphi. Creon arrives happy, for the cause of the plague has been revealed by the oracle: the undiscovered murderer of the former king, Laius, is in the city; he must be killed or banished. Oedipus is informed that there was a witness to the murder who reported that it was committed by a group of thieves. Oedipus dedicates himself energetically to discovering the murderer.

*Parodos* (lines 151-215)

The Chorus prays to many gods to avert the pestilence which is harrowing the city.

*First Episode* (lines 216-462)

Oedipus issues a proclamation ordering the murderer to confess or that he be denounced by anyone who knows him. He forbids anyone to shield or harbor him under threat of dire penalties, and curses the murderer. He expresses his determination to track him down relentlessly.

The blind prophet Teiresias is brought in, and Oedipus asks him to reveal the identity of the murderer. Teiresias professes ignorance, but when Oedipus loses his temper, taunting him for his blindness and accusing him of complicity in Laius' murder, he reveals that Oedipus is the criminal. His anger mounting, Oedipus accuses Teiresias of plotting with Creon to overthrow him, and scorns his wisdom since he did not solve the riddle of the Sphinx. Teiresias then reveals Oedipus' past and future, though the irate Oedipus pays little attention.

*First Stasimon* (lines 463-511)

Who is the murderer indicated by the oracle? Retribution is inevitable. But the Chorus cannot bring itself to believe in the guilt of their beloved king Oedipus, who aided them by ridding Thebes of the Sphinx.

*Second Episode* (lines 512-862)

Creon enters to defend himself against the charge of conspiracy

**81**

against Oedipus. While Oedipus towers in rage over him, Creon calmly urges him to be rational. He argues that it is well known that he is not ambitious for power, and that he should be judged not on impulse and in anger but by the evidence. As Oedipus rants against Creon, Jocasta enters to intervene between her brother and her husband. She urges Oedipus to have no confidence in the oracle, because it predicted that Laius would be slain by her son. But it had been reported that Laius was killed by a group of thieves at a spot where three roads met, and, moreover, her child was killed soon after birth.

When Oedipus hears that Laius was murdered at a crossroads, he recalls that he had killed a man at such a spot. In terror, he fears that he is the murderer revealed by the oracle. He orders the witness to the murder summoned. Oedipus then relates his past at Corinth, and how he had heard from the oracle at Delphi that he would slay his father and marry his mother. He resolved never to return to his "parents." In his wanderings he killed a man at a spot where three roads met. As he bemoans his fate, Jocasta convinces him that the oracle is not to be trusted.

*Second Stasimon* (lines 863-910)

Reverence for the gods is best. Prosperity leads to hybris which is punished by inevitable Nemesis. But the Chorus too is shaken in its confidence in the oracle.

*Third Episode* (lines 911-1185)

As Jocasta prays to Apollo, a messenger arrives from Corinth to announce that Polybus of Corinth is dead. Jocasta jubilantly summons Oedipus to show him new evidence of the untrustworthiness of the oracle, which had declared he would murder his father. As Oedipus expresses his conviction, the messenger reveals that Polybus was not his father. Oedipus questions him and discovers that he was given as a baby to the messenger by a shepherd of the household of Laius, the same who was the witness to the murder. Jocasta, now realizing the truth, tries to dissuade Oedipus from continuing his search. Knowing his determination to learn the entire truth, she rushes into the palace aghast.

The Chorus is overjoyed that Oedipus is a native of Thebes.

The reluctant shepherd is brought in. In the presence of the Corinthian messenger, Oedipus relentlessly forces the shepherd to reveal his origin. In horror he rushes into the palace.

*Third Stasimon* (lines 1186-1222)

All life is sorrow. See how the great Oedipus has fallen. Time reveals all.

*Exodos* (lines 1223-1530)

A messenger comes out of the palace and tells how Jocasta has committed suicide by hanging, and how Oedipus, rushing in to kill her, discovered her body and blinded himself with her golden brooches.

Oedipus comes out and bemoans his fate—the murder of his father, his incestuous marriage with his mother, and his incest-bred children. Creon, the new king, enters and addresses him with pity and kindness. Oedipus asks Creon to banish him. Before he goes he requests that he be permitted to touch his two daughters, a request which Creon has anticipated. They come in sobbing, and Oedipus bewails their future unhappiness, because of the nature of their birth. Asking Creon to care for them, he reluctantly parts from his beloved daughters. The Chorus moralizes from Oedipus' experience that no man should be counted happy until he is dead.

**INTERPRETATION**

I. The power of fate is irresistible; the irony of fate.

II. The power of the gods is supreme; man is limited; human self-confidence and wisdom are illusion before divine truth.

III. Life is tragic and full of suffering; resignation is necessary; anything can happen to anyone; even the innocent suffer; there is wisdom from suffering.

IV. But there is also personal responsibility for suffering: intellectual pride leads to punishment; "murder will out"; breaches of the unwritten laws, incest and parricide, cannot go unpunished. The character of Oedipus is partly responsible for his fall.

# OEDIPUS AT COLONUS

## BACKGROUND

About 20 years have elapsed. In accordance with another oracle, Oedipus had stayed at Thebes. But he was finally exiled with the concurrence of Creon, Eteocles and Polynices. He cursed his sons and became a wandering beggar, cared for by Antigone. Meanwhile, Eteocles has become king of Thebes and has thrust out his brother Polynices. The latter fled to Argus where he has organized an expedition against Thebes to seize the kingdom. As he is about to attack, another oracle instructs the Thebans to bury Oedipus in Thebes if they want the city to prosper.

## CHARACTERS

Oedipus
Antigone, his daughter
Ismene, his daughter
Native of Colonus
Theseus, King of Attica
Creon, Oedipus' uncle
Polynices, Oedipus' son
Messenger
Chorus of Elders of Colonus

## SUMMARY

*Prologue* (lines 1-116)

Blind Oedipus arrives at Colonus, near Athens, guided and tended by Antigone. He learns from a native that he is in the sacred grove of the Eumenides at Colonus, and that it is forbidden ground. He prays to the Eumenides for assistance.

*Parodos* (lines 117-257)

The Chorus enters looking for the stranger reported trespassing in the sacred grove. Oedipus comes forward, shocking the Chorus both by his sacrilege and appearance. He is warned out of the grove and asked to tell who he is. Reluctantly and under compulsion he tells them. They express horror when they learn his identity, and order him to leave the country at once, though they express pity for Oedipus and Antigone.

*First Episode* (lines 258-667)

Oedipus in a persuasive speech begs for asylum and convinces the Chorus to wait for King Theseus who has been summoned. Ismene suddenly arrives on horseback. Oedipus and Antigone greet Ismene lovingly. He inquires about his neglectful sons, comparing them with his devoted daughters. Ismene tells how her brothers Polynices and Eteocles had quarreled over the royal power, deposing Creon, of the expulsion of Polynices by Eteocles, and of Polynices' projected attack on Thebes with an Argive army. She also reports a new oracle that Thebes will prosper only if Oedipus is brought back. Creon is coming to take control of him, so as to possess for his own ends the deciding factor in the welfare of Thebes. Oedipus curses his sons because they did not recall him when they heard the oracle but thought only of the throne of Thebes. He offers his services to the Chorus as a future protector of Athens, if they aid him now. Instructed by the Chorus he prays and sacrifices to the Eumenides, but because of his blindness, Ismene performs the rites. The Chorus then hears with horror from Oedipus of his murder of his father, his incestuous relationship with his mother, and his incest-bred children.

King Theseus arrives, recognizes Oedipus, and at once offers his sympathy and help. Oedipus tells Theseus of the coming attempt to seize him and take him to Thebes. He begs to be permitted to remain in Attica. Theseus grants his wish, and promises him protection from harm.

*First Stasimon* (lines 668-719)

The Chorus describes in lyrical terms the beauties of Attica, particularly Colonus.

*Second Episode* (lines 720-1043)

Creon arrives, and with deceitful words pleads with Oedipus to return to Thebes with him, but the latter refuses, revealing that he knows Creon's purpose. An angry quarrel ensues, and Oedipus hears from Creon that Ismene has been seized. When Creon orders his guards to carry off Antigone, the Chorus tries to rescue her but fails. Oedipus is about to be dragged off by Creon when Theseus arrives with his bodyguard. Upon hearing what has happened, he orders Antigone and Ismene to be brought back, holding Creon as hostage for their safe return and rebuking him for his high-handed actions. Creon attempts to justify his acts on the grounds of Oedipus' crimes. Oedipus, with great feeling, proclaims innocence of wrong-doing, and rebukes Creon. Theseus then forces Creon to lead the way in rescuing the two girls.

*Second Stasimon* (lines 1044-1095)

The Chorus, anticipating the combat between Theseus and Creon's guards, prays for sure victory for their king to Zeus, Athena, and Apollo.

*Third Episode* (lines 1096-1210)

Antigone and Ismene return with Theseus to Oedipus. There is mutual joy, and Oedipus thanks Theseus. Oedipus learns from Theseus that a relative wishes to talk with him. Knowing that it is Polynices, he refuses to see his hated son. But Antigone persuades him to consent.

*Third Stasimon* (lines 1211-1250)

Desire for long life is folly, for age brings much grief and suffering, as witness Oedipus.

*Fourth Episode* (lines 1251-1555)

Polynices enters, professing to be distressed by the sad lot of Oedipus and Antigone. He tells of his quarrel with Eteocles, his plan to attack Thebes, and asks Oedipus' aid, knowing the recent oracles. He promises to take Oedipus back to Thebes. Oedipus in a crushing speech reminds Polynices of his past treatment of him, when he helped exile his father; then he curses both brothers and predicts their deaths. Oedipus orders him to begone. Before departing, Polynices begs his sisters to give him decent burial, if he perishes in the assault of Thebes, which he cannot be dissuaded from undertaking.

As the Chorus comments on the woes of Oedipus and the cyclical pattern of life, thunder is heard. Oedipus intuitively surmises his imminent death and summons Theseus. When Theseus arrives, he tells him that his end is near and that he will reveal to him in secret where he is to die. The spot is to remain the guarded secret of the kings of Athens, and it will protect Athens against Theban aggression. Then a divine summons urges him on, and he moves slowly and confidently away toward the fated place where he is to die.

*Fourth Stasimon* (lines 1556-1578)

The Chorus prays to the gods of the underworld that Oedipus may have a painless death.

*Exodos* (lines 1579-1779)

A messenger enters to announce the death of Oedipus. He relates how Oedipus prepared himself when he reached the fated spot, and bade farewell to his daughters. Thunder was heard and a divine voice called Oedipus not to delay. Before going he asked Theseus to aid his daughters. Only Theseus was permitted to be present as Oedipus mysteriously disappeared.

Antigone and Ismene enter lamenting together with the Chorus. They are apprehensive about the future but are reassured. When Theseus returns they beg to see Oedipus' tomb, but he relates that Oedipus enjoined him to keep the place secret. He agrees to send them back to Thebes.

## INTERPRETATION

I.    The central theme of this play, written by Sophocles in advanced years and produced posthumously, is the transformation in death of an essentially good man into a hero through suffering.

II.    Reconciliation between Oedipus and gods intended to teach trust in justice of gods, that man is limited, and must endure adversity, for there is divine purpose in suffering.

**87**

III. Patriotic theme: pride in Athens, particularly Sophocles' own birthplace, Colonus.

# ANTIGONE

## BACKGROUND

Polynices, son of Oedipus, led the expedition known as the Seven Against Thebes to seize the throne from his brother Eteocles. After a long siege, it was decided to settle the issue by a duel between the brothers. In the fight they slew each other, and the invaders fled. Creon, the new king, buried Eteocles with honors, but issued an edict forbidding anyone to bury Polynices, the traitor, on pain of death.

## CHARACTERS

Antigone, daughter of Oedipus
Ismene, daughter of Oedipus
Creon, King of Thebes
Eurydice, his wife
Haemon, their son
Teiresias, blind soothsayer of Thebes
Guard
Messengers
Chorus of Elders of Thebes

## SUMMARY

*Prologue* (lines 1-99)

Antigone and Ismene stand before the palace of Creon. Resolute and determined, Antigone tells the timid Ismene that she intends to flout the decree of Creon and bury Polynices, even if it costs her life. Ismene tries to dissuade Antigone from her purpose, urging the necessity of obedience to the state. Antigone is contemptuous of her advice.

*Parodos* (lines 100-162)

The Chorus hails the defeat of the Argive army and the lifting of the siege of Thebes. Polynices was guilty of treason to his country. He and Eteocles slew each other.

*First Episode* (lines 163-331)

Creon enters and declares his philosophy of the supremacy of state and country above all. He repeats his edict that Polynices is not to be buried on pain of execution. The body is being guarded to prevent burial. A guard arrives and hesitatingly announces that someone has given ceremonial burial to the corpse by strewing dust on it. Creon in a rage threatens the guard with death unless the culprit is apprehended.

*First Stasimon* (lines 332-383)

The greatest wonder in the world is man, his daring, genius, and inventiveness. But his shrewdness brings ruin if he goes counter to what is right and just.

*Second Episode* (lines 384-581)

Antigone is led in under arrest by the guard, having been apprehended repeating the burial rites. She defiantly admits her act to Creon and that it was premeditated. She glories in her act, and defends it as being in accord with eternal unwritten divine laws. She is prepared to die. Creon condemns her to death; but suspecting complicity on Ismene's part, he summons her. When she appears, she claims a part in the crime, and asks to share Antigone's fate. But Antigone harshly rejects her offer because of her refusal to aid her in burying Polynices. Despite Ismene's pleading reminder that Antigone is betrothed to his son, Haemon, Creon orders her execution.

*Second Stasimon* (lines 582-630)

A family curse dooms great houses, moving from generation to generation, as in the house of Labdacus. Intemperance and arrogance lead to ruin. Zeus is all-powerful. When the curse comes, the will of man is impotent.

*Third Episode* (lines 631-780)

Haemon arrives, and with calm self-control and deference tells Creon in a calculated speech that public opinion is against the death of Antigone as undeserved. As he pleads for her, Creon's anger and pride mount, while Haemon's demeanor is outwardly

**89**

calm. Finally, losing control, Haemon rushes out determined to die with Antigone, when he realizes his father's obdurate decision.

*Third Stasimon* (lines 781-882)

The Chorus sings of the power of love. As Antigone is being led to her death, she and the Chorus exchange sad feelings on what is going to happen to her. She recalls the past tragedies of her family. The Chorus commiserates with her, but reminds her that her downfall came from her stubbornness and temper.

*Fourth Episide* (lines 883-943)

Creon enters to hasten her departure. He orders her entombed alive. Antigone again defends her act, and bids the people and city farewell.

*Fourth Stasimon* (lines 944-987)

The Chorus reminisces on others who suffered cruel imprisonment.

*Fifth Episide* (lines 988-1114)

Teiresias, the blind soothsayer, is brought in, led by a boy. He tells Creon that the gods are angry because Polynices is unburied. The city is being polluted. He warns Creon against stubbornness and self-will. In anger Creon accuses Teiresias of having accepted bribes from the people to bring about Antigone's release. Teiresias then predicts that Creon will atone for what he has done to Polynices' body and to Antigone by the death of his son, Haemon.

Finally realizing the skill of Teiresias in foretelling the future, Creon suddenly breaks his resolve, hard as it is to alter his decree. He leaves to bury Polynices and release Antigone.

*Fifth Stasimon* (lines 1115-1152)

The Chorus joyfully sings in honor of Dionysus, protector of Thebes.

*Exodos* (lines 1153-1353)

A messenger arrives, and in the presence of Creon's wife, Eurydice, relates how first Creon gave decent burial to Polynices. Then he entered Antigone's tomb to find Antigone dead by hanging and Haemon lamenting his bride-to-be. Haemon tried to kill

Creon and then committed suicide with his sword, clinging to Antigone's body.

Creon enters, a broken, remorseful man, with the body of Haemon. He finally admits his folly. But soon a second messenger arrives to tell him that the queen has killed herself in grief over Haemon's death. Creon's cup of woe is full. He prays for death in his utter misery.

The Chorus cautions reverence to the gods, proper use of wisdom, and the dangers of pride.

## INTERPRETATION

I.   Conflict between man-made laws and unwritten divine law; between individual and state; between family and state. There is validity in both duties, but divine law is primary.

II.   Both Creon and Antigone are at fault, but Creon more so. His pride and stubbornness and intemperance led to his ruin. The main sympathy is with Antigone.

III.   Pride, despotism, and stubbornness are punished; moderation necessary.

IV.   Man is limited; reverence for the gods is needed.

V.   There is personal responsibility for suffering; wisdom comes from suffering.

# ELECTRA

## BACKGROUND

See above, pp. 69–72. In this play it is Electra who took the precaution of sending Orestes away to Phocis. She has never concealed her grief over Agamemnon's death and her hatred for his murderers. Insulted and degraded, she has begun to give up hope that Orestes will ever return to avenge their father's death.

## CHARACTERS

Orestes, son of Agamemnon and Clytemnestra
Pylades, his friend
Electra, his sister

Chrysothemis, another sister
Old Man, attendant of Orestes
Clytemnestra, Queen of Mycenae
Aegisthus, King of Mycenae
Chorus of Mycenaean Women

## SUMMARY

*Prologue* (lines 1-120)

Orestes, Pylades, and Orestes' old attendant enter. The old man points out the scenes. They are before the royal palace. Orestes instructs the old man to obtain knowledge of the situation inside the palace by entering and announcing that he has come from Phocis to report the accidental death of Orestes. He and Pylades meanwhile will honor Agamemnon's grave and then return bearing an urn supposedly containing the ashes of Orestes. They leave as Electra emerges from the palace bewailing Agamemnon's murder, her own hard lot, and Orestes' absence, for she is beginning to lose heart in her loneliness.

*Parodos* (lines 121-250)

The Chorus and Electra sing in responsive lyrics. They sympathize with her, condemn murder, urge her to cease her grief and rebelliousness, yet hope for Orestes' return. Zeus guides all. Electra cannot subdue her anguish and hatred of the murderers; she despairs over Orestes' return, lives in meanness and squalor, unmarried. There must be punishment for murder.

*First Episode* (lines 251-471)

Electra tells of her unhappy surroundings—the murderer Aegisthus on the throne, her mother, Clytemnestra, his partner in crime, married to him, their insults and mistreatment of her. The Chorus assures her Orestes will come. Her sister Chrysothemis enters, professes agreement with Electra's attitude to Aegisthus and Clytemnestra, but recommends submission to the rulers. Electra rebukes her timidity and cowardice. Chrysothemis tells her that Aegisthus is planning to imprison her in a dungeon if she does

**92**

not cease her lamenting. Electra is unperturbed. Then Chrysothemis tells her that she has been instructed by Clytemnestra to pour libations on Agamemnon's grave, for she has had a frightening prophetic dream. Urged by Electra and the Chorus, she agrees hesitatingly to substitute a lock of hair from Electra's head and one from her own as offerings to Agamemnon.

*First Stasimon* (lines 472-515)

Justice will triumph, the dream indicates. The house of Atreus has had many woes.

*Second Episode* (lines 516-1057)

Clytemnestra enters to find Electra in front of the palace. She tries to defend her murder of Agamemnon on the ground that he sacrificed Iphigenia. Electra counters that the real cause was her love for Aegisthus; and she defends Agamemnon's action on religious grounds. Electra insults Clytemnestra, who threatens punishment. Clytemnestra prays to Apollo for continued prosperity for herself and Aegisthus.

The old retainer of Orestes enters and announces the death of Orestes. As Electra is desolated, Clytemnestra eagerly asks for details, which the old man invents at length. His story is believed. Clytemnestra, overjoyed, pretends to be distressed, but finally expresses relief at Orestes' death, as she mocks Electra and goes in. Electra bewails her new unhappiness, bereft of her last hope of revenge, and prays for death. The Chorus consoles her.

Chrysothemis rushes in joyfully with news. She believes that Orestes has returned, for when she came to Agamemnon's tomb she found it newly decorated and on it a lock of hair, which she believes is Orestes'. Then Electra tells her of Orestes' reported death, and asks Chrysothemis to join her in accomplishing the murder of Aegisthus. Frightened, Chrysothemis cautions prudence, and is savagely reproached by Electra for cowardice. Electra will do the deed alone.

*Second Stasimon* (lines 1058-1097)

Filial devotion is admirable. Sin brings sorrow. The Chorus

prays to Agamemnon's soul, telling him of the sisters' quarrel, praising Electra, and hoping for her success.

*Third Episode* (lines 1098-1383)

Orestes and Pylades enter with an urn supposedly holding Orestes' ashes. Electra sadly asks to hold the urn, and then laments pathetically over his death and her own futile life. Orestes, deeply moved, questions her, expresses sympathy for her appearance and suffering, and finally reveals that he is Orestes. When he proves his identity, her grief suddenly changes to wild joy. They embrace, but he cautions her to be careful about betraying his identity by her actions.

The old retainer of Orestes comes out and firmly cautions prudence. As Electra greets him with joy, he urges Orestes and Pylades to act at once. They enter the palace.

*Third Stasimon* (lines 1384-1397)

Vengeance is about to be done.

*Exodos* (lines 1398-1510)

Electra comes out to watch for Aegisthus. Clytemnestra's death cries are heard, mingled with pleas for pity. Orestes and Pylades come out to report her death. As Aegisthus approaches with joy, they re-enter the palace. Aegisthus orders the gates of the palace opened. Orestes and Pylades are revealed standing near a covered corpse. Believing it to be Orestes' body, Aegisthus rejoices. He lifts the shroud and in horror sees the corpse of Clytemnestra. He is taken inside by Orestes to be slain at the spot where Agamemnon was murdered.

## INTERPRETATION

I.  Murder of Clytemnestra and Aegisthus accepted as justifiable homicide; all conflicts are reconciled by the triumph of justice over evil through punishment of the guilty; murder must be punished to vindicate divine justice.

II.  But basically dramatic interest is primary, not its religious or ethical significance.

III.  Tragedy of human character, particularly the psychology and personality of Electra entangled in conflicting emotions of love and hate generated by murder.

## DRAMATIC TECHNIQUE AND STYLE OF SOPHOCLES

I.   Skillfully constructed, more complex plots in single plays.

II.  3 actors; more dialogue; decreased importance of chorus.

III. Masterful use of dramatic irony.

IV.  Character drawing: the main purpose of Sophocles in the drama.

    A. "The Homer of tragedy"; varied personalities, complex human characters subtly delineated.

    B. Idealism ("men as they should be"); generally finer traits of human character with fewer faults.

    C. Character drawing through use of sharp contrasts with other characters.

    D. Development: principal characters undergo sudden change of outlook through reversals of fortune.

V.   Style: charm, grace, lucid simplicity, together with vigor, strength, dignity; Attic refinement and reserve.

## BASIC IDEAS OF SOPHOCLES

I.   Orthodox religious views (subordinated to character study).

II.  Fall of great people through character flaws; heroic dignity of man, despite imperfections.

III. When divine and human purposes conflict, the gods are supreme.

IV.  Inevitability of human suffering through character faults; human responsibility; but even innocent suffer; life is full of unexpected disaster; endure suffering.

V.   Arrogance, pride, sin lead to disaster; retribution is inevitable; moderation the best guide; reverence toward gods necessary.

VI.  Central theme: wisdom through suffering—tragedy because of human character brought about by gods, teaches humility and limitations of man.

## CHAPTER NINE

# EURIPIDES

## EURIPIDES OF ATHENS (480-406 B.C.)

I.  Born at Salamis, perhaps on day of the Battle of Salamis.

II.  Deeply influenced by Sophistic movement; philosophic interests, scholarly recluse; cosmopolitan, and most modern of the three great tragedians.

III.  Least popular as compared with Aeschylus and Sophocles in his own time, but ranked highest with later generations.

IV.  Tradition of unhappy marriages.

V.  Spent last years in Macedonia, where he died.

VI.  Wrote ca. 90 plays.

## EXTANT PLAYS (18 or 19)

*Alcestis*
*Andromache*
*Bacchae*
*Cyclops* (a satyr drama)
*Electra*
*Hecuba*
*Helen*
*Mad Hercules*
*Children of Hercules*
*Hippolytus*
*Ion*
*Iphigenia among the Taurians*

*Iphigenia at Aulis*
*Medea*
*Orestes*
*Phoenician Women*
*Suppliants*
*Trojan Women*
*Rhesus* (genuineness doubted)

## TROJAN WOMEN

**BACKGROUND**

Troy had just been captured through the strategem of the wooden horse. The captive women have been herded into huts before the walls of the burning city.

**CHARACTERS**

Poseidon, god of the sea
Athena, goddess of defensive war and wisdom
Hecuba, aged queen of Troy
Cassandra, her insane daughter who possesses gift of prophecy
Andromache, wife of dead Hector
Helen, ex-wife of Menelaus, King of Sparta
Talthybius, Greek herald
Menelaus, King of Sparta
Chorus of captive Trojan women

**SUMMARY**

*Prologue* (lines 1-152)

Poseidon stands before the walls of Troy, which he had helped build, and laments the fall of the city. As he tells sadly of the captured Trojan women who are about to be apportioned to the Greek leaders, Athena comes to assure Poseidon that she will join him in bringing disaster upon the Greeks for their sins. He agrees to cause a storm to punish the homecoming Greeks.

Hecuba awakes. She is staunch, but cannot help bewailing her woes and pain. Because of Helen's acts the Greek ships came and destroyed all that was dear to Hecuba, and now she has become a slave. She summons the Trojan women.

*Parodos* (lines 153-234)

The Chorus and Hecuba together in responsive song tell of their future slavery and separation when they have sailed from Troy to Greece as captives. They speculate fearfully on the chiefs to whom they may be allotted, and their coming life of work and shame.

*First Episode* (lines 235-510)

Talthybius enters and informs them of their future masters to whom they have just been assigned by lot. Cassandra is to be Agamemnon's concubine. Polyxena, another daughter of Hecuba, is to be sacrified at Achilles' tomb. Andromache, Hector's wife, has been given to Achilles' son; Hecuba to Odysseus. Hecuba bewails her own fate, because of Odysseus' hateful character.

On Talthybius' orders Cassandra appears; she is in an insanely joyful mood, holding a torch. She sings of her future relationship with Agamemnon. As Hecuba calms her, she predicts the death of Agamemnon, and bids them hope for this revenge. Though rebuked by Talthybius, Cassandra raves insanely about the future sufferings of Odysseus and Agamemnon. She bids Hecuba farewell and departs for Agamemnon's ships.

Hecuba in anguish tells to what a low status she has fallen in her old age from her former glory. She sorrows over the loss of her husband and sons, and her coming separation from the women of her family.

*First Stasimon* (lines 511-576)

The Chorus bewails the capture of Troy through the stratagem of the wooden horse, telling how the Trojans joyfully celebrated the supposed end of the war, but were soon overwhelmed by the Greeks.

*Second Episode* (lines 577-798)

Anromache, Hecuba's daughter-in-law, enters with her son, Astyanax, in her arms. She and Hecuba mourn over their woes.

Hecuba laments the newly-reported death of Polyxena. Andromache envies Polyxena, and wishes she were dead, rather than suffer the shame of becoming the slave of Achilles' son, not to mention his concubine. Hecuba comforts her and tells her to devote her energies to bringing up Astyanax as a future avenger of Troy.

Talthybius returns and reports with pity that it has been decided to kill Astyanax, in order to prevent the rise of an avenger, by casting him from the walls of Troy. Sadly but bravely Andromache bids a pathetically tender farewell to Astyanax and relinquishes the baby to Talthybius.

*Second Stasimon* (lines 799-859)

The Chorus tells how Troy was captured once before by Hercules and Telamon of Salamis. The Trojans used to be favorites of the gods, witness Ganymede and Tithonus. They no longer love the Trojans.

*Third Episode* (lines 860-1059)

Menelaus enters gloating over the recapture of Helen who is now held prisoner with the Trojan women. When he orders her summoned, Hecuba urges him to be merciless with her. As he threatens to kill her, Helen begs to be heard. Playing on his sympathies, she tells that she was forcefully stolen by Paris. In turn, Hecuba accuses her of lying, and insists that Helen went willingly with Paris, captivated by his charm and beauty, and that she was quite happy in Troy. Menelaus is convinced of Helen's duplicity. She begs for mercy. Swayed by her beauty, Menelaus orders her taken back to Sparta to await punishment.

*Third Stasimon* (lines 1060-1122)

Troy is being abandoned by the gods and men. Husbands and children have died in the cruel war. The women are left to suffer.

*Exodos* (lines 1123-1332)

Talthybius enters with the body of Astyanax. Announcing that Andromache has sailed, he bids Hecuba bury the baby quickly. Hecuba sadly mourns over her grandson and prepares him for

**99**

burial on Hector's shield. The Chorus mourns with her over the last hope of Troy. Talthybius returns and orders the women to be ready for the sailing of the ships. As Hecuba bids farewell to Troy, she wants to leap into the flames of the city. The Chorus laments for the fallen Troy. Hecuba prays to her dead, bewailing her lot. As the walls topple in smoke, the women turn toward the Greek ships.

## INTERPRETATION

Written in the midst of the Peloponnesian War, this episodic play arouses pathos for suffering brought about by war, and condemns the barbarity, folly and futility of war, which ruins victor and vanquished alike.

# MEDEA

## BACKGROUND

When Jason came to Colchis in quest of the golden fleece, Medea, the king's daughter, who had the powers of a sorceress, fell madly in love with him and aided him in his dangerous mission. She fled her country with him, and because of her love for Jason, slew her own brother to aid them in their flight, and later caused the death of Jason's traitorous uncle. Banished from his own land, Iolcus, Jason with Medea received sanctuary in Corinth. Here they lived peacefully for ten years and had two sons. When Creon, King of Corinth, offered Jason his daughter in marriage, he consented, for he was to be designated Creon's successor as king of Corinth.

## CHARACTERS

Nurse of Medea's children
Guardian of Medea's children
Medea, divorced wife of Jason
Creon, King of Corinth
Jason, Medea's former husband
Aegeus, King of Athens

**100**

Messenger
Chorus of Corinthian Women

## SUMMARY

*Prologue* (lines 1-130)

The Nurse prays that Jason had never come to Colchis. For then began the passionate love of Medea for Jason, on which account she committed murders. But now Medea hates Jason because of his abandoning her for marriage to the princess of Corinth. Medea is ill and emotionally unstable. She is remorseful over her crimes, and may yet commit other horrible deeds in revenge. The children's guardian enters with Medea's two sons, and tells the Nurse of more bad news—that Creon is about to banish Medea and her children. The Nurse is shocked, and fearing Medea's reaction, plans to keep the children from Medea. Medea's voice is heard bewailing her lot. The Nurse discourses on the wisdom of moderation.

*Parodos* (lines 131-213)

The Chorus inquires from the Nurse about Medea's troubles. As Medea's voice is heard lamenting, praying for death, and threatening vengeance, the Chorus with understanding consoles her and advises caution. The Nurse describes her fierce personality, and comments on the sadness of life and the soothing comfort of music.

*First Episode* (lines 214-409)

Medea enters, self-possessed, and recounts not only her own troubles, emphasizing that she is an alien, but also the sorrows of married women in general. She will find some way to avenge herself.

Creon enters and orders her out of Corinth with her children at once. He has heard of her threats of vengeance, and fears her powers. She deceitfully belittles her own cunning, vows that she will hold her peace, and begs to be permitted to remain. When he is adamant, she prevails upon him to allow her one day to prepare her departure. After he leaves, Medea reveals to the Chorus

**101**

that her purpose in gaining a day was to accomplish some grim vengeance through sorcery, whatever the consequences.

*First Stasimon* (lines 410-445)

The world is changing rapidly. Old standards are being shattered. Woman's place in society is gaining in importance. Medea is a woman of vitality and independence of mind.

*Second Episode* (lines 446-626)

Jason enters, and tells Medea she has brought banishment upon herself by her threats. He offers her money to meet her needs. Medea then assails him bitterly in a passionate speech, pointing out many reasons why his divorcing her was unjust, and her further troubles as a homeless woman with children. Jason, in an unconvincing rhetorical speech, attempts to refute her arguments, insisting that he married the princess to better the fortunes of his sons and family. He rebukes the selfishness of married women, accusing her of egoism and jealousy. Medea in turn throws up to him the fact that he married the princess secretly, and that his new bride is younger than herself, and that his purpose in marrying her was ambition. When she spurns his renewed offers of material assistance in her exile, he leaves her to settle her own problems.

*Second Stasimon* (lines 627-662)

Unrestrained love is harmful. Moderation is best, especially in love. Exile from one's fatherland is a pitiful thing.

*Third Episode* (lines 663-823)

Aegeus, King of Athens, passing through Corinth on a journey, meets Medea. She tells him her troubles and begs for asylum in Athens. He swears an oath to give her sanctuary, unaware of the crimes she has planned. After his departure Medea quickly formulates her plans for revenge. She will pretend to be reconciled to Jason's wishes, and send her sons with poisoned gifts for the princess, which will cause her death and the death of all who touch her. Then she will kill her own children to prevent their falling into anyone's hands and to deal a cruel blow to Jason.

*Third Stasimon* (lines 824-865)

Athens is a blessed land. How will it receive a murderess who has killed her own children? How can a mother coldly do such a deed?

*Fourth Episode* (lines 866-975)

Jason enters, and Medea deceitfully begs forgiveness for her recent words of hate, claiming now to understand his actions. He happily commends her change of heart. She asks him to intercede with Creon for permission that her sons remain in Corinth. She sends gifts with her children to Jason's wife, a robe and a diadem, both poisoned.

*Fourth Stasimon* (lines 976-1001)

The Chorus pities the children, who will be accomplices in Medea's crime. Poor Medea, who is about to murder them.

*Fifth Episode* (lines 1002-1250)

The children's guardian enters and announces to Medea that the decree of exile has been rescinded for her children. Medea is now torn between her love for her children and her desire to take even greater vengeance on Jason by slaying them. In this clash of emotions, she first weakens in her purpose, as her mother love masters her, but finally her grim hatred overwhelms all reason, and she is resolved to kill them.

*Fifth Stasimon* (lines 1251-1292)

Rare is the woman of wisdom. Childless people do not suffer the endless cares of those who have children. Children do not always yield the expected rewards.

*Exodos* (lines 1293-1419)

A messenger arrives and describes in detail the death of the princess and of King Creon, who clasped his daughter as she was being consumed by the poisoned robe and crown. With grim determination she rushes inside to kill her children. As the Chorus condemns Medea's action, the children's death cries are heard. Jason comes hurriedly to rescue his children from the fury of the people of Corinth. As he hears of the death of his sons, Medea miraculously appears above the house in a chariot drawn by dragons. He regrets ever having known such a barbaric woman, bemoans the loss of all he held dear, and begs for the bodies of his sons, so that he may give them decent burial. Denying his request, and predicting his future death, she leaves him a completely broken man, bearing off the bodies of her slain children in her chariot.

## INTERPRETATION

I. Uncontrolled emotions of anger and jealously overcome reason and bring disaster to all.

II. Internal conflict in Medea between emotions of mother love and desire for revenge.

III. Creates sympathy for women who suffer as inferiors under the Greek marriage customs.

IV. Character study of an emotional oriental woman, whose love turns into hate and desire for revenge. "Hell hath no fury like a woman scorned."

# HIPPOLYTUS

## BACKGROUND

Hippolytus is the illegitimate son of Theseus, King of Athens, by the Amazon queen, Hippolyte (Antiope). He shuns women, and spends his time hunting. Theseus married the young princess of Crete, Phaedra, by whom he had several children. When Phaedra first saw Hippolytus she fell madly in love with her stepson, for he was handsome and about her own age. But being a virtuous married woman, though emotionally weak, she is determined to conceal her love for Hippolytus, no matter how much she suffers from her unrequited love.

## CHARACTERS

Aphrodite, goddess of love
Hippolytus, son of Theseus and Hippolyte
Old Huntsman

Nurse of Phaedra
Phaedra, wife of Theseus
Theseus, King of Athens and Troezen
Friend of Hippolytus
Artemis, goddess of hunting
Chorus of Hunters
Chorus of Women of Troezen

## SUMMARY

*Prologue* (lines 1-120)

Appearing before Theseus' palace at Troezen, Aphrodite, resentful of Hippolytus because he ignores her worship and is a fervent devotee of Artemis, announces that she will punish him. On this day she will bring it about that Theseus will hear of Phaedra's concealed passion for Hippolytus. In this way she will cause the deaths of both Hippolytus and Phaedra.

Hippolytus enters with his fellow-hunters. They praise Artemis, and Hippolytus places a wreath at her altar, boasting of his purity. An old hunter, symbolizing the experience of age, warns him against pride and his shunning of women. The hunter is shocked at his irreverence toward Aphrodite.

*Parodos* (lines 121-175)

The Chorus has heard of Phaedra's illness. They speculate on the cause, suggesting insanity, or that Theseus loves another woman, or some trouble in Phaedra's own family, or that she is going to have a baby.

*First Episode* (lines 176-524)

The Nurse brings Phaedra out and comments on her restlessness. She is deeply distressed at her illness. Phaedra is revealed as possessed by vanity in the midst of her fevered suffering. She raves, wishing she were in some woodland or mountainous region. Suddenly realizing that she has been talking of places associated with Hippolytus, she is consumed with shame and hopes for swift death. The Nurse expresses her overwhelming love for her mis-

**105**

tress, but praises moderation in all things. She then questions Phaedra about the cause of her illness, but Phaedra maintains silence. The Nurse warns her that if she allows herself to die, her children will be harmed, for Hippolytus will succeed to the throne. At the mention of his name, Phaedra starts up. Questioning her relentlessly, the Nurse discovers that she is in love with Hippolytus.

Phaedra, having unburdened herself, is now calm. She talks of the difficulties of following the path of righteousness. She is ashamed and resolved to die because of her uncontrolled passion for Hippolytus. She reviles unfaithful wives, who besmirch the family honor. Phaedra places honor before personal happiness. The Nurse in a clever speech full of sophistry gives her many arguments against her decision, and urges her to give in to her love, and thus save her life. Phaedra weakens somewhat, torn by the conflict between her passion and her honor.

*First Stasimon* (lines 525-564)

The power of Eros (Cupid) is mighty. Even Hercules and Zeus were overpowered by Eros and loved outside their marriage ties.

*Second Episode* (lines 565-731)

Quarreling voices are heard within. The Nurse, taking matters into her own hands, has approached Hippolytus. First asking him to swear an oath never to reveal what she has to say to him, she tells him that Phaedra desires him. Hippolytus, shocked, rushes out in a towering rage, threatening to tell Theseus. He is reminded of his oath by the Nurse, but he does not feel bound by it under the circumstances. He thrusts the Nurse aside, and in Phaedra's presence bursts forth into a furious tirade against all women as the root of evil. After he leaves, Phaedra fumes against the Nurse for approaching Hippolytus, but the Nurse tries to defend herself, arguing that she did it out of love for Phaedra, and that, if she had succeeded, Phaedra would not be thus assailing her.

Her love now turned to hate, through the injury to her vanity and pride, Phaedra knows only one way to save the honor of her family and punish Hippolytus—to kill herself and drag down Hippolytus with her in death.

*Second Stasimon* (lines 732-775)

The Chorus wishes there were some escape from this mess by running far away. Poor unhappy Phaedra!

*Third Episode* (lines 776-1101)

Phaedra has committed suicide by hanging herself. At this moment Theseus arrives happily from a journey only to discover his wife's death. As he bewails this new misfortune in his sea of troubles, he observes a note tied to Phaedra's wrist. Phaedra's suicide note accuses Hippolytus of having violated her. In uncontrolled fury, he hastily prays to Poseidon to grant him one of three promised wishes by killing Hippolytus that very day. He orders him banished.

Hippolytus enters to greet his father and discovers Phaedra's body. At first his inquiries as to the cause of her death meet with stony silence. But then Theseus assails him as a corrupt man who conceals his evil intentions under the outward cloak of purity, and orders him into banishment. Hippolytus defends his innocence, emphasizing his purity and his universally known character. He is about to reveal what he knows, but his sense of honor compels him to uphold his oath to the Nurse. When he mentions the manner of his own birth from the ravished Hippolyte, Theseus in a rage orders him out at once. Hippolytus bids a sad farewell.

*Third Stasimon* (lines 1102-1150)

Life is full of chance and unexpected suffering. O, for some happiness in his life! Poor unhappy Hippolytus!

*Exodos* (lines 1151-1466)

One of Hippolytus' friends enters in haste and reports in detail how, as Hippolytus was leaving Troezen in his chariot, great tidal waves and a sea-monster sent by Poseidon frightened Hippolytus' horses. Hippolytus has been mortally wounded. Theseus is moved. and asks to see Hippolytus. As the Chorus comments on Aphrodite's success in punishing Hippolytus' pride, Artemis suddenly appears above the palace on a cloud. She tells the stricken Theseus the entire truth, and berates him for his haste in condemning the pure Hippolytus. The dying Hippolytus is brought in suffering from great pain. He converses reverently with his beloved Artemis. She consoles him with the thought that one day she will take vengeance on Aphrodite by killing one of her devotees (Adonis). Forgiving his remorseful father and embracing him, Hippolytus dies.

## INTERPRETATION

I.   Conflict between conventional standards set up by society and desire for personal happiness; between the power of sex and ascetic chastity; between uncontrolled passion and excessively controlled emotion. Moderation is desirable.

II.   Criticism of jealous, vindictive gods of popular religion who remain in conflict, while human beings reconcile their differences.

III. Psychological study of unrequited love, involving the "eternal triangle"; of uncontrolled emotions and human weakness causing tragedy; of pride, vanity, fear, jealousy, anger overcoming reason.

# ELECTRA

## BACKGROUND

Electra had been married by Clytemnestra and Aegisthus to a peasant, partly to humble her, and partly to prevent the birth of a child of Electra of high social status who might become an avenger of Agamemnon's murderers. See p. 9.

## CHARACTERS

Peasant, husband of Electra
Electra, daughter of Agamemnon and Clytemnestra
Orestes, son of Agamemnon and Clytemnestra
Pylades, friend of Orestes
Clytemnestra, widow of Agamemnon and wife of Aegisthus
Old Man

Messenger
Dioscuri, the gods Castor and Pollux
Chorus of peasant women

## SUMMARY

*Prologue* (lines 1-167)

The peasant husband of Electra stands before his hut in the country and tells of the murder of Agamemnon by Clytemnestra and her lover, Aegisthus. Orestes was secretly sent away to be brought up in safety in Phocis, and a price has been set on his head by Aegisthus. Electra was married to himself, but he swears that his respect for her social status is so great that the marriage has not been consummated.

Electra enters, meanly clad, about to fetch water. She explains the cause of her present state. There is mutual respect between her and her husband in name. As they leave, Orestes and Pylades enter, and Orestes explains that he has been ordered by the oracle of Apollo to avenge his father's death by slaying his murderers. He has come to look for Electra. She returns from the spring with water, bewailing her sad lot, the murder of Agamemnon, and the absence of Orestes.

*Parodos* (lines 168-212)

The Chorus of peasant women enters to announce to Electra that all the women of the region are to participate in a sacrifice to Hera soon. Electra declines, because of her unhappiness and wretched appearance. They console her, but she is thoroughly disheartened.

*First Episode* (lines 213-431)

Orestes and Pylades come out from their place of concealment. Orestes tells Electra that her brother is alive, and she tells the stranger of her humble marriage, and of her husband's respect for her. She hopes for Orestes' return and is grimly prepared to assist in the murder of Clytemnestra and Aegisthus. Electra then tells Orestes of her lowly position, of her mother and Aegisthus lording it over Agamemnon's realm, of Aegisthus' defiling of Agamemnon's grave, and of his mockery of a possible avenger. The peasant returns, and graciously welcomes the strangers into his hut. Orestes comments on the nature of virtue, concluding that personal worth and character, not birth, or wealth, or physical strength, is the criterion for judging the truly virtuous man. Electra sends her husband for Agamemnon's foster-father to assist in entertaining the strangers.

*First Stasimon* (lines 432-486)

Achilles came to Troy from Thessaly clad in his mighty, gorgeous armor. But the commander-in-chief of the Greek forces at Troy, Agamemnon, was cruelly murdered by his wife. Vengeance will come.

*Second Episode* (lines 487-698)

The old man arrives with food to entertain the guests. He weeps over the miseries of the family, and reports that he has seen evidence of fresh honorary sacrifices at Agamemnon's tomb. He has found some locks of hair, and surmises that Orestes has returned. Electra rationalistically [this is Euripides' criticism of the recognition scenes in the plays on the same theme by Aeschylus and Sophocles] rejects the possibility of recognizing Orestes by any similarity between her hair and his or by the shape of his footprint.

Orestes and Pylades come out of the hut. The old man recognizes Orestes by a scar on his forehead. The long-parted brother and sister embrace. As the Chorus rejoices, Orestes enquires how he is to accomplish the murders. The old man advises him. They plot the murder of Aegisthus at a coming sacrificial feast, and Electra plans to lure Clytemnestra to her hut by the false announcement that she has given birth to a son. Electra encourages the weak Orestes, planning suicide if the plot fails.

*Second Stasimon* (lines 699-746)

Atreus was blessed by Pan with a golden lamb among his flocks. But his wife was in love with his brother, Thyestes, and through collusion with her the latter obtained the animal and with it the throne of Mycenae. But Atreus, when he discovered the treachery, committed horrible crimes. Because of these happenings Zeus transformed all of nature. Yet Clytemnestra blindly slew her husband.

*Third Episode* (lines 747-1152)

As loud voices are heard from afar, Electra comes out, and a messenger reports to her in detail how Aegisthus offered hospitality to Orestes and Pylades, and how, while Aegisthus was sacrificing, Orestes slew him with an axe. As Electra and the Chorus rejoice, Orestes and Pylades enter with Aegisthus' body. Standing over the corpse, Electra recounts all his evil deeds and spurns it with her foot. The body is then concealed in the hut.

As Clytemnestra is seen approaching, Orestes weakens at the thought of matricide, blaming the oracle of Apollo for fiendish cruelty, but Electra stiffens his weak resolve. Clytemnestra arrives, guilty in conscience, and defends her murder of Agamemnon before Electra. In turn Electra accuses her adultery with Aegisthus as the basis of the crime. Clytemnestra is moved to some remorse for her treatment of Electra, now that she has heard she has had a baby. Electra asks Clytemnestra to enter the hut to perform the necessary purification sacrifices after her confinement. Electra is exultant.

*Third Stasimon* (lines 1153-1182)

Vengeance is at hand; justice is about to overtake the murderous wife.

*Exodos* (lines 1183-1359)

Clytemnestra's death-cry is heard. After the deed is done Orestes and Electra are overwhelmed with remorse over what they have done. They are apprehensive about the future, blaming Apollo for the deed. The Dioscuri (Castor and Pollux) appear above the hut as the *deus ex machina*. They reveal that Clytemnestra deserved to be punished for murder, but that the blood-vengeance ordered by Apollo was not righteous. They order

**111**

Orestes to marry Electra to Pylades. Orestes himself will be pursued by the Furies, but will be formally acquitted in Athens after due trial. The bodies of Clytemnestra and Aegisthus are to be given proper burial. The now polluted Orestes regrets his new parting with Electra, and they bid each other a tender farewell. The Dioscuri warn against injustice.

## INTERPRETATION

I.   There is both good and evil in divinities; criticism of Apollo, and the oracle; condemnation of the blood-feud and matricide.

II.   Psychological drama: realistic study of the tortured soul of Electra, her strength and weakness, how circumstances developed her into a murderess, and the psychological effects of murder.

## DRAMATIC TECHNIQUE AND STYLE OF EURIPIDES

I.   Plots complex; some use of suspense; some plays merely episodic, not organically unified.

II.   Prologues formal, non-dramatic, addressed to audience.

III.   Epilogue usually contains *deus ex machina* (in 12 plays).

IV.   Choral odes, decreased importance; tendency to become irrelevant to action and develop into mere musical interludes.

V.   Realism, uncompromising; "men as they are."

VI.   Psychological dramas (problem plays), not plays of fate or divine power.

A.   Conflicts of human emotions main interest of Euripides, either between characters or within one character ("divided soul").

B.   Tragedy of human situations primary.

C.   Tenderness and pathos principal emotions aroused.

D.   Introduction of love theme in drama.

VII.   Characters: subtle psychology of human beings; realism —epic heroes reduced to stature of ordinary persons—humble people elevated; emphasis on human weaknesses, hence especially importance of female characters (Euripides' greatest creations) in his plays.

VIII. Style: simple, lucid everyday speech; lyric beauty; but also formal rhetorical eloquence and sophistry.

## BASIC IDEAS OF EURIPIDES

I.   Keen interest in contemporary social, political, religious, and philosophical problems.

II.   Rationalism, liberalism, scepticism; criticism of orthodox formalism in religion, and conventional ethical and social standards.

III.   All extant plays on three subjects: war, women, religion.

A.   Hatred of aggressive war.

B.   Criticism of double standard with regard to women; sought to dignify the position of women.

C.   Not an atheist, but opposed to traditional anthropomorphic divinities; criticizes evils of religion, oracles, soothsaying.

IV.   Presents insoluble conflicts of life: clash of emotions, clash of reason and emotion, clash of absolute standards and relative standards of conduct.

V.   Sympathy for all human sufferings, and tolerant understanding of ordinary aspirations and emotions of human beings.

# THE DRAMA—COMEDY (OLD ARISTOPHANES

## ORIGIN OF COMEDY

The choral element originated in the phallic ceremonies to stimulate fertility at festival of Dionysus or in the ribald drunken revel in his honor (*komos*); the dramatic element in the Doric mimes. (Hence comedy—song of revelry.) There was thus impressed on comedy at the start frank indecency, particularly about sex.

## NATURE OF OLD COMEDY

I.  Poetic musical comedy, which may be compared with Gilbert and Sullivan's operas.

II.  Fantastic and unrealistic.

III.  Loose, carelessly constructed plots; broad farce and buffoonery.

IV.  Frank coarseness and obscenity.

V.  Usually a satire of important contemporary issues in Athenian life: political, social, moral issues.

VI.  Topical satire of well-known persons of the time.

## PRODUCTION OF OLD COMEDY

I.  At festivals of Dionysus, following tragedies.

II.  Contest between three poets, each exhibiting one comedy.

III.  Actors wore masks and *soccus* (sandal).

IV.  Chorus (24 in number) often wore fantastic costumes.

## STRUCTURE OF OLD COMEDY

I.   Prologue: leading character conceives "happy idea."

II.  Parodos: entrance of chorus.

III. Agon: dramatized debate between proponent and opponent of "happy idea" with defeat of the opposition.

IV.  Parabasis: coming forward of Chorus; Chorus addresses audience directly, airing the poet's views on any matter.

V.   Episodes: the "happy idea" is put to practical application.

## ARISTOPHANES OF ATHENS (ca. 446-385 B.C.)

I.   Greatest writer of Old Comedy.

II.  Little known of him; most plays written during Peloponnesian War.

III. Wrote ca. 40 plays.

## EXTANT PLAYS OF ARISTOPHANES

*Acharnians*          *Lysistrata*
*Knights*             *Thesmophoriazusae*
*Clouds*              *Frogs*
*Wasps*               *Ecclesiazusae*
*Peace*               *Plutus*
*Birds*

## BIRDS

## LEADING CHARACTERS

Pisthetaerus, old Athenian adventurer
Euelpides, a fellow-Athenian
Epops, the mysterious hoopoe (lapwing)
Prometheus, Titan, benefactor of man
Poseidon, god of the sea
Heracles, brawny hero, now minor divinity
Chorus of Birds

## SUMMARY

*Prologue* (lines 1-259)

Pisthetaerus and Euelpides are seen in a desolate spot each holding in his hand a bird, which has been serving as guide to the

**115**

kingdom of the birds. The two Athenians are discouraged. Euelpides explains that they have abandoned Athens for a quieter country. As they call upon Epops, and his servant Trochilus appears, they are seized by uncontrollable fear. When Epops appears, they explain their mission: they want his advice on where to find a quieter, more peaceful city to live in than Athens. He makes several suggestions, which they reject. Suddenly Pisthetaerus is struck with an idea. Why do not the birds build their own city between the sky and earth? They will thus become masters of gods and men alike, by intercepting the smoke of sacrifices made by men to the gods. Epops excitedly summons his wife, Procne, and the other birds.

*Parodos* (lines 260-450)

The birds of the Chorus begin to arrive one by one. Pisthetaerus and Euelpides comment on them, with topical allusions to contemporary personages in Athens. As the Chorus inquires why they have been summoned, and spy the two men, they threaten to tear them into pieces. They rush to attack, but are stopped by Epops. He asks the two Athenians to explain their plan to the birds, after a truce has been declared.

*Agon* (lines 451-675)

Pisthetaerus and Euelpides set out to "sell" their project to the birds. They argue that the birds were the first creatures of the universe, and that they once ruled all lands. They discourse on the importance of birds to man. Having stirred up the pride of the birds, they propose the building of a new city between earth and heaven. When this is completed an ultimatum will be sent to the gods and men demanding submission to the birds and divine worship from men of the birds as superior to all. The birds are completely won over. They are prepared to follow Pisthetaerus.

*Parabasis* (lines 676-800)

The Chorus comes forward and addresses the audience. They give the audience a lesson in the origin of birds and their importance to man. They next invite the spectators to come to live with

**116**

them and enjoy a life without legal restrictions such as exist in Athens. They finally expatiate on the advantages of having wings.

*Episode* (lines 801-1057)

Pisthetaerus and Euelpides return, having sprouted wings. They decide to name the new city Cloudcuckooland, and supervise the construction work. Prayers are devised for the new bird-gods. Various quacks and impostors arrive, a poet to celebrate the city in verse, a prophet with oracles, a mathematician to do surveying work, an Athenian government inspector, and a dealer in decrees, but they are all driven off.

*Second Parabasis* (lines 1058-1117)

The birds proclaim their divinity, and issue a decree setting forth penalties for those who injure birds in any way. They discourse on the carefree happiness of birds, and ask that the prize for the best play in the current competition be awarded to them, offering blessings, or evil if it is not.

*Episodes* (lines 1118-1705)

A messenger describes how the wall of the city was constructed and completed by the birds. A second messenger announces that an interloping god has entered the new realm. It is Iris, the messenger of the gods. She is shocked at the arrogance of the birds. Pisthetaerus threatens the gods with war, ordering that the city be closed to the gods and that smoke from men's sacrifices be intercepted.

A herald arrives from earth and presents Pisthetaerus with a golden crown. Many humans are desirous of dwelling in Cloudcuckooland. Pisthetaerus orders wings prepared for their reception. Several men arrive seeking wings to aid them in their activities, a parricide, a poet, an informer.

Prometheus arrives, masked and hiding under an umbrella, so as not to be seen by Zeus. He has come to offer his help, and tells them that the gods are starving and that there is dissension between the Olympian gods and the foreign (Treballian) gods. He advises Pisthetaerus that when peace envoys are sent by the gods he should

**117**

demand, as tokens of submission, the scepter of Zeus and the hand of Basileia (Royalty), Zeus' housekeeper, in marriage.

Poseidon arrives with Heracles and a Treballian god. They come as ambassadors of peace. Advised by Prometheus, Pisthetaerus states his terms. There are long, drawn-out negotiations. Heracles, having been offered dinner, immediately votes to accept the terms. Poseidon dissents. The Treballian god talks gibberish, but it is interpreted by Heracles and Pisthetaerus as a vote for peace. The terms are finally accepted, and preparations are made for Pisthetaerus' wedding to Basileia and the wedding feast.

*Exodos* (lines 1706-1765)

Pisthetaerus and Basileia enter in divine splendor, Pisthetaerus holding Zeus' lightning and thunderbolt. As the Chorus of birds adore them and joyfully sing the wedding song, the couple fly away to Zeus' palace where they are to reign.

## INTERPRETATION

I. Escapist, utopian fantasy.

II. Perhaps criticism of grandiose imperialistic schemes of Athens (Sicilian Expedition of 415 B.C.).

## CLOUDS

### LEADING CHARACTERS

Strepsiades, old Athenian gentleman

Phidippides, his spendthrift son

Servant

Socrates, Athenian philosopher, represented as master of school called "Thinkery"

Just Cause

Unjust Cause

Two money-lenders

Chorus of Clouds

### SUMMARY

*Prologue* (lines 1-262)

Strepsiades lies tossing on his bed, worried about the debts which his son has incurred because of a mania for chariot-racing. His son, Phidippides, talks in his sleep about the races. Still unable to fall asleep, Strepsiades tells of his happy early life in the country, and how his difficulties began when he married an elegant city lady. After their son was born, they quarreled about his name; his wife insisted on a name which had some reference to "horse." So they called him Phidippides (Son of Sparer of Horses), and he grew up with a passion for them. Suddenly Strepsiades has an idea. He awakes his son, and asks him to enroll in the school of Socrates next door to learn how to win lawsuits, for he expects to be sued for his son's debts. He hopes that the education in clever speaking will help him evade payment. When Phidippides refuses because school will ruin his tan, Strepsiades, despite his old age, decides to enter the school himself.

He knocks on the door of the Thinkery, and is rebuked for disturbing the studies of a disciple of Socrates. He hears about Socrates' subtle ideas, and is eager to join the school. He sees other disciples in various odd attitudes, studying a variety of subjects. Then he finally spies the master, Socrates, suspended in a basket from the roof of the Thinkery. He learns that Socrates cannot think unless he is in a rarefied atmosphere. He informs Socrates of his desire to learn to talk well enough to be able to evade payment of his debts.

*Parodos* (lines 263-509)

As Socrates prays to air, ether and the clouds, his special divinities, the Chorus of Clouds enters. The frightened Strepsiades watches the Chorus sing and dance. He learns that they are the goddesses who inspire tricky rhetoric, windy talk, and aid quacks and impostors. Socrates teaches Strepsiades about the nature and power of the Clouds, and that there is no Zeus. The Clouds according to Socrates, cause rain, thunder, and lightning, not Zeus. Strepsiades is convinced, and swears to accept no gods but Chaos, the Clouds, and the Tongue. He is ready to undergo all difficulties to learn sufficient eloquence to outwit his creditors. Socrates

**119**

administers a preliminary examination, in which Strepsiades reveals that his main interest is evasion of debts, and then they enter the Thinkery.

*First Parabasis* (lines 510-626)

The Chorus, addressing the audience, expresses Aristophanes' conviction that this is his best play, airing his views on the writing of comedy, and his pride in his art. They ask the audience for divine worship, recounting their services to the Athenians, and attack the politician Cleon.

*Episodes* (lines 627-888)

Socrates rushes out incensed at Strepsiades' stupidity and bad memory. Strepsiades comes out, and is required to lie on a bed while he is being instructed by Socrates. It is obvious that the old man is not interested in learning for its own sake, but only for the material rewards he will gain from his knowledge. His major interest is the art of false reasoning. After an unsuccessful lesson in the gender of nouns, Strepsiades is ordered to lie on the bed to ponder. He is assailed by bugs, and howls in pain. After a silence, he reveals his innermost thoughts to Socrates; he can only think of ways of outwitting his creditors, but at these thoughts he is quite ingenious. Socrates is, however, finally disgusted with him and dismisses him from the school because of his bad memory.

Strepsiades then decides to drive his son out of his home unless he enrolls in the Thinkery. He tries to teach his son some of his newly acquired knowledge. His son thinks it all quite foolish but is rapidly inducted into the school.

*First Agon* (lines 889-1112)

Phidippides is instructed by Just Cause and Unjust Cause. They quarrel and debate with each other, as each elaborates on his own merits. Just Cause exemplifies truth, justice, uprightness; Unjust Cause material success and modern ways. Each delivers a formal speech expounding his virtues. Just Cause discourses on the old education which emphasized honesty, justice, modesty, discipline, good health through physical training, morality, good manners, temperance, and respect for elders. Unjust Cause presents the merits of the new education which teaches how to discover loopholes in the laws, how to win arguments through clever speaking, how to talk oneself out of difficult situations, and the propriety of taking enervating hot baths, and practicing sexual looseness and intemperance. Just Cause finally acknowledges defeat on a technicality. Phidippides is to be instructed to talk cleverly by Unjust Cause.

*Second Parabasis* (lines 1113-1130)

The Chorus addresses the judges of the contest in comedy, and asks that the prize be awarded to this play.

*Episode* (lines 1131-1320)

Several days elapse. Strepsiades comes to inquire about his son's progress, and learns from Socrates what a brilliant student Phidippides has turned out to be. Overjoyed, he greets his son deliriously. Phidippides gives an exhibition of his ability to split hairs and quibble in the manner of the Sophists. A money-lender arrives to collect a debt from Strepsiades. He refuses to pay him because he makes an error in gender. Another money-lender is driven off by Strepsiades with the aid of the little skill he has acquired.

Some time later, in the midst of a meal Strepsiades rushes out of his house, howling because his son, Phidippides, has just beaten him.

*Second Agon* (lines 1321-1452)

Strepsiades and his son debate on the justice of a son beating his father. It is revealed that they have quarreled over the merits of Euripides, Phidippides defending him. He argues that he was just in beating his father, because his father beat him when he was a child, and his father is now in his second childhood. Strepsiades admits defeat. Phidippides then undertakes to prove that it is also just to beat one's mother.

*Exodos* (lines 1453-1510)

This is too much for Strepsiades. He suddenly admits that he

**121**

has ruined his son by following the path of evil, and he regrets his errors. Rushing to the Thinkery, with the aid of his slave he begins to demolish and burn the school, mocking and driving out Socrates and his disciples.

## INTERPRETATION

I. Satire on the new education of the Sophists and scientific research as destructive of traditional religion and morality.

II. Caricature of Socrates.

# FROGS

## LEADING CHARACTERS

Dionysus, god of wine
Xanthias, his slave
Heracles, the brawny Greek hero
Charon, the ferryman of the River Styx in the Underworld
Aeacus, one of the judges of Hades
Euripides
Aeschylus
Hades, King of the Underworld
Chorus of Frogs
Chorus of Initiates in the Mysteries

## SUMMARY

*Prologue* (lines 1-208)

Dionysus enters disguised as Heracles with lion-skin and club, but also wearing the formal tragic costume. His slave, Xanthias, is on a donkey, and carries a bundle of luggage on his shoulder. After an attempt at a few ribald jokes, Xanthias complains about carrying the bundles, but Dionysus insists that the donkey is carrying Xanthias and therefore the bundles too. They arrive at Heracles' house and knock. When Heracles sees Dionysus' odd costume, he roars with laughter. Dionysus reveals that he is consumed by a great passion for the dead tragic poet, Euripides. He is bent on going to Hades to bring him back to Athens, for contemporary tragedians are not as clever and tricky as Euripides was. He asks Heracles for directions to Hades, for Heracles once made the journey to seize the three-headed watchdog of the Underworld, Cerberus. Heracles playfully suggests three ways to reach Hades quickly; all of them involve suicide. Heracles then tells him the usual route, emphasizing the horrors and difficulties, in order to frighten Dionysus.

As Xanthias again complains about the bundles, a funeral passes by. Dionysus hails the dead man, and asks him to take the bundles along with him to Hades, but the dead man asks too high a transportation fee, and Xanthias shoulders them again. The two go on their way, and reach the banks of the River Styx. They see the old squalid ferryman, Charon, but he refuses to take Xanthias, because he is a slave and had not seen military service. After Xanthias departs on foot, Charon requires Dionysus to do the rowing.

*First Parodos* (lines 209-270)

As he does, he hears the Chorus of Frogs, singing and keeping rhythm with his rowing, using the repeated refrain, *brekekekex coax coax*.

*Episode* (lines 271-353)

After reaching the other side of the River Styx, Dionysus pays his fare to Charon, and meets Xanthias. They are both frightened by the darkness and by the sights of the Underworld. Dionysus in fear rushes to his priest sitting in the seat of honor in the audience, and begs for protection. They hear flute playing and watch in hiding.

*Second Parodos* (lines 354-459)

The Chorus of Initiates enters, singing a hymn to Dionysus, invoking his presence. With many satirical topical allusions to living persons, the Chorus asks all uninitiated to depart. They sing hymns to Athena, Demeter, and Dionysus, asking them to guide them in their joyful celebration. Dionysus then comes out of

**123**

hiding, and joins in the wild, orgiastic dance. The Chorus assails well-known Athenians of the time, and finally gives directions to Dionysus how to enter Hades' palace.

*Episode* (lines 460-673)

Dionysus knocks on the door of Hades' palace. Aeacus, one of the judges of the Underworld, appears, and taking him for Heracles, runs to summon guards to arrest him for theft. Dionysus is terror-struck. In fear he offers to change costumes with Xanthias and carry his bundles. When the exchange has been made, one of Persephone's maids appears and joyfully welcomes Xanthias, thinking him Heracles, to a feast and entertainment. Dionysus now, asserting he was merely fooling before, forces Xanthias to change costumes with him again. After this is effected, a landlady of an inn appears, accuses Dionysus, thinking him Heracles, of having failed to pay his enormous hotel bill when he was last in Hades, and threatens to summon her lawyer. Dionysus and Xanthias change costumes once again.

Aeacus now arrives with his guards to arrest Heracles. Xanthias, overpowered, offers Dionysus, as his slave, for questioning by torture. At this point, Dionysus reveals his true identity. Since there is doubt as to who is the god and who the slave, it is decided to test this by whipping each. Since both cry out in pain, and Aeacus is at a loss, he decides to take them both to King Hades for identification of the true god. Dionysus suggests it would have been a good idea to have thought of that before the whipping was administered.

*Parabasis* (lines 674-737)

The Chorus praises the Athenians, and abuses the politician Cleophon. They urge an amnesty for the reactionary revolutionaries of some years ago, who are in exile or have been disenfranchised. They then gibe at a political figure called Cligenes. Finally they urge the Athenians to honor the older citizen families above the newer ones, as pure coins are more valued than debased ones.

*Episode* (lines 738-894)

Aeacus reappears, having found out the real Dionysus. He and Xanthias have become quite intimate. A noise of quarreling is heard, and Aeacus reveals that Aeschylus and Euripides are competing for the privilege of eating free at Hades' table. Aeschylus had had the place of honor for some time, but since Euripides' recent arrival popular opinion has been in favor of Euripides. Hence, to end the dissension, Hades has proclaimed a contest as a trial of their skill. Sophocles has deferred to Aeschylus. The contest is to involve the weighing of lines in a scale from the works of the contestants. Dionysus is to be the judge.

As the Chorus sings in anticipation of the mighty verbal battle that is to take place, Euripides, Aeschylus and Dionysus come out. After the contestants warm up with a few trial gibes at each other, the Chorus prays to the Muses for aid. Before the duel begins, Aeschylus prays to Demeter, Euripides to Ether and other esoteric divinities.

*Agon* (lines 895-1098)

Euripides attacks Aeschylus for having employed silent, veiled characters at the beginnings of his plays, for using long words, bombastic language, and long choral odes, for being obscure, and for dwelling on excessively warlike themes and majestic characters. Aeschylus assails Euripides for excessive realism in language, characters, and plots, for depicting immoral love affairs, for using sophistry and rhetoric, for lack of patriotic emphasis and underplaying of military courage, for excessive emphasis on pathos and human weaknesses, and for unorthodoxy in religion.

*Episode* (lines 1099-1499)

Euripides continues the attack on Aeschylus' prologues, obscurity, repetitiousness, and poor choral music. Aeschylus criticizes Euripides for inaccuracies, monotony in his prologues, his new type of choral music, and his mingling of realistic and dignified language.

The scale is now brought out, and the contestants each quote

**125**

a verse from one of their plays into the balance. In each of three trials Aeschylus wins, for the meanings of the words he chooses involve weighty objects or ideas. At this point Hades arrives to learn who the winner is. But Dionysus still finds it difficult to decide. He then proposes to grant victory to the one who can give the best practical advice for saving the city. Euripides is vague and sophistic; Aeschylus more vigorous. Dionysus is on the point of making a choice, when Euripides reminds him that he came to bring him back to Athens. Dionysus chooses Aeschylus, quoting to Euripides the famous line from his *Hippolytus*, "My tongue hath sworn. . . ." Hades invites Aeschylus and Dionysus to a farewell dinner.

*Exodos* (lines 1500-1533)

After dinner Hades sends Aeschylus off to earth, urging him to aid his city, and giving him death-dealing gifts for various persons in Athens. He asks Aeschylus to tell these persons that Hades wants to see them soon. Aeschylus asks that Sophocles succeed him at the place of honor at Hades' table, and that Euripides be forever excluded. The Chorus bids him bon voyage.

## INTERPRETATION

I.   Fantasy on literary criticism; Aristophanes the first literary critic in history.

II.  Satire on Euripides as a dramatist and moralist; some criticism of Aeschylus.

III. Political theme: plea for unity and recall of political exiles.

## TECHNIQUE AND STYLE OF ARISTOPHANES

I.   Serious satire of contemporary issues, achieved through exaggeration and caricature.

II.  Wit and humor; unsurpassed comic imagination.

III. Remarkable poetic beauty.

IV.  Frank indecency, ribald jests, and vulgar farce.

V.   Loose plots of topical local interest.

VI.  Characters: generalized, subordinated to plot and humor.

VII. Style: varied, but essentially Attic simplicity and grace, together with poetic genius.

## THOUGHT OF ARISTOPHANES

I.   Conservative traditionalist; enemy of new ideas and new movements.

II.   Critic of intellectuals, especially the Sophists and Euripides.

III.   Critic of weaknesses of democracy, of radical social and economic theories, of radical leaders of democratic party and of their imperialistic war policy.

## CHAPTER ELEVEN

# HERODOTUS

◙

## BEGINNINGS OF HISTORY (in Ionia, 6th-5th Cents. B.C.)

I.   First uses of prose: ancient legends of past; genealogies of important families; scientific subjects.

I.   *Historia:* Greek word meaning "research," "investigation."

III.   Hampered for long time by: exclusive use of poetry as medium of expression; tendency to regard epic and mythology as true record of past; lack of adequate written records of past; religious thinking of Greeks; isolated city-state life.

IV.   Fostered by: spirit of rationalism and inquiry developed by Ionian philosophers and scientists; colonization movement and commercial life; upheaval of Persian Wars, which stimulated curiosity in modern history; scepticism of Sophists and their development of artistic prose.

V.   Predecessors of Herodotus (Hecataeus of Miletus and Hellanicus of Lesbos, ca. 500-450 B.C.) laid the foundations of history but were mainly geographers.

## HERODOTUS OF HALICARNASSUS (ca. 485-425 B.C.)

I.   Father of History; first great prose writer.

II.   The "Marco Polo of antiquity"; travelled ca. 17 years over much of the known world: e.g. Babylon, Susa, Egypt, Cyrene, Black Sea to Colchis, Asia Minor, Scythia, Greece, S. Italy, Sicily.

III.   Lived at Halicarnassus, Island of Samos, Athens; participated in founding of Athenian colony of Thurii in Italy, where he probably died.

## HISTORIA OF HERODOTUS

I.   History of the Persian Wars; but it is essentially a universal history and cultural survey of the known world in which the Greeks and Asiatics fought, from the foundation of the Persian Empire by Cyrus in 550 B.C. down to the events of early 478 B.C.

II.  Purpose: entertainment at public recitals; preservation of record of past; contrast between cultures of Greeks and non-Greeks (Barbarians).

## METHOD OF HERODOTUS

I.   Homeric qualities of style and artistic conception.

II.  Sources.

   A.  Mostly oral, gathered during his travels.

   B.  Archeological, from personal observation.

   C.  Written, works of poets, some official documents, earlier prose writers, mostly geographers.

III. Unified architectonic structure of his history.

IV.  Diffuse conversational style, with main theme of his history constantly interrupted by digressions on geography, customs and religious beliefs of peoples, irrelevant stories and folk-tales, marvels and oddities of remote times and places, human-interest stories.

V.   Speeches, debates, conversations.

## WEAKNESSES OF HERODOTUS AS A HISTORIAN

I.   Inadequate grasp of military strategy.

II.  Vague chronology, leading to errors and contradictions.

III. Faulty statistics.

IV.  Inadequate political understanding.

V.   Excessive emphasis on personalities and personal motives.

VI.  At times naïve, uncritical, gullible.

VII. Diffuseness and inclusion of much irrelevant material as digressions.

VIII. Speeches, debates, conversations unhistorical or not exact words of speakers.

IX.  Religious philosophy of history.

**129**

    A.  Instability of all human fortune.

    B.  Jealousy of gods of human prosperity; divine retribution through Nemesis destroys persons and peoples who become too big.

    C.  Personal intervention of gods in human affairs.

    D.  Belief in oracles, omens, divinely sent dreams.

## MERITS OF HERODOTUS

    I.  Indefatigable curiosity.

    II.  Conscientious and truthful; honest attempt at critical history.

    III.  Generally impartial, but at times favorable to Greeks.

    IV.  Unexcelled story teller.

    V.  Breadth of historical viewpoint; wrote a history of the civilization of the times, combining grasp of historian with that of geographer, anthropologist, ethnographer, student of comparative religion, naturalist, and sociologist.

    VI.  Humanism: interest in human personality, ambitions, and problems.

## SUMMARY
### Book I.

Introduction: his purpose in setting down his researches—to preserve a record of the great deeds of the past, in particular the causes and events of the wars between the Greeks and Persians.

1-5.  According to learned Persians, the origin of the enmity between Greeks and Asiatics was the seizure of women. The first outrage was the stealing of Greek women, including Io, daughter of King Inachus of Argos, by Phoenicians. In retaliation the Greeks seized Europa from Phoenicia and Medea from Colchis; in turn Paris (Alexander) stole Helen from Greece. The Greek expedition against Troy was, according to these Persians, interpreted by Asiatics as open hostility to all Asia.

6-15.  King Croesus of Lydia was the first in historic times to commit acts of aggression upon the Greeks, those on the coast of Asia Minor. This was the beginning of the subjugation of Greeks to

**130**

barbarians. In a digression, he relates how the family of Croesus, through his ancestor Gyges, took over the sovereignty of Lydia.

16-25. Through great military exploits Croesus' father, Alyattes, increased the Lydian Empire enormously. Digression on Thrasybulus, tyrant of Miletus, and other persons.

26-33. Croesus succeeded to the throne of Lydia, conquered all the Greek cities in Asia, and was lord of most of the peoples west of the Halys River. To his court came many famous men, including Solon the Athenian [unhistorical, because chronologically impossible] in the course of his travels. After showing Solon his great wealth, Croesus asked him who was the happiest man he had seen. Tellus of Athens, said Solon, because he had a moderately comfortable existence and a happy family life, and died in his old age fighting for his country. In second place Solon ranked Cleobis and Bito of Argos, who had great physical strength and died after performing a deed of religious and filial devotion. The gods are jealous of humans, explained Solon, and all life is unstable. No human is perfect, and no one can be called happy until he is dead. Moderation is best; wealth is not the key to happiness. After he had stated his views, Solon was dismissed by Croesus as a fool.

34-55. Shortly after Solon's departure Croesus' troubles began. He had a dream his son Atys would be killed and, despite his precautions, the dream was fulfilled. The gods have begun to teach him humility. The power of the Persian Empire, founded by Cyrus, was increasing. Resolved to check the spread of this new imperialistic power, he consulted the oracles, trusting especially one at Delphi. After he had made many precious offerings and gifts to the oracle, it advised him that, if he made war on the Persians, a mighty empire would be destroyed. Confident, he began to make military preparations, and sought alliances with Greek states.

56-58. Digression on the peoples of Greece, particularly the origins of the Athenians and Spartans.

59-64. Digression on the tyranny of Peisistratus of Athens—how he became tyrant of Athens, and regained his power, after being expelled twice, and finally established his power firmly.

65-70. Digression on Spartan history—how their misgovernment was ended by the military and political reforms of the (mythical) Lycurgus at the bidding of the oracle of Delphi; how they defeated the Tegeans of Arcadia in the Peloponnesus, after removing the bones of Orestes from Tegea to Sparta; how ultimately they became masters of the Peloponnesus and the most powerful state in Greece; and how Croesus made an alliance with them.

71-82. Croesus assumed the role of aggressor and attacked Cyrus of Persia, crossing the Halys River and marching through Cappadocia. Digression on earlier Lydian wars with the Medes, during one of which occurred the eclipse of May 28, 585 B.C. Cyrus marched to the defense of Persian territory. After an inconclusive battle at Pteria, Croesus disbanded his mercenary army. Cyrus suddenly attacked in the plain before Croesus' capital, Sardis. Victorious, he laid siege to Sardis.

82-83. The Spartans, called upon to aid Croesus, were engaged in a war with the Argives, and were unable to send assistance in time.

84-94. Sardis was finally taken after an assault by the Persian forces (546 or 541 B.C.). Croesus was captured, after having reigned 14 years. Cyrus ordered him burned on a pyre, and as Croesus stood there, he remembered in despair Solon's admonitory words on man's happiness. When Cyrus heard his story, he tried to save Croesus from burning. Croesus prayed to Apollo, and a storm quenched the flames. Cyrus then spared Croesus, showing him much respect and accepting his advice.

Croesus reproached the oracle of Delphi for misleading him and for ingratitude in view of his many gifts to the oracle. The oracle replied that it was fated for him to be punished for the sins of his ancestor, Gyges. It was Apollo who saved him from burning, and, moreover, Croesus misinterpreted the oracle, which merely stated that a great empire would be destroyed. Croesus then acknowledged his personal responsibility for his suffering, absolving Apollo of blame. Digression on the wonders and customs of Lydia.

95-106. The unification of Media, after its revolt from Assyria; the history of Media through the reign of King Cyaxares.

107-130. The birth, youth, and upbringing of Cyrus; how he overthrew his grandfather, Astyages, King of Media, after organizing a Persian army; how he founded the Persian Empire, thus ending the Median Empire.

131-140. The customs of the Persians, religious, social, dietary, political, military, legal, etc.

141-176. The growth of the Persian Empire is related, with numerous digressions, through the conquest of the Asiatic Greeks after hard struggles, of the Carian, Caunians, and Lycians.

177-187. Cyrus' conquest of Assyria. Description of Babylon, capital of Assyria, on the Euphrates River. Digression on the building construction of two queens of Babylon, Semiramis and Nitocris.

188-191. Capture of Babylon by Cyrus.

191-200. Description of Babylonia, its odd customs and its people.

201-214. Further military exploits of Cyrus, in the East, especially against the Massagetae (digression on the geography and customs of the region). How Cyrus was defeated and killed by the Massagetae under Queen Tomyris.

## Book II.

1-4. Cambyses succeeded his father Cyrus as King of Persia and invaded Egypt. The Egyptians are not the oldest people in the world, but rather the Phrygians, as proved by an experiment, according to a story related by Egyptian priests. In Memphis, Heliopolis, and Thebes, Herodotus learned about the astronomical discoveries of the Egyptians, their solar calendar, other marvels of Egypt, and that Egypt is the gift of the River Nile.

5-34. The geography of Egypt, especially the River Nile.

35-37. Egypt is a land of strange wonders and paradoxes, with its odd topsy-turvy customs, various methods of writing, religious fanaticism and rituals.

38-76. The sacred animals and methods of sacrifice of the Egyptians; the use of the scapegoat, the sacredness of the cow, and uncleanliness of the pig. Their religious beliefs are compared with Greek religion. The animals of Egypt, including the mythical phoenix, and their sacred burials are described.

77-88. The manners and customs of the Egyptians: peculiarities of diet, traditionalism and conservatism, dress, casting of horoscopes, interpretation of omens to forecast the future, medical knowledge, funerals, various methods of embalming the dead.

88-98. Other customs and oddities of Egypt, especially the Nile boats.

99-146. History of Egypt, as reported by the Egyptians themselves, with numerous digressions.

121-122. Folk-story of the imaginary Pharaoh Rhampsinitus: how clever thieves broke into his treasure-house; how one was caught in a trap; how the surviving brother concealed his identity by cutting off his brother's head; how he outwitted the king, and was rewarded by being married to his daughter.

123-124. Egyptian ideas of immortality, reincarnation of the soul. Building of the pyramid of the Pharaoh Cheops.

147-182. History of Egypt under the Saite Dynasty, from non-Egyptian sources, with numerous digressions.

**Book III.**

The expeditions and death of Cambyses (522 B.C.); the strange manner of the accession to Persian rule by Darius (521 B.C.); conditions in the Persian Empire under Darius, with numerous digressions.

**Book IV.**

1-144. The Scythian expeditions of Darius; cultural survey of the civilization of Scythia, its geography, peoples, religions, marvels and oddities.

64-72. Military customs of the Scythians: head-hunting, scalping of enemies, use of human skin of enemies for ornamental and practical purposes. Divination by willow rods; manner of execution of false diviners by burning. Burial of Scythian kings described with accuracy: human sacrifice at funeral, many persons thought to be necessary for continued happiness in afterlife killed and buried with king, including bodyguard of 50 horses and 50 men.

145-205. History of North Africa (Cyrene and Libya): geography, ethnography, customs, etc.

## Book V.

Persian conquest of Thrace, and customs and religion of Thracians; Persian negotiations with Macedonia. Outbreak of Ionian revolt against Persia (499 B.C.); spread of the revolt; digressions on Spartan and Athenian history. The Athenians and Eretrians aided the Ionian Greeks with men and ships, and participated in the burning of Sardis, capital of Lydia. Gradual suppression of the revolt by Persia.

## Book VI.

1-33. Fall of Miletus, its destruction, and end of Ionian Revolt (494 B.C.).

34-41. Digression on how the elder Miltiades of Athens had become the ruler of the Chersonese, and how his descendant, also called Miltiades, fled to Athens before the Persian advance.

42-45. After Ionia was pacified, in the Spring of 492 B.C. Mardonius, Darius' son-in-law, undertook an invasion of Europe by land and by sea, marching from Asia Minor across the Hellespont and along the coast of S. Europe, his major objectives being Eretria and Athens, who had aided the Ionians in their revolt. He subjugated Thasos and Macedonia, but his entire fleet was wrecked off Mt. Athos in a storm, and he was forced to abandon the expedition.

46-50. Darius demanded earth and water as tokens of submission from the Greeks, and prepared for war. Many Greek cities submitted, immediately, ignoring the warnings of Athens and Sparta.

51-86. Digression on the Spartan constitution; legend of the origin of dual kingship at Sparta; the rights and privileges of the kings, and the manner of their burial. Spartan history: birth and life of Demaratus, King of Sparta, and how he was deposed and exiled (491 B.C.). Digression on the insane Cleomenes of Sparta.

87-93. War of Athens against Aegina.

94-101. Renewal of Persian preparation for an attack on Greece. In 490 B.C. Darius appointed Datis and Artaphernes commanders of the Persian expeditionary force. They sailed across the Aegean conquering as they went Naxos, the Cyclades Islands, Carystus, and finally Eretria in Euboea after a short siege. Eretria was subjugated and its people reduced to slavery, without being aided by the equally menaced Athenians.

102-120. Battle of Marathon (ca. Sept. 12, 490 B.C.). The Persians then sailed for Attica, and guided by Hippias, the traitorous Athenian ex-tyrant, landed at Marathon, 26 miles N. E. of Athens. The Athenians hastened to Marathon to meet the Persian forces, led by ten elected generals, including Miltiades, recently arrived from the Chersonese, where his ancestors had lived for some time. Before leaving Athens they had dispatched a professional runner, Philippides, to Sparta with a request for aid against the Persians. When he reached Sparta, covering the 150 miles in about a day, he was informed that the Spartans, in accordance with an established Dorian religious custom, could not fight until the full moon.

Hippias, guiding the Persians at Marathon, speculated on whether he would regain his power over Athens, relying on dreams and omens.

The Athenians were joined at Marathon by their allies the Plataeans. The ten Athenian generals were divided as to whether to fight the Persians, inasmuch as they were greatly outnumbered.

Miltiades vigorously urged that they fight, and convinced the polemarch Callimachus to cast the deciding vote for battle.

Miltiades, given supreme command, deployed the Athenian troops so that the main strength was in the flanks, the center being left deliberately weak. When the Persians broke through the center, they were overwhelmed and routed by a flanking movement which joined the wings of the Greek forces. The defeated Persians soon after sailed back to Asia.

Though the Athenians were outnumbered their losses were astonishingly light, 192 men to 6400 for the Persians. 2000 Spartans arrived after the full moon on a forced march, but they came too late for the battle. They commended the Athenians and returned to Sparta.

121-131. Herodotus defends the Alcmaeonid family of the charge that they had dealings with the Persians for the purpose of betraying Athens. Stories of the Alcmaeonid family, especially how Hippocleides danced away his marriage, and how Megacles, son of Alcmaeon, won as his bride Agariste, daughter of Cleisthenes, tyrant of Sicyon, from whom were descended Cleisthenes, founder of Athenian democracy, and also Pericles.

132-140. Other military exploits of Miltiades. The failure of his aggressive expedition against Paros, as the result of which he was heavily fined, and died of battle wounds.

**Book VII.**

1-4. After the defeat of the Persians at Marathon, Darius made new preparation for attack. But he died in 486 B.C., being succeeded by his son Xerxes (Ahasuerus of the Old Testament).

5-18. Xerxes, the new king, was counselled by his advisers to war upon the Hellenes, but he had first to suppress a revolt in Egypt. When this was completed, a meeting of the council of king's advisers was held, at which a division of opinion on the advisability of a new expedition against Greece was revealed. His uncle, Artabanus, warned him of disaster, the younger Mardonius counseled war. Hesitating, Xerxes finally determined to make war following identical dreams of himself and Artabanus.

19-25. For four full years vast preparations were made. According to Herodotus, he gathered the greatest army of all times. A canal was dug through Mount Athos, bridges were built over rivers, and stores of supplies were accumulated at various places on the proposed route.

26-32. The Persian forces under Xerxes marched to the marshalling place at Sardis.

33-37. The difficulties of bridging the Hellespont. How a pontoon bridge was finally made over the strait; and how Xerxes ordered the Hellespont to be lashed and branded in order to subdue it to his will, after a storm had destroyed one of the bridges.

37-43. In April 480 B.C. the army marched from Sardis to Abydus on the Hellespont. Herodotus describes the vast size of the expeditionary forces; and the proud and arrogant spirit of Xerxes, who brutally executed the son of one of his subjects whose release from military service his father had requested.

44-56. Xerxes reviewed his entire force at Abydus. The cross ing of the Hellespont took seven days and seven nights.

57-60. The army marched to Doriscus in Thrace, where the numbering of the host took place. Herodotus' figure of ca. 2,000,-000 infantry troops, not counting other branches, is fantastic.

61-99. The names of the 61 tribes and peoples who served in the army and fleet of the Persians are then listed: especially Medes, Persians, Iranians, Anatolians, Assyrians, Egyptians, Phoenicians, Greeks, Indians, Ethiopians, Libyans, Arabians.

100-107. Xerxes reviewed the fleet, and learned from Demaratus, the Spartan traitor, the nature of the Greek people.

108-127. The army and fleet proceeded to an encampment at Therma in Macedonia.

128-137. Xerxes went sightseeing in Thessaly. Heralds returned to him from the Greeks bringing tokens of submission from some Greek peoples and cities.

138-144. It was now plain to many Greeks that the Persian expedition was directed at all of Greece, not Athens alone. But Athens took the lead in preserving the freedom of all of Greece. She was the savior of the Hellenes. The Athenians after the Battle of Marathon consulted the oracle of Delphi, and they were advised to defend Athens with wooden walls. Themistocles came to the fore, and, counseling defense by sea, convinced the Athenians after a bitter political struggle, to build a navy with the income from the silver mines at Laurium.

145-171. Congress of Corinth, 481 B.C. The Greeks who had decided to resist Persia now made peace among themselves and concluded a military alliance. Embassies were sent to various places in an attempt to secure maximum unity of the Hellenes. They did not succeed. Digression on Gelo of Syracuse, Corcyra, and Crete.

172-198. An attempt was made by the Greek forces to hold the valley of Tempe in Thessaly, but this had to be abandoned, and Thessaly was occupied by the Persians. The Greeks then took a stand at the Pass of Thermopylae in central Greece, stationing their fleet in nearby Artemisium. Herodotus now reckons up the grand total of the Persian army and navy as over 5,000,000, an utterly fantastic figure. He recounts the gigantic problems of provisioning such an army. The Persian army advanced south through Thessaly, the navy following down the coast.

198-233. Battle of Thermopylae, 480 B.C. The topography of the Pass of Thermopylae is described. The Greek forces defending the pass consisted of several thousand troops headed by the Spartan King Leonidas and his Spartan expendables. As the Persians advanced on the pass, some Greeks counselled retreat to the Isthmus of Corinth, but Leonidas held them at Thermopylae. Xerxes marvelled at the fewness of the Greeks. Then the Persian attack began, but they were unable to dislodge the Greeks, even after Xerxes' best troops, the Immortals, were sent into the assault. On the third day a Greek traitor revealed to Xerxes a secret pass over the mountains which led to the rear of the Pass of Thermopylae. In this way the Greeks were outflanked. Most of the allies managed to escape the trap and retreat. But the Spartans, Thebans, and Thespians remained to fight under Leonidas. Attacked on two fronts, the Greeks fought furiously, but were eventually annihilated to a man. Many distinguished themselves by remarkable feats of courage. The Greek dead were buried on the spot, and later commemorative monuments were erected, one containing an epitaph for the Spartans written by the poet Simonides: "Go, stranger, tell the Lacedaemonians that we lie here obeying their commands."

234-239. The Persians planned their next move. Xerxes ordered the body of Leonidas mutilated and dishonored.

## Book VIII.

1-23. While this was going on, the combined Hellenic fleet was posted at Artemisium, under Spartan leadership at their insistence, Athens yielding the command rather than endanger unity. The Euboeans, fearful for their safety if the outnumbered Greek fleet should withdraw at once, bribed Themistocles, the Athenian commander, to detain the fleet at Artemisium. He succeeded in doing this by bribing in turn the Spartan and Corinthian commanders. As the Persians sought to trap the Hellenes by a surprise enveloping movement, their plans were revealed to the Greeks by a deserter. After a preliminary skirmish, a Persian naval squadron was completely wrecked in a storm. But in the succeeding days the Greek captains decided to retreat south, after the news of the Persian breakthrough at Thermopylae was reported to them. The Persian fleet advanced south after them.

24-39. Digressions. The Persians advanced through Doris, Phocis, and Boeotia. Delphi and its oracle were miraculously preserved from the Persian invaders.

40-55. The combined Hellenic fleet anchored in the Bay of Salamis. All Attica was then evacuated by the Athenians. The composition of the fleet is then described. As the captains debated the best strategy, the Persian host entered Attica and laid it waste. They then seized Athens and devastated the Acropolis.

56-65. At first panic ensued at Salamis. But after a council of war at which Themistocles' arguments and threats prevailed, it was decided to remain there, though there was considerable support for a retreat to the more defensible Isthmus of Corinth.

66-73. The reinforced Persian fleet anchored nearby at Phalerum. At a council of war all advised Xerxes to fight a naval battle, except Queen Artemisia of Halicarnassus. Though inclining toward Artemisia's view, Xerxes accepted the advice of the majority. There followed preparations for the battle and fortification by the Greeks of the Isthmus of Corinth.

74-96. Battle of Salamis, 480 B.C. Another council of war was held at Salamis at the insistence of the wavering Peloponnesians who still favored defending the Peloponnesus. At this moment of indecision Themistocles, when it was evident that this view would prevail, secretly sent one of his slaves to the Persians. Pretending that Themistocles was pro-Persian and was plotting defeat for the Greeks, the slave in accordance with Themistocles' orders informed the Persians that the Greeks were divided and were planning flight. Taken in by the report, the Persians proceeded to bottle up the Greek fleet in the Bay of Salamis, so that retreat was impossible. Unaware of this, the Greeks were still debating flight, when Aristides the Just arrived and informed Themistocles of the Persian maneuvers. When the trap was confirmed by a deserting Persian ship, the Hellenic fleet girded itself for battle. In the furious battle, most of the Persian ships were disabled, the Athenians and Aeginetans bearing the brunt of the fighting. Queen Artemisia among the Persian forces especially distinguished herself in Xerxes' eyes as he watched the battle from the shore. The Persian rout was complete, and many of their ships were intercepted as they sought to flee.

97-106. After the naval battle was over, Xerxes, fearing that the Greeks might seize the Hellespont and cut off the escape of his armies, determined to retreat. The news of the Persian defeat hard upon the heels of the report of the destruction of Athens cast the capital of Xerxes, Susa, from joy into deep gloom. At Mardonius' request it was decided to leave him with an army in Greece to make an assault on the Peloponnesus. Digression on the revenge of Hermotimus the eunuch.

107-120. The remnants of the Persian fleet retreated at full speed toward the Hellespont, pursued by the Greeks as far as Andros, where the majority of the captains agreed that it would be better for Greece to permit the Persians to cross the Hellespont and leave them in peace. But in secret Themistocles sent the same slave he had sent before the battle of Salamis to advise Xerxes of the Greek decision not to attempt to destroy the bridges over the Hellespont. Xerxes retreated through Boeotia to Thessaly. Here Mardonius chose sufficient troops for the projected attack on the Peloponnesus, and Xerxes and his armies retreated across Macedonia, Thrace, and the Hellespont to Sardis.

121-125. Tremendous thanksgiving offerings were made by the Greeks, and Themistocles was voted the outstanding hero of the war.

126-132. During the winter and spring of 480-479 B.C. Arta bazus, a Persian general, captured Olynthus and unsuccessfully besieged Potidaea in the Chalcidice. The Persian fleet mustered at Samos, while a Greek navy under Spartan command gathered at Delos.

133-144. Mardonius wintered in Thessaly. After consulting oracles, he sought to win over to the Persian side the Athenians, as a preparatory move in his planned attack on the Peloponnesus. Digression: legends of the origin of the Macedonian monarchy, Mardonius sent Alexander of Macedon as his ambassador to Athens to offer friendship and an alliance. Spartan envoys arrived in Athens to argue against such an Athenian move. The Athenians summarily rejected the proposals of Mardonius.

**Book IX.**

1-89.   Rebuffed, Mardonius advanced south from Thessaly into Attica. The Athenians requested aid from Sparta, which was sent with some hesitation. Mardonius retreated to Boeotia. The Hellenes advanced north, defeating the Persian cavalry. After 12 days of maneuvering on both sides, the armies met at the Battle of Plataea (Sept. 479 B.C.), which resulted in an overwhelming victory for the combined Greek forces of 50,000 men.

90-113.   Meanwhile the navies of the Greeks met the Persian fleet at the Battle of Mycale (Sept. 479 B.C.), winning another brilliant victory.

114-120.   At the end of 479 B.C. the Athenians besieged and early in 478 B.C. captured the strategic stronghold of Sestus on the Chersonese.

## CHAPTER TWELVE

# THUCYDIDES

🔲

## THUCYDIDES OF ATHENS (ca. 460-400 B.C.)

I.   Wealthy Athenian family; moderate democrat.

II.   One of 10 generals of Athens in 424 B.C.; instructed to relieve Amphipolis, under Spartan attack; failure to do so resulted in exile from Athens for 20 years.

III.   Travels to all theaters of the Peloponnesian War; return to Athens in 404.

IV.   Profoundly influenced by Sophistic movement, both in thought and style.

## HISTORY OF THE PELOPONNESIAN WAR

I.   History of the conflict between the Athenian Empire and Sparta and her allies from 431-411 B.C.; the work ends abruptly and was unfinished at the time of Thucydides' death.

II.   Purpose: to provide an instrument for predicting the behavior of states, classes, and individuals under similar conditions in the future, through an accurate record and realistic analysis of the events of this war.

## METHOD OF THUCYDIDES

I.   Sources
   A.   Keen personal observation
   B.   Official documents
   C.   Literary sources, critically appraised
   D.   Trustworthy oral sources

II.    Annalistic method; chronology by summers and winters.

III.    Rhetorical speeches and dialogues: not the exact words of the speakers, but contain the general purport of their marks, and reflect the opposing motives and viewpoints of the antagonists at each critical issue of the war, together with the political principles and ethics of the times.

IV.    Style: antitheses; balance and contrast; symmetry; rhetorical; highly abstract diction; compact and concentrated; poetic and archaic; austere and obscure.

V.    Tested accuracy of narrative, and generalizing analyses.

VI.    Digressions: never irrelevant, always historical.

VII.    Influence of the drama: "the most tragic of historians."

## MERITS OF THUCYDIDES AS AN HISTORIAN

I.    First scientific historian; critical and sceptical.

II.    Impersonal; impartial.

III.    Penetrating knowledge of mass psychology and human nature.

IV.    Professional knowledge of military strategy.

V.    First attempt at accurate chronology.

VI.    Dramatic skill in narrative.

VII.    Political and social realism.

VIII.    No religious causes, only scientific observation.

## THOUGHT OF THUCYDIDES

I.    Mechanistic, materialistic view of history; law of human nature; individuals, classes, states act not in accordance with laws, customs, ideals, principles, or divine influence, but by self-interest and advantage, by what benefits them and what is expedient.

II.    Human nature is uniform, and behavior is motivated by circumstances; men will behave the same way under the same conditions.

III.    Therefore, it is possible to predict the future ("My history is a possession forever"), for similar conditions will recur, and history will repeat itself. There is no rigid determinism, for if

**145**

events can be predicted, human beings can guide history. Chance is operative only in minor events.

IV.   War is inevitable, for peoples strive for higher material standards, and evolve new forms of society, which upset the balance of power and bring about conflict between old and new social forms.

V.   Strength and weaknesses of two systems: Athenian democracy and Spartan authoritarianism.

VI.   Admiration for moderate Periclean democracy, involving political unity of all classes, and defensive imperialistic policy, as bringing out the best in human nature and leading to highest material progress; opposed to radical democracy, after death of Pericles, for the exclusive interest of the lower classes, and its hyper-imperialistic policy, as leading to internal disunity, social decay, and weakness in war.

VII.   Brutalizing effect of war on all.

## COMPARISON OF HERODOTUS AND THUCYDIDES

| Herodotus | Thucydides |
|---|---|
| 1. Vast historical canvas | 1. Local subject |
| 2. Lived after events treated | 2. Contemporary |
| 3. Often forced to rely on interpreters in foreign lands | 3. Nearly all the warring states spoke Greek |
| 4. Pioneer | 4. Profited by mistakes of Herodotus |
| 5. Inadequate military knowledge | 5. Experienced in warfare |
| 6. Faulty chronology | 6. Accurate chronology |
| 7. Lucid conversational style | 7. Compact, abstract, obscure, rhetorical style |
| 8. Imaginary speeches, or not exact words of speakers | 8. Admittedly not exact words of speakers, but contain general tenor of remarks |

| | |
|---|---|
| 9. Record of past for entertainment | 9. Didactic purpose, as guide to future |
| 10. Often uncritical and naïve | 10. Mercilessly critical, sceptical, insistent on truth |
| 11. Irrelevant digressions, folktales, human interest stories | 11. Few digressions, but always historical and to prove a point |
| 12. Traditional religious philosophy of history | 12. Political realism; concept of uniformity of human nature |
| 13. Human touch | 13. Penetrating psychological analysis of human nature |
| 14. Epic quality | 14. Dramatic quality |

## SUMMARY

**Book I** (covers 435-432 B.C.: events leading up to war; basic and alleged causes).

1. Introduction: he began to write at the beginning of the war, which was the most important event in Greek history up to that time.

2-18. Analysis of past Greek history and society to prove that the Peloponnesian War was the greatest event in Greek history. Primitive Greece was weak because of early migratory tendencies and lack of unity. There was no common Hellenic action before the Trojan War. Naval power, destined to become of paramount importance in Greek history, began with Minos of Crete, who cleared the sea of piracy, an occupation previously not frowned upon. Fortified towns were built, which grew gradually in size and prosperity.

Agamemnon was commander of the Greek expedition to Troy because of his superior wealth and naval power. The Trojan expedition was not a great one, because Greece was at the time poor, and the number of men involved was limited. With the gradual stabilization of Greece, wealth was acquired, and naval power

**147**

grew. Hellenic navies of the past were small, but those cities which possessed navies became powerful and rich. Land warfare was insignificant.

The unity of Hellas at the time of the Persian wars was short-lived. When the Persians were successfully repelled, two hostile blocs developed, one led by Athens, a great naval power, the other by Sparta, a strong land power. Thus, until the Persian Wars, events in Greece were of small scope, because of the disunity of the Greeks and absence of great concentrations of wealth.

19. The Spartan league consisted of independent states, ruled by pro-Spartan oligarchies. The Athenian Empire, the most powerful force in Greece, was based on naval might of Athens, which exacted heavy tribute from its subjects.

20-22. There is a need for critical examination of the evidence of the past. The errors of his predecessors in the writing of history are due to lack of critical ability. Early history is uncertain because of the lack of trustworthy evidence; reliance on tales and legends is utterly foolish. The Peloponnesian War, tested by actual facts, was the greatest ever known.

The speeches incorporated in his history do not contain the exact words of the speakers, but sentiments proper to the occasion, and the general tenor of the remarks made. He does not employ a subjective approach, or use chance information, but relies on personal observation and trustworthy oral sources. It is difficult, however, to trust eyewitnesses, because they vary in their reports, or are prejudiced. His purpose is to present an accurate and true picture of the events, not for the purpose of entertainment, but to provide a tool for predicting the future, when similar events occur. "My history is an everlasting possession, not a prize composition which is heard and forgotten."

23. The principal cause of this great and disastrous war was the growth of Athenian power and Sparta's fear of Athens.

24-55. The growing inevitability of war, and the immediate, alleged causes. The first of these was the Athenian intervention in

**148**

the dispute between Corinth and Corcyra. Invited by the common people of Epidamnus, Corinth interfered in the internal affairs of Epidamnus, a colony of Corcyra. War was declared between Corcyra and Corinth, and fearing the growing preparations of Corinth, the Corcyreans sent envoys to Athens to establish an alliance with her. At a meeting of the Athenian Assembly the Corcyrean and Corinthian ambassadors presented their cases. As a result, the Athenian people formed a defensive military alliance with Corcyra, because it was believed that war with Sparta was inevitable, and Corcyra, in addition to possessing a large navy, was in a strategic spot. Athenian ships despatched to defend Corcyra were embroiled in a naval engagement between Corinth and Corcyra.

The Corinthians accused the Athenians of breaking the truce of 445 B.C. between them and the Peloponnesians by attacking the Corinthian navy. The Athenians protested that their intentions were purely defensive on behalf of their ally, Corcyra.

56-66. The second alleged cause was the Potidaean affair. When Athens sought to prevent a revolt of her subject, Potidaea, a former Corinthian colony, the Potidaeans sent envoys to Sparta who returned with a promise of military assistance if Athens attacked her. Thus encouraged, Potidaea and other neighboring cities revolted from Athens. The Peloponnesians sent the promised aid. After heavy engagements, the Athenians blockaded and besieged Potidaea, with Corinthian and Peloponnesian garrisons inside.

67-71. At this point Thucydides begins his analysis of the contrast between conservative, authoritarian Sparta and dynamic, democratic Athens. A meeting of the members of the Peloponnesian League and all others who had grievances against Athens was summoned by Corinth at Sparta. The Corinthian envoys, after numerous grievances against Athens had been set forth, complained of Sparta's delay and inaction in the face of the hostile intentions of Athens now clearly revealed in the Corcyra and Potidaea incidents. They stressed Sparta's characteristic conservatism, its ignorance of external affairs. Athens, they said, had succeeded in encroaching on many Greek cities and enslaving them, because of Sparta's inaction and dilatory defensive policy. The Athenians are the opposite of the Spartans—active, aggressive, enterprising, intelligent, radical, taking risks even when they are weak, while Sparta acts weakly even though strong. The Corinthians urged the Spartans, in view of the nature of the enemy, to give up their policy of inaction and old-fashioned ways for a policy of aggressiveness and originality. They urged them to invade Attica, and not forsake their allies, since they were the leaders of the Peloponnesian League.

72-88. An Athenian embassy at Sparta attempted to prevent the Spartans from making a rash decision, but without success, despite the cautious views expressed by King Archidamus. The Spartan Assembly, by a large majority voted to stand by the allies and declare war, on the grounds that the truce of 445 B.C. had been broken, but primarily because Sparta feared the ever-increasing might of Athens.

89-117. History of the 50-year period (Pentecontaetia) from the end of the Persian Wars to just before the beginning of hostilities between Athens and Sparta: the capture of Sestus (479/8 B.C.); rebuilding of Athens, including new walls despite Spartan objections; construction of Piraeus, the harbor and naval base of Athens, and building of the Long Walls connecting it with Athens, under the guidance of Themistocles; formation of the Delian Confederacy; growing power and imperialistic policy of Athens; increasing mistrust of Athenian aggressiveness by Sparta; hostile acts of the allies of Athens and those of Sparta.

118-125. The Spartans received enigmatic assurances of success from the Delphic oracle, and summoned a meeting of their allies to put the question of war before them. The Corinthians took the lead in urging military action to prevent inevitable enslavement by Athens. War preparations lasted a year.

126-138. Meanwhile, diplomatic exchanges took place. Claims and counterclaims were made on both sides, especially concerning the failure to drive out religious pollutions in their respective cities. The Spartans hoped to stir up internal discord and to effect the banishment or discrediting of Pericles, the leader of the Athenian democrats. Events of earlier years connected with the curses and pollutions affecting both cities are detailed, especially the treasonous dealings of Pausanias the Spartan and of Themistocles the Athenian with Persia. The horrible death of Pausanias in Sparta, the flight of Themistocles to Persia and his death there, together with an analysis of his greatness are outlined. "Such was the end of Pausanias the Lacedaemonian, and Themistocles the Athenian, the two most famous Hellenes of their day."

139-146. Sparta made political demands on Athens concerning Potidaea, Aegina, Megara, and even demanded the breakup of the Athenian Empire. An assembly was held in Athens at which Pericles spoke. He urged them not to yield to any of Sparta's demands, reminding them that they had great military power and internal unity. They need not fear war, because of the greatness of their navy. Let them trust to Athens and the sea, not to the land of Attica, which Sparta can and will invade and occupy. The Athenians will free their allies if Sparta does the same. They are willing to arbitrate the dispute, for Athens does not want war. But war is inevitable, and preparations must be made.

**Book II** (events of 431-429 B.C.).

1-17. Events preceding the first campaign. War broke out in desultory fashion in the Spring of 431 B.C. When Thebans attacked an Athenian ally, Plataea, and openly violated the truce of 445 B.C., Athens sent aid to her ally and prepared earnestly for war. Preparations on both sides; strengthening of alliances. In Greece the greatest sympathy lay with Sparta, for she proclaimed herself the liberator of the Hellenes from the empire of Athens. While at a meeting of the Peloponnesian allies at Corinth King

Archidamus of Sparta made a cautious speech, at Athens Pericles expressed supreme confidence in Athenian victory, listing her material resources and elements of her power. He advised all the people of Attica to forsake the country districts and gather inside the walls of the city. The Athenians followed his advice, many reluctantly, crowding the city with refugees from the country regions.

18-33. First campaign of the war: Spartan invasion of Attica; Athenian naval attack on the Peloponnesus.

34-46. Pericles' "Funeral Oration." In the winter after the first campaign, in accordance with ancestral custom, a public funeral was held for the Athenian war dead. Pericles delivered the funeral oration. Instead of dwelling at length on the heroism of the dead soldiers, he seized the occasion to depict in idealized terms the democratic society and the empire for the preservation of which they had laid down their lives. He begins by pointing out that the deeds of the living, not words, are the best tribute that can be offered to those who died for Athens. He has a few brief words for their forefathers, who preserved Athens free, for their fathers, who founded the empire, and for the living who improved and strengthened the empire.

The burden of his speech is, however, an anaylsis of Athenian democratic society: 1. originality of Athenian government; 2. majority rule; 3. political and legal equality of citizens; 4. recognition of merit, equality of opportunity, even for the poorest; 5. individualism in private life unrestrained, tolerance of others; 6. self-directed respect for authority and for written and unwritten laws; 7. provisions for relaxation through public games and sacrifices; 8. high standard of living; 9. foreigners welcomed to Athens; 10. the education of Athenians is liberal, not exclusively military, but this does not weaken their courage and skill in war, for their courage is voluntary, not enforced by law; 11. moreover, they have leisure for the pursuit of personal happiness and for the cultivation of the arts of peace, for enjoyment of beauty and development of the mind; 12. all Athenians are, and are encouraged to be, active citizens and have a fair idea of politics, taking part in debates and policy-making; 13. in her foreign affairs Athens does not act from motives of self-interest; 14. versatility and adaptability of individual Athenian; 15. Athens is universally admired by her enemies and subjects, and her power extends over many lands and seas.

Such is the city for whom these men gave their lives; the living should cherish and struggle to preserve it. They died in a noble cause, not hesitating to risk their lives through selfish motives. Every citizen should daily fix his eyes on the greatness of Athens and become filled with love of her, for the greatness of Athens was achieved by men of courage who did their duty. The sacrifice which the dead made has been repaid to them in fame and glory, for they have an eternal memorial erected to them in the hearts of men. Their courageous example should be emulated by all who love freedom.

He cannot therefore commiserate the parents of the dead, but would comfort them with the honor that has come to them, however hard their loss. Those who are still young enough should have other children for their own happiness and for the state. Those who are too old should be comforted by the happiness they have had living in Athens, by the glory of the dead, and by the thought that death will cut short their sorrow. The sons and brothers should emulate the dead. The widows should not, in their sorrow, display more than natural women's weakness, so that they will not "be talked about for good or evil among men." The children of the dead will be supported at public expense.

47-54. No sooner did the campaign of 430 B.C. open than a mysterious plague broke out in Athens. It raged for a year, and the fatalities were enormous. Among the dead was Pericles. The origin and causes of the plague were unknown. Thucydides, who recovered, gives a clinical analysis of the symptoms and the course of the disease as he observed them. There was no remedy for it, and the misery was increased by the presence of an abnormally swollen population. Moral and legal restraints collapsed in Athens during the plague. (Some modern theories of the nature of the disease, none satisfactory, are: bubonic plague, typhus, smallpox, ergotism, i.e. poisoning from fungus growth on rye.)

55-70. Campaign of 430 B.C. The despairing Athenians unsuccessfully sued for peace, accusing Pericles of misleading them. At a meeting of the Assembly he defended his policies, but was fined. He was, however, soon re-elected general, but died of the plague in 429 B.C. Appreciation of the greatness and integrity of Pericles, and of his basic policy to maintain the empire through naval power and not to enlarge it during the war.

71-103. Campaign and events of 429 B.C.

**Book III** (events of 428-426 B.C.).

1-25. Campaign of 428 B.C. especially the revolt of Lesbos from Athens.

26-88. Campaign and events of 427 B.C. When Mytilene, on the Island of Lesbos, fell to Athens, there was a long debate in the Athenian Assembly as to how to treat the revolting city. It was spared from total destruction in the nick of time. The Spartans, however, when Plataea capitulated to them, razed the city to the ground and put the inhabitants to death.

In Corcyra there was fierce and merciless fighting between the democratic and oligarchic factions. At first the oligarchs were victorious, but a popular counter-revolution overthrew them.

81-84. The Peloponnesians and the Athenians rushed to aid the opposing factions in Corcyra. When the Peloponnesians retired, and the popular party sighted the Athenian vessels, they proceeded to massacre all the oligarchs they could find. The revolutionaries were pitiless, massacring all their enemies in a bloody purge.

The conflict between oligarchy and democracy assumed critical proportions in all Greek cities, the democrats hoping to receive Athenian assistance, the oligarchs Spartan. The war led to internal revolutions in many cities, and factions relied on outside assistance to solidify their revolutions. The war caused men to act from motives of a lower type than would be deemed proper in peacetime. War and revolution altered moral principles, corrupted all, even transformed values and the meanings of ordinary words of language; party ties were stronger than family ties.

The revolutionary ferment was caused by the desire for power and the self-interest of the party leaders. The crimes committed were monstrous; the spirit of revenge was fierce, knowing no bounds imposed by law or religion. Everyone distrusted everyone else; antagonisms were sharp. Force, not intelligence, prevailed in this fierce contest for power and survival. The principal causes of the violence in Corcyra were the desire for revenge against their former oppressors on the part of the democrats, covetousness for material gain on the part of the poor at the expense of the rich, and hatreds of the party leaders for one another. Revenge triumphed over justice and the finer traits of human nature.

89-116. Campaign and events of 426 B.C.

**Book IV** (events of 425-423 B.C.).

After two more years of fighting, a year's truce was agreed upon in the Spring of 423 B.C.

**Book V** (events of 422-416 B.C.).

1-83. Hostilities were renewed in 422 B.C. In 421 B.C., after 10 years of fighting, peace was agreed upon, and Sparta and Athens formed a 50-year alliance. The Spartans and the Athenians technically adhered to the terms of the peace treaty and alliance by not invading each other's territory for about 7 years. But the Spartan allies were dissatisfied with her move, and hostilities broke out, soon after peace was declared, in various parts of the Greek world. Actually there was no peace; the treaty was violated in various ways on both sides. The Spartan allies were in open hostility to Athens. Meanwhile, the war parties in both Athens and Sparta agitated for renewal of hostilities. New militant leaders arose on both sides.

84-116. When the war party came to power in Athens, the radical democrats abandoned Pericles' defensive policy, and undertook an aggressive, expansionistic imperialistic policy. An expedition was sent to annex the neutral Dorian Island of Melos. The Athenian forces landed on the island, and sent envoys to negotiate surrender. A dialogue ensued which reveals in the stress of war the abandonment of abstract principles of justice, and displays the political morality of the Greeks of the time, who openly proclaimed the Sophists' doctrine, "might makes right."

The Melians saw the issue as one of war or slavery for themselves, the Athenians cynically insisted that the discussion be orientated around the question of preserving the city. The Athenians then quite frankly admitted that Melos had not injured Athens and that she had been neutral in the war. It was not a question of justice, but of power and expediency. The Melians countered that, speaking only in terms of expediency, it is to the best interests of Athens not to continue aggressions, for the Athenian Empire may some day fall and the consequences for Athens would be terrible. The Athenian envoys replied that Athens would face this contingency when it came. Meanwhile their most serious enemies were their own subjects who might revolt. They urged surrender in the interests of their empire and the preservation of Melos. For then Athens would be richer and the Melians would not be destroyed.

The Melians preferred neutrality and friendship with Athens, but the Athenians rejected this, for their subjects might interpret her inability to annex Melos as a sign of weakness. For that reason they could not permit any state, however insignificant, to remain free. The Melians then pointed out that this policy was against Athens' best interests, for all neutrals would regard her with enmity and strengthen their defenses. The Athenians countered that their real enemies were not all neutrals but only the islanders who might endanger her naval supremacy.

The Melians then submitted that if Athens used force to preserve her empire and her subjects used it to revolt, it was understandable if they attempted to use force to preserve their freedom. To which the Athenians replied that it was not a question of honor but prudence, for it would not be a disgrace to yield to an overwhelming force. The Melians admitted that the odds against them were heavy, but if they fought there was hope that they would remain free. The Athenians replied that hope was self-delusion, and that power was victorious. In turn, the Melians pointed out that their hope was not blind, for they counted on the gods to aid the righteous and the Spartans to aid fellow-Dorians. The Athenians replied that even the gods act on the principle of "might makes right"; and as for the Spartans, they act only on the basis of self-interest in international affairs. The Melians asserted that it was to the best interests of the Spartans to aid them; for otherwise their allies would not trust them. The Athenians countered that the Spartans would not undertake the risk to save a small island, if they had to face Athenian naval might. The Melians fell back on the conviction that somehow or other Sparta would aid them.

The Athenian ambassadors summed up, in their renewed demand for surrender, by advising the Melians not to rely on hope and not to be motivated by any false sense of honor, for there was no dishonor in yielding to such an overpowering force as Athens, who would make her an honorable tribute-paying ally. The consequences of resistance would be inevitable ruin. The Melians chose to fight. After a long siege, the city surrendered to Athens. The women and children were sold into slavery, the men were put to death, and the island colonized by Athenian settlers.

**Book VI** (events of 415-414 B.C.): Sicilian Expedition.

(The next venture under the new aggressive imperialistic policy of Athens was the attempt to add Sicily to the empire. It was undertaken at the instigation of Alcibiades, a young kinsman of Pericles and disciple of Socrates, wealthy, brilliant, impetuous, ar-

**157**

rogant, egotistic, and ambitious. The purpose was not only to enlarge the empire, but also hem in the Peloponnesus from the west and cut off aid to Sparta. It failed utterly because of Athenian self-confidence in the face of so vast a project, disunity among the population and generals as to the purpose of the expedition, and the weakness of some of the generals.)

1-5. Early inhabitants of Sicily; Greek colonization of the island.

6-18. The expedition was undertaken on the pretext of aiding an ally, the Sicilian city of Segesta. She was at war with Selinus, and when Selinus appealed to Syracuse for aid, Segesta summoned Athens. Athenian envoys were dispatched to Sicily and were convinced of the ability of Segesta to support an expedition with financial help. At a meeting of the Athenian Assembly Nicias, who was weak but of unimpeachable integrity, tried to dissuade the Athenians from undertaking the expedition. The gifted, but reckless and corrupt, Alcibiades eagerly urged the attempt to conquer Sicily. The expedition was voted with high enthusiasm, and Nicias, Alcibiades, and Lamachus were elected generals.

19-26. Nicias, hesitant and pessimistic from the start, warned the Athenians of the need for vast preparations, hoping to discourage the venture, and even offering to resign his command. But the population, convinced by Alcibiades' demagogy, voted his recommendations for huge expenditures and gave *carte blanche* to the generals.

27-29. As the expedition was on the point of sailing, an event occurred which cast gloom over the undertaking. The numerous *hermae* in the city, square religious symbols of fertility and prosperity, were mutilated one night by vandals, perhaps pro-Spartan reactionaries, perhaps drunken rioters. One of the persons implicated in this act of impiety and in other religious crimes unveiled in the investigation was the general Alcibiades. But he was permitted to sail.

30-32. Despite the disquiet aroused by the mutilation of the *hermae* and the cloud hanging over Alcibiades, the huge armada sailed from the Piraeus in great splendor and high hopes.

33-41. When reports of the expedition reached Syracuse, an assembly was called there. Confusion and dissension were great, but preparations for defense were voted.

42-61. The fleet reached its mustering place, Corcyra, and sailed for Sicily. But it was clear from the start that there was disunity among the three generals as to the purpose of the expedition and the strategy to be employed. They seized Catania, north of Syracuse, as a base of operations. At this point the Athenian state trireme "Salaminia" arrived to bring Alcibiades back to Athens for trial. Long digression on the affair of Harmodius and Aristogeiton and the overthrow of tyranny at Athens. En route Alcibiades escaped from custody and deserted to Sparta. He was tried *in absentia* and condemned to death.

62-71. Deprived of the brilliant and adventurous Alcibiades, Nicias and Lamachus did not put into effect Alcibiades' plan for an immediate assault on Syracuse. Though the Athenians came off victorious in a skirmish near Syracuse, Nicias undertook a policy of delay, engaging in minor military activities in various parts of Sicily. In this way one year was wasted by the Athenian expeditionary forces.

72-88. The dispirited Syracusans sent for aid from the Peloponnesians. Much time was consumed in military and diplomatic maneuvers.

89-93. When the Spartans hesitated to send aid to Syracuse, Alcibiades addressed the Spartan Assembly in a brilliant, Macchiavellian speech. Calling himself a true Athenian patriot, he advised the Spartans to send aid to Syracuse, and gave them the benefit of his military knowledge by advising them simultaneously to harass Athens itself by building a permanent fort at Decelea as a base of operations. The Spartans were convinced by his arguments, and voted to send reinforcements to Syracuse under the command of Gylippus.

94-104. In the spring of 414 B.C. reinforcements arrived from Athens. With these the Athenians descended in force from Catania and seized Epipolae, the heights near Syracuse, where they rapidly constructed a powerful fort. The strategy of Nicias and Lamachus was to cut off Syracuse completely from the mainland by a circumvallation operation. The desperate Syracusans then began to build counter-walls. In the skirmishes connected with the walling operations, Lamachus foolishly exposed himself and was killed. Left in sole command, Nicias, ill of a kidney ailment, and lacking confidence in the entire undertaking, made serious blunders. As the Syracusans began to sue for peace, he permitted Peloponnesian ships under the command of Gylippus with reinforcements to land. After Gylippus fought his way into Syracuse with aid, it became clear that the circumvallation could not be completed and that Syracuse could not be besieged by land.

**Book VII** (events of 414-413 B.C.): Sicilian expedition (contin.)

1-7. Gylippus landed with reinforcements on the Sicilian coast, and succeeded in fighting his way into the city through the incomplete encircling wall.

8-15. Nicias, unable to cope with the situation wrote back to Athens requesting that new reinforcements be sent or that the expedition be recalled, and asking to be relieved of his command because of his chronic illness.

16-25. Upon receipt of Nicias' letter, the Athenians voted huge reinforcements and elected two new generals, Demosthenes and Eurymedon. The following spring (413 B.C.) the Syracusans, advised by Gylippus, built up a naval force. They then attacked and defeated the Athenian fleet which was anchored in the Great Harbor of Syracuse. Continued skirmishing.

26-41. Demosthenes and Eurymedon, sent to reinforce Nicias, proceeded slowly. Meanwhile, the Syracusans improved their warships so that they were superior in ramming tactics, and won another naval victory over the Athenians.

42-46. Upon the arrival of Demosthenes and Eurymedon, new vigorous tactics were adopted by Demosthenes. But a night attack by land on the Syracusan cross-walls ended in confusion and rout. The Athenians were cut off from their base in Catania.

47-59. Demosthenes urged immediate retreat to Greece of the entire expeditionary force. But Nicias, who had been in favor of such a move for a long time, now hesitated, and it was decided to remain. Another naval engagement in the harbor ended in a new Athenian defeat. The Syracusans now planned to capture the entire Athenian navy and to prevent the escape of the expeditionary force either by sea or by land. As part of their strategy they bottled up the mouth of the Great Harbor with sunken ships. Eurymedon was killed.

60-68. The Athenians held a war council and planned to retreat either by sea, if they could fight their way out of the sea blockade, or by land.

69-87. As the Athenian plan became clear to the Syracusans, they began to man their ships. Nicias, realizing the critical nature of the coming naval engagement, exhorted the captains, reminding them in trite phrases of the cause for which they were fighting —democratic Athens—and of their wives and children and gods. The Athenian fleet proceeded to the mouth of the harbor dogged by a detachment of the Syracusan navy. The fiercest engagement of the war now took place, for the stakes were very high. All through the violent and confused naval battle, the two armies on the shore watched with bated breath their respective navies decide the issue. Not being able to participate, the anxiety of the Athenian soldiers was almost unbearable as they watched, their hopes being alternately raised and dashed down. Finally, the Athenian vessels broke and fled to the shore. The panic was indescribable. Demosthenes and Nicias decided on another attempt to break the sea blockade the next morning, but the sailors refused to embark, paralyzed by their defeat.

It was therefore decided to escape by land at night. The Syra-

**161**

cusan general Hermocrates sent spies to spread among the Athenian soldiers the notion that the roads were being guarded by Syracusans and that it would be fatal to attempt a retreat by night. Believing this falsehood, Nicias and Demosthenes decided to remain another day to make adequate preparations for the retreat. Meanwhile, the weary Syracusans, who had been celebrating the naval victory, had time to recuperate and block all the roads.

The Athenian army began to move under a pall of gloom, the whole force being in tears because of the shame of their defeat and because they could not bury their dead or rescue the sick and wounded who were left behind. The 40,000 troops remembered from what splendor they had fallen, and feared capture and enslavement. Seeing the low morale of the troops, Nicias went among them, buoying up their hope, for hope was all he could offer them in their desperate plight.

They proceeded in two divisions, headed by Nicias and Demosthenes. For several days the army advanced, continually harassed by the Syracusan infantry and cavalry, and in desperate need of food. Their desperate situation increased, and many soldiers were wounded on the march. By a clever strategem they gave the Syracusans the slip. But the following morning the Syracusans and their allies pursued them and caught up with Demosthenes' division which was six miles behind Nicias' force. Demosthenes' troops, hopelessly surrounded, surrendered under a guarantee of personal safety.

The troops under Nicias, when informed of the surrender of their comrades, refused to do the same. Constantly assailed by missiles, and in dire need of provisions, they pressed forward. When they reached a river, all discipline broke down as they rushed into it for the purpose of assuaging their thirst and to cross to the other side. Here they were trapped and slaughtered in great numbers by the Syracusans. Nicias capitulated. He and Demosthenes were executed by the Syracusans, against the wishes of Gylippus. The surviving prisoners were marched to Syracuse and

**162**

put into a concentration camp at the bottom of a deep quarry. Crowded into a small area, suffering from intense sun during the day and extreme cold at night, with no sanitary facilities, with corpses lying about unburied, and with a starvation diet, the prisoners suffered acutely. Finally, the Syracusans sold some of them into slavery; the remainder were left to perish in the quarries. From this greatest action of the war, few returned. "Thus ended the Sicilian expedition."

**Book VIII** (unfinished; events of 413-411 B.C.).

Internal disorder ensued in Athens after the Sicilian disaster. An oligarchical revolution, through a coup d'état, brought into power the Council of 400, which governed despotically and sought to make peace with Sparta. Finally, the oligarchs were deposed. and a government by 5,000 of the wealthiest citizens succeeded to power, forming a regime which was a compromise between oligarchy and democracy. Alcibiades was recalled from exile.

## CHAPTER THIRTEEN

# HISTORY AND SOCIETY

## 404-323 B.C.

▣

## GENERAL CONDITIONS IN GREEK WORLD

I.   Greece never recovered from the loss of wealth and man-power caused by the Peloponnesian War.

II.   Growing economic and political crisis.

A.   Inflation; growing gap between large number of poor and few rich.

B.   Fierce internal class struggle in many Greek city-states.

C.   Distress and disillusionment caused growing individual-ism (concern for self and family), in contrast with citizenship ideal of 5th century; increasing detachment from affairs of gov-ernment on the part of many, and development of professional politicians; avoidance of civic responsibilities.

III.   Increase in militarism; development of mercenary soldiers.

IV.   Government: revival of democracy in some states; nu-merous oligarchies; military despots supported by professional armies; loose and unstable leagues and federations.

## ATHENS IN THE AFTERMATH OF THE PELOPONNESIAN WAR

I.   After peace was declared with Sparta, the democratic gov-ernment was overthrown by an oligarchy of the Thirty Tyrants, supported by Sparta.

II.   The Thirty instituted a bloody reign of terror, which resulted in a counter-revolution in 403 B.C. and the restoration of democracy.

III. Trial and execution of Socrates in 399 B.C.

## SPARTAN HEGEMONY (404-371 B.C.)

I. Sparta, the "liberator" of the Greeks from Athenian tyranny, now stepped into Athens' shoes, dominating many states by setting up pro-Spartan oligarchies, and by Spartan garrisons and Spartan governors.

II. Development of a coalition against Sparta headed by Thebes, Athens and Corinth; organization of Second Athenian Confederacy.

III. Development of powerful, aggressive Thebes, under Pelopidas and Epaminondas.

IV. Battle of Leuctra, 371 B.C.: victory of Thebes over Sparta; end of Spartan invincibility; Sparta humbled and weakened by Thebes.

## THEBAN HEGEMONY (371-362 B.C.)

I. Intervention of Thebes in Peloponnesian disputes.

II. Coalition against Thebes, led by Athens and Sparta.

III. Battle of Mantinea, 362 B.C.: death of Epaminondas, the architect of Theban power.

IV. Exhaustion, chaos, confusion in Greece, bordering on anarchy.

## RISE AND HEGEMONY OF MACEDON (359-336 B.C.)

I. Macedon, military monarchy north of Hellas, whose leaders had become Hellenized.

II. Philip II, King of Macedon; skillful diplomat; through policy of "divide and conquer" and lavish bribery he played upon Greek disunity and confusion in order to absorb most of Hellas under his power.

III. Demosthenes, by his speeches (especially his *Philippics*) and policies finally organized resistance against Philip's intervention and annexations.

**165**

IV. When Philip threatened Athenian spheres of influence, Athens, led by Demosthenes, declared war; alliance of Athens and Thebes.

V. Battle of Chaeronea, 338 B.C., near Thebes in Boeotia; rout of Greek forces by Philip; loss of Greek freedom; political bankruptcy of city-state form of government.

VI. Assassination of Philip.

## ALEXANDER THE GREAT (336-323 B.C.)

I. Succeeded his father, Philip, at age of 20; tutored by Aristotle.

II. Invasion of Asia (334 B.C.); conquest of Persian Empire (331 B.C.).

III. Continued expeditions and conquests to the East; crossed the Khyber Pass into the Punjab of India; refusal of his soldiers to go farther.

IV. Death of Alexander at Babylon, 323 B.C., at age of 33.

V. Policies and achievements of Alexander the Great.

A. Spread of Hellenism over Asia and N. Africa.

B. Building of many cities, especially Alexandria in Egypt.

C. Racial and cultural fusion of upper classes of natives with Greco-Macedonian conquerors.

D. Led to new type of culture, Hellenistic, characterized by fusion of Greek and Oriental cultures, and large monarchies with little or no political freedom.

## CHAPTER FOURTEEN

# PLATO

◙

## BEGINNINGS OF WORLD PHILOSOPHY AND SCIENCE (ca. 625-420 B.C.)

I. Founders of Materialism: first to abandon religious-mythological explanation of world; first scientific-philosophical attempts to arrive at objective truth about the universe, its nature and composition (cosmology); reliance on sense perception; attempt to explain how change occurs; principle of unity of matter, and search for single, primal material substance as ultimate reality of universe.

   A. Milesian School (Ionia, birthplace of science and philosophy).

      1. Thales ("Father of Philosophy"): water, ultimate reality.

      2. Anaximander: infinite (formless matter); theory of evolution and natural selection.

      3. Anaximenes: air, material first principle; change through rarefaction and condensation.

   B. Heraclitus of Ephesus: fire, ultimate material principle; permanence (Being) is illusion of senses; only change (Becoming) is true ("all is flux"), as reason proves; change is conflict of opposites, and all things contain conflicting opposites ("strife is the father of all things"); principle of relativity.

   C. Empedocles of Agrigentum: doctrine of 4 elements, (earth, air, fire, water); matter eternal, uncreated, indestructible;

**167**

change through reconciliation of opposites; cause of motion through external material forces of love (attraction) and hate (repulsion).

D. Leucippus of Miletus and Democritus of Abdera: atomic theory; atoms, indivisible solid units of matter, ultimate physical principle; infinite in number, different sizes and shapes, invisible; change by recombinations of atoms in empty space through natural law or chance.

II. Founders of Idealism: non-reliance on sense perception; denial of all change; search for eternal, abstract, non-material truth.

A. Pythagoras and Pythagoreans (S. Italy): ultimate principle, number abstractions; religious-philosophical sect, main interest mathematics and mysticism; distrust of sense perception and concrete things; eternal, abstract, rational truth through mathematics; body inferior to soul ("body is prison or tomb of soul"); ascetic purity and control of body by reason; reincarnation of souls; principle of permanent release from reincarnation through development of reason and contemplation of ultimate reality; emphasis on harmony, order, proper proportion through mathematical study.

B. Eleatic School (S. Italy).

1. Xenophanes: unity (oneness), ultimate reality; the One is God (pantheistic); attack on polytheism and anthropomorphism of traditional religion.

2. Parmenides: Father of Idealism; sense perception is illusion and leads to opinion; no truth in Becoming (the changing material world perceived by senses); only truth is Being (pure abstract thought, unchanging, eternal, perceived by reason).

3. Zeno: the world of sense perception is illusion; there is no motion or change; static universe; need to distinguish appearance from reality.

## ANAXAGORAS OF CLAZOMENAE

I. Taught in Athens; expelled for views on religion.

II.  Matter is indestructible, change is recombination of infinite elements.

III.  Causative agent of motion is *Nous* (Mind, Reason, God).

IV.  Sharp distinction between soul and body (mind and matter).

## SOPHISTS

Extreme scepticism produced by these conflicting and irreconcilable views of the pre-Socratic philosophers prepared the way for the Sophists.

## SOCRATES OF ATHENS (469-399 B.C.)

I.  Early life as sculptor; left Athens only on military service several times; ugly and grotesque appearance; remarkable physical endurance; mystic; devoted his mature life to teaching, without fees, his concepts of proper conduct.

II.  Socratic Problem: Socrates wrote nothing. His thinking is known largely through the works of his disciples Plato and Xenophon. In most of Plato's dialogues Socrates is the mouthpiece through which Plato expounds his own philosophy. How, then, can Socrates' views be distinguished from those of Plato? Is the Socrates of Plato's dialogues the historical Socrates, or the idealized product of Plato's artistry and imagination?  What is the pure essence of Socrates' teaching as distinguished from that of his pupils?

III.  Socrates is the "Father of Ethics." Turning his back on the Ionian materialistic physical science, Socrates transformed philosophy from the study of the external universe to the study of the inner life of man and his relations to other human beings. Abandoning scientific truth, he concentrated on ethical truth, seeking to establish absolute, universal, unchangeable standards of conduct.

IV.  Happiness does not consist in material rewards or bodily pleasures, but perfection of the soul, which is all-important. "Virtue is its own reward."

V.  True virtue is not enforced or conventional conduct, or

derived from sense-perception, but self-directed morality, based on reason and understanding.

VI.  Virtue is knowledge: no man intentionally does wrong; improper conduct is the result of ignorance of true knowledge; virtue is teachable and can be learned by reason.

VII.  Objective standards of conduct, valid for all, can be derived rationally by the formation of general concepts or precise definitions. This is achieved by inductive reasoning, through observation of particular instances of behavior and pruning away unessential and temporary qualities in order to arrive at the permanent essence.

VIII.  Dialectic method: question and answer method of learning and teaching; realization of ignorance was for Socrates the first step to knowledge; constantly professing personal ignorance ("Socratic irony"), he sought through the give and take of conversation to expose ignorance, and to test all presupposition through elimination of error, testing of theories to perfect and purify them through reason; he constantly stressed the need for critical self-examination ("know thyself"; "the unexamined life is not worth living").

## PLATO OF ATHENS (428/7-348/7 B.C.)

I.  Wealthy, aristocratic family; active in political life of Athens in youth.

II.  Disciple of Socrates for ca. 10 years.

III.  Abandonment of political activity; disillusionment with democracy and oligarchy after excesses of the Thirty Tyrants (see p. 164) and execution of Socrates in 399 B.C.; traveled for ca. 10 years.

IV.  Academy founded in Athens by Plato ca. 388/7 B.C.; first university in world; unbroken existence for ca. 900 years; here Plato taught and wrote his philosophical works.

V.  Two trips to Sicily; attempt to put his political theories into practice at Syracuse failed.

## WORKS OF PLATO

| | | |
|---|---|---|
| *Alcibiades* | *Hippias Minor* | *Phaedrus* |
| *Apology* | *Ion* | *Philebus* |
| *Charmides* | *Laches* | *Politicus* |
| *Cratylus* | *Laws* | *Protagoras* |
| *Critias* | *Letters* | *Republic* |
| *Crito* | *Lysis* | *Sophist* |
| *Euthydemus* | *Meno* | *Symposium* |
| *Euthyphro* | *Parmenides* | *Theaetetus* |
| *Gorgias* | *Phaedo* | *Timaeus* |

## DIALOGUE FORM AND STYLE

I.    All the works of Plato, except the *Letters* and the *Apology,* which is largely a monologue, are philosophic dialogues. The Platonic dialogue is an argumentative conversation dramatic in form. The number of persons in the dialogues vary from a minimum of 2 to a maximum of 9. The principal speaker in most of the dialogues is Socrates, who serves as the mouthpiece of Plato.

II.    Imbedded in most of the dialogues are myths, which serve as allegories or parables.

III.    Elegant, graceful poetic prose; sense of humor; skill in character delineation.

## BASIC THOUGHT OF PLATO

I.    Theory of Ideas

A.    Plato is a philosophic dualist. He makes a sharp distinction between the material world, perceived and known through the senses, and a super-sensory world apprehended by reason. The material world is correlated with matter, body, sense perception, many, opinion, particulars, becoming; the world of ideas with mind, soul, reason, one, truth, universals, being.

B.    He rejects the concrete material world as a source of true knowledge. It yields relative, individual truth (opinion) obtained through the senses. Concrete particulars contain opposites (e.g. an object will be heavy to one person, light to another;

**171**

opinion will vary about a woman's beauty). Such truth is, therefore, subjective, temporary, changing.

C. True reality is the super-sensory world of abstract ideas, apprehended only by reason, objective, eternal, unchanging truth. Ideas (universals, absolutes) have an independent or temporal character. E.g. Beauty, Justice, Heaviness, Smallness, Courage. Concrete particulars exist only insofar as the Ideas participate in them; they are copies of Ideas. All particulars, even all human beings, might cease to exist, but the world of Ideas would continue to be.

D. Idea of the Good. As all particulars are subordinated to and derive their existence from the Ideas, so all Ideas, forming a pyramid, are subordinated to the highest idea, the Idea of the Good, which stands at the apex. This supreme concept, the one absolute reality (or God), self-sufficient and perfectly harmonious, is the creative cause of the universe. It is the end of all, pure reason, absolute virtue, from which flow all other Ideas and through them the imperfect material world.

II. Soul and Human Nature

A. As the body is mortal and physical, it should be subordinated to the soul, which is divine and immortal.

B. The soul contains three elements: reason, good emotions, bad emotions. The souls of all persons are unequal at birth, having varying compositions of these three elements.

C. Since man is a composite of conflicting elements, body vs. soul, emotions vs. reason, the good and just man is developed through a harmony of these opposites. This is achieved through the dominance of the soul and reason, and the disciplining of and subordination of the body and emotions to the soul and reason.

D. Doctrine of Recollection. Since true knowledge cannot be acquired through the senses, all learning and knowledge is recollection by the divine, immortal soul of knowledge which it possessed before it entered the body.

III.  Ethics

A.  Happiness is not pleasure, or material success through power and wealth, for this is subjective, temporary, and relative, and caters to the body and emotions.

B.  True happiness is virtue, conscious, self-directed goodness through knowledge and reason (virtue is knowledge). The highest pleasure is intellectual, knowledge of absolute truth, which is goodness.

C.  Virtue is its own reward.

IV.  Political theory (see pp. 216–217).

# APOLOGY

**BACKGROUND**

In 399 B.C., in the wake of the disaster suffered by Athens in the Peloponnesian War, Socrates was formally indicted on two charges: corrupting the youth, and introducing new divinities. Actually these were pretexts. He had made many personal enemies by questioning and criticizing conventional religious and moral standards; in the popular mind he was confused with the Sophists and physical scientists. But the principal source of animosity against him was political: the radical democrats regarded him as subversive of democracy both because of his belief that the government should be in the hands of trained experts and because many of his disciples were anti-democratic, e.g. Alcibiades, Critias, Plato, Xenophon. The jury consisted of 501 citizens chosen by lot from a panel of 6,000. The law required that the trial be concluded in one day. There being no lawyers or public prosecutor, both plaintiff and defense delivered their own speeches and did their own cross-questioning. Socrates' accusers, Meletus, Anytus, and Lycon, completed their case against him. Then Socrates spoke in his own defense (*apologia*). Plato, who was present, wrote down his version of the speech some time later.

**SUMMARY**

17A-18A.  Introduction. His accusers have spoken persuasively but falsely. He himself, despite the warnings of his accusers, is not an eloquent speaker, unless by eloquence is meant truth. He will speak in his accustomed manner, informally and extemporaneously, as has been his custom in speaking to his fellow-citizens in places of public assembly. This is his first appearance, at the age of 70, as a participant in a law suit, and he therefore asks the jury's indulgence if he employs an unjudicial manner of speaking.

18A-24A. Refutation of popular opinion of him. There have been false rumors long current which are more dangerous than the present charges—that he is a sophist, scientist, and atheist—rumors broadcast by anonymous persons and by Aristophanes' burlesque of him in the *Clouds* (see pp. 118–122).

Though it is true that he was interested in physical science in his youth, he now denies that he knows anything about that subject. Nor is he, like the Sophists, a teacher; he accepts no fees. Yet there is nothing wrong in the true teacher accepting money, for specialists in teaching human excellence are admirable and enviable, like Evenus of Paros, whose fee is 5 minae (ca. $500 in present purchasing power).

He admits that he does possess a certain kind of wisdom but of a strange kind—human wisdom, which is admission of ignorance. A friend of his consulted the oracle at Delphi to find out who was the wisest man, and was told that Socrates was. Believing that the oracle had presented him with a paradoxical riddle, for he believed himself to lack all wisdom, and not wishing to disbelieve the oracle, he concluded that the god Apollo had imposed a mission upon him. He therefore set about trying to discover the meaning of the riddle, hoping to find a man wiser than himself.

Thus he went to politicians and by conversing with them discovered that he was wiser than this group, for they confidently believed that they were wise, but he proved that they were not truly wise. In this respect he considered himself wiser than the

**174**

politicians, for he admitted his ignorance. The result was that he incurred the enmity of these democratic politicians. Despite growing unpopularity, he felt that he must obey Apollo, and went on in his search, only to find that the oracle was correct, for those reputed the wisest were the most ignorant. He went to poets and had the same experience, discovering that they did not know the meaning of their own writings. When he went to the artisans, he discovered that they possessed wisdom which he did not possess— skill in their occupation. But this wisdom was vitiated by their belief that, because they were experts in their field, they were therefore also experts in more important matters (e.g. politics). He felt that he was better off than the artisans because of his intellectual humility.

Because of his divine mission he has incurred many enemies. But he possesses no wisdom, for only the god is wise. The oracle, he realized finally, meant that only the man who has intellectual humility, like Socrates, is wise. He has felt it incumbent upon him, in obedience to the oracle, to show people that they are not wise, though they appear to be. His devotion to his divine mission has completely absorbed his energies, and he is in complete poverty as a result.

Young men of the leisure class who have listened to him examining and exposing the pretenders imitated him. Many people in their anger at these youths have blamed Socrates for corrupting the young men, but he assumes no responsibility for them. The truth is that they do not like having their ignorance revealed. This is the real reason for the enmity of Meletus, Anytus, and Lycon against him.

24B-27E. Refutation of the formal charges, that he is a corrupter of the youth and is unorthodox in religion. He cross-questions Meletus, trying to show that the charges are a pretext, since Meletus does not know the real meaning of them. When Meletus declares that he is the only corrupter of the youth in Athens, he points out that this implies that everyone else in Athens

**175**

improves the youth. But this is the job of a specialist, just as training horses requires an expert. He likewise points out that it would be against his own interests to corrupt his fellow-citizens, for he would be injured in turn by them. Moreover, since he believes that "virtue is knowledge," he cannot have corrupted them intentionally, and should be re-educated out of his ignorance, rather than punished.

Concerning the assertion of Meletus that he teaches atheism to the youth, he points out that this contradicts the indictment, which merely accuses him of being unorthodox and believing in new divinities. He disavows the scientific views of Anaxagoras, and through the dialectic method insists that he believes in divine forces.

28A-34B. Digression on his life. Like Achilles, he is not afraid of death, for he believes he has acted in accordance with right and his principles. Dishonor in deserting one's post is more to be feared. He is merely acting in obedience to Apollo, not calculating the dangers of death, which may in fact even turn out to be the greatest good for man. He will not disobey the god. If released on the condition that he cease his questioning, he will refuse, since he must persist in teaching philosophy in obedience to Apollo, rather than cease in obedience to men. He teaches the unimportance of material things and the importance of virtue and the soul.

His mission to teach true virtue has been the greatest blessing ever bestowed upon Athens. He will never alter his ways, no matter what they do to him. If they kill him as a public nuisance, they will injure themselves more than him, for by doing so they will be sinning against Apollo. He is the gift of the god to Athens, and a successor to him will be difficult to find. He is a sort of gadfly sent to stir the sluggish beast which is the state into virtuous action. If they kill him, the beast of the state will slumber in a dishonorable peacefulness.

He has devoted himself to his mission so faithfully that he has had little time for active political life. Ever since he was a child he has possessed a divine sign (his *daemon*) which warned him when he was not to do something. It warned him not to go into politics, for it is a dangerous activity. His mission could therefore be fulfilled only in private life. On two occasions in his life when he was involved in politics, he alone refused to do what he regarded as unjust, even at the risk of his life. He has not corrupted the youth, for he never professed to teach anything. There are many present in the courtroom who will be character witnesses for him and will testify that he has never corrupted anyone.

34C-35E. Peroration. He will not follow the customary practice of bringing in his family in order to play upon the emotions of the jury. Such conduct would be a discredit to Athens and disgraceful to himself. He asks no personal favors of the jury, but only objective justice, for they have sworn to judge honestly. Asking them to act on any other motives would be inviting them to commit perjury, which would be an act of impiety.

(At this point the jury balloted and brought in a verdict of guilty by a vote of 280-221. The victorious accusers then demanded the death penalty. According to Athenian law the jury determined the penalty, after the defendant had proposed a counter-penalty.)

36A-38B. The counter-penalty. He expected the verdict of guilty, but not by so small a majority. He regards the vote therefore as a victory. As a counter-penalty he ironically suggests as his just deserts for his services to Athens—a pension for the rest of his life. He cannot suggest a penalty, for that would be an admission of guilt. He is not afraid of death, which may be a good. He rejects imprisonment or a fine, which he cannot pay because of his poverty, or exile, for he would surely not be tolerated in another city if his fellow-citizens cannot tolerate him. He refuses to stop talking in exile or in Athens, for it would be disobedience to Apollo; nor will he stop examining and criticizing people. Finally, because his friends urge him to and offer surety, he suggests a fine of 30 minae (ca. $3,000 in present purchasing power).

(The jury voted the death penalty by a much larger majority, 360-141).

38C-42A. Informal address to the jury. He is not disturbed by the death penalty. He is an old man, and would have died soon anyway. To those who have condemned him he states that he is not sorry for the uncompromising manner in which he addressed them and for his refusal to plead for mercy, since he acted in accordance with principle and righteousness. He prophesies that those who condemned him will be plagued by others like him, who will censure them for their evil lives much more mercilessly.

To those who voted to acquit him he tells that his divine voice made no sign of opposition when he was speaking. Therefore, he is convinced that what has happened is good. As for death, it is either the end, and therefore good, because he will sleep quite peacefully, or, if there is an immortality, it is even a greater good, for he will be able to see and talk to the great men of the past who have suffered unjustly, and to continue his questioning in Hades of those who are reputed to have wisdom. Moreover, they do not put one to death there for asking questions.

No evil can happen to a good man. He asks one favor of his accusers and condemners—that they punish and reprove his sons, if they neglect virtue for material things or become pretenders. This will be justice to him. Whether it is better to live or die, the god only knows.

# PHAEDO

## CHARACTERS OF THE DIALOGUE

Echecrates of Phlius in the Peloponnesus, a Pythagorean

Phaedo of Elis, philosopher, a favorite of Socrates; narrator of the dialogue

Apollodorus of Phalerum, disciple of Socrates

Simmias of Thebes, disciple of Socrates

Cebes of Thebes, disciple of Socrates

Crito of Athens, oldest friend of Socrates and his admirer
Socrates

## SUMMARY

57A-59C. Prologue. Scene: Phlius in the Peloponnesus.
Echecrates asks Phaedo to relate an eyewitness account of the
last day of Socrates' life. He was executed a month after the trial.
The execution was delayed a month until the return of the sacred
ship from Delos. The persons who were present in the prison cell
on the last day of Socrates' life are listed. Orders for the execution
have been issued.

59C-70C. Socrates' attitude to death: the philosopher is ready
and willing to meet death, so that the soul may be released from
the prison of the body, but, on the other hand, the philosopher
will not commit suicide. His friends and disciples have learned of
the return of the sacred ship from Delos, and have assembled at
the prison earlier than usual. Socrates asks someone to take home
his tearful wife. He comments on the intimate relationship between pain and its opposite, pleasure. He has spent his month's
imprisonment turning Aesop's fables into verse and writing a hymn
to Apollo.

In reply to a question, Socrates remarks that the true philosopher
gladly accepts death, though he must not commit suicide. Suicide
is unlawful, because, although death is a great blessing, he may not
open the door to death himself. For men are the property of the
gods, the guardians of men, and must await their bidding as to
this matter. In answer to Cebes' argument that, if the gods are
men's guardians, the philosopher should not be willing to leave the
service of such good masters by dying, Socrates maintains that the
good man is not grieved at death, for there is immortality and great
happiness in the afterlife for the real philosopher. True philosophy is a pursuit and practice of death, for it aims at liberating
the soul from the tomb of the body. Death is the separation of
the soul from the body. Material pleasures affect the body and

should be despised by the philosopher who should be concerned with the exclusive pursuit of the pleasures of the soul, wisdom and knowledge, to the acquisition of which the body and its demands are hindrances. Perfect wisdom can be attained only when the soul is released from the body, and the mind attains absolute truths (ideas), without sense perception.

The body, with its desires and weaknesses, is a source of much trouble and impedes philosophy. Pure wisdom can come only after death has released the soul. Hence he rejoices at his coming death. True philosophy is the practice of dying; death is no evil and is not to be feared. The true philosopher possesses true courage and temperance, for the multitude endures evils only to avoid greater ones and foregoes pleasures only to enjoy greater ones. The masses are motivated by fear and self-indulgence. The only true virtue is wisdom. Since he has practiced this all his life, he looks forward to death with eager anticipation.

Very well, replies Cebes; but since immortality of the soul is implied in the position Socrates has taken, how can we prove that when the soul leaves the body it does not disappear but rather continues to exist?

70C-77D. First Proof of Immortality.

A. Argument from analogy of opposites. The ancient tradition of reincarnation of souls implies the continued existence of the soul after death. The argument for immortality here is based upon the principle that all things and processes generate their opposites. If there is dying, there must be rebirth, otherwise everything would die out completely. Therefore, the living are generated from the dead, and the souls of the dead exist somewhere and are reborn.

B. Argument from the theory that learning is recollection. If learning is recollection, the souls must exist before birth in the human body. The doctrine of recollection rests upon the Theory of Ideas. The souls once knew the Ideas (abstract concepts) before birth, and since concrete particulars appear to strive after some absolute, we recollect the Ideas after birth. Therefore, the souls exist before birth. The entire argument depends upon the validity of the Theory of Ideas.

In answer to Cebes' hesitation Socrates asserts that complete proof is obtained by combining both of the above arguments.

77D-78B. Digression on the need to eliminate the fear of death at all costs.

78C-84B. Second Proof of Immortality.

By considering the soul's own nature we can decide whether the soul can be dispersed after death or whether it survives intact. Ideas are unchanging and eternal; concrete particulars are tem· porary and changeable. Concrete things are perceived by the senses; the invisible ideas apprehended by reason. Since the soul is invisible, it resembles the idea, and is therefore immortal and unchanging, while the body is mortal and dissoluble. Some souls are weighted down by bodily attributes because of addiction to material things and do not readily leave the earth at death. The souls of those who have practiced true philosophy and have restrained the body go up to commune with the gods. Therefore, we must constantly purify our souls from contact with the body and corporeal desires, and must follow reason only, resisting enslavement of the soul to the body. If we do this, we need not fear dispersal of the soul at death.

84C-88B. Socrates welcomes objections to his arguments. Simmias is not convinced; there is a flaw. If the soul is the harmony of the parts of the body, as harmony is to a lyre, it is conceivable that the soul may perish before the body does, as when harmony disappears upon the smashing of the lyre. Cebes admits that it has been proven that the soul exists before entering the body, but he is not convinced that there is proof that the soul exists after death.

88C-89A. Echecrates the auditor and Phaedo the narrator of the dialogue comment on what has preceded.

89A-91C. Despite the consternation of all, Socrates composedly warns against the danger of becoming haters of argumentation because of the serious objections that have been raised. This would be fatal to the truth, for the only salvation is to continue the investigation and blame the inadequacy on oneself, not upon argumentation and the search for the truth.

91C-95A. Socrates refutes Simmias' objection that the soul may perish before the body. Simmias is convinced that if learning is recollection, then the soul is not a harmony, and that the soul guides the body and not the body the soul.

95A-100A. Cebes' objection, that it is necessary to prove that the soul is eternally indestructible, not merely that it exists before birth, for otherwise the soul might be said to perish after death, has raised the whole question of the origin (generation) and decay (change) of all things. In his youth Socrates had a passion for natural science. He investigated these problems a long time, but after much speculation as to the causative agents of generation and decay, he gave up such attempts, concluding that he was not temperamentally suited for such studies. He rejected the search for material causes through sense perception as deceptive, for it offered to his mind no real explanation. In his discontent with materialistic interpretations of the universe, he came upon Anaxagoras' theory of Mind as the ultimate principle. After reading Anaxagoras' book, he was bitterly disappointed, for he concluded that with Anaxagoras Mind as the basic cause was itself a physical and material cause. He was all the more disappointed because Anaxagoras made no attempt to explain the purpose behind the orderly universe and human behavior. All these explanations had not plumbed to the basic cause of events at all, which he was convinced was not physical. So he gave up the study of physical phenomena and began to develop his own method, turning from sense perception to general definitions and concepts which he judged to be closer to truth.

100B-107B. Third Proof of Immortality: Theory of Ideas.

Socrates then proceeds to elaborate the Theory of Ideas in great detail in order to offer a final proof of the immortality of the soul. The cause of all material things and particulars are the Ideas, and the concrete thing exists only insofar as the Ideas participate in it, e.g. Beauty, Greatness, Smallness, Duality. Only Ideas, or universals, can be known.

Two opposite Ideas can co-exist in the same concrete object, but Ideas are mutually exclusive; they cannot co-exist in one another, while particulars always contain opposites. Moreover, there are things which are not exact opposites (e.g. snow and heat; cold and fire; three and even), but they contain opposite Ideas, and so cannot co-exist, but repel each other. The cause of life in the body is the soul, which brings to the body the Idea of life. The opposite of life is death. Therefore, the soul cannot co-exist with death, and what will not admit death is itself deathless, and what is immortal is indestructible. When death enters the body the soul withdraws, since it contains the opposite of death, namely life. By its very nature the soul cannot co-exist with death.

Cebes is now completely convinced; Simmias hesitatingly agrees, but he has misgivings, for the only real "proof" offered depends on the validity of the Theory of Ideas.

107B-114C. Myth of the Afterlife.

Therefore, since the soul is immortal, it should be the greatest concern of humans while they are on this earth. Hence, the importance of attaining virtue and wisdom. When the body dies judgment is passed on the souls and they are separated. The true philosopher's soul will go to the "real earth" (heaven), which is above, where it will commune with the gods, living happily in sublime beauty. The others will be sent below the earth to Tartarus. Tartarus is described, especially its rivers, Acheron (Sorrow), Styx (Loathing), Cocytus (Lamentation), Puriphlegethon (Burning). Incurable sinners are cast into the depths of Tartarus and never return. The less guilty are eventually purified and cleansed of their guilt in Acheron, and undergo reincarnation. The truly pure souls, who have learned wisdom and true virtue, and who have subjugated the body, live beatifically in the earth above the level of the earth of human existence.

114D-118D. Last Moments of Socrates.

Having concluded, Socrates goes to bathe himself in order to spare the women of his family this trouble after his death. He urges his friends not to mourn for his body, since his soul will be happy. After his bath Socrates says farewell to his sons and the women of his family. The jailer, in tears, announces that the time has come. Crito says that, though it is sunset, customarily the condemned is permitted much more time before drinking the hemlock poison. But Socrates sees no gain in delay. When the cup of poison is brought in, he is given exact instructions by the administrant. Jokingly, he asks if he may make a libation out of the cup, since he is going on a journey, but he is told that just enough has been prepared to cause death. Without hesitation he drains the cup of poison.

At this moment his friends burst into uncontrolled weeping. Socrates rebukes them. When the poison begins to take effect, he lies down and covers himself entirely. As death approaches, he uncovers his head and asks Crito to fulfill for him a vow he had made to the god Asclepius.

# SYMPOSIUM

## CHARACTERS OF THE DIALOGUE

Apollodorus of Phalerum, narrator, who heard the conversation from

Aristodemus, disciple of Socrates

Phaedrus of Athens

Pausanias of Athens

Euryximachus of Athens, a pedantic physician

Aristophanes, the comic poet

Agathon, the tragic poet

Socrates
Alcibiades

## SUMMARY

172A-174A. Preface. Apollodorus of Phalerum narrates to a friend the conversation on love which took place at the banquet and drinking party (symposium) given many years before (in 416 B.C., a few months before the Sicilian Expedition) by the tragic poet Agathon at his house to celebrate his victory in the dramatic contest. Apollodorus had heard what happened long ago from Aristodemus, an eyewitness, and had only recently recounted the entire discourse to Glaucon.

174-178A. Prologue. Aristodemus met Socrates, unusually well-groomed, on his way to Agathon's dinner party. Socrates asked him to join the party, even though he was not invited. On the way Socrates fell into a mystical trance, and Aristodemus went on alone, only to find that Agathon had tried unsuccessfully to invite him. Dinner was served without waiting for Socrates, and he did not arrive until they were half-way through. After dinner the drinking began. All agreed to drink moderately, since they had not yet recovered from the preceding day's celebration. A proposal to pass the time in discussion was approved. The topic proposed by Euryximachus, the praise of Eros (Love), was approved by all.

178A-180B. Speech of Phaedrus. The god Eros deserves to be honored before all other gods because of his antiquity. He is the source of many blessings, especially the love of a man for another man, when it serves as a stimulus for noble and courageous deeds in the lover for the purpose of winning favor in the eyes of his beloved. An army (e.g. the Spartan army) composed of such lovers, vying to win each other's commendation, would be invincible. Homosexuality is commendable because of its military value. For the lovers will die to protect each other, as Alcestis for her husband, and above all as Achilles gave up his life to avenge

Patroclus. These were highly honored by the gods, who did not so treat Orpheus for his failure to offer up his life for Eurydice. Eros is the chief cause of virtue and happiness, defined as military prowess and courage.

180C-185C. Speech of Pausanias. There are two kinds of love, and these must be distinguished before we can praise the best type. There is a heavenly and beautiful love, and a vulgar, ugly, and base love. The latter type, which the common people enjoy, is bodily, unstable, temporary, and merely satisfies lust. It is both heterosexual and homosexual. The noble and heavenly love is purely homosexual love, of men for boys in their 'teens. Men of the common people ought to be prevented by law from indulging in such love, for they have vulgarized and degraded pederasty, and brought it into disrepute. Such love must be a permanent affection, and be directed to the soul of the beloved, his good character and intelligence. Such a love is beautiful and noble, if carried on with grace, and is to be praised and fostered, though there are many who frown upon it. The lover will grant any favor to his beloved that aims at virtue and wisdom. Such love is of great value both for the individual and the state.

185C-188E. Euryximachus' speech. It was Aristophanes' turn, but being seized with hiccoughs, he asks Euryximachus to speak next. Euryximachus recommends several remedies, and begins his speech. Continuing where Pausanias left off, he agrees that there is a good and bad Eros. Speaking as a physician, pedantically and with technical terminology, he enlarges the scope to embrace all nature, and gives Eros a cosmic significance. There are good and healthy elements in the body, as well as bad and ugly ones. The body is full of these warring opposite elements. The science of medicine consists of effecting a love or harmony of these opposites, and is thus the art of love. It is the same in the art of music. All nature is full of opposites, and in each sphere, meteorology, astronomy, religion—proper proportion, harmony, blending is the key to perfection. This is the great significance of love. The

**186**

greatest love brings temperance and concord, and hence supreme happiness.

189A-193D. Aristophanes' speech. Aristophanes, cured of his hiccoughs, warms up with some humorous banter before beginning. His speech is pure comic fantasy, in the true Aristophanic vein. Love does possess a great healing power. For, originally humans were of three sexes—double male, double female, and half-male, half-female. Their shape was globular and they possessed two sets of all limbs and organs (like Siamese twins). When these mighty humans threatened Zeus, he decided to weaken them by splitting them in two. Apollo stitched their wounds together, and they had the general appearance of normal men and women. Each half of the original composite person sought out and embraced the other half with a passionate yearning for the original unity. Thus came about the love of man for man, of woman for woman, and that of the opposite sexes. Love is then a search for the other half and a desire for wholeness of the two original parts. The love of a male for a young boy is not degenerate but a mark of courage and original virility. In all love, of whatever kind, the lovers desire to remain ever with each other, and would be happy if they could be permanently fused together. Veneration for Eros will thus bring healing to man and eternal happiness.

193D-197E. Agathon's speech. Socrates delays Agathon's speech with some argumentation, and is rebuked. Agathon's speech begins. It is a highly artificial praise of love, superficial, flowery, full of dazzling verbal brilliance. Eros is the most beautiful and best god, the youngest, for he is associated with youth, tender, soft, pliant, graceful. Love has all the cardinal virtues, justice, temperance, courage, and wisdom. His greatest blessings are beauty, goodness, peace, friendship, courtesy, and good-fellowship among men.

198A-201C. Interlude. Socrates professes ignorance of the subject of love, but desires to speak the truth, not fine phrases in order to win applause. Employing the dialectic method with

**187**

Agathon, he establishes a proper definition of love first—that it is a desire to possess the object of one's affection which is not yet possessed. Love is not possession but a wanting of what is still lacking. Eros is a desire for beauty and goodness.

201D-212C. Socrates' speech. Having established these points, Socrates pretends that he learned of the nature of love from the prophetess Diotima of Mantineia. She taught him that love is itself not good and beautiful. There are means between opposites, and love is of this kind, as right opinion is midway between ignorance and intelligence. Love cannot be a god because gods are perfectly beautiful and happy, whereas love is a desire for these things. Love is intermediate between mortal and divine, a superhuman spirit mediating between gods and men, and harmonizing the universe. He is the son of Poverty and Plenty, and hence poor, but always passionately desirous of the beautiful, good, and wise. He is alternately desirous and satisfied; a mean between wise and unwise, for he is a seeker after beauty, and hence also after wisdom (philosopher).

The value of love for mankind consists in that it impels us to the love of the beautiful, which is the possession of the good and happiness. Through this effort to attain wisdom we reach happiness. Though all persons wish to possess permanently the good and be happy, not all are true lovers.

Love is not only a desire to possess the beautiful, but also a natural desire of all to procreate beauty. People procreate children and love their offspring because of a desire for immortality. The soul too procreates and produces offspring, brain-children, and yields a higher form of immortality, for wisdom and ideas are less perishable than mortal children. The love of mind for mind, soul for soul, produces a more lasting marriage than physical love. Its offspring are truly immortal, for they are wisdom and spiritual values. The love of a man for a beautiful youth with a beautiful character and mind creates a "marriage of minds." He teaches him true virtue and begets in his mind ideas, wisdom, good laws, poetry.

But there is even a higher stage of love. The first stage in mounting the ladder of love is the love of one beautiful body. After that we can pass on to the love of all beautiful bodies and things; then to love of all beautiful pursuits; then to love of all beautiful sciences. Finally we reach the highest form of love, love of Absolute Beauty, all truth, eternal and perfect. This is the closest to immortality a human being can attain.

212D-222B. Alcibiades' speech. At this point Alcibiades, very drunk, enters to congratulate Agathon. When he catches sight of Socrates, he puts a garland on his beloved master too. Alcibiades objects to the soberness of the gathering, and drinking is renewed. He is asked to add his voice in praising love. Instead, he delivers an encomium on Socrates himself. In his drunken state he compares him to a statue of Silenus. He is a mocker, charming men with his divine words into a wild ecstasy, disturbing their souls and enslaving them, and making them ashamed of themselves. Externally he is like Silenus, seeking out erotically handsome young men like Alcibiades, but he is solely interested in their souls and minds. And like Silenus he is physically ugly. But internally he is sheer wisdom and beauty, temperance and virtue. He is also physically hardy and courageous in battle, completely original and inimitable.

222C-223. Epilogue. More revelers arrive and there is a mighty uproar. Some of the guests leave. Aristodemus fell asleep. Upon awakening at dawn, he discovered only three still awake, Agathon, Aristophanes, and Socrates, still drinking and carrying on a discussion. But soon Agathon and Aristophanes dropped off to sleep. Socrates covered them, and followed by the faithful Aristodemus, he went out, bathed, and continued in his usual activities the whole of that day.

## PLATO'S VIEW OF LOVE (Socrates' Speech)

Love is the striving of the philosopher (lover of wisdom) for happiness and immortality through wisdom. The journey of the soul upwards to ultimate achievement takes one, starting half-way between ignorance and knowledge, and between mortality and divinity, first to love of beautiful persons and objects. Beauty arouses the desire to procreate beauty, not merely to possess the beautiful person or object. The desire for parenthood is a yearning for immortality. Spiritual parenthood of soul through soul is nobler and more productive of immortal offspring, wisdom and goodness. Love is then a climb to beauty, first physical, then mental. On the highest rung of the ladder the lover reaches abstract beauty itself (pure wisdom, the Idea of the Good), the attainment of which grants immortality to the philosopher.

# REPUBLIC

## GENERAL OUTLINE

I.    Books I-II, 354C. What is justice?

II.    Books II, 357-V, 471. Origin of the state; development of the ideal (just) state; education and life in the ideal state.

III.    Books V, 471-VII, end. Philosopher-kings and the ideal state.

IV.    Books VIII and IX. Actual (unjust) states and individuals.

V.    Book X, 595A-608B. Philosophy vs. poetry.

VI.    Book X, 608C-end. Rewards of justice; immortality.

## CHARACTERS OF THE DIALOGUE

Socrates

Glaucon, brother of Plato

Adeimantus, brother of Plato

Polemarchus, son of Cephalus

Cephalus, wealthy Syracusan businessman resident in the Piraeus

Thrasymachus of Chalcedon, Sophist

Others present who are mute: Lysias (the orator) and Euthydemus, sons of Cephalus; Niceratus; Charmantides; Cleitophon.

(The conversation is supposedly narrated by Socrates to four persons on the day after it took place.)

## SUMMARY

Book I, 327-331D. What is justice? Cephalus' view (that of wealthy, retired businessman—respect for property, wealth as a means to goodness, honesty, telling truth, meeting financial obligations). Socrates, having gone down to the Piraeus, the seaport of Athens, with Plato's brother, Glaucon, in order to participate in the religious ceremonies in honor of the Thracian goddess Bendis, is on his way back. He is spied by Polemarchus, who induces him to stay, and invites him to the house of his father, Cephalus, a retired alien businessman.

The aged Cephalus converses amiably with Socrates about the advantages of old age, provided one has acquired good character and a contented mind. Since Cephalus has inherited most of his fortune, and has no overpowering desire for wealth, Socrates asks him what the greatest advantage is that he has obtained from his wealth. Cephalus tells of his increasing concern over the after-life as he grows older, and that the chief value of wealth lies in its smoothing the way for a happy after-life, for it makes it possible to be honest, truthful, and to pay one's debts. After questioning he admits that justice does not always consist of meeting one's financial obligations, and excuses himself to attend the sacrifices.

I. 331E-336A. Polemarchus' view. Polemarchus suggests that justice is giving every one his due, helping one's friends and injuring one's enemies. Socrates methodically reveals the inadequacy of such a definition, and proceeds to show that justice cannot involve injuring a human being, for by its very nature justice involves goodness and virtue, and therefore it can only improve others. Socrates thus seeks to lay down the principle that justice is not relative, but absolute and objective. Just conduct should not vary subjectively according to circumstances. He thus rejects the principle of doing unto others as they would do to us. It is never right to harm anyone, even our enemies. In injuring a human being, we injure justice. Goodness excludes harm, which injures character.

I. 336B-347E. Thrasymachus' view. Thrasymachus, the Sophist, charges in at this point of the argument, fiercely and impolitely, and offers to express his view of justice—for a fee. (For him justice is political, and involves struggle between the strong and weak. The weaker serve the interests of the stronger. Egoism and success are the dominant drives of human beings; injustice is strength, justice weakness. Might makes right. The ruling power imposes laws upon the weaker to promote self-interest or class interests. Right and wrong in the abstract is meaningless; force and power, not abstract morality, is justice.) Justice is the interest of the stronger. Laws are made for the interest of the ruling power. Socrates attempts to break down this view by casuistry, and forces the snarling Thrasymachus to modify his definition by admitting that there is an art of ruling which involves the knowledge and ability to rule without mistakes. On the analogy of the crafts, the craft of ruling has a purpose outside of itself, namely the interest of the governed, not the interest of the ruling power.

Thrasymachus, appealing to history, shows that rulers have governed only for their own selfish interests. He accuses Socrates of being naïve in believing that justice and honesty pay. Injustice, he asserts, is more profitable. The most successful and admired men are those who practice despotism on a large scale, declares Thrasymachus, returning to his original position. Socrates asserts that injustice is not more profitable than justice. He insists on distinguishing between the proper function of every craft, how it benefits the objects it deals with (in government, the weak), and the material rewards obtained. Material rewards are demanded by rulers, as by craftsmen, because they are basically reluctant to rule, finding it irksome and troublesome.

I. 347E-354C. Thrasymachus maintains that justice is a defect and the mark of a fool, injustice a virtue and the mark of the superman in character and brains. Injustice reveals strength and produces happiness. Assailing this view, that injustice and selfishness brings success, through wealth and power and happiness, and that a life of injustice pays more than one of justice, Socrates argues that going to extremes, as the superman does, is not a sign of intelligence and good character, for there is a certain just proportion and harmony in all things. Unlimited self-assertion of the individual is not always conducive to strength, as in group actions. Unlimited power may cause disunity of purpose and therefore weakness, just as would happen within a man's soul if each element had unlimited authority. Injustice causes disunity and hatred, justice order and unity and strength. Justice is therefore a virtue. Thrasymachus is forced to admit that justice, not injustice, is the mark of superior character and brains.

Does justice or injustice lead to happiness? All things have their proper functions (virtues). The virtue of the soul is justice. Therefore, only the just man is the happy man. Injustice does not pay, for it brings unhappiness. The just man is the wise and good man, not one motivated by selfish interests. Right makes might.

Book II, 357A-367E. Dissatisfied, Glaucon and Adeimantus desire to learn the nature of justice for its own sake, not justice that is practiced through fear, social convention, or the expectation of material rewards and good reputation.

Glaucon presents the popular view of the origin of justice (Social Contract Theory). Moral and religious conduct are artificial human conventions followed reluctantly by tacit consent through fear and force. Justice is a compromise by the weak, who, fearing harm at the hands of the strong, enter a social contract only because injustice may lead to retaliation and suffering. They choose this as the lesser of two evils because of the lack of power to do wrong. If these conventions were removed, human nature would be revealed in the raw as egoistic and unjust self-interest.

Men would do wrong if they could escape detection. Wrongdoing pays if you can get away with it. Therefore, people act justly only under compulsion. Which is happier, the perfectly unjust man who is thought by the public to be perfectly just, or the perfectly just man who is regarded as unjust and has an evil reputation and miserable existence?

Adeimantus presents the position of contemporary morality and religion. Justice is practiced not for its own sake but for anticipated rewards, respectability and material rewards in this life and in the after-life. Wrongdoing can be atoned for by bribing the gods through sacrifices. The effect of this position is to encourage immorality and put a premium on injustice, for one can obtain these rewards by merely seeming just in the public eye and bribing the gods for atonement, masking one's wrongdoing with a cloak of respectability. Injustice pays, since you can buy your way out of the consequences; honesty does not pay, but dishonesty does, if you maintain an outward reputation for honesty. What if there are no gods? If there are, one can do wrong and avoid divine punishment by sacrifices and purification ceremonies. Therefore, injustice is to be preferred to justice. Only weakness prevents injustice. What is justice for its own sake? How can it be explained as divorced from material rewards? How does it benefit a man; how does injustice harm a man if one dismisses the restraining elements of social reputation and divine rewards and punishment?

II, 367E-372A. To understand the nature of justice, says Socrates, we must first study the composition of society. By studying justice in the state, we will be able to understand it in the individual. People are born with innate differences which fit them for different occupations, and they achieve greatest success by working at one trade only. Many types of specialists are needed for a community to exist. Society is not an unnatural, artificial, expedient arrangement (Social Contract Theory), but rather a natural one. For men are not born self-sufficient or completely alike. To supply the material needs necessary for existence specialization and division of labor are necessary. One element of justice is then division of labor, specialization of function, mutually interdependent classes, and harmonious co-operation.

II, 372A-374E. The primitive state was small, and the citizens lived modestly in idyllic innocence, even if this entailed an animal-like existence. For the satisfaction of needs above the simple economic level of existence unnecessary luxuries were introduced. The enlargement of society was thus necessitated in order to include more specialists to provide for the luxuries. The expansion of the territory of the state to support this increased population led to warfare. The desire for luxuries accounts for warlike aggression. Because of war a new class of warrior specialists must be added to the state. This will be one element of the guardian class in the ideal society.

II, 375A-376E. Society needs these professional soldiers (guardians) for aggression, to protect the city against invasion, and to maintain order within the city. Their virtue will be courage, and they will be like watchdogs, combining the qualities of fierceness to enemies and gentleness to fellow-citizens. But they must have the philosophic element in them also (love of wisdom), for some of them will become rulers.

II, 376E-392C. The education of the guardians must be controlled by the state. Elementary education should have as its principal aim the training of a sound mind in a sound body, through gymnastics and "musical" training (literature, music, art).

But existing literature must be rigorously censored, for much is immoral, and misrepresents the gods and heroes, inculcating evil ideas. Even if these stories were true, they should be suppressed, for they show the intrigues, feuds and warfare of the gods, whereas these should not be revealed in conflict. Moreover these myths present the gods as responsible for evil, and in addition increase the fear of dying, inculcating weaknesses and emotionalism.

The early years in education are of great importance because

**195**

of the pliability of the mind. One must begin with stories, but these must be carefully prepared to achieve the desired effect on character development. They must reveal a true concept of divinity, as characterized by perfection, goodness, unchangeableness, truthfulness, beneficence. There must be no presentation of the ideas of hereditary guilt or of gods causing evil. Divine forces are not responsible for evil, but only for what is good. If the former is allowed to be taught, it will be disastrous to the good society.

The use of fictitious stories to teach young people raises the question of whether it is proper to present them as if they were true. Lying is in general wrong, but it is permissible for the ruling classes to tell "white lies" when it is for the benefit of society. The purpose of these stories is to inculcate respect and obedience for superiors, harmony, bravery, willingness to die. They should not present any terrifying concepts of an after-life if people are to be trained to die willingly. Heroes should not be shown mourning over the loss of friends, if endurance of suffering is to be developed. Nor should gods be shown lamenting; nor should too much laughter be presented or aroused. The qualities to be developed are truthfulness, self-control, obedience, control of appetites, piety. Hence it is necessary to censor literature very carefully.

III, 392C-398B. The question of whether to allow tragedy and comedy arises. For guardians must not play many parts; they must be themselves always (specialists). In acting, only certain types of characters should be permitted to be impersonated, types not inferior to themselves. Since imitation by children of characters created by an author leads to identification by the child with the character, this may be harmful and leave a permanent mark on the character of the actor. Therefore, the form and style of literature, as well as its contents, must be carefully censored. Narrative literature is best; the drama is to be carefully controlled to avoid imitation of inferior types. The simple, unified style of writing is preferable to the complex, diffuse style.

III, 398C-400C. There must be a rigid censorship and limitation of types of music and meter in poetry, and of musical instruments. Courage and temperance must be instilled, and therefore certain effects are to be avoided, as those produced by dirges, laments, and by poetry and music which cause effeminacy and sluggishness.

III, 400C-403C. Literature, music, art ("musical" education) have a great influence on character. The aim of "musical" education is to inculcate rhythm, harmony and temperance of the soul, and thus develop good moral character. Proper "musical" education and proper gymnastics constitute the first stage to knowledge of Ideas, for the harmonious soul and beautiful body in the concrete individual are copies of the Ideas. Censorship of all arts is therefore necessary to prevent the inculcation of harmful qualities which will corrupt the soul. Rhythm and harmony produce grace of body and mind, and recognition of and sensitivity to beauty in the concrete. This is the first step to the recognition of Ideas. The individual who possesses a harmonious soul in a beautiful body stimulates a noble love in others like himself. Thus through love of beauty harmony is increased.

III, 403C-412B. There must be carefully regulated physical training for the professional soldiers. They must lead a simple life and develop health, temperance, self-reliance. Good physical training produces harmony in the soul too. There must be no drunkenness. This rigorous physical training must be extremely simple, harmonious, balanced, and develop endurance. Hence they must be trained to live ascetically without luxuries and refinements.

Digression on excessive addiction to physicians, law-courts and judges. It is a sign of a badly educated society to require justice from others instead of practicing it, and health from physicians instead of training oneself to possess it. But since judges and physicians are necessary, they should be specialists. The good judge must be a man of virtue. The function of doctors in the good society is to cure the physically and mentally sound, to leave the physically unsound to die, and to put to death the mentally unsound. We should aim, however, to live so that there will be the least possible need for these two kinds of specialists.

The combination of mental and physical training avoids excessive development of either aspect of a human being and causes greatest harmony of the soul. "Music" alone produces softness, gymnastics alone hardness of the soul. A proper proportion of ferocity and gentleness is needed in the soldier class. Too much bodily training without mental discipline results in the starving and atrophy of the rational faculty and the ability to acquire knowledge. A person so trained becomes an ignorant brute. The purpose of this early education, up to the age of 20, is to bring the two elements of body and soul into harmony in perfect proportion.

III, 412B-Book IV, 421C. How are the rulers to be selected from among the trainees? There must be a careful selection of those to be trained to rule, based on merit. The principal test is a sense of duty to the commonwealth, based on inward conviction, and a lack of self-interest. Those will be chosen who cling to this ideal despite all temptations and annoyances. There must be constant supervision to detect divergences, and frequent testing by ordeals and temptations. Thus, in addition to the farmers and craftsmen, the producing class, there will be a supreme small class of guardians, who will make decisions, and a large class of auxiliaries to the guardians, the soldiers, who will carry out and enforce these decisions.

Allegory of the Metals. Justice is the happiness of all classes through harmonious co-operation. In the ideal society all men are brothers, but they are fashioned of different materials, some more precious than others:

> gold—philosopher-kings or guardians
> silver—soldiers or auxiliaries
> iron and bronze—farmers and craftsmen.

Children will generally be like their parents. If, however, there are mutations, e.g. an iron child from a parent of gold, or a silver child from a parent of iron, the offspring will be demoted or elevated in class.

The upper classes will not be despotic rulers but friends of the citizens and gentle to them. They will own no property. They will be supported by the producing class, live their lives on a common pattern, own no precious metals. Their happiness is not personal material gain, but doing their duty to society and maintaining harmony. The purpose of the ideal society is not the happiness of one class but of the entire community. Personal happiness, through power and wealth, is destructive of community welfare, and therefore of virtue and justice.

Book IV, 421C-427C. The abolition of private property and the rule of communal living applies only to the two upper classes. But there shall not be excessive riches or poverty in the rest of society, for too much luxury causes softness and poor workmanship, and too much poverty unrest and class warfare. Such a state, though not rich, will by clever diplomacy be a match for many richer states in war. For other states fight for wealth, and are thus disunited internally and amongst themselves. Unity is to be maintained by good education carefully guarded against change. The size of the state shall be not too small or too large. If it went beyond due measure in size, unity could not be maintained. The guardians shall be charged with maintaining respect for laws and superiors. Only basic laws, not petty legal regulations, shall be their concern. Religious matters are to be left to the Delphic oracle.

IV, 427C-434D. The cardinal virtues of the state.

| Class | Metal | Virtue |
|---|---|---|
| Philosopher-kings | Gold | Wisdom — knowledge of what is good |

| Soldiers | Silver | Courage—knowledge, through conviction of what to fear and what not to fear |
|---|---|---|
| Farmers and artisans | Iron and bronze | Temperance — self-control, consent to be governed, willing subordination to upper classes. |

Justice, the highest virtue, is specialization, differentiation of function, and unity and harmony of all. Justice in society, civic virtue, exists when each class does its own proper work and minds its own business, not interfering in the affairs of other classes.

IV, 434D-441C. Applying our investigation to the individual we find that there is no difference between the just man and the just society. The individual contains three elements in his soul: reason (whose function is wisdom), good emotions (whose function is spirit or honor and courage), base emotions (whose function is to cater to bodily appetites). States are like the individuals that compose them: the state is the individual writ large. Since a person reacts often in contradictory ways to the same situation, there must be more than one element in the soul. For example, when we thirst for drink on occasions, we inhibit our desire for drink, because we know that we may be injured thereby, as in an illness. Therefore, there is not only an appetitive element in the soul desiring pleasure, but also a rational one. Similarly, it can be shown that there is a third element, emotional, but of a higher type than the appetites, with which it is often in conflict. This third element often joins with reason against the appetites.

IV, 441C-445B. Virtue in the individual. The individual is like a miniature society. If each part of the soul practices its own proper virtue, the soul will be healthy. A healthy individual soul is like a healthy society. Reason, whose virtue is wisdom, should rule and be the guide; good emotion should aid reason with courage and obey it; base emotion should subordinate itself and practice

200

temperance and self-control. These three elements are brought into proper accord by gymnastics and "music," by mental and bodily training. Unanimity, concord, harmony amongst the three elements eliminate internal discord between ruler and subordinates. Justice is internal harmony of all parts of an individual and of society. The unified person who practices self-mastery is not at war with himself, and enjoys health and happiness. His internal harmony leads to outward justice. Injustice is discord, internal strife in an individual and in society, the warring elements usurping each other's proper functions. Virtue is the health of the soul. Justice is a state of health, injustice of disease. Therefore, just as no one would desire a diseased body, so no one desires injustice, since it implies a diseased soul. Therefore, it is ridiculous to ask whether injustice ever pays, even if we escape detection and punishment, or if justice pays, even if no one rewards it.

IV, 445B-Book V, 457B. Equality of Women. Women and children are to be held in common by the two upper classes (guardians). Women are to have the same tasks and opportunities as men in the upper classes, with certain limitations. For this they must have exactly the same education and upbringing as the men, however revolutionary such an idea may be. This involves mental training, as well as physical and military discipline for women. It may be argued that men and women have different functions in society, since they have different natures, but this is a superficial view and mere verbal hair-splitting, for some women are by nature more like some men than they are like other women. Sex is no criterion for distinguishing function in society, except in reproduction. Women are capable of performing all tasks men are, and vice versa, though women are weaker. They will therefore be philosopher-rulers, soldiers, or workers, according to their ability.

Book V, 457B-466D. "Communism" of the guardian classes. For the purpose of producing maximum unity in the two upper classes they are to have neither private property, private homes, or families. The purpose of this regulation is to abolish all personal interests and to restrict them to the common interest in duty to the state. Persons interested in material things are not fit to be members of the upper classes, which should not need to be concerned with material things. In this way the principal source of discord will be eliminated and they will achieve the highest unity, living like one big happy family.

This is not to say that, if women and children are held in common, that there is to be promiscuity. On the contrary, sex relations are to be carefully regulated by the rulers. Mating is to be controlled to breed the best types. Eugenic reproduction is all the more important in human beings, if we take the trouble to breed animals carefully. Another purpose is to keep the number of citizens as constant as possible. Couples are paired off at the proper season and under proper supervision by the rulers. Reproduction is limited to the established breeding ages of 20-40 for women, 25-55 for men. Outside these ages reproduction is forbidden, though above the maximum ages unofficial unions are permitted, but not for the purpose of child-bearing. Children belong to the state and are reared in state nurseries. Infanticide of defective children is necessary. Children and parents will not know each other. Thus all members of the upper two classes will regard each other as members of one family.

V, 466D-471C. Warfare. Men and women are to fight side by side in battle. Children are to be taken to watch actual battles to test their characters and to inure them to warfare. Cowardice involves demotion to the working class. The rewards for bravery in battle are increased breeding opportunities and other greater recognition. Humane regulations for warfare among Greeks are set down: No Greeks are to be enslaved in war; there is to be no plundering of corpses of dead enemies; no devastation or plundering by Greeks. Since the Greeks are like a single people, strife among them should be avoided. Foreigners may be treated differently.

V, 471C-474B. Philosopher-kings. The advantages of such a

society are many, but is it possible for such a state to come into existence? The state we are constructing is a theoretical, ideal society. Theory is never completely realizable in practice; the actual always falls short of the truth. The ideal is a standard to aim at, and to hold up as a gauge for measuring and judging the actual. What is the least change that is necessary to transform the actual state into an approximation of the ideal state? Until philosophers are kings or kings become philosophers, the human race will never have surcease of its troubles. Neither the abstract theoretical philosopher, nor the practical politician can solve the problems of society; there must be a unity of thought and action of wisdom and power. Reason must rule, if we are to come close to the ideal society.

V, 474B-480. The true philosopher and the two worlds of opinion and Ideas. Some are born to study philosophy and be leaders in society; others are not, and are meant to be followers. True philosophers, who ought to be rulers, should not be mere part-time curiosity seekers or amateur philosophers, but rather, as true lovers of wisdom, should have an insatiable curiosity to know all truth and reality (Ideas), not merely part of wisdom. The amateur philosopher loves concrete particular beautiful things and therefore has relative knowledge; the true philosopher loves absolute beauty and truth. The former is like a dreamer who cannot distinguish the copy from the real; the true philosopher is wide awake, for he does not confuse the Idea with the particular. He has knowledge; others have false opinion. Opinion lies midway between not-being and being, between ignorance and knowledge. Knowledge concerns being (Ideas), opinion what lies between absolute knowledge and absolute ignorance, namely the world of the senses and concrete objects. Opinion is relative, varying, and confused. Knowledge achieved by reason is absolute and unchanging. Opinion is the knowledge the masses have, relative, sensory truth, not absolute rational truth. The true philosopher (lover of wisdom) loves the Ideas.

Book VI, 484A-487A. The qualities of the true philosopher, who knows absolute truth and to whom the state is to be entrusted: permanent love of abstract Ideas; love of all true knowledge; love of truth; absorption in pleasures of the soul, with little concern for the body; temperance; generosity; courage; justice; gentleness; pleasure in learning; good memory; balance and harmony of mind.

VI, 487B-497A. The fate of true philosopher in actual society. In practice philosophers become either perverted individuals, or are corrupted, or become useless to society. The true philosopher, who adheres to his principles, has no recourse except to stand aside from politics, powerless, for public opinion regards him as an impractical starry-eyed idealist. Moreover, if he entered politics, he would inevitably be corrupted and be forced to abandon what he knows to be the truth; and so, to save his soul he isolates himself from government in his ivory tower.

Parable of the Ship of State. The captain of the ship (the people) is incapable of navigating the vessel by himself. The sailors (professional politicians), who have never learned the art of navigation (governing), quarrel about which one is to take the helm. They first beg the captain to be permitted to steer, and if they do not succeed, they kill those who have been assigned the helm. Then they drug the captain, mutiny, and seize the ship for their own pleasure. The true pilot, who knows the art of navigation, and should have the authority to steer, whether the others like it or not, will be thrust aside in the confusion as an idle star-gazer. Thus the true philosopher is useless to society.

The fault in this situation lies in public opinion, not in the philosophers themselves. For the public ought to request such men to rule them. In actual society (Athenian democracy) men become rulers by begging the public to choose them. A sick society must summon such a doctor, as a sick man calls his physician.

But the greatest harm to the reputation of philosophy is done by the majority of philosophers who become corrupt. For abandoning the love of truth, when they enter politics, they bring philosophy into disrepute. The true philosopher is a rare plant, and hence very easily destroyed. For he is easily seduced from philosophy by material things, wealth, power, position. Such a man is very easily corrupted, and the more gifted and able he is (as Alcibiades), the greater his own corruption and the greater the harm he does to society. Public opinion corrupts these men, for they cannot resist it and they learn to cater to it, instead of being guided by reason. Being susceptible to flattery, he becomes like the masses, guided by opinion and appearance.

Moreover, the Sophists, who are mercenary, teach people the opinions of the masses, not truth. They study the whims and tempers of the mighty beast (the people), systematize this knowledge, call it wisdom, and teach it to others. Truth, honor, goodness, justice are equated by them with the shifting whims of the people; the opposites with what the great beast dislikes.

So the philosopher, when he comes into contact with the masses, begins to do only what they will acclaim. Therefore, the true philosopher, guided by absolute truth, will be thrust aside by the masses. To maintain his integrity he must resist the temptations they offer him and remain aloof from actual society. Otherwise he will be corrupted, and do the greatest harm to his state.

Hence, too, miserable people, the false philosophers (Sophists), attracted to philosophy because of the dignity of the position, enter the field, and cause additional dishonor to the name of philosophy.

The worthy disciples of philosophy will thus be a tiny remnant, which stands aloof from the practical, corrupting world of politics, though this is actually their greatest mission in life.

VI, 497A-502C. There is no actual society adapted for the participation of the true philosopher. Firstly, philosophy must be brought back into repute; and the education of the true philosopher must be carefully organized to create the perfect philosopher with perfect knowledge. Such men must rule, whether they like it or not, and the people must obey them, whether they like it or not. The public must be convinced, when they discover their true nature, to accept such men and obey them. At present the public judges philosophy by what they think of the corrupt philosophers and the false pretenders. Such a true philosopher, knowing absolute truth, will order society well according to the ideas; without him, no state can be happy. Such philosophers will have to start with a clean slate, and remake society according to the principle of absolute justice. Such men are rare, but one is enough to bring into existence the ideal society, if the people obey him willingly. The ideal state is possible of creation.

VI, 502C-509C. The Idea of the Good. It is indeed difficult to find such men, for the combination of necessary qualities is hard to unite in one person. The intellectual discipline necessary to protect the philosopher is, moreover, exceedingly arduous for most people. Especially difficult of attainment is the highest knowledge, the Idea of the Good, the end of all knowing, the one absolute truth which stands above all the Ideas as their unifying principle, Beauty, Justice, Goodness, Truth, the source of all knowledge and moral values. The Good is not pleasure but knowledge itself. It can only be mystically glimpsed; it can never be actually described. It is like a divine revelation.

There can be no sight without light, unless the sun illumines objects. The eye is dependent upon the sun, which is the source of light. So the Idea of the Good is to the mind's eye as the sun is to the physical eye. It sheds light on all wisdom. The soul is like the eye, and it sees the truth only insofar as the Idea of the Good shines upon it. It is the highest truth, like a radiant sun, the source of all truth and beauty, of all Ideas, but greater than all of them. The Idea of the Good is thus to the intellect as light is to the visible world. The mind's eye (intelligence) cannot see the light (truth) unless the sun (Idea of the Good) illumines all knowledge.

VI, 509D-511E. The Divided Line (the four stages of education). The lower stage of knowledge is in the visible world, changing and relative and perceived by the senses, with the aid of the light of the sun. In this sphere natural objects are closer to the truth than reflections of them and works of art and literature. The individual has cognition of the latter through imagining, conjecture, guesswork; of the former through opinion or belief (conventional notions, common sense, correct belief without knowledge). The higher stage of knowledge is in the intellectual world, eternal and absolute, perceived by the mind with the aid of the Idea of the Good. In this sphere the level above natural objects consists of the objects of mathematics, which involve abstract thinking and understanding based upon uncritically accepted hypotheses. Higher than this level is that of Ideas, perceived by higher reason, and involving knowledge or intelligence, all in the light of the first principle, the Idea of the Good. This unified Idea of the Good stands at the apex of the entire knowable universe, and is glimpsed through the ultimate science, dialectics, the study of the interrelation of Ideas, without the senses and without arbitrary hypotheses; it involves philosophical self-conversation through question and answer until the beatific vision of truth is glimpsed.

|  |  | OBJECTIVE | SUBJECTIVE |
|---|---|---|---|
| Idea of the Good | Intellectual World | Ideas | Higher Reason (Knowledge, Intelligence) |
|  |  | Objects of Mathematics | Abstract Thought, Understanding, Working with Axiomatic Hypotheses |
| Sun | Visible World | Objects of Nature | Belief or Opinion, Common Sense, without Knowledge |
|  |  | Images, Works of Art and Literature | Imagining, Conjecture, Guesswork |

Book VII, 514A-521B. Allegory of the Cave. Human beings live, as it were, in an underground cave, chained in such a way that they cannot move and that they must look at a wall. Behind and above them light (truth) streams into the cave from outside. Thus they see only the shadows of reality projected on the wall (the visible world, not the intellectual world). If they are released from their chains and begin to "see the light," they will at first be blinded by its brilliance. Some will prefer to go back to the comfortable falseness of the shadows, finding the truth hard to face. To reach the sun (Idea of the Good) it is necessary to climb a steep ascent. The rise to true knowledge is arduous, steep, and long. No one who has truly attained the beatific vision of true knowledge would want to go back to the perception of the shadows. In fact, if he does go down into the cave again, it will take a long time for his eyes to become accustomed to seeing in the darkness. And thus he would appear ridiculous to those who are trained to regard the shadows as truth.

The senses are our prison, and the climb upward from the lowest stage of education through sense perception to the highest, up to the Idea of the Good, the unified ultimate source of all truth, is exceedingly difficult. Those who have seen the beatific vision will be reluctant to go back to the shadows.

The capacity for learning is innate and exists in the soul; it cannot be put there. Education is a gradual conversion (turning around) of the soul from the shadows toward the truth. The art which will effect this conversion is education, the gradual freeing of the soul from the body. The best minds must be compelled to acquire this knowledge and then be forced to go back into the cave, get used to the shadows, and do their duty to society by ruling and bringing happiness to all classes. The state in which the rulers are the most reluctant to govern is the best administered one. For the rulers will guide not for personal advantage but because of a stern necessity to do their appointed duty.

VII, 521C-531C. Curriculum of Higher Education (Abstract Thinking). In the lower stage of education (up to the age of 20) the principal subjects were gymnastics and "musical" training (see pp. 195–198). For the next ten years subjects are studied which involve non-sensory learning as a training in apprehending absolute truth. The purpose of mathematics in education is not essentially for any practical value (though, since most of the trainees at this level will remain soldiers, it will be useful in the art of war), but rather to train the mind to apprehend Ideas, and to screen out, through the difficulty of the subjects, the weaker minds.

1. Arithmetic: study of abstract number.

2. Plane Geometry: valuable because it is based upon universal, self-evident truth (axioms).

3. Solid Geometry: a new study in Plato's time. He stresses the need for encouragement of new sciences by the state through public administrators.

4. Astronomy: not astronomical observations for practical purposes, but the laws of motion of perfect mathematical bodies; a branch of pure mathematics, involving the beauty of the heavens, the harmony of perfect spheres in perfect motion and proportion.

5. Harmonics: the science of sounds, as a theory of harmony of sounds.

6. Dialectics: the coping-stone of the sciences; the one true science as compared with mathematics, just as opinion is a higher stage than conjecture. For here only the intellect, without any sense perception, is used until the one perfect unity and harmony is reached, the Idea of the Good, the end of the intellectual world. This study involves independent thought, self-conversation, without unexamined hypotheses, all in the light of the Idea of the Good. It affords a synoptic view of all sciences, knowledge, reality in one unified process.

VII, 535A-541B. Program of Studies. Recapitulation of the qualities needed by prospective philosopher-king (see p. 203). Summary of the educational program: up to the age of 17 or 18—literature, music, elementary mathematics; from 17 or 18 to 20—physical and military training only; from 20 to 30—mathematical studies; from 30-35—dialectics.

Plato warns that students should not be introduced to discussions involving dialectics at too young an age, for it may do them harm, if they are not ready for philosophy. Such premature study may corrupt them, for they may indulge only in verbal gymnastics, not true study of ideas.

From the ages of 35 to 50 the philosopher is to have practical experience in minor offices and commands, not only for the experience in governing, but also to test him by exposing him to the seductions of the material world.

From the age of 50 on he will alternately rule and study. It does not matter whether we produce one or more such philosopher-rulers, male or female. A start could be made in constructing such a state by sending out of a city all over the age of 10, and beginning the process of re-education, without the corrupting influence of the children's parents.

Book VIII, 543A-550C. Degenerate Societies. Timocracy. Plato assumes that the ideal society, headed by an intellectual elite, has been constituted, but since in the world of concrete existence nothing can remain perfect, he traces the gradual decline of society through a cycle of various progressively worse societies, indicating the types of individuals which characterize these societies.

The ideal society will cease to be perfect when the ruling class becomes disunited. This will happen when the stock degenerates and the ruling class begins to acquire private property. In a revolution the soldiers will oust the philosopher-kings; reason will be dethroned, and ambition and love of honor will dominate. There will be respect for authority, but only through force, and the working class will be enslaved. Personal interest will be strong, directed toward family and property. There will be no mental training for the soldier ruling class; each will be ambitious to excel all in honor.

The dominant individual in this society will be warlike and aggressive, uncultured, self-willed, fond of music, not a good

**210**

speaker, harsh in his attitude toward slaves, obedient to authority, ambitious for office, proud of military and physical prowess, eager for wealth. He will be dominated by the second element of the soul. But as time goes on he will become arrogant and over-ambitious for wealth.

VIII, 550C-555B. Oligarchy (Plutocracy). The introduction of private property inevitably leads to increasing growth of wealth. Competitive ambition for honor gives way to overwhelming passion for wealth, and timocracy is overthrown. Political power is based now on property qualifications; the poor do not vote or hold office, even though some poor might make good statesmen. Such a society is highly disunited, for it breeds class warfare between rich and poor. It will be weak in war, not only because it is a disunited society, but also because the rich must rely on the poor to do the fighting for them. Such a society breeds paupers and dangerous criminals Love of money dominates; ambition dies out.

The dominant individual in this society is so constituted that reason and ambition have been subjected to greed for wealth, one of the base appetites. The profit motive is primary. He is miserly, and has no mental cultivation, has corrupt tendencies, which he suppresses through fear or which he covers up with a cloak of respectability. He is a disunited personality, yet he is not dominated by the worst passions. His miserliness prevents him from attaining any ambition beyond additional wealth.

VIII, 555B-562A. Democracy (Athenian: see p. 57). The concentration of wealth in a plutocracy, and the growth of the poor through the political policy and selfish interests of the rich lead to revolt. Such a society is readily subject to civil war, and the degenerate and weakened plutocrats are overthrown by the toughened common man.

In a democracy there is unlimited personal freedom for all, including freedom of speech. There are no property qualifications for voting or office-holding. Unlimited self-interest is rampant, and a great variety of types are developed. There are no duties or obligations. Decisions are temporary and for the moment, subject to change by the clever appeals of demagogues. It is anarchy with variety, and unlimited disunity. All are regarded equal, even if by nature they are unequal.

The dominant individual in this society is guided by the lowest appetites, which he cannot control, excessive desire for food and sex. He has lost possession of his soul. He is insolent, anarchic, wasteful, impudent. He makes no distinction between necessary and unnecessary appetites, for all are regarded as of equal importance. Therefore, the principal drive is pleasure for the moment. He has no organized unified principle of living. In such a society liberty is synonymous with anarchy, and equality failure to discriminate between equal and unequal.

VIII, 562A-Book IX, 576B. Despotism. Democracy is finally ruined by excessive liberty permitted by unscrupulous leaders. This complete liberty is anarchy, in which there are absolutely no controls, and no respect for authority. From this, state despotism, the opposite of liberty, is generated. At such a stage there are three classes: the rich; the rural masses, who are not interested in politics; a powerful class of political parasites who dominate politics, consisting of idle hangers-on, spendthrifts, and ruined persons. These professional politicians make legal assaults on the wealth of the rich. To defend themselves the rich form a reactionary party. The masses then set up a champion of their interests (a demagogue). He starts out as the people's champion, but in the end turns into a despot, enslaving all, even the masses themselves. Because of the vigorous measures taken by the party-leader of the masses, attempts will be made on his life. He requests and receives a bodyguard to protect him, and soon becomes absolute master. Power corrupts him. Though he begins as the champion of the people's rights, he tries to remain in power by every possible means. He even provokes wars to divert the attention of the people. When criticism of him begins, he is forced to do away with his closest advisers, and soon incurs the enmity of all. To remain in power he builds up a professional army loyal to himself. To suport his expensive regime he must increase taxes to such an extent that even the masses are full of unrest. But the people cannot now get rid of their own creation. They have fashioned a monster, and they are his slaves.

The despotic man is dominated by the lowest and most shameless emotions, such as are revealed only in horrible dreams. Reason has become completely subjugated. He is drunken, lustful, insane, completely dominated by base appetites and pleasures. He does what he likes, plunders everyone; nothing is sacred to him, and he is never satisfied with what he has plundered, always wanting more. His life is corrupt, and he has not a real friend in the world. He is hated and feared by all alike. He is the perfectly unjust man, as the true philosopher is the perfectly just man.

IX, 576B-588A. The just life is happier. The unjust man does not possess true freedom, which does not consist of complete power to act arbitrarily. Since the emotions dominate him and he has no internal harmony, he cannot make decisions for his whole person. He is beset with fears of all kinds, and cannot move about freely. He is not really rich, because he can never satisfy his desires. The happiest man is the good and just man who is master over himself, whether he is recognized as such or not.

Every successful man will praise his own type of life as "happy." But the best judge is the philosopher, who has the widest experience and the deepest knowledge and insight into the values of all types of life.

Finally, there is a difference between pure and illusory pleasures. Sensual pleasures are impure, negative, and deceptive, because they involve the absence of pain, which will return with the end of pleasure (e.g. eating). The pleasures of the mind are true, positive, absolute, eternal. The only genuine pleasures are rational and belong to the higher element of the soul, not to the two irrational parts.

IX, 588B-592B. Justice is profitable, for injustice leads to

**213**

internal disharmony and loss of self-mastery, and allows the animal part of man to subdue the divine and human element (reason). Therefore, injustice is to man's own best interests, as it is to the best interests of society to be governed by the philosopher-kings. Thus the body, wealth-seeking, desire for honors and power should be subordinated to soundness of mind. It is doubtful whether the just man will in practice be able to participate in the policies of actual societies.

Book X, 595A-602B. Attack on poetry and art in education. We must exclude all dramatic poetry from the ideal society. All art is representation *(mimesis)*. The actual bed is a copy of the Ideal Bed; but the painting of a bed is still farther removed from reality. It is at third remove from the truth, for it is an imitation of an imitation of the Idea. Similarly the tragic poet represents, through language, rhythm, and music, the actions of men at third remove from the Ideas. The same is true of Homer. To represent human conduct implies knowledge of what is good. If that is so, why are not poets men of action in public life? They really do not know what is good, and therefore cannot be true educators. All poetry is merely a representation of a likeness of reality. The poet writes only in the world of opinion, to please the ignorant multitude. Art and literature are not to be taken seriously.

X, 602C-608B. Psychology of the drama. Just as the senses are subject to illusions, so too are the emotions. Dramatic poetry is illusion, and appeals to the emotions, not to the reason, which checks the emotions. Dramatic poetry, being illusion and stirring the emotions, strengthens them to the detriment of reason. Dramatic poetry is therefore harmful, and should be banished from the ideal state. Further, it corrupts even the best men, for they are emotionally moved by poetry, a thing which would not happen to them in real life under similar circumstances. Since the emotions are strengthened by the drama, the dramatists, and Homer too, are to be excluded. The only poetry to be permitted will be hymns to the gods and the praises of good men. Poetry and philosophy are at war, for poetry's purpose is to give pleasure, not aiming at the truth. Therefore, poetry corrupts goodness and justice.

X, 608C-612A. Further proof of immortality (see pp. 180–183). The good benefits and preserves, the evil corrupts and destroys. Everything has its peculiar evil which tends to destroy it, since it is the opposite of the essential nature of that thing (e.g. disease for the body, rust for iron). If there is something whose peculiar evil cannot destroy it, that must be immortal. Such is the soul, whose special evil is vice. Vices deprave the individual but do not utterly destroy his soul. Therefore the soul is immortal.

X, 612A-613E. Rewards of justice in this life. Justice is rewarded in this life and injustice punished by the gods. If the just man suffers in this life, it is due to sins committed in a former life. But his sufferings will profit him in the end. As for men, even they, on the whole reward justice more consistently than the opposite. Justice triumphs, evil is punished.

X, 613E-end. Vision of Er. But more important are the rewards and punishments in the afterlife. Er, the son of Armenius, was slain in battle, but on the twelfth day after, he returned to life on the funeral pyre, and told what he saw in the other world.

The souls go on a long journey until they reach two openings in the earth, corresponding to two in heaven. There they are judged, and some are sent to heaven, some into the earth. Souls continuously come down from heaven and up from the earth. They have been in heaven or inside the earth for a thousand years, and have been rewarded or punished ten-fold for their deeds, once every hundred years. Now, assembling in a meadow, they are ready for reincarnation. Some incurable sinners can never be cleansed, and can never return from Tartarus, where they are everlastingly scourged and tortured.

The assembled souls, ready for reincarnation, proceed on a journey. They see the entire harmonious arrangement of the universe, and finally come to the three Fates, Clotho, Lachesis, and Atropos, who guide the motion of the universe. The souls stand in front of Lachesis and are informed that a great variety of choices of new lives is open to them. They have free choice of their new lives, and the responsibility is with the chooser, not with the gods or chance. Hence the supreme necessity of a life of virtue, wisdom, and justice in this life, so that the choice of one's future life a thousand years later will be a better one.

Curiously enough, however, in most cases the choice is based on experiences in the soul's previous life. E.g., Orpheus chose the life of a swan because he hated women; Ajax chose the life of a lion, bcause he did not want injustice done to him again; Agamemnon the life of an eagle, so that he could continue to be a mighty bird of prey, and so that he would not suffer as he did before; Thersites the life of a monkey, so that he could continue his idle chattering; Odysseus the life of a private man because he had learned the evils of ambition.

When their lots have been approved by the three Fates, they finally go to the river Lethe (Forgetfulness). Here they drink and forget what they knew in the past, and are then reborn.

Hence virtue and the good life are profitable. Moreover, we have a duty to unborn generations, for by living justly and virtuously in this life we influence the lives of future generations.

## PLATO'S SOCIAL AND POLITICAL THEORIES

I.    Attacks contemporary politics, the Sophists, individualism in all its forms, democracy as unstable and based on ignorance, factionalism, class struggle, love of wealth and power, individual freedom, change, majority rule.

II.    The ideal state is based on absolute justice, which involves unity, single-mindedness, specialization of function by all, professional administrators, professional soldiers, and workers; "one nation, indivisible, with duties and justice for all."

III.    Ideal happiness in the state is the performance of one's duty to society to the best of one's native ability. Man is the servant of the state. True freedom is discipline to the whole, not the pursuit of personal happiness. Each class has its special function. The individual must be subordinated to the interests of the entire state.

IV.　　Government should be in the hands of an intellectual elite. Reason (philosopher-kings) aided by force (soldiers) must rule, and the irrational (workers) must be suppressed or trained in self-control.

V.　　"Like man, like state; the state is the individual writ large." Hence the need for compulsory, state-controlled education for the two upper classes to train leaders and a professional army.

VI.　　Emancipation of women, abolition of family and home for two upper classes; eugenic breeding, not community of wives.

VII.　　Abolition of private property for two upper classes; not economic communism, but more like an ascetic monastic life. The two upper classes are to enjoy true leisure to fulfill their duties, with no worries concerning material goods and none of the distractions of personal possessions.

VIII. No "art for art's sake"; strict censorship of art and literature.

## CHAPTER FIFTEEN

# ARISTOTLE

◙

## ARISTOTLE OF STAGIRA (384-322 B.C.)

I.　　Born in N. Greece, at Stagira in the Chalcidice; hence often called "the Stagirite."

II.　　His father Nicomachus, physician to King of Macedon.

III.　　Student of Plato at the Academy for ca. 20 years.

IV.　　Left Athens after Plato's death; lived in Asia Minor and in Mytilene on the Island of Lesbos.

V.　　Tutor of Alexander the Great ca. 3 years, 343-340 B.C.

VI.　　Lyceum established by him in Athens ca. 335 B.C.; second university in world. His school is often called the Peripatetic School because Aristotle was in the habit of walking around the courtyard of the school while he lectured.

VII.　　Anti-Macedonian feeling in Athens on the death of Alexander (323 B.C.) caused him to leave Athens so that the Athenians might not "sin twice against philosophy."

VIII.　　Died in Chalcis in Euboea the next year.

IX.　　Universal knowledge (Dante: "The master of those who know"); classified all known fields of knowledge; founder of biology, psychology, formal logic, syllogism (deductive reasoning), scientific method, philosophical terminology; Father of Naturalism.

## EXTANT WORKS

I.　　Treatises on Logic (*Organon*)
　　　　*Categories*
　　　　*On Interpretation*

*Prior Analytics*
*Posterior Analytics*
*Topics*
*On Sophistical Refutations*

II. Philosophy of Nature
*Physics*
*On the Heavens*
*On Generation and Decay*
*Meteorologica*

III. Psychology
*On the Soul*
*On Sensation*
*On Memory*
*On Sleep*
*On Dreams*
*On Divination by Dreams*
*On Longevity and Short-
ness of Life*
*On Life and Death*
*On Respiration*

IV. Biology
*History of Animals*
*On the Parts of Animals*
*On the Motion of Animals*
*On the Walking of
Animals*
*On the Generation of
Animals*

V. *Metaphysics* (First
Philosophy)

VI. Esthetics
*Rhetoric*
*Poetics*

VII. Ethics
*Nicomachean Ethics*
*Magna Moralia*
*Eudemian Ethics*

VIII. Political Science
*Politics*
*Constitution of Athens*

## STYLE

Only ca. ¼ of Aristotle's prolific writings has survived. Practically nothing of his popular (exoteric) works exists; the extant writings are his scientific (esoteric) treatises, in the form of lecture notes. The style of the latter works is dry, precise, formal, objective, and impersonal, filled with technical terminology.

## ARISTOTLE VS. PLATO

I. Aristotle's debt to Plato's thought is far greater than his disagreement with it.

II. Opposed Plato's Theory of Ideas and emphasis on mathematical study.

III. Postulated a changing dynamic universe as opposed to Plato's static view.

IV. Greater reliance on observation through senses; more practical common-sense point of view, less other-worldly.

V. Combined mysticism and science, idealism and materialism.

VI. Aristotle's philosophy is Platonism modified by common sense.

## BASIC THOUGHT OF ARISTOTLE

I. Metaphysics (First Philosophy; nature of Being).

A. Aristotle rejects Plato's Theory of Ideas, for he cannot accept the independent existence outside the mind of universals or absolutes. The material world, perceived through the senses, and ideas are not separate from one another. His basic principle is that the universal (Idea, form, essence) exists only in the particular, not apart from it. Ideas are copies in the mind of concrete things. Ideas cannot exist without matter, nor matter without Ideas. There is, therefore, no supreme Idea of the Good, to which all else is subordinated, but a great variety of Ideas independent of one another.

B. The real world is dynamic, changing, full of movement and flux. The basic problem of philosophy is to explain motion and change. Sense perception and observation are important, but true knowledge is grasp of the essence (form) of things. For matter cannot exist without form, and form is knowable by reason and logic, not sense perception. Science employs sense perception to describe and catalogue, but more important is reason to explain causes of facts and their relationship to entire system of knowledge, and to establish universals (Ideas, forms, essences). But the first principles of all sciences are axiomatic, self-evident truths, grasped by intellectual intuition and requiring no proof. Hence his science is a refined Platonic idealism, employing both induction from experience and deduction from universal self-evident truths.

C. Doctrine of Causation (Four Causes), to explain change and essence.

1. Material Cause—the type of matter involved.

2. Efficient Cause—the cause of motion, the producer of change.

3. Formal Cause—the essence, idea, universal concept in the object.

4. Final Cause—the purpose or end of change.

For example, a statue is made of marble (material cause) by a sculptor (efficient cause) into the shape of a horse (formal cause) for the purpose of decorating a temple (final cause).

Viewed statically, change is broken down into Matter (particular) and Form (universal); there is no Matter without Form or Form without Matter. Matter is what becomes and changes; Form is what Matter becomes and what gives unity and purpose to Matter. Viewed dynamically, change is analyzed as the passage of Potentiality (Matter or Becoming) into Actuality (Form or Being). All things strive to become their proper form, for which they are fitted by nature (e.g. acorn into oak; child into adult). Motion is the constant striving of matter toward higher and higher forms, from formless matter to matterless form (God.) Hence, the end toward which all things move is logically the cause of all motion.

D. God. Pure perfect form and reality; static perfection, eternal, unchanging; completed actuality, without matter; self-sufficient and self-explanatory; ultimate source of all change and development in the universe; pure knowledge, reason, without activity; the ultimate Efficient Cause, Formal Cause, Final Cause of the universe; the final end and the absolute logical beginning of all; the First Cause, the prime mover, though unmoved ("the unmoved mover"); pure happiness, contemplating its own wisdom and perfection.

E. Teleology. There is a rational plan, design, purpose in the universe; nothing is aimless or useless, everything has a purpose. All things develop and move to an end, the idea for which they exist, which is the real cause of all motion. Logically, there

**221**

is a development and evolution from lower to higher forms up to the ultimate end, God. All things are for the best.

II. Scientific Method.

    A. Aristotle rejects sophistry (as false reasoning) and dialectic (as reasoning yielding probability from accepted but unproved premises).

    B. Formal logic (Analytics) to demonstrate truth, the tool of science. This involves true premises and true reasoning. Aristotle's most important contribution is the doctrine of the syllogism, employing deductive reasoning from universal to particular. E.g.,

        Major Premiss: All matter occupies space.

        Minor Premiss: A table consists of matter.

        Conclusion: A table occupies space.

He employed both inductive and deductive logic, over-emphasizing the latter, and often beginning with self-evident truths.

III. Soul. Unified, single, indivisible; it is the Form of the body, and cannot exist without the body with which it has an organic functional connection. Probably no belief in personal immortality.

IV. Ethics. See below.

## NICOMACHEAN ETHICS

### SUMMARY

**Book I, 1-3.**

The subject and the nature of Ethics.

    1. All human knowledge and activity aim at different goods, which are their ends. Some goods are superior to others; achieved purposes are better than activities. The ends of minor arts are subordinate to the ends of more inclusive master arts which are more desirable and for the sake of which the others are pursued.

2. Most ends lead to further activity, but there must be a supreme good *(summum bonum)* which is desired for its own sake, not as a means to new ends, and to which all other desires are subordinated. This knowledge is of great importance as the good to aim at in all human activities. This is the all-embracing master art—political science, the end of all other human sciences and the regulator of all human life, the supreme good of man. Ethics is thus a branch of political science.

3. Ethics can never be an exact science. Because of varieties of opinions, we can in this field only approximate the truth; probability is as far as we can go. Since judgments of the validity of ethical truths depend on broad factual experience of life, the young are not good judges in ethics. It takes maturity, living experience, and reason to benefit from the study of ethics.

## Book I, 4-12.

The good for man.

4. The supreme good to be attained by man is generally acknowledged to be happiness. But people disagree as to what constitutes happiness: the average man regards it as consisting of pleasure through material goods, wealth and honor; the Platonists as an abstract absolute good, which is the source of all other goods. There is of course a difference between deductive and inductive reasoning. In ethics we proceed inductively from observed facts, not deductively from abstract ideas. "The fact is the starting-point." The basis of ethics is thus relative knowledge, not absolute truth. A prior good moral training is essential in ethical reasoning.

5. There are three types of living: sensual; political; contemplative. The masses of the common people identify happiness and the good with sensual pleasures and enjoyment; this reveals a slavish and bestial taste. Superior people identify happiness with honor, or political life. But honor, not being self-sufficient as an end, is not something proper to man, for it depends on those who bestow the honors, not on the person who receives them, and

therefore can be taken away. Even virtue and happiness are not identical, for virtue is compatible with complete inactivity, and even with suffering and misfortune. Such a life cannot be a happy one. The contemplative life, which is true happiness, will be treated below. Money-making is not an end in itself, and therefore not happiness.

6. Criticism of Plato's Idea of the Good. However difficult it is to criticize Plato's views, the truth demands prior allegiance. There are various types of goods, not one universal Idea of the Good. The goods are all relative, e.g. to time, place, person. Thus there is not one science of the good, but many sciences of the good in various fields, e.g. medicine, war. The idea and the particular are not separately existing entities. The Idea of the Good and particular goods are not separate. The good cannot be more good for being eternal. Despite the arguments of the Platonists about absolute and secondary goods, there is no single Idea of the Good. The practical and attainable (not the ideal) good varies with different activities and arts, e.g. weaving, carpentry, medicine, military strategy.

7. The good in each activity and art is that for whose sake all else is done, the end or purpose of that activity. There is more than one end of activity, but the supreme good is the final end which does not lead to further desire or activity; it is desirable in and of itself, being self-sufficient. Happiness is the supreme good, for this is desired for its own sake and not for something else. The final and self-sufficient good, the end of all activity, is happiness. Moreover, man has a proper function peculiar to himself. It is not merely vegetative (for this applies to animals too), nor sensory (for this applies to lower animals too), but rather active use of the rational faculty. The function of man is an activity of soul in accordance with reason. Since this is man's proper function (or virtue), it follows that the function of man is an activity of soul in accordance with virtue, the best and most inclusive virtue, judged by the criterion of a complete life of a man. Reminder that

complete precision in ethics is unattainable, as not possible in this subject. For ethics is a practical, not a pure science. The methods of ethics vary; the facts, or first principles, can be obtained by perception, by induction, or by habituation, or in other ways that are suitable.

8. Goods are divided into three classes: external goods; goods of the soul; goods of the body. The truest goods are those of the soul, and thus the end of human life must be a good of the soul. Happiness is a sort of good living and good acting. Happiness is an *activity* in accordance with virtue, not merely a moral state of inactivity, for good results must be produced, and this implies activity. Such virtuous activity brings pleasure in itself to lovers of virtue. For pleasure is derived from noble actions, not merely noble states of being. Virtuous actions are in themselves pleasant, good, and noble. Happiness is the best, most pleasant, and noblest thing in the world. But happiness requires also external goods, without which noble actions are impossible.

9. What is the source of happiness? It is acquired by learning or training, and is something divine in nature. It can be acquired by all, except those who are morally hopeless, with effort and will, for it is not a matter of chance. The definition of happiness agrees with the end of political science, for political science aims at effecting good and noble acts in citizens. Animals cannot be happy, for they cannot perform virtuous acts; nor can children be happy since they are too immature to act in this way.

10. Solon had asserted that we should call no man happy until he is dead. But since happiness is an activity, death cannot involve happiness. Further, Solon's view conceives happiness as dependent upon the ups and downs of chance and fortune. Happiness and virtuous activities are something permanent and stable. Despite the chances and accidents of life true nobility shines through, for happiness consists of virtuous activities. The virtuous and happy man will bear misfortunes of life gracefully and with resignation, but he will not be made unhappy thereby, even though

**225**

external goods are essential to happiness. Thus again, the happy man is the living man whose activities are in accordance with complete virtue and who is provided with external goods for a complete lifetime.

11. Are the dead affected by the misfortunes and good fortunes of friends and relatives? Only to a slight degree, but not so much as to affect happiness.

12. Happiness as a final goal is not something to be praised but rather honored. Praise belongs to subordinate things and virtues, not to the supreme and perfect good and to first principles, just as praise does not belong to the gods.

Book I, 13. Types of virtue.

If Happiness is activity of soul in accordance with perfect virtue, knowledge of the nature of virtue is one of the keys to happiness, both in ethics and politics. Virtue (or excellence) is not of the body but of the soul, of which virtue is an activity. The soul has two faculties: rational and irrational. The irrational faculty itself has two parts: the vegetative (involving nutrition and growth), which is not exclusively human and therefore not involved in human virtue; and the emotional or desiring element, which resists the rational faculty, but is also capable of obedience to it as its superior. There are therefore two kinds of virtue (or excellences): intellectual virtues (e.g., wisdom) and moral virtues (attained when the emotional element obeys reason; e.g., temperance generosity).

## Book II, 1-4.

Moral virtue in general.

1. Intellectual virtue (excellence) is perfected by teaching. Moral virtue (excellence) is created as the result of habit, by training the emotional element to subordinate itself to the rational faculty. Therefore moral virtues are not inborn; they are not inplanted in us by nature. People are born neither moral nor immoral, but amoral. If this were not so, habit and environment would have no effect at all on moral excellence. Humans are born

with a capacity for acquiring and perfecting good character by habit and practice. This differs from man's sensory faculties, for here he is born with the potentiality and later exhibits the activity (as in seeing and hearing). Virtues are like the arts (e.g. like learning to play an instrument) in that we acquire skill by practicing them. Similarly in the state we are made good by forming good habits of conduct. So also in the case of virtues we become just or unjust, brave or cowardly, temperate or self-indulgent by doing the corresponding acts. States of character arise from corresponding activities. Hence the supreme importance of forming the right habits from early youth.

2. Since ethics is not a pure, theoretical science, but a practical science, we must examine the nature of right and wrong actions, not expecting scientific accuracy in this field. Each concrete case involving virtue must be examined on its own merits. But there is a general rule to follow: excess and deficiency in all things are destructive while the intermediate preserves. So in the moral virtue, as, e.g. temperance, courage, the mean (moderation) preserves them.

3. In the field of moral virtues pleasures and pain are involved. The right education is to train people to feel pleasure in moderate (and therefore virtuous) activities, and to feel pain in unvirtuous actions. Hence the importance of habit, for it is more natural and easier to take pleasure in the wrong things and be pained by the right things, as e.g. in eating, sleeping. The rule of pleasure and pain in moral actions involves training to feel pleasure and pain rightly or wrongly.

4. Virtue is not knowledge itself, nor merely doing virtuous acts. It is rather a combination of the two: just and temperate action involves knowledge of what the person is doing, deliberate choice of the action for its own sake, and a fixed moral state. That is, the virtuous act is not merely an accidental one, but habitual and conscious. Justice and temperance are produced by doing just and temperate acts, not by the possession of theoret-

ical knowledge. All the talk in the world will not make a good man unless he practices virtuous acts.

## Book II, 5-9.

Definition of moral virtue.

5. What is virtue? The soul consists of three elements: emotions; faculties; states of character. Virtue must be one of these three. It is not emotion, for emotion, considered abstractly, is neither good nor bad, and it does not involve deliberate choice, but is uncontrolled impulse. For the same and other reasons virtue is not a faculty (abstract capacity for feeling emotion). Virtues are states of character involving conscious choice of the mean of a given emotional state in a given situation.

6. What is the nature of a state of character? Every excellence enables the object which possesses it to perform its function well. So in man moral excellence or virtue will be the state of character that enables a good man to perform his proper function. It is true that the intermediate or mean stands between the extremes of excess or deficiency. But in ethics there is no absolute mean in a particular act which can be set down as a fixed rule for all (e.g., not everyone will eat exactly the same amount of food). The mean is to be regarded relatively to the individual concerned. What is temperance for one person will be vice for another. Every art is properly practiced when it follows the mean, avoiding excess and deficiency. So also in moral acts, excess and deficiency are vices, the mean is virtue. Excess or deficiency constitute failure, the mean success. Hence it is easy to fail, for evil is varied and infinite, and difficult to succeed, for virtue is limited to the intermediate state.

The characteristics of virtue then are:

a. State of character involving deliberate moral choice;

b. The choice of the mean relative to the individual;

c. The mean as determined by reason, in accordance with the reason of a man of practical wisdom. The rule of the mean does not apply to every action and emotion. Some do not involve both excess and deficiency, but only excess or deficiency, e.g. malice, theft, murder, adultery. Therefore they must be avoided entirely, not practiced in moderation.

7. Particular virtues:

| Excess | Mean | Deficiency |
|---|---|---|
| rash confidence | courage | cowardly fear |
| self-indulgence | temperance | insensibility |
| prodigality | liberality | miserliness |
| vulgarity | magnificence | niggardliness |
| vanity | proper pride | undue humility |
| ambition | proper ambition | lack of ambition |
| irascibility | good temper | lack of irascibility |
| boastfulness | truthfulness | self-depreciation |
| buffoonery | wittiness | boorishness |
| obsequiousness or flattery | friendliness | quarrelsomeness or surliness |
| bashfulness | modesty | shamelessness |
| envy | righteous indignation | maliciousness |

8. All three states are opposed to each other, the extremes being more opposed to each other than to the mean. The extremes are not equally opposed to the mean state in all cases. Sometimes the deficiency, sometimes the excess is more opposed to the mean. E.g., cowardice is more contrary to courage than rashness. For we tend more naturally to one extreme than to the other, e.g. towards self-indulgence rather than to its opposite.

9. Hence, it is difficult to act virtuously, because it is difficult to find the mean relative to us—to do the right thing, with reference to the right person, to the right extent, on the right occasion, from correct motives, and in the proper fashion. Therefore, since it is a difficult matter to hit the mean, the simplest of practical rules is to avoid the lesser of two evils, the extreme which is most contrary to the mean, namely the course that tends to give us pleasure in a particular situation, and is therefore most tempting.

Sometimes then we will move toward the excess, sometimes toward the deficiency.

## Book III, 1-5.

Voluntary nature of moral purpose; responsibility for actions.

1. The element of voluntary or involuntary character of emotions and actions must be studied. Involuntary actions are those done under compulsion from the outside, or through ignorance. Some actions involve a mixture of the voluntary and involuntary, as when a man is forced to commit a base act by a tyrant who threatens to kill his kin. The latter is to be classed with voluntary acts. All voluntary and involuntary acts must be judged with reference to a particular act, not in the abstract. Whether we praise or condone such acts depends on the ends for which they are done, for noble or base ends. There are, however, some acts which a good man would not do under any circumstances, even at the pain of death. However, as a rule, we should blame our own moral weakness, not external pressure, for wrong actions.

Acts committed through ignorance are non-voluntary, unless pain and regret follow, in which case the acts might be called involuntary. The wicked, unjust man acts through ignorance and mistaken moral purposes, and ignorance of universal principles. Involuntary acts are the result of ignorance in a particular situation. Such acts may be pardoned, but not the former, for they are the result of general bad moral character. Since there are many elements in an act, only a madman could be ignorant of all the particulars. A person may be said to act involuntarily if he is ignorant of some of the particular aspects of an act, and feels regret and pain afterward. Voluntary actions are those done of one's own free will and choice, and with full knowledge of all the particulars involved. Involuntary acts of all kinds should be avoided.

2. The most important element in virtuous acts is general moral purpose, not mere volition or the action itself. Acts of

**230**

children, animals, or those done on the spur of the moment involve volition but not moral choice and purpose. Moral purpose is not desire, emotion, wish, opinion. It is voluntary, and decided by previous deliberation; it involves reason, self-control, what is in our power and possible, choice of accepting or avoiding actions directed toward the good.

3. Moral purpose involves deliberate choice of possible things which we have the power to do by our own efforts, not external and unchangeable things (as the material universe, the rising and setting of the sun), or irregular, uncontrollable events (as rain, snow), or accidental events (as finding a treasure). Deliberation is concerned with means of acting, not ends or purposes of actions, which are assumed as first principles.

4. The choice of the means is directed toward the end. The object of choice is the good in an absolute sense, but in practice it is what appears to be good to the individual in a concrete situation, judged by the standard of the behavior of the virtuous man.

5. We are responsible for actions, both good and bad, for we exercise voluntary choice of means and the power to refrain from acting. Therefore, Socrates' dictum, that no one does wrong willingly, is false. Hence, the justification of rewards for good acts and punishment for evil acts. Even ignorance is punished, if due to vice or negligence, as in the acts of a drunkard and where ignorance of the law is concerned. In both such cases the individual had the power initially to avoid the difficulty. Unjust and self-indulgent persons cannot plead that they have become habitually so and therefore are not responsible for demoralization. They had the initial voluntary choice of avoiding the formation of bad moral habits. All vices are to be blamed, whether of soul or body, when these arise through our own power to avoid or choose the wrong or right path. Virtues and vices are both voluntary; hence we are personally responsible for both.

**231**

**Book III, 6-9.**

Courage.

6. Courage is a mean between fear and confidence. All evils are objects of fear. Some evils it is right and proper to fear, e.g., disgrace. Some it is not right and proper to fear, e.g. poverty, disease. But courage is not to be confused with not fearing evils in general. True courage is rather fearlessness in the face of a noble death (especially in war).

7. More generally, true courage is the manner of facing evils—fearing the right things, from the right motives, in the right manner, and at the right time. The courageous man does this with nobleness as the positive end of courage, not merely as an escape from evil or through fear of disgrace. Excessive fearlessness is a form of insanity or foolhardiness, akin to cowardice. Excessive fear is cowardice. Suicide is cowardice, not courage at all, for complete escape from evil is sought thereby.

8. False kinds of courage: 1) courage of citizen-soldier —inspired by fear of punishment and promise of rewards, not by a sense of nobility; 2) experience—knowledge of when no danger is really present, as in the case of professional soldiers. Such turn cowards when real danger overwhelms them; 3) blind emotion—lacks moral purpose, and is not motivated by nobleness; 4) sanguineness—comes from confidence in previous victory and from a sense of superiority, not from noble motives. Such people will turn cowards when they do not succeed; 5) ignorance—changes at once to cowardice when the facts are discovered.

9. Courage involves facing what is painful, but the end achieved is pleasant, as in the case of the victorious boxer. The happier a person is, the more painful will be death, and the more courageous he will be in meeting death.

**Book III, 10-12.**

Temperance.

Temperance is a mean between bodily pleasures (too much

and too little) that affect the sensual appetites, particularly taste and touch. Delight in such things is slavish and beastlike. It is natural to eat and touch, but excess is licentiousness and self-indulgence. We need not fear the extreme of deficiency here, for such insensibility is inhuman. The temperate man will desire such pleasures in moderation, so long as they are within his means and consistent with noble conduct. Self-indulgence involves more voluntary conduct than cowardice and is therefore more blameworthy, since it is easier to avoid. Self-indulgence is akin to childishness. In the temperate man the rational element controls the appetitive one.

**Book IV.**

Other particular virtues: liberality, magnificence, pride, ambition, good temper, friendliness, truthfulness, wit, shame.

**Book V.**

Nature of Justice.

**Book VI.**

Intellectual Virtue.

**Book VII.**

Continence, Incontinence, and Pleasure.

**Books VIII-IX.**

Friendship.

**Book X, 1-5.**

Pleasure.

1. It is important to study pleasure, for in education proper training involves pleasure in doing the right thing, pain in doing the wrong; in the development of character we must learn to enjoy what is right and be pained by what is wrong. Some say pleasure is the supreme good, others that it is utterly bad. The second view is incorrect, for it is not consistent with the facts of experience.

2. Pleasure is the supreme good, is the view of some. It

is one of the goods, but not the supreme one. Common experience shows pleasure to be a good.

3. The view that pleasure is wholly bad is utterly false. There are various types of pleasures, some moral, some immoral. Therefore, pleasure in the abstract is not the supreme good; some pleasures are desirable, some undesirable.

4. Pleasure is something complete and whole at any given time. It is not a process in the formative state, involving time and development; it is an end in itself. Every sense performs activity upon its proper objects, and the perfection of this activity involves the best-conditioned sense organ in relation to the noblest and most beautiful object. This activity will be the most pleasant, for it is the most complete. Pleasure is a concomitant of the activity. No one can feel pleasure continuously, for humans are not capable of continuous activity. Pleasure completes activities, and thus per-fects life. Without activity there is no pleasure; every activity is perfected by pleasure.

5. There are different kinds of pleasure, e.g. the pleasures that perfect the activities of the senses and those of the mind. The pleasure involved in each activity intensifies the activity. The various pleasures are not interchangeable, for a particular pleasure may hinder activity in a field to which it is alien (e.g., listening to music while studying), for the more pleasant activity drives out the less pleasant, very much like pain. Pleasures differ from one another, as do activities, in goodness and badness, some being superior to others. Species of animals differ in their pleasures; human beings differ from one another in their pleasures. The high-est pleasures, however, are those which appear to the good man as desirable. Hence the activities of the perfect and supremely happy man and the pleasures that perfect these activities are the pleasures proper to man.

**Book X, 6-9.**
Happiness.

6. What is the nature of happiness, which is the end of human life? Happiness is self-sufficient activity desirable for its own sake, not for a further end. Such are virtuous activities which are performed for their own sake. Therefore amusements involving bodily pleasures do not constitute happiness, however common this notion is. These are not what a good man would value, for they are not activities in accordance with virtue. Moreover, amusement would be a silly and childish end for the supreme good of man, and finally amusement is not an end in itself, but relaxation for the sake of future activity. Serious things are superior to the lighter things that take place in amusements. Slaves can amuse themselves, but they cannot be happy, for they are not free, and do not have the leisure necessary for virtuous activities.

7. Happiness is activity in accordance with the highest virtue of man, reason, which is the highest and most divine element in man. It is therefore the contemplative activity of philosophic wisdom. For reason is the highest faculty in man, the most continuous form of activity which he is capable of, the most pleasant activity, and it is self-sufficient. Leisure is indispensable for happiness. Contemplative activity has its proper pleasure, which heightens the activity. Such a contemplative life is something divine. Life according to reason is the highest end of human existence, the pleasantest, the best, and happiest.

8. The moral virtues make one only less happy than the life of reason. But they are emotional or bodily in origin, and therefore inferior. Practical wisdom is associated with moral virtues, theoretical with contemplative activity. A life of pure reason is something separate from emotions, though it needs external goods, but less than the moral virtues do. That perfect happiness is contemplative activity appears from the nature of the gods who are supremely happy, but whose activity, since they are perfect, does not consist of moral acts, but rather of contemplation. The lower animals cannot therefore be called happy, for they cannot contemplate. External goods are necessary to the happy man

(e.g. food, health), but not in excess, merely enough to make virtuous acts possible. This can be tested not only by the authority of the wisest men, but also by observation of the facts of experience. The man who lives in accordance with reason will be the happiest and dearest to the gods, as being most like themselves.

9. Mere knowledge is not enough in ethics; the practice of virtue is the end. Theory does not make men good, particularly the masses, who are motivated in their actions by fear of punishment and bodily pleasures. Virtue requires a person who is by nature predisposed to good character, but it is habit which inculcates virtuous actions.

The right laws and state-controlled education are needed to train people to act virtuously, not only in youth but in maturer years. We cannot abandon this to the family, for there is not sufficient compulsive power there. Individualism in education and character training is wrong; public control through legislation is best, as in Sparta. Individual methods and individual attention are better than mass education, for each individual is different. But the teacher must know universal principles first.

Legislation is necessary for these ends. Such legislation should be prepared by real statesmen, not by sophists (theoretical college professors), nor by empirical politicians who have no theory. Experience must be combined with knowledge. By collecting, studying, and comparing the various constitutions of states it will be possible to determine what harms or preserves states, and what is the best type of society. Consideration of the political implications of virtue is necessary, for ethics is a branch of politics.

## PRINCIPAL IDEAS OF ARISTOTLE'S ETHICS

I. The *summum bonum* (highest good) of all human activity is happiness, which consists of continuous intellectual activity, contemplation of acquired theoretical wisdom.

II. As means to this end, external goods (health, moderate wealth) are necessary, for they facilitate leisure and a life of reason.

**III.** Another means to happiness is moral virtue, which involves the control of the appetites and emotions by reason. Moral virtue or good character is acquired not by knowledge but by exercise and habit to inculcate self-control.

**IV.** Virtue is moderation, the golden mean. Though happiness is not sensory pleasure, asceticism is wrong. The emotions must not be suppressed entirely; they must be trained to moderation by reason. The mean is not absolute but relative to each individual and each situation.

**V.** Virtuous acts involve conscious choice and fixed moral purpose. Hence man is responsible personally for moral actions.

# POETICS

## SUMMARY

### 1-5. General introduction to poetry.

**1.** Poetry, like all the other arts, is a mode of imitation (*mimesis*). (The function of the poet or artist is to imitate, through media appropriate to the particular art, not particular historical events, characters, emotions, but the universal aspects of life [form, essence, idea] impressed on his mind by observation of real life. Poetry is an act of creation, for it imitates mental impressions; it is therefore an idealization, not a direct copy of human life. It is closer to reality than the concrete situation, since the universal is truer than the particular.) All arts, e.g. poetry, music, differ from one another in 1) the media they employ; 2) the objects they imitate; 3) their manner of imitation; 4) their proper function (end, purpose).

Media of imitation. (Greek) poetry employs language, rhythm, and harmony (music). In dancing, rhythm alone is used; in playing an instrument rhythm and harmony. Epic poetry employs language and rhythm; lyric poetry employs language, rhythm, and harmony; tragedy and comedy the same three media as lyric, but at times only language and rhythm (in the dialogue of the actors), at times all three combined (choral lyrics). It is not the use of meter that makes poetry, but rather the element of imitation of the universal. A person who writes a scientific subject in verse is not a poet.

2. Objects of imitation. Human beings in action, their characters, acts, emotions. The persons imitated will be either higher than average (idealism), average (realism), lower than average (caricature). Tragedy imitates persons better than average, comedy those worse than average.

3. Manner of imitation: 1) completely indirect imitation, as in straight narrative; 2) partly indirect and partly direct, as in epic, which contains both narrative and speeches of character; 3) entirely direct action, as in the drama, where the entire incident is acted out before the audience. "Drama" means "action."

4. Psychology of artistic creation and enjoyment of art. Works of art are created because it is instinctive in man to imitate, and because of the human instinct for rhythm and harmony. People enjoy observing works of art for various reasons: 1) there is pleasure in seeing imitated certain things and events (e.g. murder, dead body, operation) which would be painful to observe in real life; 2) from art we often learn something new, and people take pleasure in learning; 3) if there is nothing new to be learned from the imitation, there can be pleasure in the recognition of what we know; 4) there is pleasure in observing the technical perfection of a work of art.

Origin and development of tragedy and comedy (see pp. 60, 114).

5. Comedy. This involves the imitation of lower types of men whose faults are ridiculous. What is ridiculous is ugly, and consists of faults, acts, or deformities which do not cause pain to anyone (e.g. funny mask, pie-throwing, slipping on a banana peel). The history of the development of comedy is obscure.

Epic vs. tragedy. They have the same objects of imitation—

actions of men of a higher type. But they differ in: 1) manner of imitation, which in epic is a combination of direct and indirect narrative, in tragedy direct action; 2) media of imitation, for epic does not have music or spectacle; 3) verse form, which in epic is single (dactylic hexameter), in tragedy varied; 4) length, which in epic is not fixed, in tragedy is approximately one day. Tragedy is more complex than epic, for it contains all the elements of epic, and in addition music and spectacle. Therefore a good judge of tragedy is also a good judge of epic.

## 6-22. Tragedy.

**6.** Definition of tragedy: 1) objects: imitation of serious action, complete in itself so far as size is concerned; 2) media: rhythm, language, and melody (Greek tragedy is poetic drama, employing alternation of dialogue and choral odes); 3) manner: direct action, not narrative; 4) purpose: to arouse pity and fear and effect a pleasurable catharsis (purging) of these two emotions.

(Interpretations of "catharsis": 1) Plato rejects tragedy on the ground that it arouses pity and fear and makes men emotionally weak; Aristotle believes that tragedy purges away these emotions and makes men stronger; 2) medical [or "vaccination"] theory—pity and fear are often present in persons to excess; by applying more of the same there will be a pathological release which will be pleasant and benefit persons by restoring proper emotional balance; 3) vicarious experience theory—we take pleasure in experiencing the emotions involved in such a fictitious scene without being personally harmed; 4) sadistic theory—we enjoy seeing others suffer, and there is added pleasure because we know it is only a play, not real life; we feel superior to the characters who suffer; 5) we tend to identify ourselves with one of the characters in the play; when the drama is over, we take pleasure both because it has not really happened, and because we realize that our own troubles are minor as compared with what has happened in the tragedy.)

**239**

Six elements of tragedy: 1) spectacle (scenery, costumes); 2) music; 3) diction; 4) character; 5) thought; 6) plot. Order of importance of these elements: 1) plot (for tragedy is not mere character study, but a dynamic portrayal of life; good plot is necessary to produce the tragic effect of pity and fear); 2) character (must be subordinated to the action); 3) thought; 4) diction; 5) music; 6) spectacle. The last two are the least important, since the tragedy may be read.

**7.** Proper construction of plot. It must be a complete whole, having a beginning, middle, and end. It must be neither too short nor too long, so that we may grasp both the separate parts and the unity of the whole in a single memory span. The natural limit in size is one that provides a change in the hero's fortunes with proper dramatic causation.

**8.** Unity of action (the only one of the "three unities" which Aristotle insists upon). A unified plot does not consist of disconnected events about the same hero, but rather of organically unified events in which all the parts are absolutely necessary and in perfect order. There must be one central theme, as in the *Iliad* and *Odyssey*.

**9.** Philosophical nature of poetry. The poet imitates not what actually happens, but what might happen, what is probable, and would befit a particular type of individual. The poet therefore imitates ideal truth, the universal and typical. Hence "poetry is something more philosophic and of graver import than history." Hence, too, plot, not verse form, is the heart of tragedy.

The worst plots are episodic ones, in which the sequence of events has no dramatic causation, since they are neither probable nor necessary. The best plot is one that arouses pity and fear, in the most powerful manner, through incidents that are unexpected but necessary and probable and linked together in sequence by cause and effect.

**10.** Mechanism of the tragic plot: 1) simple plot—single continuous movement of events without reversal (peripety) or discovery (anagnorisis); 2) complex plot—in which a change in the hero's fortune is attended by reversal or discovery or both.

**11.** Parts of plot.

**A.** Reversal (peripety)—change that occurs when opposite of what was intended turns out.

**B.** Discovery (anagnorisis)—change from ignorance to knowledge, from love to hate, or vice versa. The best form of discovery is that which arouses pity and fear most, namely that associated with peripety, being necessary or probable, dramatically caused, effecting love or hate, involving reversal which brings happiness or misery.

**C.** Suffering—murder, torture, injury, etc.

**12.** Quantitative elements of tragedy: prologue, episode, exodos, parodos, stasimon (see pp. 60–61).

**13.** Ideal tragic character and plot.

    **A.** Plot.

        1. Complex.

        2. Must arouse pity (what we feel when someone suffers more than he deserves for his faults and mistakes) and fear (what we feel when suffering happens to someone like ourselves).

    **B.** Character.

        1. Must pass from happiness to misery (not the reverse).

        2. Must not be perfectly virtuous and just.

        3. His downfall must not result from vice or baseness.

        4. His downfall must come about because of a flaw of character (tragic flaw) and error in judgment.

        5. Must belong to distinguished family, so that the fall will be all the greater.

The simple unhappy ending is best in tragedy. The double ending, happiness for the good and unhappiness for the evil, is less desirable, and is a concession to popular taste.

**14.** Methods of arousing pity and fear. It is not artistic to effect this by staging (as a storm). The best means is through the incidents of the plot—when a murder or other horrible deed is about to be perpetrated by a person on a blood relative who is unknown to him and whose identity he discovers just in the nick of time.

**15.** Character. There are four things to aim at: 1) good in performing the proper functions of that character; 2) true to type; 3) true to life; 4) consistent and unified throughout. All acts and words should be the probable or necessary outcome of the inner character. It is necessary to portray character flaws naturally, but the character as a whole must be made better than average (idealized).

The *deus ex machina* is not an artistic device. If it is used it should be employed only to explain past events beyond the knowledge of the characters, or future events necessary to the story.

**16.** Types of discovery. There are six types of discovery: 1) by signs, tokens, or marks on the person; 2) by arbitrary direct discoveries invented by the poet; 3) through awakened memory; 4) through logical reasoning; 5) through wrong sophistical reasoning which reaches the correct result; the best is 6) discovery that grows in a probable manner out of the incidents themselves (as in the *Oedipus Rex*).

**17.** Practical hints for composition: 1) visualize the scenes as they would be when performed; 2) get outside yourself, feel the emotions personally; act out the story yourself (the poet must be a good actor and have a touch of madness in him); 3) first make an outline of the plot (universal form), then fill in the necessary episodes.

**18.** Complication and denouement. The complication is all that precedes the crisis, the change in the hero's fortune; the denouement (unravelling) is all that follows the crisis to the end of the drama.

There are four types of tragedy (viewed from the major emphasis): 1) complex (involving peripety and discovery); 2) of suffering; 3) of character; 4) of spectacle. All four should be properly combined to achieve the best effect. Tragedy should not be too long or attempt to cover an epic story. The chorus should be an integral part of the play, almost one of the actors, and not perform mere unessential musical interludes.

**19.** General observations on thought and diction.

**20.** Diction. The parts of speech are analyzed.

**21.** Types of words in poetry: from the point of view of structure, simple or complex; in meaning, ordinary, foreign, metaphor, ornamental; in form, coined, lengthened, shortened, altered (poetic).

**22.** Use of diction in poetry. There must be clarity without vulgarity, achieved by combination of the ordinary and the unfamiliar. It is bad to make excessive use of metaphors and foreign words, nor must the language be entirely prosaic. Moderation is necessary, otherwise the effect will be ludicrous. The most important element is mastery of metaphor.

**23-24.** Tragedy and epic compared.

**A.** Likenesses: 1) epic too must be a complete whole and possess unity of action (not, as in history, a chronicle of all events in a given period, whether causally related or not); 2) epic has the same types as tragedy—simple, complex, character, suffering; 3) epic has the same parts, except melody and spectacle; 4) epic uses peripety and discovery; 5) epic employs the same thought and diction.

**B.** Differences: 1) length—epic is longer than tragedy; 2) the epic meter is solely dactylic hexameter; 3) objectivity of epic poet; 4) media—only language and rhythm; 5) combination of indirect and direct manner (narrative and speeches); 6) more room for the marvelous and improbable in epic, since it is listened to or read, not performed and seen.

**25.** Solutions of problems of literary criticism.

**A.** The poet should not be expected to be scientifically correct. Apparent faults and impossibilities are permissible if they serve the ends of poetry and create a desired effect. They are not serious if the poet in describing something makes a technical error through ignorance.

**B.** Our impression of an impossibility or error may be wrong, for the poet may be treating things ideally or realistically, or vice versa.

**C.** We must not attribute to the poet errors that he puts into the mouths of his characters, for such error may be true to the character's type.

**D.** As for language, it must be remembered that a poet is permitted greater license.

**E.** We cannot criticize a supposed error, unless we know what the poet really intended.

**F.** Poetry often deals with probable impossibilities.

**26.** The highest form of poetic imitation. Which is the higher and more dignified form of imitation, epic or tragedy? The argument that, since tragedy appeals to the masses, it is vulgar is false. The degrading of tragedy is due not to the dramatic poet but to the overacting of the performers. For tragedy may produce its proper effect by being read. Hence the performance is not the criterion. Tragedy has everything that epic has, and more (music and spectacle); it can be both acted and read; it is more concentrated and more effective; it has greater unity. Thus tragedy is the highest form of poetic art.

## CHAPTER SIXTEEN

# HELLENISTIC SOCIETY

## 3 2 3 - 3 0 B .C .

◘

## POLITICAL, SOCIAL, AND ECONOMIC CONDITIONS

I.   At the death of Alexander the Great his great empire disintegrated, various parts falling into the hands of his generals.

II.   Few large monarchies (such as the Kingdoms of Macedonia, Seleucid Syria, Ptolemaic Egypt, Pergamum) and federations of cities replaced the numerous independent, now politically decadent, city-states of the Hellenic world; political freedom and the citizen-soldier ideal came to an end; with loss of interest in public affairs there developed extreme individualism, greater emphasis on personal economic and social concerns, and the concept of a world society (*cosmopolis*) to replace devotion to the city-state (*polis*) of Greek society.

III.   Alexander's conquests and policies had brought into being a new culture, called Hellenistic, shared by the upper classes of Greece and the Oriental world, involving a fusion of Greeks and non-Greeks, of Greek culture and Oriental culture. New cultural centers sprang up outside of Hellas, especially Alexandria, Pergamum, Antioch, Rhodes.

IV.   Endless disastrous warfare and struggle for power among the great Hellenistic powers; severe economic crises, resulting in increasing impoverishment of the masses everywhere and concentration of wealth in the hands of the few; intense class struggles, frequent revolutions.

V. This political and economic instability led to intellectual confusion, uncertainty of the future, fear, moral decay, depopulation; Greek culture tended to lose its creativeness and to look back to the past.

VI. Roman intervention and gradual conquest of the entire Hellenistic world, 200-30 B.C.

## HELLENISTIC LITERATURE

I. Largely escapist, written for small cosmopolitan intellectual elite; divorced from politics and social and economic problems.

II. Numerous works of research and scholarship.

III. Alexandrianism: dominant literary style, characterized by "art for art's sake," artificiality, sophistication, shallowness, erudition, bookishness, romantic love, perfection of form.

IV. The authors most important for world literature were Theocritus, the founder of pastoral poetry (see pp. 52–53), and Menander, the outstanding author of the New Comedy. This type of comedy replaced the Old Comedy, being non-personal, non-political, and dealing realistically with the scandals and love affairs of the leisure class of the Hellenistic world. Menander's works are largely lost, but are known through the imitations and adaptations of the Roman authors Plautus and Terence.

## HELLENISTIC SCIENCE

This was the great age of Greek science, represented by such familiar names as Archimedes and Euclid. Brilliant discoveries were made in mathematics, mechanical devices, geography, astronomy, medicine, biology.

## HELLENISTIC PHILOSOPHY

I. Separation of ethics and politics; main purpose to develop practical ethics, not to solve problems of world but to provide personal escape from evils; narrow, individualistic, subjective.

II. Stoicism

A. Founded by Zeno (ca. 330-260 B.C.); school at Athens in Painted Stoa.

B. Developed and was modified over a period of five centuries, so that its original materialism was eventually abandoned for Platonic idealism.

C. Aim: to teach personal happiness, to produce wise man who can be happy, and maintain inner peace and contentment, in a world full of troubles.

D. The entire world is a single cosmic interconnected machine; everything happens through rigid determinism and predestination; there is no chance.

E. God is in the entire universe (pantheism), synonymous with Providence, Reason, Virture, Nature; the human soul is immortal and derived from God; reason and virtue are the proper nature of man.

F. There is purpose, design, harmony, beauty in the universe; there is no evil in the universe, but incorrect thinking makes it so.

G. The purpose of life is not pleasure and material things but reason and virtue.

H. Happiness and freedom in a world in which everything is predestined and perfect consists of: living in harmony with nature; making oneself self-sufficient and tranquil by complete suppression of all emotion and by freedom from external circumstances and material things; by using one's will-power to accept whatever happens, interpreting everything as good, accepting and enduring pain; by subordinating oneself voluntarily to the world order, and accepting one's assigned place in society; doing one's duty thoroughly in the place in society allotted to one; by not altering external circumstances but adapting and resigning oneself to them.

I. Concept of brotherhood of man, and natural innate rights of man.

III. Epicureanism

**247**

A. Founded by Epicurus (342-270 B.C.); school at Athens, The Garden.

B. Aim: to teach personal happiness, mental calm and tranquillity, through escape from the evils of the world, banishment of superstition and fear of the gods and death.

C. Knowledge of science to end fears. Atomic theory (see p. 168); uncompromising materialistic philosophy; natural law; no spontaneous generation; indestructibility of matter; all change through the fortuitous combination of atoms in constant motion; theory of the evolution of man and society; sense perception is the infallible source of all knowledge.

D. Religious views: the gods have no power, there is no divine creation, no divine providence, no design, no fate; no personal immortality; the gods exist outside the universe, live calmly and in perfect happiness, and are contemplated and adored as serene ideals.

E. Ethics (egoistic hedonism): the highest good is pleasure, which is the absence of pain and fear; use one's free will to avoid all activities which disturb pleasure; the highest pleasure is mental calm and tranquillity, achieved through reason and knowledge of nature; physical pleasures should be simple and enjoyed in moderation; avoid marriage, family ties, politics, ambition for wealth and power; friendship is the best social pleasure; virtue and justice are practiced, not for their own sakes, but to maintain tranquillity and avoid punishment.

## CHAPTER SEVENTEEN

# ROMAN CIVILIZATION

### To 30 B.C.

## ITALY

I.   Apennine Mts. run through the length of the Italian Peninsula coming down to the seacoast on the eastern (Adriatic) side.

II.   Important plains on the western side: Etruria, Latium, Campania. "Italy faces the west." Fertility of Italy.

III.   Only navigable river, Tiber, from seacoast to Rome; only two considerable harbors, Naples in Campania, Tarentum in Magna Graecia (S. Italy).

IV.   Effects of geography: Italy easier to unify than Greece; commerce retarded; slow cultural development.

## SETTLEMENT OF ITALY

I.   Gradual infiltration of Italic tribes (ca. 2000-1000 B.C.), coming probably from Central Europe, speaking an Indo-European language; principal branches of Italians: Latins, Umbrians, Sabines, Samnites.

II.   Settlement of Etruria by Etruscans from Asia Minor (ca. 1000 B.C.).

III.   Colonization of seacoast of S. Italy by Greeks (ca. 750-550 B.C.).

IV.   The Italians of the 1st Cent. B.C. were the product of a fusion of original inhabitants, Italic peoples, Etruscans, Greeks, and Gauls (from S. France).

## ROME

City in northern Latium, on Tiber River; built on seven hills; inhabited by fusion of natives, Latins, Sabines, Etruscans; strategic position of Rome.

## ROMAN KINGDOM (traditional dates: 753-509 B.C.)

I.  Romulus traditional founder of city of Rome and her first king.

II.  Seven kings; Etruscan conquest; several Etruscan kings of Rome, the last of whom, Tarquin the Proud, was overthrown by a revolution which ended the monarchy.

III.  King chosen for life; powers limited by Senate (advisory council of aristocrats) and Popular Assembly (fighting men).

## ROMAN REPUBLIC (500-30 B.C.)

I.  Political Developments

A.  The king was replaced by two annually elected chief executives, the consuls; gradual increase in number of officials, elected annually with one or more colleagues possessing the same powers: praetors (judicial officials), aediles (public welfare), tribunes (protectors of plebeians, non-aristocratic citizens), quaestors (treasury officials). In a crisis a dictator was chosen for six months. The Senate became the decisive political power.

B.  Class struggle between patricians (aristocrats) and plebeians (509-287 B.C.): the plebeians gradually won legal and political equality, with right to hold office, elect officials, become senators, participate in making of laws. But the principal result was that the rich plebeians and aristocrats merged to form a new ruling class, the Senatorial Order. The Republican government remained essentially aristocratic because office-holding was expensive and officials received no pay.

II.  Territorial Expansion

A.  Gradual conquest (509-264 B.C.) of all Italy S. of Rubicon River; formation of Roman Military Federation, in which all peoples retained local autonomy but relinquished control over

**250**

foreign affairs to Rome, and contributed quotas of soldiers to the Roman army; establishment of colonies of Roman citizens in strategic spots in Italy.

B.   Conquest of Western Mediterranean (264-146 B.C.); defeat of Carthage in disastrous Punic Wars during which Italy was invaded by the famous Carthaginian general Hannibal; annexation of Rome's first overseas provinces, Sicily, Corsica and Sardinia, Spain, Africa.

C.   Conquest of the Eastern Mediterranean (200-30 B.C.); Roman intervention in the affairs of the Hellenistic states; conquest and annexation of Macedonia, Greece, Asia Minor, Syria, Judea, Egypt.

D.   Provincial administration: provinces ruled by annual Roman governors (proconsuls, propraetors) with arbitrary power; paid heavy tribute to Rome; exploited by governors, tax-collectors, Roman money-lenders and business men.

## EARLY ROMAN FAMILY LIFE AND CHARACTER

I.   Large household (*familia*) ruled by head called *paterfamilias;* purity and solidarity of family life.

II.   Suppression of individualism through inculcation of *pietas,* obedience to *paterfamilias,* devotion to the state, submission to gods.

III.   Patriotism; physical toughness; military courage.

IV.   Conservatism; respect for tradition, the customs of the ancestors.

V.   Roman women subordinated to men, but their position in the family and in society was higher than that of Greek women.

## EARLY ROMAN ECONOMIC LIFE

I.   No extremes of wealth.

II.   Basically agricultural; commerce and industry negligible.

III.   Problem of landless poor partially solved by distribution of conquered lands and citizen colonies in Italy.

IV.   Slaves relatively few in number.

**251**

## EARLY ROMAN RELIGION

I.  Family Religion: worship of vague protective spirits (Lares, Penates, Janus, Vesta) who were supposed to guard the farm life and welfare of the household; *paterfamilias* acts as priest of family.

II.  State Religion: worship of anthropomorphic divinites, borrowed from Etruscan and Greek sources, which were supposed to protect the entire state and its territories; religion controlled by priestly officials.

## EFFECTS OF ROME'S CONQUESTS (264-133 B.C.)

I.  Economic: growth of large estates in Italy owned by Senators; worked by large slave gangs; ruin of Italian peasants, who flocked to Rome; increase in wealth and luxury; growth of commerce and industry.

II.  Social: besides the wealthy Senatorial Order, the poverty-stricken city masses (*plebs*), the numerous slaves, there grew up a new powerful class, the Equestrian Order, composed of financiers and businessmen.

III.  Political: supreme power of Senate; pro-senatorial activity of tribunes, who were nominally the protectors of the plebeians; corruption of Roman officials.

IV.  Religious: confusion, scepticism, superstition, because the agricultural family religion served no purpose in urban life, because of the introduction of Greek religious ideas, because the state religion became a political tool of the Senate, and because growing individualism was not satisfied by the community spirit of earlier Roman religion.

V.  Family life: breakdown of solidarity and purity of family life through growth of individualism; growth of immorality, divorce, childlessness.

VI.  Cultural: adoption by the Romans of Greek (Hellenistic) culture, its individualistic spirit, religious views, literature, art, philosophy, educational system, amusements, language. "Captive

**252**

Greece made her barbarian captor captive." The principal effect was a changed emphasis on the individual and the growth of a desire for personal happiness, wealth, power.

## CENTURY OF REVOLUTION AND CIVIL WAR (133-30 B.C.)

I.     Supremacy of the Senate challenged by reformers and military leaders.

II.     Reorganization of army: professional volunteer army replaces citizen-peasant militia; armies loyal to generals, not state; independent power of generals and use of military force in politics, as by Marius, Sulla, Pompey the Great, Caesar, Antony, Octavian.

III.     Attacks on the Roman Empire, especially by the Germans and eastern peoples; revolt of Italian allies (90 B.C.) compelled Rome to grant Roman citizenship to all Italy; disastrous uprising of slaves (73 B.C.).

IV.     Ruthless internal revolution and civil wars; bloody elimination of political enemies by proscriptions.

V.     New conquests by Pompey in the East and Caesar in Gaul; annexation of Egypt by Augustus.

VI.     Growth of personal political power: dictatorship of Sulla (82-79 B.C.); First Triumvirate (Caesar, Pompey, Crassus), 60-50 B.C.; dictatorship of Caesar (49-46 B.C.); Second Triumvirate (Octavian, Antony, Lepidus), 43-32 B.C.

VII.     Final destruction of power of Senate by Caesar and Octavian (Augustus).

VIII.  The Roman Republic was destroyed because the Senate was unable to solve the political, social, and economic contradictions engendered by the Roman conquest of the civilized world, because the city-state Republic was not adapted to ruling a great empire, and because the continuous warfare of this century impelled most people to abandon the little liberty they enjoyed for peace and security.

**253**

## EARLY PERIOD OF ROMAN LITERATURE (240-70 B.C.)

I.   Translation of Homer's *Odyssey* into Latin by Livius Andronicus, a Greek slave from Tarentum.

II.   Epics on Roman themes by Naevius and Ennius.

III.   Adaptations and imitations of the Greek New Comedy by Plautus and Terence.

IV.   Imitation of Greek tragedy by Roman writers.

V.   Creation of a new literary type, satire, by Lucilius.

## GOLDEN AGE OF ROMAN LITERATURE— CICERONIAN PERIOD (70-43 B.C.)

I.   Lucretius' *De Rerum Natura,* didactic epic on Epicurean philosophy.

II.   Catullus' lyric poems.

III.   Cicero's oratorical writings, popularizations of Greek philosophy, and letters.

IV.   Caesar's historical works (*Gallic War; Civil War*).

V.   Sallust's historical works.

## CHAPTER EIGHTEEN

# LUCRETIUS

◙

## TITUS LUCRETIUS CARUS (ca. 99-55 B.C.)

I.   Almost nothing known of him.

II.   Principal extant authority on Epicureanism and Greek atomic theory.

III.   Elizabeth B. Browning: "He died chief poet on the Tiber side."

## DE RERUM NATURA (On the Nature of Things)

I.   Didactic epic poem (in dactylic hexameter) on the scientific views of Epicureanism, the materialistic philosophy of the Greek thinker Epicurus (see p. 248).

II.   Purpose: addressed to the Roman aristocrat Memmius, it seeks to convert the reader to Epicureanism, to teach mental tranquillity, and dispel fear of the gods and death through science.

III.   Influences: Homer, Empedocles, Thucydides, Euripides, Epicurus, and the Roman epic poet Ennius; no influence of Alexandrianism.

## SUMMARY

*General Outline*

Books I-II:   Atomic theory

Book III:   Mortality of the soul

Book IV.   Sense perception; thinking; reproduction and love

**255**

Book V: Origin of the world; origin and evolution of man and civilization

Book VI: Natural phenomena; disease

## Book I.

1-145. Invocation to Venus (creative power of nature). O mother of the Aeneadae (Romans), through whose fructifying power all living things come into being and reproduce, O sole mistress of the nature of things, help me to write these verses on nature for the enlightenment of Memmius! But first beseech thy lover, Mars, to cease from bloody war and bring peace to the Romans, so that I and Memmius may have peace of mind, the one to write, the other to read these verses.

Listen, while I explain to you the nature of heaven, the gods, and atoms. Human life lay crushed beneath religion until a man of Greece (Epicurus) dared courageously to oppose it, traversing with reason the entire universe and establishing the laws of nature. Thus religion in turn was conquered to the benefit of man. Think not that this venture is sinful. It is rather religion that has caused sinful deeds, as witness the pitiful sacrifice of Iphigenia at Aulis by her own father, Agamemnon, because of his ignorance of science. "So great the evils to which religion could prompt!"

Even you may at times desert the Epicurean view, frightened by the tales of the priests about punishments in afterlife. But there is a fixed limit to human existence, and speculation about immortality and reincarnation of souls, as by Ennius, is false and harmful. I must, therefore, explain not only astronomy and the laws of nature, but also the nature of the soul, however difficult and laborious a task it is to attempt to explain for the first time in Latin verse the discoveries of the Greeks.

146-214. Scientific knowledge of the laws of nature will dispel superstitious fear. The basic principle, out of which all else flows, is that nothing can be created out of nothing by divine power. There is no spontaneous generation; all living things, animals and plants, spring up and develop from atoms in an orderly fashion, according to fixed laws of nature, and there is a fixed natural limit to their growth.

215-264. Nothing can be reduced to utter nothingness. Matter is indestructible. If matter could be destroyed, the whole universe would have disappeared a long time ago. And how could new things constantly grow and develop? All things are dissolved into atoms, which are indestructible, and these atoms are then recombined into new forms. For rain fructifies the earth, whose produce feeds animals, which in turn nourish humans. Nothing is utterly lost.

265-328. It is not sound to question the existence of atoms because they cannot be seen. We can prove the existence of invisible atoms by the analogy of invisible winds, smells, heat, cold, sounds, the unseen drying of clothing, the imperceptible wearing away of a ring or a stone, the imperceptible growth and decay of living things.

329-482. Besides atoms, there is also void, without which there could be no motion, birth, or growth of things. Things apparently solid are actually porous; sounds pass through walls; things of the same size are of unequal weight (as a piece of lead and wool) because the lighter has more void in it. All objections to the existence of void are false. Many other proofs of its existence can be adduced by any inquisitive person.

Nature, then, consists of body and void in which matter moves. Besides these two there is no third substance. Whatever can be perceived by the senses is body, whatever cannot is void. All other things are either essential properties or accidents of matter or void. Time and actions are not essential properties, and do not exist by themselves, but are accidents of matter and void on given occasions. Without body and void nothing can happen.

483-634. Bodies are either atoms or clusters of atoms. But atoms themselves are solid and indestructible. The solidity and singleness of atoms cannot be perceived by the senses but must

GREEK AND ROMAN CLASSICS

be deduced by reason. Body and void are independent and mutually exclusive. Thus body must be solid, without void, eternal, and indestructible. All things are made up of atoms, and are ultimately dissolved into atoms. Unless nature had set a limit to the divisibility of matter, nothing could come into being, for all things would long ago have been utterly destroyed, considering that things are more quickly broken down than renewed. Atoms cannot be soft, for then we could not explain hard things. They are hard, solid, and single. If atoms were soft, the world and its contents could not exist continuously. Common sense supports this view that there is some ultimate unchangeable matter, as the regular continuity of various species of animals, controlled by the laws of nature, proves.

Atoms, though finite, have parts. But matter is not infinitely divisible. For the parts of the atoms cannot exist separate from it; the atom is an eternal union of these parts, but it is impenetrable and indestructible.

635-920. Attack on Heraclitus and the Stoics who assert that fire is the primal element. Fire cannot explain the variety of things. Moreover, these philosophers deny void; and if fire can be extinguished, then it can be utterly destroyed and things can be created out of nothing. Then too this view is against the evidence of the senses, which are the ultimate criterion of all knowledge.

All those philosophers who believe the primal substance to be fire, air, earth, or water, are in error. Equally wrong is the great genius, Empedocles of Sicily, who posited a combination of all four elements. All these thinkers have gone astray in their theories of the primal substance, for they deny void and maintain infinite divisibility and softness of matter. Moreover, the first elements cannot themselves be perceived by the senses, nor can they be transmuted into something else, as is necessary with the theories of earth, air, fire, and water. Things change by the combination and recombination of atoms and the motion of matter in void. Equally false is the view of Anaxagoras, for it can be proved that substance does not have the same inherent nature as the things which are produced by combinations of the primal substance. This view involves assigning to the primal substance the secondary qualities that belong to the things composed of it.

921-950. I am aware of the difficulty of the subject, but I am inspired by the great hope of praise and by love of the Muses to enter untrodden paths, so that I may release the mind from religion. This I essay to do with the charm of my honeyed verses, as physicians smear the rim of the cup when they want to give children bitter medicine to cure them. Similarly, the bitter pill of science will more easily be swallowed because of the charm of my sweet verses.

951-1051. The universe is infinite in extent. Void or space is infinite, for otherwise all matter would long ago have settled in a mass at the bottom, and nothing could come into existence. Thus atoms are continuously in motion in infinite space. Finally, matter too is infinite, forming things through endless fortuitous clashings and rearrangements of atoms.

1052-1117. Do not believe the Stoic view that all things are attracted to a center; there can be no center in an infinite universe. Nor are there creatures in the antipodes who walk head downward, enjoying day while we have night, and vice versa. Even if there were a center, things would no more necessarily be attracted to it than repelled by it. For space is infinite, and if matter were finite, all matter would in an instant be broken up into separate atoms, and nothing could come into existence.

## Book II.

1-61. It is pleasant to be safe while others are in distress, as when one watches from a distance persons on the sea in a storm or in a furious battle. But nothing is more pleasant than to look down from the lofty citadel of philosophy upon men blindly wandering in error from the true path, struggling for position, power, and wealth. Miserable are they, living in darkness and danger, for they do not see that true happiness requires but little—freedom from pain and fear. Truly, little is needed to banish pain from the body, not wealth and luxury. Nor can wealth, power, armies and navies banish from the mind the fears of religion and death. It is only the wisdom of philosophy, knowledge of nature, that can remove these idle terrors.

62-166. I shall now explain motion, and how things come into being from and are dissolved into atoms. All things change, being in constant motion, but the sum of matter is eternally the same. Single atoms are in constant turbulent motion in infinite space through their own weight or the impact of other atoms. The hard atoms at times rebound back into space, at others become entangled with one another, forming dense aggregations with little void between them. Those that rebound into space continue to move, as can be seen by the analogy of motes in the sunbeam. Thus atoms in motion form small bodies, and these combine to form larger ones until we perceive them by our senses.

The velocity of complex sunlight and heat is obstructed by objects in their path. But the single atoms travelling through perfect void move at a far greater speed than light.

167-183. Some people, in ignorance, believe that the regularity and perfection of nature imply divine providence and design. Aside from the proofs of science, the imperfection of the world argues against this view.

184-293. Despite the Stoic view, nothing naturally moves upward. All matter naturally falls downward, as many instances prove. Falling atoms, in their downward course, swerve ever so slightly, otherwise they would never join, and nothing would come into being. The collisions of atoms cannot be thought to take place because heavier and lighter atoms fall at unequal speed, for in void (vacuum) all objects fall at the same rate of speed. Hence only "swerve" can explain this. There is no rigid determinism in the motion of atoms, for how else can we explain free-will than by the doctrine of a minimum of "atomic swerve"?

294-333. Matter was never more or less condensed than now, and motion is constant, for the sum of matter cannot be changed, nor matter escape from or enter the universe. Despite constant motion of atoms, the whole universe seems to be at rest, for we cannot see the individual atom. Similarly, a flock of sheep or an army seen from a distance seems to be at complete rest, though the individual sheep or soldiers are moving.

334-568. Atoms, infinite in number, are individual and of different shapes, as humans, animals, and plants all differ from one another. Some atoms are larger than others, some are fine, some are smooth, some hooked. Pleasant sensations are caused by smooth atoms, unpleasant ones by hooked atoms. Some are tooth-like, some jagged. Differences in the types of atoms explain different types of substances and varying effects on the senses. But the number of shapes and sizes of atoms is limited, for otherwise some atoms would be infinite in size. Besides, there is a fixed limit to all things, and thus there must be a fixed limit to types of atoms. But atoms of like shape are infinite in number, for otherwise all matter would be finite.

569-729. The conflict between destruction and production is everlasting. Nothing exists eternally; some things are always disintegrating, some things always coming into being. Every day the birth cries of babies are mingled with laments for the dead.

All things are made up of a greater or lesser variety of atoms. The earth possesses the greatest variety of atoms, and hence she is properly called Mother Earth, the parent of gods, men, and animals. But this is mere symbolism, for the gods are immortal and perfect and self-sufficient, and enjoy complete calm, not concerning themselves with the affairs of men, nor heeding their prayers. We may use the name Neptune for the sea, Ceres for corn, Bacchus for wine, Mother of the Gods for earth, so long as we do not bring in religious associations. The earth is senseless matter, producing many things because it receives into it many kinds of atoms.

Animals, plants, humans differ from one another, and therefore are made up of different elements, which unite to produce varied things. Yet there are laws of the union of atoms, and fixed limits, not an infinitely varied combination of them; otherwise there would be monstrous beings of all kinds. Living things reproduce after their kind, and originate and grow from fixed types of atoms. The same principle applies to inorganic matter. Thus all types of things remain distinct.

730-864. Atoms have no color or other secondary qualities. They are unchangeable and fixed. Color is due to changes in the types of atoms, their position and motion. Many arguments are given to support this view, including the point that if one divides a thing into small enough parts the color gradually disappears. Further, atoms are devoid of heat, cold, sound, flavor, odor, for these are temporary, secondary qualities that cannot belong to immortal atoms.

865-1022. All things that are alive and that possess sensation are composed of atoms which are themselves devoid of sensation, e.g. worms from excrement, cattle from water and plant life, humans from animals. Nature changes food into living bodies possessing sensation by recombinations and motions of atoms. But only certain shapes and types of atoms in certain arrangements and motions produce sensation in living things. If the atoms had sensation, they would be subject to destruction. Sensation can then come from what has no sensation itself. It cannot exist in a body until it is begotten, for the elements of the body are previously scattered in nature. Life and sensation depend on the arrangements of the atoms, and death may be caused by a severe blow which disturbs the arrangement and motion of atoms essential to life. Pain occurs when atoms are disturbed, pleasure when they return to their proper place. Thus atoms have no sensation themselves. Atoms cannot have emotions or think; this is an absurd notion. Death, or the end of sensation, is the disarrangement and dispersal of the various types of atoms and their motions that make up the body and the sensory part of a living thing.

1023-1174. Hear a great new truth, difficult as it may be for new truths to gain acceptance and easy to take for granted old ones, just as the wondrous spectacle of the heavens is casually accepted. Since space is infinite, and atoms unlimited, so there must be other worlds beyond ours. For just as ours is a fortuitous combination of atoms, there must be other such combinations elsewhere, other worlds, inhabited by men and animals. There is no single specimen of anything; everything belongs to a species. By analogy, there must be other worlds and heavens too.

There is no divine intervention in the universe. For the gods are completely tranquil and self-sufficient, and cannot therefore supervise these numerous worlds and their natural phenomena. How can we believe that Jupiter hurls lightning if it strikes temples of Jupiter, desert places, and innocent people, passing by the guilty?

Our world came into being, received accretions of matter. But all things, by a law of nature reach maturity and then begin to decay, losing more matter than they take in. So our world will eventually decay and be completely destroyed. Even now the earth is exhausted and has lost her ancient lush fertility. The farmer and vineyard planter shake their heads in sorrow at the small yield, sigh for the good old days, and pray to the gods, not comprehending that all things must decay and pass away.

## Book III.

1-30. O Epicurus, who has shed light on the darkness of error, my beloved guide and master, thy philosophy has unveiled the entire universe, made the nature of things intelligible, and dispelled fear of the blessed gods and afterlife.

31-93. Next I shall explain the nature of the soul, and thus abolish the fear of death, which tortures people, and is the source of all evils. Some men assert that they know the soul is not immortal, but in adversity they return to religion. It is the fear of death that drives men to commit crimes in order to attain power and wealth with which they hope to prolong life and attain happiness. Hence come civil war, murder, hatred of relatives, envy of others, betrayal of friends, country, parents, and many other evils. All these follies can be dispelled by knowledge of nature.

94-322. Mind and soul form one integrated whole, and they are an organic, material part of the body, no less than a foot, or the head, or eyes. The mind, which is the ruling organ of the entire body, is situated near the heart, while the soul is spread throughout the entire body. Yet the two are united and function together in violent emotions, affecting also the body. The mind and soul are material (atomic), and affect and are affected by the body in an integrated fashion. The mind and soul are composed of exceedingly small, smooth, round atoms, for the mind can move very speedily. The whole mass of these atoms weighs very little, witness the fact that at death there is no appreciable decrease in weight when these leave the body.

323-416. The soul is contained in the body; the two cannot be separated without mutual destruction. Body and soul cannot have sensation separately, but only when joined. The body is not born without the soul, nor does it continue to exist after death. The two are a joint nature. Body and soul have sensation when joined; the soul cannot have sensation alone. Sensation is then an accident of the body. Decocritus' view that atoms of the soul and body alternate with one another is false; the atoms of the soul are relatively few. The mind is more important for life than the soul, for if the mind is injured death results, but not so if the soul is.

417-829. Next, 28 arguments are given for the mortality of the soul (or mind; the two are now used synonymously), the most important of which are: 1) the body is the vessel of the soul, and when the body perishes, the atoms of the soul spill out, scattering like smoke or steam; 2) the soul is born with the body, matures with it, and decays with it, as we can see in the child, the adult, and old man; 3) both mind and body are subject to disease and pain, and often disease of the body affects the mind; 4) wine affects body and mind alike; 5) epileptics are affected both in mind and body; 6) since both body and mind can be healed by medicine, the latter must be mortal, for something immortal is not subject to change in any way; 7) often in a dying man sensation is gradually lost, e.g. in the hands and feet, proving that the soul is gradually scattered and therefore mortal; 8) just as eyes and ears decay when separated from the body, so the soul, which is also an organ of the body, decays when detached from the body; 9) the body rots away when the soul leaves it, the soul being broken up and leaving the body piecemeal, for no one feels the soul going out entire; 10) if the soul can exist alone, it must have all five senses, but there cannot be sensation without body; 11) something that is immortal cannot be divided, but we see limbs which have been cut from a man still retain sensation and motion for a while, and the parts of a snake which has been cut into pieces continue to move; 12) if the soul is immortal, we should remember our former existence; 13) each species of living thing retains its own peculiar qualities, and the young are not as wise as the adults of the species, so that there is no transmigration of immortal souls into other living things; 14) the soul is not immortal because it is subject to destructive influences—it suffers with the body, and has also its own ailments, worries, remorse, fear, insanity, lethargy.

830-1094. Since the soul is mortal, death is nothing to us. Just as we felt no distress from events which happened before our time, so when body and soul have been separated we shall not be affected by events of the future, even if the whole world collapses in ruins. Supposing that the soul has sensation after death, this would not affect us, for our identity consists of an integrated unity of body and soul. Even if through the fortuitous motions of atoms our own bodies should be reconstituted at some time in the future, this would be nothing to us once our identity had been snapped asunder. It is probable that in infinite past time our bodies did exist before, but we remember nothing of the past. We have nothing to fear of the future after our death, for we will have no sensation, once our identity has been destroyed.

Those who deny sensation after death and yet fear what will happen to their bodies when they decay or are burned or devoured by beasts are foolishly projecting their present consciousness into the time after death. They will not be there to mourn themselves after death, nor does it matter in what manner our bodies are destroyed.

Some are unhappy because they will be deprived by death of the sweetest things in life, home, wife, children. But they forget that after death they have no concern for such things. Others complain that the dead sleep forever without cares, while the living are left miserable with grief over the loss of a beloved one. If the dead sleep peacefully, why mourn unceasingly for them?

Men say as they drink wine, "Enjoy the present moment; it is irreplaceable." As if, after death they will be tortured by thirst or similar desires. Death is like an everlasting sleep during which we have no sensations or desires.

If you have had a pleasant life, why not be satisfied and leave like a well-fed guest; but if you have had unhappiness in life, why hesitate to leave it, for there is nothing new under the sun that you might wait for to change your fortune? If an old person laments coming death, he should be censured for desiring more than is his due of happiness, or for not having taken full advantage of his life. It is a law of nature that old things must give way and relinquish their atoms to create new things; all is change, constant decay and generation. Generations come and go; no one lives forever. Just as we had no concern with all past time, so will the future be for us, nor is there anything appalling in this thought.

All the stories of horrors in Tartarus, of Tantalus, Tityos, Sisyphus, the Danaids, Cerberus, the Furies, are false. They are merely reflections of people's cares, worries and disappointments in real life. But guilty consciences and fear of punishment after death make a hell on earth for fools.

**266**

Great and powerful men had to die, like Xerxes, Scipio, Homer, Democritus, even Epicurus, the mightiest mind of all time. Why then should you fear to die, since you waste your life anyway in idleness, groundless fears and delusions?

Men feel a burden of worries pressing their minds, and, for want of anything serious to do, try to flee from themselves, all in vain. If they knew what the cause of their malaise was, they would abandon all else to study the nature of things.

Why lust after life amid cares and dangers? Death is inevitable for all, and life creates no new pleasures. The future is uncertain; it brings both good and bad fortunes. Besides, no matter how one has lived, the same everlasting death awaits all.

**Book IV.**

**1-25.** Same as Book I, 926-950.

**26-468.** Psychology of sense perception; theory of images. All things emit from their surfaces in constant rapid streams films having the shape of the things which produce them. These films float in the air, are separately invisible, and of extreme fineness. Besides, there are also self-created films of varied shapes floating in the air. They move at tremendous velocities, and are the explanation of how all the senses perceive, of sight, taste, smell, hearing, touch. We do not see the films, but they stimulate sensation in us by their constant stream. They are reflected by mirrors. When we have illusions, it is not the senses that are responsible, but the opinions added by the mind to the perception of the senses, as many observations prove.

**469-521.** Complete scepticism is wrong. The ultimate source of all knowledge is sense perception, which is infallible. All true reasoning depends on the evidence of the senses. The evidence of each of the senses is equally valid and trustworthy.

**522-721.** Sound (including echoes) can be explained in the same way, through atomic particles which strike the ear; so also the sense of taste, varieties of taste reactions, and smell.

**267**

722-1036. The mind apprehends when extremely fine atomic films, floating about with great velocity, enter the body. We have ideas of monstrosities which never existed (e.g. centaurs, Scylla, Cerberus) because films, flying about, fortuitously join together. So also can be explained visions of the dead which we perceive in sleep.

With regard to the sense organs and other parts of the body, there must be no teleological explanation of them. They were not made so that we might use them, but uses were found for them by humans. To think otherwise is to confuse cause and effect. It is different with things that men create for a specific purpose, e.g. weapons of war, beds, etc.

All living things require food because they are constantly losing matter through exertion, breathing, etc. Food replenishes the lost matter.

Walking takes place in the following manner: films of walking stir the mind, which then stirs the soul, which in turn stirs the body to move.

Sleep takes place when part of the soul leaves the body, the remainder withdrawing deep into the body. During sleep people and animals dream subconsciously of what has occupied them during their waking hours. Emotional drives and desires also appear in dreams, causing physical reactions.

1037-1287. Sexual desire should be suppressed or diverted, for it causes worry and pain. Entanglement in love should be avoided; in any case, moderation is essential, else it becomes an all-consuming passion, ruining health and fortune. Independence is lost, and the lover is a prey to jealousy and worry. Unrequited love leads to even greater ills.

Avoid becoming entangled in the nets of love by using your reason and by not being blind to the defects of the beloved, as most men are. Women are all alike. But at times there is genuine love on the woman's part. Natural, physical causes of hereditary resemblance in reproduction, and of sterility are explained. Sometimes women without beauty endear themselves to their husbands by their character and charm, or simply by habitual association.

**Book V.**

1-54. No one can adequately praise Epicurus, who is more divine than traditional Greek and Roman gods, because he discovered the true philosophy, and freed people through reason from fear, superstitions, passions that bring unhappiness. He deserves to be ranked among the gods for disclosing the nature of things and of the gods themselves.

55-90. I shall now explain the temporary nature and origin of the world, the origin and evolution of animals and men, the origin of religion and superstition, the movements of heavenly bodies without divine intervention.

91-508. The earth is mortal; it had a beginning in time and will some day come to an end. The world is not divine in whole or part; it is simply inanimate matter.

The gods dwell in abodes outside our world, not in it. The gods did not create the world, and so there is no need to praise them for it. Moreover, the gods are completely blessed, and do not need anything from man, nor do they trouble themselves about man and the universe. The world came into being through natural causes, by the fortuitous combination of atoms in constant motion. Finally, the world is too imperfect and too full of human miseries for us to imagine that it is a work of divine creation.

The parts of the world, earth, air, fire, water, are separately mortal, grow and decay; hence the entire world, the sum of these, must be mortal. Therefore there was a beginning and there must be an end of the world, the earth, seas, and heaven alike. The origin of the world is of fairly recent date, for the arts and sciences are still in the process of development. The world will end when one of the ceaselessly warring elements, earth, air, fire, water, conquers the others.

The world was not created by divine design, but came into being by the fortuitous combinations of disordered atoms, producing first earth, then the ether, the outermost sphere of the world, then the heavenly bodies, then the seas.

509-771. Natural explanations of the movements of the stars, sun, moon; of the heat of the sun, the alternation of day and night, the lengthening and shortening of day and night in different seasons, the light of the moon, eclipses of the sun and moon. The earth is stationary; the sun, moon, and stars are about the same size as they appear to the senses.

772-924. I now return to the infancy of the world. First came grass, then trees, lastly animals. The latter grew directly out of the ground and were nursed by the earth. All of men's needs were supplied by the earth in the perpetual springtide of the new world. Mother earth then produced all living things, birds, animals, men. But as it grew older, it ceased bearing animals from age; for time changes everything, even the earth.

At this time the earth produced many types of monsters, whose species perished completely, through natural selection. Only those species survived which were fitted to survive in the struggle for existence, to adapt themselves to the environment, to protect themselves, or to be useful to man. Complex creatures of fable, combining parts of different animals, such as centaurs, Scylla, the Chimaera, cannot have existed; they are figments of the imagination.

925-1240. Early man was hardier than now, leading a migratory, food-gathering existence. There were no stable communities, no agriculture; men lived off the natural produce of the earth, acorns, berries, river and spring water. They dwelled in caves and forests, not possessing fire, clothing, or laws. Each person was an isolated individual, living for his own selfish ends. There was no family life or marriage. They slept on the ground, not fearing the darkness, through habit. The greatest danger to them came from wild beasts. Death came, as it does now, to all; but war did not destroy thousands, nor shipwrecks, as happens now. Often lack of food or poisonous berries would cause death; now it is luxury and premeditated poisoning that kills many.

In time they developed homes, skins of animals for clothing, fire, and family life. Thus they were softened physically and emotionally, and therefore to protect themselves and their helpless wives and children they gave up their individualism by making compacts of friendship (Social Contract Theory).

Men then developed language because of necessity. It is wrong to suppose that one man invented language, as many believe. Fire was not brought down by Prometheus, but men learned its use from lightning and the friction of trees. They learned cooking from the effect of the sun's heat.

Civilization developed through the genius of men of intellect. The earliest rulers were kings, men outstanding for brains, beauty, strength. They built cities; people attained power in proportion to beauty and strength. But later gold was discovered, and power was transferred to the wealthy. True happiness, however, comes from a simple life and a contented mind. The struggle for power and ambition for fame is fraught with great danger, envy, and eventual downfall. To achieve happiness and independence it is better to be a private man than a powerful ruler.

Kings were overthrown by violent revolutions, and anarchy ensued. To terminate this state, constitutions, laws, and elected officials were established. Men began to obey these for fear of punishment, and those who escape are tortured by conscience.

The origin of religion was in the visions men had in sleep of divine beings, and in ignorance of the true explanation of natural phenomena. What unhappiness and fears they brought upon themselves when they assigned such powers, through ignorance of science, to the gods! True religion consists in contemplating all things with peace of mind. The awesomeness of the universe, great human and natural catastrophes impel men to prostrate themselves before the gods.

1241-1457. Metals were discovered through forest fires; tools and weapons were made. Bronze was at first more valued than gold; now the opposite is true. Weapons grew in strength until iron was discovered. New methods and terrible instruments of warfare were perfected.

Then weaving was invented, and men first performed this work until it later became woman's function. Then settled agriculture and the clearing of forests developed. Music was devised by imitating birds; instruments were invented—things to delight the simple life of the carefree rustics of this time, together with dancing and other merriment. But later men tired of such simple pleasures, and more elaborate ones came into being. Luxury displaced simplicity, bringing in its train cares, unhappiness, and war.

The calendar was devised by observation of the sun and moon. Then came walled cities, private property in land, the art of navigation, international treaties, invention of the alphabet, and poetry. All the practical and fine arts by slow degrees were advanced step by step until perfection in each was attained.

## Book VI.

1-42. Athens bestowed many gifts upon mankind, but none greater than the glorious Epicurus, who, when men were provided with the basic necessities of life and great luxuries, but were yet miserable, purged men's hearts of terrors and fears with true wisdom and the true guide to happiness.

43-95. I shall now explain natural phenomena, thunder, lightning, winds, storms. These are not caused by the gods in wrath, for they live a blessed unperturbed existence. Ignorance of these truths leads to superstition, vain fears, a miserable existence.

96-378. Natural explanation of thunder and lightning, and of their effects.

379-422. This is the nature of the thunderbolt, and not the superstitions people are taught. Why, if Jupiter hurls the thunderbolt, are innocent people so often struck by lightning; why does it strike in solitary places or the sea; why is there no thunder when the sky is unclouded; how can he hurl the thunderbolt in so many places at one time; why does it strike the temples of the gods; why does it strike mountain tops so often?

423-1089. Natural explanations of hurricanes, rain, the rainbow, snow, hail, frost, earthquakes, volcanoes, the rising and flood of the Nile, poisonous vapors coming from the ground, odd phenomena, the magnet.

1089-1286. Natural explanation of the causes of disease. Description of the plague at Athens in 430-29 B.C. (imitating Thucydides' description—see pp. 153–154).

## STYLE AND SPIRIT OF LUCRETIUS

I. Eloquent, passionate sincerity; dynamic energy; intensity and enthusiasm; reforming missionary zeal; optimism.

II. Uncompromising realism; dogmatic, intolerant of opposing views; rationalism, mental independence.

III. But also pity, tenderness, melancholy, tragic pathos, and compassion for suffering.

IV. Colossal imagination; deep feeling; majestic grandeur and sublimity.

V. Love of nature; sense of the grandeur of nature.

VI. Moral fervor; satirist of the follies of men.

VII. Many dry sections; repetitions; rugged, archaic style.

## LUCRETIUS AS A SCIENTIST

I. Genuine scientific spirit and curiosity.

II. Many faulty and crude scientific theories.

III. His science was a means to an end, to establish a basis for Epicurean ethics.

IV. No experimentation; acute empirical observation together with inductive logic.

V. Not interested in scientific truth for its own sake; therefore accepts alternative explanations of the same phenomena, so long as no divine influence is involved.

VI. Excessive use of analogies.

VII. Father of anthropology.

## CHAPTER NINETEEN

# CATULLUS

◻

## GAIUS VALERIUS CATULLUS (ca. 84-54 B.C.)

I.  Born at Verona, in northern Italy; wealthy family.

II.  Introduced to fashionable society of Rome.

III.  Love affair with Clodia (the Lesbia of his poems), an emancipated woman of the decadent Roman aristocracy, married, older than himself, corrupt and faithless. The love affair passed from infatuation, passionate and tender love, to estrangement and doubt, to reconciliation, to agonizing disillusionment and final renunciation.

IV.  Member of staff of Memmius, governor of province of Bithynia, 57 B.C. Visited grave of his beloved brother in the Troad.

V.  Returned to Verona and summer estate at Sirmio, then to Rome; death at ca. 30 years of age.

## LYRICS (116)

I.  Greek influence: early Greek lyric poets and Alexandrian poets.

II.  Alexandrianism of longer lyrics (see above, pp. 245–246).

III.  Style of shorter lyrics: spontaneous and naïve simplicity and directness; sophisticated literary intellectualism; intense, passionate emotion (love, hate, sorrow, friendship); uninhibited, frank, and natural self-revelation; intensely personal, sensitive, sincere; tenderness, grace, elegance, wit, irony; "Tenderest of Roman poets nineteen hundred years ago" (Tennyson); "the Heine of Roman literature."

## Lesbia Cycle

No. 51. (Adaptation of one of Sappho's poems. See p. 48).
Lesbia, like a god or even more than divine is he who sits near you
and hears your lovely laughter. When I see you, I am speechless,
swept with waves of emotion, my ears ring, my eyes lose their sight.

No. 5. Let us love with abandon, Lesbia, disregarding all
gossip. Life is a short brilliant light; death is eternal night. Let us
kiss innumerable times, so that none may be able to count the
number of kisses and thus try to blight our happiness with the
evil eye.

No. 7. I shall be satisfied with as many kisses, Lesbia, as there
are sands in the desert, stars in the sky. Thus no malicious person
will be able to count the number or cast the evil eye upon us.

No. 3. I mourn the death of Lesbia's pet sparrow. It was a
lovable devoted creature. Now it has gone to cursed Hades, which
devours all pretty things. Lesbia's eyes are red with weeping over
her loss.

No. 43. What lack of taste and good manners to compare my
Lesbia's real beauty and refinement with the qualities of the provincial lady Ameana!

No. 8. I must be cold to Lesbia as she is to me. The days of our
beautiful mutual love are over, days of unsurpassed happiness and
brightness. I must suppress my anguish and misery and be firm.
Farewell, Lesbia! But you will be sorry, for no one will make love
to you. I must steel myself and be firm.

No. 72. You used to say, Lesbia, that I was your only love.
I loved you then with the pure love of a father for his son. But
now, though I know your true character, my passion grows. This
is not strange, for though I desire you more, I respect you less.

No. 75. I have been reduced to such a state, Lesbia, on account
of you, that I could no longer respect you, if you reformed, nor
cease to love you, even if you did the worst.

No. 85. I hate her and I love her. I don't understand it, but
I feel it, and am tortured.

No. 76. If one can take pleasure in recalling one's merits, kindnesses, fidelity, reverence for the gods, I deserve a better reward. My love was complete, but she was ungrateful and destroyed it. Why the torment, then? Cease to be miserable over this love, however difficult it is to abandon love so suddenly. This is the only way to regain peace of mind. Ye gods, have mercy on a pious man! Take this plague from me! I am completely listless and joyless. I do not want her love; I desire to be finally cured of this illness.

No. 11. (Furius and Aurelius have been sent to him by Lesbia to effect another reconciliation.) Furius and Aurelius, my friends, who would go to the ends of the earth with me, go to Lesbia with a little message. Tell her to go on living in her wanton profligacy. My love for her is completely dead, crushed like a flower by a passing plowshare.

## Trip to Bithynia and Return

No. 101. O my dear brother, I come over many lands and seas to thy grave to pay my last respects to your silent ashes. Take these funeral offerings, wet with your brother's tears. And forever, hail and farewell (*ave atque vale*)!

No. 46. Spring is here! It is time to say farewell to Bithynia and set out for the coastal cities of Asia and thence home. Farewell, dear friends!

No. 31. How happy I am to be safely back in beautiful Sirmio! There is no place like home after long travels and labors. Welcome, lovely Sirmio! Let there be universal rejoicing and laughter now that I am home.

## Occasional Poems

No. 9. Welcome home from Spain, Veranius, my dearest friend! What joy to see you, talk with you about where you have been, kiss you! I am the happiest man in the world!

No. 13. Fabullus, come to dinner at my house, but bring your own food, a pretty girl and wit, if you want a good time. For my purse is full of cobwebs. I shall give you my affection, and a rare exquisite perfume belonging to Lesbia. When you smell it, you will pray to become all nose.

No. 45. Love idyl of Acme and Septimius. Septimius expresses his undying, unchanging love for Acme. Love sneezes a good omen. Acme kisses his eyes and vows her love. Love sneezes again. With such good omens they love each other dearly, completely devoted. They are the happiest and most blessed mortals.

No. 49. Most eloquent of the Romans, Cicero, I thank you, I who am the worst of poets as you are the best of lawyers.

No. 22. Suffenus is a charming and witty person, but he is one of the worst of poets. He writes reams of the absurd stuff and is very proud of it. He is as clumsy in writing as he is delightful in talk. Yet he delights in writing and is very conceited about his work. We are all like Suffenus in some ways: we cannot see our own faults.

No. 12. O napkin thief, this is no joke; it is bad manners and bad taste. If you don't want to be attacked by my verses, send back my napkin, which has a sentimental value to me. It was sent to me from Spain by dear friends.

No. 23. Arrius had the nasty habit of adding "h" to words beginning with vowels; it was probably an inherited trait. What a pleasure when he left Rome for Syria. But suddenly a message came that since Arrius crossed the Ionian Sea its name has been changed to "Hionian."

## CHAPTER TWENTY

# FOUNDATION OF ROMAN EMPIRE— AUGUSTUS

## 30 B.C.-14 A.D.

▣

## PRINCIPATE OF CAESAR AUGUSTUS

I.    After the defeat of Antony and Cleopatra at the Battle of Actium and their subsequent suicides in Egypt, Octavian, Julius Caesar's grandnephew and adopted son, was sole ruler of the Roman world.

II.    In 27 B.C. he proclaimed the "Restoration of the Republic," a political compromise between the absolute military leader, supported by the army and the business interests, and the still powerful members of the Senatorial Order; the hollow shell of the old Republic was restored, with its annually elected magistrates, Senate, and Popular Assemblies.

III.    But within the framework of the "Restored Republic" Augustus became *de facto* emperor, possessing control over civil affairs through his tribunician power and over the armies, provinces and foreign affairs through his proconsular power; he was also senior senator and *pontifex maximus* (head of the state religion). He was thus far more powerful than the early kings of Rome; but he preferred to be called by the unofficial title *princeps* (chief).

## POLICIES OF AUGUSTUS

I.    *Pax Romana* (Roman Peace) enforced through the

Roman armies and the collaboration of local aristocracies throughout the empire.

II.     Imperial civil service, a paid bureaucracy drawing on all classes of the population.

III.    Economic stabilization of the empire.

IV.     Reform of provincial administration; improved conditions; lessening and regularization of exploitation.

V.      Defense of natural boundaries of empire, Rhine and Danube Rivers in the north, Euphrates River in the east.

VI.     Standing professional army of 300,000 men, loyal to the emperor; establishment of Praetorian Guard, imperial bodyguard of 9,000 picked soldiers.

VII.    Attempt to revive the old Roman religion; establishment of emperor worship.

VIII.   Attempt to limit the rampant individualism of the dying Republic by social and moral reforms, by which he hoped to raise the declining birth rate, lessen immorality and luxury; back-to-the-land movement.

IX.     Beautification of Rome, the capital of the empire.

X.      Imperial patronage of literature.

## GOLDEN AGE OF ROMAN LITERATURE— AUGUSTAN PERIOD

I.      Imperial censorship; restricted freedom of expression.

II.     Literary patronage; literature in the service of the new order of Augustus; Maecenas, Augustus' friend, the great literary patron of the period. Writers were brought into the literary circle of Maecenas, guaranteed security, and urged to employ their talents in support of the new regime.

III.    Great stress on perfection of form.

IV.     Principal themes of Augustan literature: peace; the glories of Rome's heroic past; nationalism and imperial mission of Rome and Italy; praise of the beauties of Rome and Italy; praise of Augustus and the imperial family; glorification of agriculture;

stress on old Roman virtues (devotion to state, military courage, religious devotion, purity in morals); revival of religion and morals.

V. Tendency to idealize the pre-civil war past of Rome and the Augustan Age.

VI. Decline in oratory and objective history; abandonment of socio-political scope of pre-Augustan literature.

## CHAPTER TWENTY-ONE

# VERGIL

▣

## PUBLIUS VERGILIUS MARO (70-19 B.C.)

I.   Born in the village of Andes, near Mantua, in northern Italy; moderately well-to-do family.

II.   Educated in the towns of northern Italy, Rome, and Naples, where he came under the influence of Epicureanism.

III.   In the political disorders attending the Battle of Philippi in 42 B.C. his estate near Andes was confiscated, but it was subsequently restored through the intervention of Maecenas.

IV.   Becomes member of the literary circle of Maecenas; abandons most of his Epicurean views.

V.   Falls mortally ill while on visit to Greece for· purpose of completing the *Aeneid*; buried at Naples.

VI.   Orders *Aeneid* destroyed in his will, but it is published in unfinished state at the direction of Augustus.

## WORKS OF VERGIL

Early Minor Poems
*Eclogues* (*Bucolics*)
*Georgics*
*Aeneid*

## AENEID

## LITERARY INFLUENCES ON AENEID

I.   Homer's *Iliad* and *Odyssey*.

   A.   Books I-VI (wanderings of Aeneas) from *Odyssey*.

B. Books VII-XII (battles of Aeneas in Italy) from *Iliad*.

C. Borrowing of language, phrases, lines, entire episodes.

D. Some examples of borrowing from *Odyssey*: storm and shipwreck; hero directed to royal palace by Venus (Nausicaa), graciously entertained by Dido (Alcinous), relates story of his wanderings at banquet, remains with Dido (Calypso), visits Hades; he is directed to Hades by the Sibyl (Circe); in Hades Palinurus (Elpenor) asks to be buried, angry Dido (Ajax) refuses to talk with him, Deiphobus (Agamemnon) tells how he was murdered through the connivance of his wife, Anchises (Teiresias) predicts the future.

E. Some examples of borrowings from *Iliad*: battle scenes, attack on the ships, catalogues of troops and chiefs, armor of Aeneas (Achilles) made by Vulcan (Hephaestus), funeral games for Anchises (Patroclus), broken treaty, midnight reconnoitering by Nisus and Euryalus (Diomedes and Odysseus), unsuccessful embassy to Diomedes (Achilles), quarrel of Turnus and Drances (Agamemnon and Achilles), slaying of Pallas by Turnus (Patroclus by Hector), duel at end between Aeneas and Turnus (Achilles and Hector).

II. Other early Greek epics (Cyclic Epics).

III. Greek tragedy, especially Euripides' plays, *Trojan Women, Hecuba, Hippolytus, Medea*.

IV. Alexandrian poets, especially Apollonius of Rhodes, author of the romantic epic, *Argonautica*.

V. Roman poets, especially Ennius, Catullus, Lucretius.

VI. It must be remembered, however, that Vergil is a creative imitator, and that he refashioned and unified all this borrowed material and combined it with original ideas to create a great Roman epic poem.

## COMPARISON OF "ARTIFICIAL" EPIC (AENEID) WITH "NATURAL" EPIC (ILIAD; ODYSSEY)

| *Early Oral Epic* | *Later Written Epic* |
| --- | --- |
| 1. Recited to listening audience | 1. Read by educated persons |

2. Repetitions
3. Simple and direct

4. Rapid, diffuse

5. Objective narrative; extrovert

6. Individualism; sacrifices of hero for personal glory; emphasis on physical prowess

7. Emphasis on past
8. Purpose: pleasure of narrative

9. No romantic love
10. Some humor

2. Variation
3. Complex, learned, importance of details

4. Compact, economy of means

5. Subjective, allusive, suggestive, symbolical; introspective, philosophical

6. Subordination of hero to higher end; sacrifices for social ideal; emphasis on moral stature of hero

7. Past used to explain present
8. Purpose: didactic and moral, but also pleasure of narrative

9. Romantic love
10. Uniformly serious

## BACKGROUND OF AENEID

After the fall of Troy Aeneas, Priam's son-in-law and second in command to Hector, became the acknowledged leader of the surviving Trojans. A divine mission was imposed upon him to build a new city destined by fate. Not knowing where the promised land was, but constantly guided by the hand of fate, the Trojans set out under Aeneas' leadership in 21 ships to find the destined new home. Aeneas was accompanied by his father, Anchises, and his son, Ascanius, whom he had rescued from burning Troy. They wandered through the Mediterranean for seven years until they arrived on the coast of western Sicily. Here Anchises died. The *Aeneid* begins at the moment the Trojans are about to sail north from Sicily to Italy.

## IMPORTANT PLACES

Alba Longa. Town in Alban Hills near Rome, traditionally founded by Ascanius.

Carthage. Phoenician seaport in North Africa; kingdom of Dido.

Cumae. Greek colony, north of Naples, where Aeneas landed and consulted the Sibyl.

Hades. Also called Erebus, Orcus. The underworld, with its rivers and divisions.

Italy. Also called Ausonia, Hesperia.

Latium. Plain of west central Italy, inhabited by the Latins.

Laurentum. Capital of the kingdom of Latinus in Latium.

Lavinium. Mythical city built by Aeneas in Latium.

Mt. Olympus. Supposed home of the gods in northern Greece.

Pallanteum. Mythical city of King Evander on the site of Rome.

Rome. City on the River Tiber, traditionally founded by Romulus.

Sicily. Large island S. W. of Italy.

Tiber. River in northern Latium.

Troy. Also called Ilium, Dardania, Pergama, Teucria. (See p. 10).

## PEOPLES

Etruscans (Tuscans, Tyrrhenians). People living in the plain north of Latium.

Greeks. Also called Achaeans, Argives, Danaans, Pelasgians.

Latins. Inhabitants of Latium.

Phoenicians (Carthaginians). Sea-faring people from eastern Mediterranean; inhabitants of Carthage.

Rutulians. A tribe of the Latins.

Trojans. Also called Aeneadae, Teucrians.

## PRINCIPAL CHARACTERS OF THE AENEID

Acestes. King of western Sicily.

Achates. Armor-bearer and faithful attendant of Aeneas.

Aeneas. Son of Venus and Anchises; King of the Trojans.

Amata. Queen of the Latins; wife of King Latinus.

Anchises. Aged father of Aeneas.

Anna. Devoted sister of Dido.

Ascanius (Iulus). Young son of Aeneas and Creusa.

Camilla. Warrior-maid; Volscian ally of Turnus.

Creusa. Wife of Aeneas; daughter of Priam.

Dido (Elissa). Daughter of Belus, Phoenician king; Queen of Carthage.

Evander. Greek prince, King of Pallanteum on the Tiber; father of Pallas.

Euryalus. Courageous Trojan youth, friend of Nisus.

Hector. See p. 10.

Hecuba. See p. 10.

Helen. See p. 10.

Laocoön. Trojan priest of Apollo and Neptune.

Latinus. Weak-willed King of the Latins.

Lausus. Son of Mezentius, Etruscan chief.

Lavinia. Daughter of Latinus and Amata; Latin princess destined to marry Aeneas, but bethrothed to Turnus.

Mezentius. Exiled Etruscan tyrant, ally of Turnus.

Nisus. Courageous Trojan youth, friend of Euryalus.

Pallas. Young son of Evander.

Priam. See p. 10.

Romulus (Quirinus). Descendant of Aeneas; son of Mars; traditional founder and first king of Rome.

Sibyl (Deiphobe). Prophetess; priestess of Apollo at Cumae.

Sinon. Greek spy.

Sychaeus. Prince of Tyre; murdered husband of Dido.

Turnus. Chief of the Rutulians.

**GODS (see pp. 329–331).**

Apollo

Cupid

Diana

Fates

Iris

Mercury

Minerva

Neptune

Vulcan
Venus
Juno
Jupiter
Lares and
    Penates
Mars (Mavors)

### Chronology of the Aeneid
### (*ca. 3 months*)

Books  I-IV  ........................ca. 45 days
Books V-VI  ........................  23 days
Book VII  ........................  4 days
Books VIII-IX  ....................  4 days
Book X  ............................  1 day
Book  XI  ........................  13 days
Book XII  ............................  1 day

## SUMMARY
## Book I.

A. Prologue. Central theme—the fulfillment of destiny; the trials and tribulations of Trojan Aeneas, driven by fate and Juno's anger, his wanderings from Troy, and his battles in Italy until he founded a city (Lavinium), becoming the ancestor of the Latins and the Romans. Invocation to the Muse. Why did Juno in her anger cause so much suffering for a hero distinguished for his devotion to duty?

B. Rich and powerful Carthage, of Phoenician origin, was Juno's favorite city, and it was her fond hope to make it mistress of the world. But she had heard of the destined rise of a new people, from Trojan origin, which would in the future destroy Carthage. There were other reasons for her hatred of the Trojans: the judgment of Paris, the descent of the Trojans from an illegitimate son of Jupiter, the displacement of Hebe by the Trojan boy Ganymede as cupbearer of the gods. Therefore, she drove the remnants of the Trojan people over the seas for many years, keeping them from their fated new home in Latium.

C. As the 21 Trojan ships sail from Sicily, Juno, eternally angry and frustrated, and jealous of her power, plots a new disaster to keep them from Italy. She goes to Aeolus, King of the winds, and bribes him to cause a furious storm. As the storm rages, Aeneas, terrified, wishes he had died fighting for Troy. The Trojan ships are scattered; one is sunk. At the height of the storm Neptune rises from the deep and, angry because his waters have been disturbed, orders the winds to return to Aeolus. They meekly obey his superior power, and the storm subsides. Aeneas anchors with seven ships in a quiet harbor on the coast of Africa. As the weary Trojans prepare food, Aeneas, accompanied by the faithful Achates, slays seven deer, and distributes meat and wine equitably among his people. Then he cheers them up, reminding them of what they have already been through, and the glorious future that lies in store for them, suppressing his own anxiety and discouragement.

D. Meanwhile, Venus, Aeneas' mother, approaches Jupiter on Mt. Olympus, and tearfully berates him for the suffering of the Trojans and of her son Aeneas to whom Italy and great empire had been promised by fate. Benignly Jupiter reassures her, prophesying the founding of Lavinium by Aeneas, the victorious war he will fight in Italy, the building of Alba Longa by Ascanius, the birth of the twins Romulus and Remus from Mars and how they will be suckled by a she-wolf, the building of Rome, the world empire of the Romans, the conquest of Greece by the Romans, and finally the coming of Augustus, who will bring peace to the earth. He then sends Mercury to Carthage to soften the hearts of Dido and her people toward the shipwrecked Trojans.

E. The next morning Aeneas, accompanied by Achates, sets out to reconnoiter. On his way he is met by Venus in disguise as a huntress, who informs him where he is, and recounts Dido's past

**287**

—her happy marriage to Sychaeus in the Phoenician city Tyre, the cruel murder of her husband by her greedy and tyrannical brother Pygmalion, her oath to remain faithful to the memory of Sychaeus, her flight from Tyre with other Tyrians, the building of the new city Carthage. As she predicts the safety of his lost ships, he realizes her identity. Aeneas then proceeds to Carthage, miraculously made invisible by Venus, and mingling with the inhabitants gazes with envy at the growing city which is being industriously built in a magnificent style by the people. He enters a temple and sees, with deep melancholy, paintings on the walls depicting scenes from the Trojan War.

F. Queen Dido arrives at the temple to dispense justice. Suddenly Aeneas is amazed and overjoyed to see the captains of his lost ships, who have been arrested by the Carthaginians, come in to beg aid from Dido for their journey to Italy. Dido graciously apologizes for their treatment by the sentries, expresses admiration for the Trojans, and promises unstinting aid, even welcoming them to settle in Carthage permanently. Completely reassured, Aeneas suddenly becomes visible, made unusually handsome by Venus. He first addresses Dido, thanking her for her kindness and promising eternal gratitude, and then greets his friends. Dido, herself a refugee who has learned from her own misfortune to pity others, is generous with her hospitality to the shipwrecked Trojans. A banquet is ordered in their honor. Aeneas, good father that he is, sends for his son Ascanius. But Venus substitutes Cupid in disguise for the boy, so that she may frustrate any of Juno's schemes against the Trojans by causing Dido to fall in love with Aeneas. At the banquet Dido, already attracted to Aeneas, fondles Cupid, imagining him to be Ascanius, and is inflamed with overmastering love for Aeneas. She prolongs the banquet, seeking to be with Aeneas, by asking him many detailed questions about incidents in the Trojan War. Finally, she asks him to tell the entire story of the fall of Troy and of his seven years' wanderings.

## Book II—Aeneas' Story

A. Aeneas hesitates to relate the story of the fall of Troy because of the sadness of the event and the lateness of the hour, but he complies with Dido's request. After ten years of unsuccessful war, the Greeks built a huge wooden horse, spreading the rumor that it was an offering to Athena for their safe return to Greece. They then filled the horse with picked men and pretended to sail away. The Trojans were overjoyed at the departure of the Greeks. Opinions were divided as to what to do with the horse; some urged that it be dragged into the city, others that it be destroyed. At this point Laocoön harangued them, reminding them of Greek treachery and warning them to fear the Greeks bearing gifts. He then hurled a spear into the horse.

B. But at this very moment Trojan shepherds dragged in a Greek who had surrendered to them. This was Sinon, who had been left behind for the sole purpose of convincing the Trojans to drag the horse into the city. By clever acting he played upon the Trojans' sympathies and pity, telling them a well-rehearsed tale of his dissatisfaction with the Greek leaders and how he had escaped when they were about to offer him up as a sacrificial victim. When he was questioned about the horse, he pretended that he was revealing a Greek secret by telling the Trojans its purpose. It was built, he said, to ensure their safe return to Greece, and was made large enough to prevent its being taken into the city through the gates of Troy. If the Trojans should drag it into their city, it would harm the Greeks and protect Troy, and ensure ultimate revenge against Greece. The Trojans were completely convinced by Sinon's lies, and their conviction was reinforced by a horrible occurrence. Two huge serpents appeared from the sea, seized and crushed to death Laocoön and his two sons.

C. The Trojans tore down the walls and dragged the horse into the city, despite unfavorable omens and the warnings of Cassandra. During the night, Sinon released the Greeks concealed in the horse. and the others, who had returned in their ships, entered

**289**

the city. In his sleep Aeneas saw a vision of Hector, who told him to flee the doomed city and find a new home for the gods and people of Troy. He awakened to find the city in flames, and rushed to arm himself, ready to die in battle, despite the dream and the futility of the sacrifice. He gathered a group of warriors, and they battled fiercely, performing mighty deeds of valor and killing many Greeks, though without hope, for the city was obviously falling. The slaughter was appalling. Aeneas survived the exploit, and then rushed to try to save Priam's palace. Mounting to the roof of the palace, he saw Achilles' son, Pyrrhus, break into the palace, where the trembling women of the royal family were huddled. The aged King Priam donned his armor to defend the palace, but Hecuba dissuaded him, and forced him to seek asylum at an altar with the women. But when Pyrrhus slew one of his fleeing sons before his own eyes, the old man rebuked him sharply and weakly hurled a spear at him. At this Pyrrhus brutally slew Priam at the very altar.

D. Horrified, Aeneas remembered his own father, his wife Creusa, and his son Ascanius. He found himself completely alone. Suddenly he spied Helen hiding in a small temple, in fear of both the Trojans and the anger of her former husband, Menelaus. In fury, Aeneas decided to kill her as the cause of their woes, to avenge the deaths of his people. But suddenly his mother Venus appeared and deterred him from the deed by revealing the awesome scene of the gods assisting in the destruction of the city. She urged him to rescue his own family. He rushed to his father's house, but the aged Anchises resolutely refused to leave, fearing that he would be a burden because of his advanced age. He urged Aeneas to take the others out of the city, but rather than abandon his father, Aeneas decided to remain and die. As he prepared for battle, Creusa held up little Ascanius and asked to go forth with him to die. But suddenly a flame appeared on little Ascanius' head, and Anchises joyfully prayed to Jupiter for another omen. Thunder and a falling star convinced him. Anchises was now prepared to go.

E. Taking his father, who held the little images of the gods (Lares and Penates) in his hands, on his back and his son by the hand, Aeneas safely led them out of the city. But Creusa, who followed behind, was lost. In despair he left his father and son in a safe place and rushed back into danger to find her, calling her name again and again. Suddenly the ghost of Creusa appeared to him. She told him that it was fated for her to die at Troy, prophesied his future wanderings and his marriage to an Italian princess. Saddened, he returned to Anchises and Ascanius, only to find a large group of Trojans prepared to follow him into exile. Lifting up his father on his back, he led them to nearby Mt. Ida.

## Book III—Aeneas' Story (continued)

A. The surviving Trojans, now called Aeneadae (followers of Aeneas), sailed the following summer to find a new home, guided by fate. They landed in Thrace, and began to build a city. But presently they found the grave of Priam's son, Polydorus, whom the king of Thrace had recently killed for his wealth. And so they left the land hastily, and sailed thence to Delos, where they consulted the oracle of Apollo for advice as to where to establish their new home. When they were told to search for the land of their earliest ancestors, Anchises interpreted this to mean the Island of Crete. And so they sailed joyfully through the Cyclades Islands to Crete. Here they built another city, but presently a plague and famine overtook them. And one night the sacred images of the Trojan gods appeared to Aeneas in a vision and revealed that Crete was not the destined land meant by Apollo, but rather the western land, Hesperia (Italy). Anchises confirmed that one of the earliest Trojan ancestors, Dardanus, came from Italy.

B. And so they sailed again, driven by a storm to the Strophades, small islands west of the Peloponnesus. Here they landed to eat, but the inhabitants, the half-woman, half-bird creatures called Harpies, swooped down on their food, defiling everything.

**291**

They fought them off, and were cursed by their leader Celaeno. Hastily they left, sailing up the coast of Greece, and, passing Ithaca and other islands, reached Actium. Thence they sailed north to Buthrotum in Epirus, where to his surprise Aeneas found Priam's son Helenus ruling the region with Andromache, dead Hector's wife, as his spouse. After a tearful and loving reunion, he learned how this came about. Helenus, who was a prophet, gave him detailed instructions on how to proceed to the destined land in Italy, telling him what to avoid and where to land.

C. Thence they proceeded northwest, and soon sighted the S. E. coast of Italy, but since they had been warned by Helenus to land on the west coast and avoid the straits of Messina, where they would be endangered by Scylla and Charybdis, they continued sailing west. They finally reached Sicily where they rested at the foot of Mt. Aetna, terrified by the rumblings of the volcano. Here they discovered a follower of Odysseus, Achaemenides, who had escaped from the cave of the Cyclops Polyphemus. At his pitiful pleading that they not leave him at the mercy of the Cyclops, they took him along with them. Catching sight of Polyphemus and the other Cyclopes, they fled, hugging the shore of Italy, until they reached Drepanum in W. Sicily. Here they were kindly received by King Acestes, and here Anchises died. Thus Aeneas concluded his story.

## Book IV.

A. Dido, now hopelessly in love with Aeneas, confides her feelings to her sister Anna. She is, however, resolved to abide by her oath to her dead husband, Sychaeus, and prays that she may die if she violates it. But Anna convinces her by many arguments to give in to her love for Aeneas. After this her love becomes an all-consuming passion, and she completely neglects her duties as queen of Carthage. After Juno and Venus agree to their union, each for her own reasons, the Carthaginian and Trojan leaders go hunting in the mountains. Juno causes a storm, and Dido and

Aeneas come alone to a cave, where the union is consummated, Now Dido abandons all modesty and openly flaunts her love for Aeneas.

B. But rumor of their affair spreads far and wide, and ultimately reaches the ears of Jupiter himself. He promptly despatches Mercury to Aeneas to remind him of his high destiny and to order him to depart for Italy. Mercury finds Aeneas, not only forgetful of his mission, but even supervising the building of Carthage. Aeneas is quickly brought back to his sense of duty by Jupiter's message, and prepares to depart, ordering the captains of the ships to prepare for departure in secret. He is at a loss, however, how to break the news to Dido. But she, having discovered the secret plans, comes to him in a frenzied passion and reproaches him bitterly for abandoning her, entreating him to change his plans or postpone them, and threatening suicide. Aeneas, suppressing his emotions, admits his indebtedness to her but insists that he never intended to marry her, and that duty calls him to Italy against his will. Bereft of reason, she raves, assails him for ingratitude, swears vengeance, and finally faints.

C. Aeneas, struggling with the conflict between duty and his emotions, goes to supervise the preparations for departure. Meanwhile, Dido, distraught, sends Anna to him with repeated messages bidding him to stay, but to no avail. Finally, insane with hopelessness, she resolves to die. She orders a funeral pyre built on which, she pretends, she is going to perform a magic ceremony to solve her problems, by burning an image of Aeneas and all that reminds her of Aeneas. Unable to sleep, she is remorseful over the violation of her oath to her husband. Aeneas, meanwhile, is warned again in a dream by Mercury to depart at once. He gives the order for the ships to sail. At dawn, when Dido sees the Trojan ships on the sea, she raves insanely, and then utters a curse on Aeneas, praying that an avenger may arise from her people (Hannibal is meant), and that their descendants may be eternally at war with one another. Then she rushes out, climbs the pyre, and plunges a sword into herself. As Anna laments over her sister Dido, who still lingers, Juno takes pity on her, sending Iris to cut off a lock from her head and release her soul.

**Book V.**

A. Aeneas on the high seas catches sight of the fire from Dido's funeral pyre and surmises what has happened. A storm drives the Trojans again to Sicily, where they are once more graciously received by King Acestes. Here Aeneas proclaims a festival to commemorate the first anniversary of the death of his father Anchises. Proper sacrifices are made at his tomb. Then, nine days later, athletic contests are held to round out the event, with gifts for all and prizes and wreaths for the victors. The events are a galley race, won by Cloanthus; foot race, won by Euryalus with the aid of his friend Nisus; boxing contest, won by the aged Sicilian Entellus; archery contest, won by Acestes; cavalry display of young boys, headed by Ascanius.

B. Suddenly news is brought that the Trojan ships are burning. (Juno had sent Iris in disguise as a Trojan woman to stir up discontent among the women, who, after seven years, are tired of wandering. She agitated them, suggesting that they remain in Sicily, and they set fire to the ships.) The men rush down to the shore, but the ships are beyond human aid. Aeneas immediately prays for aid to Jupiter, who sends a rainstorm. All the ships are saved but four.

C. Disheartened, Aeneas takes stock of the situation. His father Anchises appears to him in a dream, advises him, and bids him come to the Elysian Fields in Hades to see him. Aeneas then decides to leave a colony of Trojans in Sicily, and take along to Italy only the most hardy. After the colony is well established, the remainder set sail again. Venus, meanwhile, fearing Juno, begs Neptune not to hamper the voyage of the Trojans. He consents, but demands the life of one Trojan. Palinurus, Aeneas' pilot, falls asleep at the helm and falls overboard.

**Book VI.**

A. The Trojans reach Cumae, and disembark joyfully, in Italy at last. But Aeneas at once climbs the hill to Apollo's temple to consult the Sibyl, Deiphobe, in her cave. At his request she predicts his future in Italy—fierce war with the inhabitants, a sturdy leader to oppose him, great hardships. Nothing daunted, he asks to be guided to the underworld to see Anchises. She tells him of the difficulties, and that he will be permitted to descend if he can find and pluck a golden bough hidden in a nearby forest. He first gives proper burial to his comrade Misenus, and then goes to seek the golden bough, which he brings back to the Sibyl.

B. After proper sacrifices, Aeneas is guided by the Sibyl and enters the underworld, startled by many horrible creatures. The two reach the river Acheron, where Aeneas sees the ferryman Charon, and a numerous throng of souls belonging to unburied persons, which may not cross for a hundred years. Among these he sees the pilot Palinurus who begs for and is promised decent burial, the Sibyl assuring him that this will be done in due time. Charon is at first insolent to Aeneas, but when he sees the golden bough he readily grants them passage on his boat, and they are ferried across. On landing after crossing the Styx they see Cerberus, whom the Sibyl drugs so that they may pass.

C. When they enter the realm of Hades they see the sights of the underworld: first the souls of those who died in infancy, of those who died falsely accused, and of suicides. Next those who died of unrequited love, among them Phaedra. Here he sees too the soul of Dido, and weeping with pity begs forgiveness. But she turns away without speaking to him, and rejoins the soul of her husband Sychaeus. Next he comes to the abode of famous warriors of the past, and sees a great number of them. Among these he sees Priam's son Deiphobus, who tells him how he was treacherously murdered on the night of the fall of Troy by Menelaus with the connivance of Helen, his wife after Paris' death. Aeneas and the Sibyl then come to the gate of Tartarus. The Sibyl describes the region to him and the punishments assigned to the sinful there, mentioning many famous sinners and their punishments.

D. Then they proceed to the Elysian Fields, where the blessed dwell in beauteous surroundings. Aeneas is directed to Anchises, who greets him with deep affection. Anchises explains to Aeneas the presence of innumerable souls waiting at the river Lethe. They are awaiting reincarnation after being purged of their sins over a period of 1,000 years. Then, mounting a hill, he reveals to Aeneas the souls of his descendants and the destiny of his people: outstanding among these are his Italian-born son by Lavinia, Silvius, Romulus, the founder of Rome, the other great kings of Rome, the future greatness of Rome, her conquests, and finally Augustus, who will rule a great empire. Other peoples, says Anchises, will be greater artists, orators, scientists; the Roman destiny will be to rule the world. He points out too the soul of Marcellus (Augustus' first son-in-law, who died while the *Aeneid* was being written). Finally, having instructed Aeneas about his duties in Italy, he escorts Aeneas and the Sibyl out of Hades.

## Book VII.

Thence the Trojans sail north along the coast of Italy, passing Circe's realm. They enter the mouth of the river Tiber. Second Invocation to the Muse. The coming battles of the Trojans and the Italians. Aged King Latinus has an only daughter, Lavinia. Queen Amata had offered her in marriage to her favorite, Turnus, prince of the Rutulians. But there were many omens warning against the marriage. An oracle, morever, predicted to Latinus that Lavinia was fated to marry a foreign prince.

B. Aeneas and the Trojans land on the shore of the Tiber River, where the curse of the happy Celaeno is humorously fulfilled. Aeneas is convinced that they have now reached the fated spot. He despatches envoys to King Latinus, while he begins to plan the building of the new city. The Trojan envoys are graciously received by Latinus, who hears their purpose and welcomes them to Italy. Recalling the oracle, he immediately offers Lavinia's hand to Aeneas in marriage.

C. Juno, in anger and frustration, decides to delay the success of Aeneas' undertaking by causing a war between the Trojans and Latins. She unleashes the horrible fury Allecto from Hades, and sends her to stir up strife. Allecto goes first to Queen Amata and inflames her with enmity toward the marriage of Lavinia and Aeneas, from which she is unable to dissuade Latinus. Next Allecto visits Turnus and inspires him with fury for war. Turnus begins to mobilize his people. Finally Allecto stirs up animosity on the part of Latinus' people against the Trojans. The first blood is shed when the Trojans rescue Ascanius from the fury of the Latins. All clamor for war with the Trojans—the Latins, Turnus and the Rutulians, and Amata and her followers. Latinus, unable to deter them, relinquishes his royal command. When Latinus refuses to declare war, Juno herself opens the dread gates of the temple of Janus, symbolizing the beginning of war. Preparations begin.

D. Invocation to the Muse. Catalogue of the Italian forces, their leaders and places of habitation, among them Mezentius the Etruscan tyrant, Turnus, and the warrior-maid, Camilla.

## Book VIII.

A. As the Italians mobilize for war, Turnus sends an envoy to secure aid from Diomedes who had settled in S. Italy. Aeneas is troubled, but in a dream he sees the god of the Tiber River, who advises him to seek an alliance with the Greek king Evander, ruling at Pallanteum (on the site of future Rome). Aeneas travels up the Tiber and is welcomed by King Evander and his son Pallas. He points out that they are both at war with the Italians. An alliance and aid are promised by Evander, who explains to him the origin of the annual sacrifice to Hercules which he is engaged in celebrating. Hercules had slain the giant Cacus nearby. Evander then points out the places of interest in his city (the future Rome).

B.  Meanwhile Venus goes to her husband Vulcan, and with a forced show of affection obtains from him a promise that he will make a suit of armor for Aeneas. He commences the work.

C.  Evander gives Aeneas whatever forces he can spare, led by his son Pallas, but he advises him to seek aid from the Etruscans, who had recently overthrown the tyrant Mezentius now living in refuge with Turnus. Aeneas and Pallas take leave of Evander and reach Etruria. Here Venus brings Aeneas the completed set of armor, including a wondrous shield, decorated with scenes from the future history of Rome, e.g., Romulus and Remus nursed by the she-wolf; the seizure of the Sabine women; the siege of Rome by Lars Porsenna; the saving of the Capitol from the Gauls; Catiline's punishment; the Battle of Actium; the triumphs of Augustus.

## Book IX.

A.  Juno sends Iris to urge Turnus to attack the camp of the Trojans in the absence of Aeneas. Acting under standing orders, the Trojans assume the defensive, barring themselves in the camp. Exasperated, Turnus prepares to fire the ships. But the ships are miraculously turned into nymphs, as Jupiter had predicted, and plunge into the water. Believing that the Trojans are now cut off from escape, Turnus and the Rutulians bivouac on the plain before the camp during the night.

B.  Sentries are posted by the Trojans. The friends Nisus and Euryalus boldly agree to reconnoiter to find Aeneas. They set forth their purpose at a council of the chiefs, and their courage is applauded. All are moved to tears by the devotion and charm of the two youths. They set out in the darkness, and falling upon the sleeping enemy, slay many of them. As they proceed on their journey, they are spied by a troop of horsemen. They flee to the woods for protection, but Euryalus loses his way. Nisus retraces his steps, to find Euryalus captured. From his hiding place Nisus slays two of the enemy with his spears. In revenge the leader slays Euryalus. Nisus then rushes forth from his place of concealment, fights his way to the leader, kills him, and is slain in turn. Thus bravely died the friends Nisus and Euryalus.

C. At dawn the Rutulians expose the heads of Nisus and Euryalus to the Trojans. There follows heart-rending lamentation by the Trojans, especially by the mother of young Euryalus. The Rutulians and their allies then attack the camp with fire, seeking to break into the fortifications. Many Trojans perish. The boy Ascanius slays with an arrow Turnus' brother-in-law, who has taunted the Trojans with cowardice. But Apollo appears in disguise to caution him to abstain from further fighting. Some Trojans now daringly open the gates to meet the Rutulians. Horrible slaughter ensues as the Rutulians rush in. As Mars inspires the Rutulians with renewed courage, the Trojans lose heart. Pandarus shuts the gates, locking Turnus inside. After slaying mighty Pandarus, Turnus flings himself like a lion at bay at the Trojans. They finally surround him, but he escapes death by flinging himself from the battlements into the Tiber.

**Book X.**

A. Jupiter summons the gods in council on Mt. Olympus and bids them put an end to their strife over the Trojans and the Latins. Venus pleads for the Trojans, complaining of the victories of Turnus, and detailing the long suffering of the Trojans. Juno, with bitterness and scorn, assails the Trojans and Venus' aid. Zeus, at a loss, proclaims that fate, not the quarreling gods, will decide the issue.

B. As the Rutulians attack the camp again, the Trojans defend themselves from the battlements. Meanwhile, Aeneas, having successfully concluded an alliance with the Etruscans, is returning to the rescue with 30 ships, including a force of Etruscan warriors. Catalogue of Etruscan ships.

Sailing in the moonlight Aeneas is accosted by the new nymphs, recently his ships, who reveal to him the danger to the

**299**

Trojans in the camp. The following morning he orders his forces to be ready for instant action. When the Trojans in the camp catch sight of Aeneas approaching, they are cheered. Turnus and his men prepare to prevent a landing, but the Trojans disembark speedily. Turnus then orders an immediate assault on the reinforcements. A fierce, indecisive conflict ensues.

C. Evander's son Pallas rallies his retreating men with a vigorous speech. He himself sets an example by performing deeds of heroism, slaying many of the foe. On the other side, Lausus, Mezentius' son, leads the opposing forces. As the battle sways back and forth, Turnus rushes to the aid of Lausus and the Latins. His men retire as Turnus advances to face Pallas, whom he slays with his spear. Turnus removes Pallas' sword-belt, and the boy's comrades remove his body. When news of Pallas' death reaches Aeneas, he furiously fights his way toward Turnus, mercilessly and brutally slaying all in his path. As Ascanius and the Trojans break out of the camp and Turnus is hemmed in on two fronts, Juno is permitted by Jupiter to rescue Turnus and delay his death. Juno descends at once and creates a phantom in the shape of Aeneas, which Turnus pursues until he comes on a ship on the shore. At once the ship bears him off miraculously, as Turnus despairs of his reputation.

D. Mezentius slays many of the Trojans and their allies, but the battle is still indecisive. Aeneas comes out to face him, and wounds him. But he is rescued by the aid of his son, Lausus. Aeneas meets and slays the young Lausus, pitying him. Mezentius laments his son's death, and though wounded returns on horseback to meet Aeneas. He is rapidly unhorsed and slain by Aeneas, but before dying requests decent burial for himself and Lausus.

## Book XI.

A. The victorious Aeneas erects a military trophy with Mezentius' arms, and urges his men to prepare to march on Laurentum, the stronghold of the Latins. There is great mourning over Pallas, as Aeneas sends his body, escorted by 1,000 men, to his father Evander. An embassy arrives from Laurentum, and a truce for twelve days is declared for burial of the dead and consideration of peace. Pallas' body is brought in mourning to his father Evander, who asks for vengeance upon Turnus. The Trojans and Latins bury their dead with the customary ceremonies.

B. The Latins are disunited on the issue of continuing the war, many blaming Turnus for their woes. Meanwhile, to add to their cup of woe, the envoys sent to Diomedes return with his refusal to join them and his advice to sue for peace from Aeneas. At a general assembly of the people, King Latinus proposes peace and a grant of territory to the Trojans. Defying Turnus, one of the nobles supports Latinus, and advises that Lavinia be given in marriage to Aeneas. Berating their lack of courage, Turnus offers to decide the issue by meeting Aeneas in single combat.

C. At this moment news is brought that the Trojans and Etruscans are advancing upon Laurentum. In the consternation Turnus rouses the people to defense and battle. He entrusts to the warrior-maid Camilla and her cavalry the task of holding the combined Etruscan and Trojan cavalry forces, while he himself prepares an ambush for the Trojan infantry. On Mt. Olympus Diana, the patroness of Camilla, orders one of her nymphs to kill anyone who slays her favorite.

D. The cavalry forces meet, and a wild see-sawing battle ensues, in which the Amazon-like Camilla distinguishes herself, slaying many. The Etruscans rally, and Camilla is finally slain; her slayer is in turn killed by Diana's nymph. At Camilla's death the Latin cavalry retreats to Laurentum, slaughtered by the pursuing enemy. As panic grows in the city, Turnus, abandoning his ambush, rushes back to the city. Both armies bivouac before the city for the night.

## Book XII.

A. Seeing the Latins in dire straits Turnus declares that the issue over Lavinia's hand and peace will be settled by a duel between himself and Aeneas, despite the pleadings of Latinus and Amata. After Aeneas accepts the challenge, preparations are made for the contest. Juno, fearing for Turnus' life, advises his sister, a nymph, to prevent the duel. Latinus and Aeneas solemnize the terms of the duel and the peace treaty by oaths and sacrifices. But Turnus' sister stirs up the Latins with pity for Turnus, and one of them throws his spear, slaying one of the allies of the Trojans.

B. With this the battle is renewed fiercely; Aeneas is wounded by an arrow and withdraws. Turnus, taking advantage of Aeneas' absence, slays many of the enemy. The arrow is removed from Aeneas with the miraculous aid of Venus, and Aeneas returns to the fray, seeking Turnus. The latter's divine sister keeps him out of danger. While Turnus and Aeneas continue the slaughter of their enemies in the titanic struggle, Aeneas decides on a surprise attack on Laurentum. Leaving his allies to hold the enemy, he and the Trojans assault the city. There is panic inside, and Queen Amata, believing Turnus dead, commits suicide by hanging.

C. At this Turnus, in order to spare the city, offers single combat again. He rushes to the city, ordering his men to cease fighting. Aeneas prepares to meet him as the Latins and Trojans look on. The duel begins. They fling their spears at each other, and then fight with swords. When Turnus' sword is shattered, he flees, pursued by Aeneas. Turnus' sister, Juturna, and Venus intervene to aid their kin with weapons. The champions face each other again. Jupiter now, as Turnus' fate approaches, orders Juno to cease intervening against the Trojans. Juno reluctantly consents, on the condition the name "Trojans" be abandoned and the combined people be called Latins. Juturna retires, abandoning Turnus to his fate, as one of the Furies is sent to terrify Turnus. The duel continues. The two heroes mock each other, and Turnus hurls a huge rock at Aeneas, but misses. Aeneas then wounds Turnus, who begs that his body be given to his kin for burial. Moved to pity, Aeneas is about to spare his life, when he spies on Turnus' shoulder the sword-belt of Pallas. In fury he slays Turnus.

## STYLE AND TECHNIQUE OF AENEID

    I.   Homeric influence (see above, pp. 38–39).

        A.  Invocation to the Muse

        B.  Story begins *in medias res*

        C.  Use of supernatural as divine machinery

        D.  Similes, lengthy, taken from nature, animal life, everyday life, but also political field

        E.  Epic question

        F.  Speeches (often rhetorical)

        G.  Catalogues of names

        H.  Balanced contrast

        I.  Meter: dactylic hexameter

    II.   Subjectivity, allusiveness, introspection, symbolism.

    III.  Exquisite verbal art and perfection of form.

    IV.  Complex, learned, compact.

    V.  Stately, majestic (Tennyson: "Wielder of the stateliest measure ever moulded by the lips of man"; Dante: "You are my master and my author; you are the only one from whom I have taken the beautiful style that has made me famous").

    VI.  Dramatic power; psychological insight.

## THOUGHT AND SPIRIT OF VERGIL

    I.   Vergil reflects the contradictions of the Augustan Age; he synthesizes the old in literary tradition and Roman life with the new elements of Augustan policy; there is thus a dualistic habit of mind in him, indistinctness and fuzziness of thought, combined with mysticism.

    II.  Stresses Roman nationalism and imperialistic destiny, glorification of the Emperor Augustus, revival of old Roman religion.

    III.  At the same time he has a tragic, pessimistic view of life, and a broad human sympathy; his tenderness, pathos, melancholy are outstanding; he sees both joy and suffering in life, but views it as a tragic paradox; he has a horror of war, reflecting the yearning for peace in the Augustan Age, and intense pity for suffering in general.

IV. Religion: fusion of Homeric divine machinery, fate, Roman religion, Greek philosophy (modified Stoicism, Platonism).

V. He places great emphasis on character. His characters are more generalized than Homer's, less individualistic, more symbolical. His ideal character (Aeneas) is a combination of Roman and modified Stoic qualities, possessing deep sense of devotion to duty *(pietas)*, wisdom, moderation, control of emotions, ability to endure adversity, but also human defects and weaknesses (pity, anger, love, discouragement). Heroism for Vergil is not Homeric military prowess, but strengthening of character, overcoming of natural human weakness through suffering and experience.

## CHAPTER TWENTY-TWO

# HORACE

◧

## QUINTUS HORATIUS FLACCUS (65-8 B.C.)

I.    Born at Venusia, in southern Italy; father of freedman (ex-slave) status, but provided his precocious son with best available education.

II.    Educated in best schools at Rome; student at Athens, where he was influenced by the Greek lyric writers and Epicurean philosophy.

III. Officer in the army of Brutus defeated by Octavian and Antony at the Battle of Philippi, 42 B.C.

IV.   Worked in Rome as clerk; became Vergil's best friend.

V.    Joined the literary circle of Maecenas, who bestowed on him an estate in the Sabine Mts. near Rome ("Sabine Farm"). After this he abandoned some of his Epicurean beliefs, and lived a life devoted to leisure and writing.

VI.   Satirist, lyric poet, moralist, literary critic.

## WORKS OF HORACE

*Epodes*
*Satires*
*Odes*
*Epistles* (includes the famous *Ars Poetica*)
*Carmen Saeculare*

## ODES

Book I, 1.   (Dedication to his patron Maecenas).  O Maecenas, my patron and friend, people have various ambitions in life: victory in athletic contests; election to political office; wealth; farming; sailing the seas as a trader; loafing in the country near a stream with a bottle of wine; soldiering; hunting. As for me, association with the Muses elevates me above the masses. If you, Maecenas, rank me with the lyric poets, my head will strike the stars in pride.

I, 4. Spring and the west wind have returned. Ships are sailing again, and the herds and farmers come out to the fields. Venus, the Graces and nymphs are dancing again, and the lightning of Vulcan is seen. But let the coming of Spring remind you that death is inevitable for rich and poor alike. Life is short; enjoy it now.

I, 5. Who is the lad now making love to you, Pyrrha? Poor naïve, unsuspecting fellow, wait 'til he discovers your fickleness! I escaped from your clutches with difficulty, but, though somewhat battered, I am safe.

I, 9. See how winter holds all in its grasp. Pile the fire high, and pour forth wine more generously. There's no use worrying about the weather, for the gods control it at their will. Don't worry about the future; each new day is so much gain. Dance while you're still young. Go out to the public squares of an evening where many a lad and his girl are making love to each other.

I, 11. Don't worry about how much time we have left to live. Be content with whatever time the gods give you. Be wise, drink wine, don't make long-range plans. Time flies, enjoy today, don't trust the morrow.

I, 14. O Ship of State, new dangers threaten. Hasten to port. You are in grave danger, your rigging and equipment gone or damaged. Beware, the gale is strong. O my new love and care, avoid the treacherous waters.

I, 22. He who is upright and without sin needs no weapons to protect himself, wherever he may be. The proof is that while I was wandering in the Sabine woods one day, singing of Lalage, a horrible wolf saw me and fled, though I was unarmed. In whatever place in the world I may be, I will always love my "sweetly laughing, sweetly prattling Lalage."

I, 24. Quintilius is dead, he who was without peer in honor, loyalty, truthfulness. You, Vergil, mourn him more than all others. But there must be a limit to one's sorrow, for he cannot be brought back from the dead, even if you played music more sweetly than Orpheus. What we cannot change becomes easier to bear if we learn to accept it.

I, 31. Don't grieve overmuch, Albius, for heartless Glycera, who has abandoned you for a younger lover. She is not worth it. Unrequited love is a common thing; moreover, Venus delights in bringing together persons not suited for each other. I, too, had a similar experience once.

I, 38. I hate the luxury of the Persians, O my slave. I want no expensive garlands. Simple myrtle will do for both of us, as I drink beneath the vine.

Book II, 2. "The wise man alone is rich" (Stoic paradox), O Sallust, as you know, for you have no excessive greed for wealth. Proculeius will be immortal because of his generosity to his brothers who had lost their wealth. If one curbs one's greedy desire for wealth, one will be a greater master than the ruler of broad lands. Avarice grows by indulgence to it, as dropsy does. True virtue, wisdom and happiness do not belong to the powerful and wealthy king of Parthia, but to him who disdains the lure of wealth.

II, 3. Remember to maintain a level head both in difficulties and prosperity. For death is inevitable, no matter how you have lived, whether gloomily or with joyful abandon. The shade of a tree, the racing brook are meant by nature to be enjoyed. Be happy with wine, perfumes, and roses, while you may. You can't take it with you; an heir will inherit your unused wealth. We must all go to Hades, whether we be rich aristocrats or poor and of lowly birth. There is no return when once we have crossed the Styx on Charon's bark.

II, 10. You will live best by not going to extremes. By following the policy of the Golden Mean you will avoid envoy for excessive wealth and the degradations of poverty. Too much prominence and wealth are attended by the greatest dangers; for when the fall comes, it is all the harder. All is change; life is full of ups and downs; nothing ever remains the same. Therefore, be hopeful when in trouble, anxious when prosperous. There is always a silver lining in the offing. Trouble cannot last forever, for nothing remains the same. Apollo is the god of plague, but also of music. Be brave in difficulties, cautious in prosperity.

II, 13. The man who planted you, O tree, had a criminal murderous character. He put you on my estate so that you might fall on the head of your innocent master. We little know when and how death will strike and what dangers to avoid, for death is something unforeseen. I almost went to Hades, to the Elysian Fields, where I might have seen Sappho and Alcaeus singing their songs, and the souls marveling at both, but mostly at Alcaeus' political and military themes. Even Cerberus, the Eumenides, Prometheus, Tantalus, and Orion are charmed by their sweet music.

II, 14. O Postumus, death is inevitable. No amount of piety or sacrifices will stop advancing age or death. Pluto is merciless, conquering all. We must all cross the gloomy Styx, be we kings or needy tillers of the soil. We seek to escape death in various ways, but in vain. We all must see Cocytus, the Danaids, and Sisyphus in Tartarus. We must leave our lands, home, wife, property. The rare wine which you, in your miserliness, have stored away, your heir will wantonly enjoy.

II, 16. Peace and contentment is everyone's prayer. This cannot be bought with wealth. Political power and wealth will not drive away the cares of the mind. He lives well who lives on a little, undisturbed by fear or greed. Life is short. Why then should we aim at so much? You cannot escape yourself by travelling from place to place. Care follows you wherever you go, swifter than the wind. Life is full of change; nothing is perfect in every respect.

Be happy now, don't worry about the future. Learn to smile at misfortune. No one can have everything. You have herds of animals and wealth. To me fate has granted a small estate, the inspiration of the Greek Muse, and scorn for the envious crowd.

Book III, 2. The young men of Italy should toughen up and learn courage in military service, so that they will be dreaded by our enemies. It is sweet and glorious to die for one's native land. Everyone must die, brave man and coward alike. But the courageous man will become immortal; his soul will beat a path to heaven. There is a reward too for those who do not do the fighting, but know how to keep state secrets. We must not consort with the sinner. Justice, though slow, always overtakes the guilty.

III, 9   Horace: When I was your lover, I was happier than the king of Persia. Lydia: When you loved me I was more famous than the mother of Romulus. Horace: Now musical Chloe is my mistress, and I would gladly die for her. Lydia: Now Calais is my love, and I would gladly die twice for him. Horace: What if I discard Chloe and welcome you back? Lydia: Though Calais is handsome and you are very fickle, I'll gladly live with you forever.

III, 26.   'Til recently I have been a hardy and successful campaigner in the battle of love. But now I'm through. Hang my weapons (lyre, torch, crowbar) on the temple wall. O Venus, strike with your lash haughty Chloe.

III, 30.   I have erected a monument more enduring than bronze or the pyramids of Egypt. Nothing will ever destroy it. I shall not altogether die; a great part of me will be immortal. I shall grow with the praise of posterity, as long as Rome exists. I, who rose to fame from low estate, shall be famous for having been the first to adapt Aeolian song to Italian verse. O Muse, place on my brow the laurel wreath.

## STYLE OF THE ODES

I.   Greek influence: early Greek lyric poets and Alexandrian poets.

II. Exquisite technical perfection and polish of form and language; commonplace ideas inimitably stated ("what oft was said, but ne'er so well expressed"); practical common sense wisdom, proverbial statements.

III. No profound imagination, thought, or feeling; more reflective than emotional; humor, mild irony; easy-going urbanity; individualist.

IV. Self-revelation and self-criticism.

V. Love poems adaptations from Greek models; national and patriotic themes.

## SATIRES

I. Satire the only type of literature created by the Romans. The creator of satire was Lucilius. Horace was indebted to him, but dropped his bitter tone and political themes.

II. Verse form: dactylic hexameter.

III. Style of Horace's *Satires*: genial, tolerant, urbane; humorous; prosaic and conversational; non-political, non-personal, but general and typical; self-revelation.

Book I, 3. (On Tolerance). Singers are odd people. If you ask them to sing, they are reluctant; if you don't, it's difficult to stop them. Such a man is Tigellius, odd and highly inconsistent. Have I no faults then? Yes, but not as bad. Some are smug and self-satisfied, loving to censure others and ignoring their own faults. This unrestrained habit of criticizing leads to mutual criticism. While people look for some trifling external fault in a friend, they ignore his hidden gifts. We should, on the contrary, be as blind to a friend's faults as a lover is to his beloved's blemishes, or as indulgent with them as a father is with his son's shortcomings. Let us rather strive to turn bad qualities into good ones, even at the risk of exaggerating a bit.

But we do the opposite, stupidly turning good traits into faults. We must remember, however, that everyone has faults and is exposed to such evil censure. We must then be mutually tolerant of each other's faults, indulgently trying to see the best in each other. We must know how to discriminate between lesser and greater faults, not assigning equal censure to all, especially when a friend commits a slight pardonable social offense.

The Stoic view that all faults are equal and deserving of equal censure is unreasonable and repugnant to common sense. The moral code developed through a process of slow evolution; there is no natural, absolute justice. Thus there must be a distinction between the penalties we assign to lesser and greater crimes. The Stoic, if he were king, would punish all faults with death. Is the Stoic, as he believes, already a king? No. Is he a potential king among men? Well, I have my doubts, when boys pull his beard and jostle him in the streets as he is on his way to a cheap bath. I prefer to remain a private man, happier than the Stoic, ready to tolerate my friend's shortcomings.

I, 6. (On Ambition). You, Maecenas, do not, as most men, judge a man by his birth instead of his worth. The proof is your friendship for me, the son of a freedman. Many a man of low social rank has lived an upright life and won high political distinction; contrariwise, many an aristocrat has toppled from distinction. Though people as a whole look up to those of high social rank, ambition for political power is undesirable. For envy increases, there is no peace of mind, no privacy, and people gossip about men in politics.

People talk about me because of my humble origin and because I am your friend. But I am proud of this, because you judge men not by their fathers' status but by their own worth. Moreover, I am proud of my father, who moulded my character for the best and gave me a fine education in Rome. If I had my life to live over again, I would choose to have my own father rather than be the son of a wealthy aristocrat. For great wealth is irksome and restricting; one must live on a grand scale. As it is, unlike rich men, I can go anywhere I please, eat simple food, sleep untroubled by social obligations, live calmly and at leisure. These I would not

**311**

enjoy if I were ambitious for wealth and power, and if my ancestors had been senators.

I, 9. (The Bore). Horace, strolling in Rome, is accosted by a bore, who foists himself upon him and cannot be shaken off. The bore discourses on his own merits as a poet, dancer, and singer. After some time the bore announces that he is a defendant in a law suit and must go to court. He begs Horace to accompany him, but when Horace refuses he abandons his case to follow him. It is obvious soon that the bore wants an introduction to Maecenas. Presently a friend of Horace, who is a practical joker, comes along, but refuses to rescue Horace, and runs off. By luck the plaintiff in the law suit spies the bore and hails him off to court as a crowd gathers. Thus was Horace rescued by Apollo.

II, 6. (Country Life). Horace is satisfied with his small Sabine Farm, and prays to Mercury to preserve his blessings permanently, for he is not desirous of increasing his property and wealth. Life in the country is exceedingly pleasant, while in Rome there are law courts, jostling crowds in the streets, innumerable social obligations, political intrigue. His personal friendship with Maecenas leads people to try to reach Maecenas through him for political favors or to pump him for information. All the while he yearns for the quietness of his country estate, his books, leisure, simple food, congenial friendly gatherings, serious philosophical conversation. When someone brings up the question of wealth and luxury, a neighbor of his relates in detail the fable of the country mouse and the city mouse.

## HORACE'S PHILOSOPHY OF LIFE

I.      Eclectic (and therefore inconsistent): Epicureanism, Stoicism, Peripatetic views; dilettante and opportunist.

II.     Life is short and uncertain; death is inevitable; there is no personal immortality, except through great achievements in life.

III.    Enjoy the present moment (*carpe diem*) with wine, love, song.

IV. Moderation (Golden Mean) is necessary for happiness: don't be overly ambitious, avaricious, or extravagant; live a simple life with peace of mind and economic security; be content, don't worry.

V. Be content with your lot and optimistic; resign yourself to what can't be changed.

VI. Pleasures of the country life; love of nature.

VII. Friendship is important.

VIII. Asceticism is wrong; over-indulgence equally so.

IX. Patriotism, duty to country, military courage.

X. Conventional Roman religious views.

## CHAPTER TWENTY-THREE

# ROMAN EMPIRE

## A.D. 14-476

▣

## FIRST TWO CENTURIES (A. D. 14-180)

I.  Julio-Claudian Dynasty (A.D. 14–68): Tiberius (Augustus' stepson), Caligula, Claudius, Nero.

A.  Increasing despotism and suppression of civil liberties.

B.  Trial and execution of Jesus of Nazareth in Roman Province of Judea, during reign of Tiberius.

C.  Conquest of new territory, especially Britain (A.D. 43) in reign of Claudius.

D.  Disastrous consequences of arbitrary whims of some of the emperors, particularly Nero, and of palace intrigues.

E.  First persecution of the Christians, during reign of Nero.

II.  Year of the Four Emperors (A.D. 68-69): civil war and rebellion.

III.  Flavian Dynasty (A.D. 69-96): Vespasian and his two sons, Titus and Domitian.

A.  Restabilization of administrative and financial efficiency of the empire.

B.  Destruction of Jerusalem (A.D. 70) and dispersion of the Jews, during reign of Vespasian.

C.  Eruption of Vesuvius (A.D. 70): burial of Pompeii and Herculaneum.

D.  Despotism of Domitian.

IV. The "Good" Emperors (A.D. 96-180): Nerva, Trajan, Hadrian, Antoninus Pius, Marcus Aurelius.

A. Empire at its greatest territorial extent (A.D. 117); conquests by Trajan of new provinces in Europe and the East.

B. Growing importance of the provinces; decline of Italy.

C. Growing economic and social crisis.

D. First barbarian invasions, during the reign of Marcus Aurelius.

## SILVER AGE OF ROMAN LITERATURE (A.D. 14-180)

I. Oppression and restraints on freedom of expression during the first century; increased freedom during age of the "Good" Emperors.

II. Influence of increasing importance of the provinces: change from nationalism of Augustan Age to internationalism, cosmopolitan, broad interest in all mankind.

III. Stagnation of thought; artificial show-pieces; dilettantism; learning; epigrammatic style; rhetorical emphasis.

## CENTURY OF DECLINE AND ANARCHY (A.D. 180-284)

I. Empire-wide revolution ends privileges of Rome, Italy, and the ruling class of the empire, which is replaced by military leaders supported by peasant armies.

II. Extension of Roman citizenship to all free men in the empire (A.D. 212).

III. Fifty years of anarchy; renewed barbarian invasions.

## ORIENTAL DESPOTISM (A.D. 284-350)

I. Restabilization of the empire by Diocletian; end of principate; absolute monarchy; end of local self-government in empire, complete centralization; beginnings of serfdom.

II. Recognition of Christianity by Constantine the Great.

## DISINTEGRATION OF THE ROMAN EMPIRE (A.D. 350-476)

I. Barbarian invasions of the 4th and 5th centuries; loss of provinces.

**315**

II.  Separation of the empire into West and East.

III.  Fall of the West (A.D. 476) to Odovacer; Italy becomes German kingdom.

IV.  Survival of the empire in the East (Byzantine Empire) until A.D. 1453.

## CHAPTER TWENTY-FOUR

# JUVENAL

◙

## DECIMUS JUNIUS JUVENALIS (ca. A.D. 60-140)

I.  Little known of him; probably born at Aquinum near Rome.

II.  Disappointed in military career; perhaps exiled by the Emperor Domitian to Egypt.

III.  Wrote 16 *Satires*.

## SATIRE III—Rome

My friend Umbritius was abandoning Rome for the little town of Cumae near Naples. Any place is better to live in than Rome. Everything is at a price here, and beggars roam in sacred spots. "At Rome," said my friend, "corruption reigns supreme. The honest man is doomed to failure. And so, I am leaving my native city before I grow too old, abandoning it to corrupt, successful people, who were catapulted from insignificance to greatness by luck. Only lying, hypocrisy, crime, and blackmail succeed in Rome.

"Those most in favor with the rich are foreigners, Greeks, Orientals. Rome has become a city of foreigners, who have imported their native manners and customs. These are successful in Rome because they have quick minds, ready tongues, impudence, and can do anything, even fly to heaven. I, who was born in Rome, count for nothing. The Greeks are skilled in flattery, acting any part demanded of them, fawning on the rich. They hold nothing sacred; a Stoic philosopher brought about the death of his friend and pupil. We Romans cannot compete with them.

"At Rome men are judged by their wealth, not by their moral character. The poor men's clothes are the butt of ridicule and laughter. It is hopeless for the poor man to advance himself. The cost of living is great and standards are high. Splendor and luxury are everywhere; the poor must ape the rich. Money rules all.

"Tragic fires are frequent at Rome. The poor man suffers most from a fire, for he loses what little he possesses, and no one will help him. The rich man's plight causes general alarm, and his friends aid him in replacing what he has lost. In the country rents are low, and one can become a property owner for what it costs to rent a dark hole in Rome.

"It is so noisy only the rich· can sleep. The rich man can make his way at ease through the great crowds, borne in a litter by his slaves. But the poor man is crushed, jostled, trampled on. There are great dangers too in the street—men racing about with portable kitchens on their heads, clothing torn, wagons loaded with stone breaking down and burying passers-by who are on their way home to their expectant families.

"The dangers of the night are as varied. Under open windows lurks constant death, for many things are thrown out at night. Drunks accost, insult, and beat one to a pulp. Thieves lurk in the streets.

"There is a shortage of iron in Rome; most of it has gone to forging chains for criminals. The prisons are full. But it is time to leave now. When you decide to abandon Rome for Aquinum, I shall be glad to come visit you."

### SATIRE X—The Vanity of Human Wishes

Few people in the world know what constitutes real happiness. Most pray for blessings that bring about their ruin. The usual ambitions are eloquence, physical strength, wealth, political power, military glory, long life, beauty.

The famous athlete Milo died as the result of his great strength.

Wealth causes many to be strangled or poisoned or to be attacked by the emperor. Soldiers are not sent to confiscate the property of a man living in a garret. The poor man can travel at night without a care, while the rich man trembles for his life. This drive for riches caused the philosopher Democritus to laugh perpetually, the philosopher Heraclitus to weep constantly at the vanity of human wishes. What would have been their reaction at the luxury and pretense of Rome! It is indeed vain to pray for wealth.

Political power causes envy and headlong ruin. Mighty Sejanus fell from his high position at the command of Tiberius. The fickle Roman populace, eager only for cheap bread and amusements, applaud the momentary favorite of the emperor and trample on yesterday's hero. Would you wish for Sejanus' wealth and power? So too died Crassus and his son, Pompey the Great and his sons, and Caesar. Few kings and tyrants die a natural death.

Every schoolboy longs to be a great orator. But Demosthenes and Cicero, the greatest of them, died miserably, the former a suicide, the latter murdered by Mark Antony's soldiers.

Many prize military glory above all. Hannibal brought ruin to his native Carthage by his vast military ambitions, and suicide for himself. Death overtook the mighty conqueror Alexander the Great, and King Xerxes of the Persians. "The paths of glory lead but to the grave."

Many pray for long life. But old age is filled with unhappiness of all kinds—physical ugliness, inability to enjoy the pleasures of youth, deafness, constant illness and ailments, paralysis, senility, the deaths of all one's relatives. Truly a gloomy existence! Some old people, as King Nestor, have actually prayed for death. What did it profit Priam to live to a ripe old age, when he was forced to see the destruction of his power and the deaths of his sons? Witness the fall of Marius, Pompey the Great, and others.

Mothers pray for beauty for their sons and daughters. But beauty and chastity are a rare combination. Many dangers confront the beautiful person; often beauty leads to corruption, demoralization, and crime.

What then is there left to pray for in order to achieve happiness. A sound mind in a sound body; courage not to fear death; ability to endure hardship; and, above all, virtue.

## STYLE AND SPIRIT OF JUVENAL'S SATIRES

I.     His satires are motivated by fear and hatred of Domitian, bitter disappointment in life, contempt for humanity at large, especially women.

II.     Savage cynicism, fierce, grim, remorseless invective; somber pessimism; sardonic humor.

III.     Exaggeration; reveals only the seamy side of Roman life.

IV.     Realism; good portraiture; pictorial power.

V.     Little constructive criticism to correct the evils he portrays.

VI.     Grand, majestic style; rhetorical; frequent epigrammatic statements.

VII.  Moralist; Stoic viewpoint.

## CHAPTER TWENTY-FIVE

# TACITUS

## CORNELIUS TACITUS (ca A.D. 55-120)

   I.    Distinguished Roman family.

   II.   Lawyer; long political career, including consulship and provincial governorships.

   III.  Became historian late in life; greatest Roman historian; last great classical writer.

## WORKS OF TACITUS

*Dialogue on Orators*
*Agricola*
*Germany*
*Histories* (covering events of the years A.D. 68-96)
*Annals* (covering events of the years A.D. 14-68)

## HISTORICAL METHOD AND THOUGHT OF TACITUS

   I.    Sources

      A.  Literary; earlier historians

      B.  Public records

      C.  Oral

      D.  Personal observation

   II.   Insufficiently critical of sources; often accepts what is probable; often accepts conflicting evidence and points of view, unwilling to sacrifice any, leaving matters undecided.

   III.  Annalistic method.

**321**

IV.　　Rhetorical speeches, some historical, some an approximation of what was said on the occasion.

V.　　Moral purpose of history: glorification of virtue and good deeds, condemnation of vice and evil deeds; didactic purpose: instruction by examples of good and evil characters; contrast between evils of 1st cent. A.D. and improved conditions of 2nd cent.

VI.　　Political bias: opposition to despotism of Roman emperors; anti-democratic; favors moderate aristocratic Republic, but resigns self to monarchy, hoping for good emperors.

VII.　　Tendency to debunk; cynical, gloomy, tragic viewpoint.

VIII.　Confused philosophy of history; chaotic view of world; mildly Stoic, believing in fate and predestination; but also accepts freewill, chance, and divine intervention; superstitious.

## MERITS OF TACITUS AS HISTORIAN
I.　　Search for truth; sincerity.

II.　　Realism; great dramatic skill in narrative.

III.　Psychological insight; vivid character studies.

## WEAKNESSES OF TACITUS AS HISTORIAN
I.　　Unessential learned digressions.

II.　　Contradictions and inconsistencies due to: 1) confused philosophy of history; 2) conflict between facts and his prejudices; 3) conflicting evidence of his sources.

III.　Use of gossip, rumor, innuendo, anecdote, speculation, even though he mistrusts them, to cater to public taste for these.

IV.　Some speeches not exact words of speakers.

V.　　Sets down hidden motives of historical characters.

VI.　Inadequate knowledge of military strategy.

VII.　Limited viewpoint: concentrates his attention on imperial court.

## STYLE AND SPIRIT
I.　　Unique and personal style.

II.　　Brevity; compactness; sustained vigor and dignity.

III.    Obscurity; startling, vivid effects, especially through understatement; irony; sarcasm.

IV.    Pessimism; cynicism; somber gloom; melancholy.

V.    Rhetorical; epigrammatic statements.

VI.    Archaisms; poetical color (influence of Vergil).

VII.    Realism.

VIII.    Dramatic skill; psychological insight; tragic manner.

## ANNALS (his greatest work)

A year by year treatment of the events from the death of Augustus (A.D. 14) to the death of Nero (A.D. 68); not preserved entire.

## Summary of Typical Selections

Book I,1-8. After the establishment of the Roman Republic, with its principle of political equality, limitations on political freedom and usurpations of arbitrary power were rare and of short duration, until Augustus seized permanent power upon the defeat of Antony. Excellent histories of the Republic and the Augustan Age have been written, but the reigns of Tiberius, Caligula, Claudius, and Nero were not recorded in a trustworthy fashion, for histories of these reigns were written in fear or hatred of these emperors. I shall treat them objectively, without partiality or bitterness.

Augustus, favored by the general yearning for peace, by bribing the soldiers and the people with gifts and the surviving Senatorial families with honors, gradually, without appreciable opposition, became supreme ruler. Freedom was abandoned for security and peace.

Augustus sought to bolster his reign by establishing a dynasty, but in his old age he was forced by circumstances to select his stepson Tiberius as his successor. Few were left who remembered the political equality of the old Republic. All classes submitted to Augustus. When he was near death, some talked of restoring the Republic, but no one did anything. There was much concern at the possibility that Augustus' wife, the mother of Tiberius, would have a powerful influence over the new ruler. And when Augustus died there were rumors that Livia had a hand in hastening his death to further her own ambitions through Tiberius.

The first crime of the new reign was the murder of Augustus' grandson, Agrippa Postumus. Officially, he was put to death in accordance with Augustus' orders, but probably Tiberius and Livia ordered him killed.

When Tiberius succeeded to power, the most eminent men vied with one another in servility to him, acting out the farce of joy at Tiberius' succession and sadness at Augustus' death. Everyone swore fidelity to Tiberius. Though maintaining a pretence at Republic forms, Tiberius left no room for doubt that he was emperor. He pretended indecision, too, for he feared his nephew Germanicus, and desired thus to win the support of both the Senate and the masses for himself. At the first meeting of the Senate the will of Augustus was read, and then honors were heaped upon Augustus, Tiberius, and Livia by a servile Senate. On the day of Augustus' funeral it seemed ridiculous to some that the body of Augustus, autocrat and prince of peace, should be protected by a guard of soldiers.

I, 72-74. In the second year of his reign Tiberius revived the law of treason in a new form, employing it to suppress freedom of speech, because of the circulation of anonymous verses attacking him. But soon the interpretation of the law was extended so broadly that it became the most abominable legal device ever invented, involving many in charges of treason for the most trivial acts. Worse, it gave rise to the profession of informers, who became wealthy and powerful by denouncing persons who made remarks that could be interpreted as treasonable.

III, 65. The historian's task is to preserve from oblivion virtuous and evil deeds and characters, to hold up examples of conduct for the future. This period was filled with shameful deeds, and was blackened by the lowest depths of servility to the emperor, with men vying to outdo one another in slavery to Tiberius.

Tiberius himself, though a tyrant and enemy of civil liberties, despised the Senators because of their servility to him.

IV, 32-35. The events of these times cannot be compared in scope and drama with the history of the Republic. My history is of narrower scope, for there were no events of tremendous significance; yet they deserve attention. Despite the Republican façade, the principate was an outright monarchy. Hence concentration on the rulers themselves is of prime importance, so that examples of conduct may be set forth. The endless succession of despotic acts and treason trials may be monotonous and dry reading, but such was the period. Every vicious person will see his own character mirrored here.

In A.D. 25 Cremutius Cordus was prosecuted on a charge of treason for writing a history in which he praised Brutus and Cassius, now dead almost 70 years. After defending freedom of speech and tolerance in an impassioned oration, he committed suicide. His book was ordered burned by the Senate; yet copies were secretly preserved. By trying to suppress truth and works of genius, tyrants call attention to these works and give their writers a passport to immortality.

XIV, 60-65. In A.D. 62 Nero divorced his young innocent wife and married the evil Poppaea, who brought about the banishment of Octavia on a trumped-up charge. But the public clamor was so great that Nero was forced to issue an order for her recall, following a violent demonstration in her behalf. Poppaea, however, continued to intrigue against the helpless Octavia, playing on Nero's fears, so that he devised a scheme to get Octavia out of the way permanently. He ordered one of his criminal henchmen, the same who had accomplished the murder of his mother for him, to confess publicly that he was guilty of adultery with Octavia. Then he formally banished her again, and in a few days ordered her to commit suicide. When she pleaded for her life, his soldiers horribly killed her and sent her head to Poppaea. The Senate promptly decreed thanks to the gods.

Nero murdered others through fear or desire for their wealth, until a conspiracy was formed against him, unsuccessful as it was.

XV, 33-44. In A.D. 64 Nero, whose passion for fame as a singer was unbounded, made his public debut in the theater of Naples. He planned a concert tour of Greece and the Orient, but suddenly cancelled it, proclaiming that the public clamored jealously for him to remain at Rome. He squandered the wealth of the treasury on unbounded luxuries, public entertainment, and committed numerous indecent acts in public.

In this year the most disastrous fire in Roman history devastated Rome. The fire spread rapidly and could not be checked; many died in the conflagration. Nero was munificent in his aid to the stricken population. It was rumored that while Rome burned Nero ascended the stage of his theater and sang of the destruction of Troy. And many believed that Nero himself ordered the city burned, so that he could rebuild it and rename it after himself. Many famous buildings and priceless works of art were destroyed in the fire.

Afterwards Nero built a magnificent new palace of tremendous size and splendor, and undertook other expensive projects. The city was rebuilt under his supervision, with regulations designed to prevent fires from spreading so rapidly. But everything he did could not still people's suspicions that the city was fired by his orders. Therefore, he sought to divert suspicion by employing the Christians as scapegoats. Though few believed they were guilty of burning the city, they were persecuted with unimaginable cruelty. A public spectacle was made of their suffering, until finally compassion was stirred up for them, for it was evident that they were killed only to satisfy the cruelty of Nero.

XV, 60-64. In A.D. 65, infuriated by the conspiracy of Piso, Nero instituted a blood purge. Many were mercilessly killed, including the aged Seneca, the Stoic philosopher, who had been his tutor and minister. There was no real proof that he was involved in the conspiracy, but Nero thirsted for his blood. Seneca, undaunted by the accusation, was ordered by Nero to commit suicide. Calmly and stoically he addressed his sorrowing friends, holding up his life as a model to them. Then he bade a tender farewell to his young wife, who resolved to die with him. But Nero's soldiers ordered her life saved. Seneca's veins were opened, and, as his life slowly ebbed away, he dictated his farewell address. But it was necessary to administer poison and to place him in a hot bath in order to bring about his death.

## HISTORIES

Book I, 1-4. Much has been written about Roman history of the past. Those who wrote during the Republic were inspired by the spirit of freedom. But when all power was surrendered to Augustus after the Battle of Actium, genius and truth died with liberty. Two groups of writers developed, those who flattered and fawned upon the emperors, and those whose hatred of them rankled inside. Thus neither group wrote objective history. I myself have no feeling for or against any of the emperors to be treated here; I owe, in fact, much in my career to some of them. Freedom of speech has returned, and the truth may now be told.

There were in the period under discussion great battles, civil war, cruelty, emperors put to death, foreign troubles, numerous natural catastrophes, and other great calamities and evil conditions—a truly melancholy period. Yet the picture is brightened by examples of personal integrity and honor.

After the death of Nero there was much rejoicing, but no sooner was it over than a terrible secret of the Empire was discovered—that emperors might be chosen elsewhere than at Rome. Meanwhile, there being no emperor, the flame of liberty was kindled again at Rome, giving people new hope, but the degenerate masses and corrupt hangers-on waited for what would happen.

## GERMANY

13-27. The Germans always carry weapons after they have reached manhood. Those of distinguished parentage are from early age designated as future chiefs. Each chief is surrounded by a large body of picked youths; his prestige is gauged by the number of his followers. The Germans are very warlike, and their courage is motivated by blind obedience to their chiefs. They hate peace, so that, if their native states are in a condition of prolonged peace, they go over to warring tribes in order to be able to continue fighting. The nobles despise work, preferring to live off war booty. When they are not fighting, they indulge in hunting, idleness, sleep, feasting. The chiefs are accustomed to receive liberal gifts from their tribes.

The Germans have no cities, being rugged individuals; they live in rude wooden dwellings. They wear crude clothing as a rule, many even the skins of wild animals. Their women wear the same type of clothing.

Their marriage customs are very strict. Monogamy and conjugal fidelity are almost the universal rule. A wife is purchased by the husband, and she presents her husband with armor as a symbol of their common life of danger. Divorce and second marriages are rare. The women live an uncorrupted simple life. Adultery is very rare, and is severely punished. Limitation of children and infanticide are regarded as infamous. Their children are healthy, and their family life is a very close type. There is no need for wills. Family feuds are common, but disputes over homicide are often settled by money payments. Lavish hospitality is part of their code.

Drunkenness is not regarded as disgraceful, and drunken quarrels are common. Important decisions are taken at drunken feasts, but they reaffirm them the next day. Beer is the common drink; food is simple.

Their sports are hazardous. They have a passion for gambling, often staking their personal freedom in the heat of gaming.

Their slaves are not of the Roman type; they are serfs who live independently but give a share of their produce to their owners. They have no knowledge of lending money at interest. Land is communally owned, and is redivided on occasions. There is so much land that intensive cultivation is unnecessary.

Their funerals are simple; they are buried with their weapons in mound tombs unadorned with monuments.

## CHAPTER TWENTY-SIX

# ST. AUGUSTINE

## RELIGIOUS DEVELOPMENTS

I.    Roman state religion, cold and formalistic, steadily declined during the Roman Empire, though maintained by the Senatorial aristocracy.

II.    Roman family religion maintained a strong hold among country folk *(pagani)*.

III.    From the time of Augustus it was customary to worship the living emperor; deification of emperor and members of imperial family.

IV.    Superstitions, fatalism, astrology, magical practices flourished in the Roman Empire.

V.    Numerous Oriental mystery cults appealed to the masses of the Empire; these had orgiastic rituals, initiations (often by baptism), intense emotional appeals, and offered hope of personal immortality.

## SPREAD OF CHRISTIANITY

I.    Especially among lower classes in urban centers.

II.    Because Christians refused to worship the emperors, there was repression of the religion, including violent anti-Christian riots and organized imperial persecutions.

III.    Finally in 311 A.D. Christianity was declared a legal religion; the "Edict of Milan" issued by Constantine in 313 A.D. granted complete religious freedom to Christianity.

IV.   Constantine was converted to Christianity in 312 A.D., and granted numerous privileges to the Catholic Church.

V.   Pagan worship was officially abolished by the Emperor Theodosius in 395 A.D.

## AURELIUS AUGUSTINUS (354-430 A.D.)

I.   Born in Province of Numidia, son of pagan father and Christian mother.

II.   Teacher of Grammar and Rhetoric in N. Africa; professor in Rome and Milan.

III.   Converted to Christianity in 387 A.D.

IV.   Bishop of Hippo in Numidia 395-430 A.D.

## WORKS OF ST. AUGUSTINE

His literary output was enormous, consisting of philosophical and grammatical works; polemical works; moral and theological works; apologetic works. His two most famous works are *Confessions* and *The City of God*.

## THE CITY OF GOD

### BACKGROUND

In 410 A.D. Rome was captured and sacked by the Goths under Alaric, the first time in 800 years that Rome was occupied by foreign troops. The pagans blamed the Christians and their abandonment of the traditional gods for the disaster. *The City of God,* in 22 Books, was written by St. Augustine between 416 and 426 to defend and console the Christians.

### Book I.

1-29.   The subject of this work is the defense of the the Christian religion against the pagans. The earthly city is possessed by the enemies of God, who attribute the sack of Rome to the Christians and their prohibition of worship of pagan gods. But some pagans saved their lives by seeking asylum in Christian churches. In all wars cities supposedly protected by pagan gods have been sacked. Acts of clemency by the Goths were influenced by Christ's name.

Christians suffered in the sack of Rome because all men sin somewhat, particularly in failure to reprove sinners through expediency, thus failing to aid them toward eternal life. Suffering tests the pious and their love of God. The saintly did not lose their faith and godliness when they lost their worldly goods in the sack of Rome. True treasures are the riches within, which cannot be plundered. Many Christians lost their lives; what is important, however, is whether they lived good lives. They will receive resurrection and eternal life. True Christians who have been led into captivity will be true to their religion under stress. Christian women who were violated by the barbarians were not contaminated thereby. Those who committed suicide committed a sin, for suicide is akin to homicide. Sin may not be committed to obviate sin. Suicides are denied the better life after death. The violence done to Christians is part of the disciplining experience of the earthly life imposed by the secret judgments of God — to test Christian perfection and to correct their imperfections. There are due rewards in the eternal life.

30-36. The capture of Rome has not corrected the vices of the Romans and their indulgence in profligate pleasures. The Romans desire to live without moral restraints, for they lust after power and luxuries. Thus they blame not themselves but the saintly Christians for their calamities. God moderated the destruction of Rome and spared the lives of the survivors. The sons of the Church are present even now among the wicked; some day they will be converted, just as there are false Christians in the Church of God. The City of God and the City of the Devil are commingled in this world and will remain so until the last judgment.

## Books II-X.

Rome suffered many calamities before the time of Christ. From its foundation there have been corruption, vice, disasters and calamities. The greatness of the Roman Empire is not due to pagan gods or Fate but to God. The pagan gods do not ensure eternal life after death but only the true God.

**331**

## Book XI.

1-16. There are two cities — the earthly and the heavenly — which are intertwined in this world. Man can attain knowledge of God through the mediation of Jesus Christ. The authority of the Scriptures and faith are the indispensable guides. Thus we know that God created the world, and also angels. God is the Father, the Son and the Holy Ghost. Some angels fell from the light of goodness of their own free will, being uncertain of eternal blessedness.

17-34. Sin is contrary to nature; it originates in the will, not in God the Creator. A separation was made between holy and unclean angels, who turned away from righteousness of their own free will. All things created by God are good; nothing in nature is evil. The divine Trinity — the Father, the Son and the Holy Ghost — are indivisibly united and co-eternal. The holy angels know God in his essence, and they know themselves better in God than in themselves. There are two different and dissimilar communities of angels, those of light and those of darkness, both good by nature, but the latter depraved by their will. Thus the whole world is divided into heaven and earth, into spiritual and material. Here the origin of the two human communities is to be found.

## Book XIV.

1-9. The sin of Adam altered human nature for the worse, and this flaw was transmitted to all humans, who are, accordingly, liable to sin and subject to death. Men would have been hurled into eternal death, had not the grace of God saved some. Thus there are two cities: one composed of those who live after the flesh, the other of those who live after the spirit. The will of man is of paramount importance. He who lives according to God should hate vice and yet love the sinner, for no one is evil by nature. He who loves God and his neighbor as himself, not according to man (i.e., in the flesh), but according to God, is through this love a man of good will. The citizens of the City of God fear eternal punishment, desire eternal life, rejoice in hope and good works. The citizens of the earthly city, who live according to man, are overwhelmed with evil emotions.

10-28.  Adam and Eve fell into vice of their own will, though their nature was created good. The true and good nature of man can be restored only by God's grace. "This is the great difference which distinguishes the two cities . . . the one guided and fashioned by love of self, the other by love of God." For their disobedience our first parents were justly punished through a hard life and death. Sexual lust is an evil difficult to overcome, yet it is necessary to control lust as well as anger by wisdom. Yet procreation is a blessed gift of marriage, instituted by God; it is not the punishment of sin. So long as the will is in control, chastity is preserved and there is no lust. True blessedness cannot be enjoyed in the present life. This was possible only in Paradise before man fell into sin. Evil is brought about by free will, and good is restored by God's grace. Thus the two cities have been formed by two loves: the earthly by love of self and contempt of God; the heavenly by love of God and contempt of self.

## Book XVIII.

1-9.  In the older philosophies the supreme good was found to exist in this life and in men themselves. For the City of God eternal life is the supreme good, eternal death the supreme evil. To attain the former and escape the latter one must live rightly. Man cannot attain the supreme good in this life, as the Greek and Roman philosophers held. Since in this life we are a battlefield in which virtue wars with vice, we must strive to prevent the soul from succumbing to the flesh, and fight against sin. But salvation is to be attained only in the world to come. Though life in the earthly city is full of distress of all kinds, it is most commendable to the citizens of the City of God. Everything in this life is precarious and many things may tempt us.

10-21.  Only in the afterlife shall the citizens of the City of God attain complete happiness and eternal peace—the supreme good—

by grace of God, both in the spirit and in the body renewed by resurrection. The highest form of peace, the peace of the heavenly city, is the perfectly ordered and harmonious enjoyment of God, and of men with one another in God. To attain eternal peace man must have a divine Master, whom he obeys without misgiving. The divine Master inculcated two precepts — love of God and one's neighbor — so that man finds three things to love: God, oneself, and one's neighbor.

Slaves should not disturb their station, but serve with good will and attain a higher form of freedom through love and righteousness. The worst form of slavery is the servitude of men to their own lusts, not physical slavery to a master. Both the earthly and the heavenly city seek peace in the things necessary to mortal life. The heavenly city, however, using those on earth as a means to a higher end, obeys the laws of the earthly city and is in harmony with it, except in matters of religion. The heavenly city while on earth unites citizens of all nations, all tongues, all cultures, preserving these diversities as not hindering the worship of the true God. The citizens of the City of God in this earthly pilgrimage to eternal peace, despite the sorrows of life, are blessed in the hope for the future life.

22-28.  The only true God is the one the Christians serve. Many devious efforts have been made to discredit Christ, to no avail. The people alienated from God is a wretched one, even when they enjoy earthly peace. But the citizens of the City of God should enjoy this peace so long as the two cities are commingled on this earth. Prayers should be said for temporal rulers. The City of God will enjoy perfect peace in the final eternal peace to come. But the wicked shall inherit eternal misery, a second eternal death, which is to be their punishment in the last judgment.

**Book XXII.**

1-10.  God will accomplish the blessedness of the City of God. Despite sin and evil, everything tends toward just and good ends that are preordained. God has promised eternal blessedness and resurrection to the pious, and everlasting punishment to the wicked.

The Romans loved Romulus, founder of Rome, and believed him to have become a god. Christians love Christ because they believe him to be God. The City of Christ has numberless followers and martyrs among all the peoples of the world. Numerous miracles throughout the Roman Empire have been wrought so that the world might believe in Christ and his ascension to heaven. The deaths of martyrs, too, are miracles that attest the faith that preaches the resurrection of the flesh to eternal life.

11-28. In the resurrection all bodily blemishes will be removed and all men will be exquisitely beautiful and youthful. "Not a hair of your head shall perish." From the hell on earth, to which the whole human race because of original sin is condemned with all the miseries and ills of life, there is no deliverance except by the grace of the Savior Jesus Christ. There are many blessings, however, on this earth, as a solace for our miseries: the wonders of reproduction, the marvelous creations of the human mind, the wonders of the human body, the beauties of nature and the universe. Some philosophers attack the reality of the resurrection of the body. But now the whole world believes it, as was predicted by God.

29-30. In the City of God the blessed finally will partake of the peace of God. There they will be rewarded with the beatific vision, seen "face to face", what we now "see through a glass, darkly." In the City of God there will be eternal happiness, untainted by evil, and the blessed will have eternal leisure to contemplate and praise God. God will be the final reward of virtue. The will of man will now be truly free, taking delight in not sinning. This is the highest freedom of the will — not to be able to sin. This is the gift of God to the blessed. The greatest joy of the City of God will be the celebration of the grace of Christ. This will be a perpetual Sabbath. "There we shall rest and see, see and love, love and praise" without end.

# BASIC THOUGHT OF THE CITY OF GOD

I.    Man's suffering is due to sin and his will, not to chance or fate.

II.    History shows that from the original sin of Adam and Eve two communities evolved. — the earthly city and the heavenly city — whose values differ profoundly.

III.    The earthly city, descended from fallen angels, consists of the enemies of God, who are characterized by pride, sinfulness, selfishness, disharmony, war, hate, vice, devotion to material goods, happiness in this life and in men themselves.

IV.    The citizens of the City of God — the followers of Christ in the Catholic Church — are descended from the holy angels, and live in the spirit, being characterized by humility, virtue, love of God and neighbor.

V.    The two cities are commingled in this life and can co-exist, sharing temporal things but are irreconcilable in matters of religion. Christians should accept and enjoy the temporal blessings of the earthly city, particularly peace and prosperity, treating it as a pilgramage toward eternal blessedness in the afterlife.

VI.    The adherent of the City of God, through love of God and Jesus Christ the Savior, righteousness, faith and charity, will be rewarded by the grace of God both in this life and with the supreme good of man — resurrection, the beatific vision of God, and eternal peace and blessedness in the afterlife.

# MYTHOLOGY

## ORIGIN OF EARTH AND GODS

*Chaos.* The Greeks did not think of the universe as springing into being by an act of divine creation, but rather as developing through a long evolutionary process of countless ages. Not being able to conceive of a time when nothing existed, Greek fancy postulated as the starting point of this development Chaos, the primeval state of things when matter was in shapeless confusion in the dark abyss of infinite space. (Milton: "void and formless infinite.")

*Ge* (Gaea; Latin: *Tellus, Terra Mater*). Mother Earth, who emerged from Chaos; nourishes all creatures in life, and receives them again in death. Mother of numerous offspring, especially Uranus, heaven personified.

*First Divine Dynasty:* Ge and Uranus (Earth and Heaven). Out of their prolific union there issued a large progeny of enormous size, chief among them the Titans, nature deities of mighty strength, personifying such phenomena as earthquakes, volcanic eruptions. The most important Titans were Oceanus (conceived of as a river encircling the earth), Cronus, Iapetus and his sons Prometheus and Atlas. Fearing their titanic power, Uranus imprisoned them inside Ge. Armed with a sickle by his mother, Cronus escaped, overpowered Uranus, severely mutilated him and deposed him from power, liberating his fellow Titans.

*Second Dynasty:* Cronus and his sister-Titan, Rhea. Cronus identified by the Romans with Saturn), an agricultural divinity, has developed erroneously into Father Time. Fearful of Uranus' curse that Cronus would be overthrown by one of his children, he swallowed the first five, Hestia, Demeter, Hera, Hades, Poseidon.

Rhea rescued her last child, Zeus, who eventually dethroned Cronus and compelled him to disgorge his brothers and sisters. There followed the great Battle of the Titans and Gods, which resulted in the overwhelming victory of Zeus, representing intelligence, over the Titans, representing brute force. Cronus was banished to the West (Isles of the Blest or Italy), and the remaining Titans were confined again in Tartarus, except Atlas, who was assigned the eternal task of supporting the heavens on his shoulders, the shifty Oceanus who remained opportunistically neutral, and Prometheus who aided Zeus because he favored intelligence and was opposed to force.

*Third Dynasty*: Olympian gods, headed by Zeus and Hera. The children of Cronus redivided the universe, Zeus receiving the sky, Poseidon the sea, Hades the underworld. The Olympian gods, so-called because they were supposed to live on the summit of Mt. Olympus, the highest peak in Greece, eventually consisted of twelve divinities: Zeus, Hera, Hestia, Poseidon, Demeter, Athena, Ares, Hephaestus, Aphrodite, Apollo, Artemis, Hermes, each with well-defined spheres of power. They were conceived as anthropomorphic, human in form and behavior. They married, had children, acknowledged Zeus as their king, held their councils in his palace on Mt. Olympus, and feasted on ambrosia and nectar, the food and drink of the gods. They were fashioned by the early Greeks in their own image.

## OLYMPIAN GODS

| Greek Name(s) | Roman Counterpart | Functions | Attributes |
|---|---|---|---|
| ZEUS (son of Cronus, therefore called Cronides, Cronion) | JUPITER (Jove) | King of gods; god of sky, heavenly phenomena (rain, thunder, lightning); hospitality protected by him | sceptre; thunderbolt; eagle; aegis (his protective breastplate) |
| HERA (sister and wife of Zeus) | JUNO | Queen of gods; patron divinity of marriage | Iris (rainbow), her messenger |

338

| HESTIA (sister of Zeus) | VESTA | Goddess of fire in hearth; domestic life | |
|---|---|---|---|
| DEMETER (sister of Zeus) | CERES | Goddess of grain, agriculture | |
| POSEIDON (brother of Zeus) | NEPTUNE | God of sea; horses | trident (3-pronged spear) |
| HEPHAESTUS (son of Zeus and Hera) | VULCAN | God of fire; smith of gods; forger of armor of gods and heroes | anvil and forge; lame; Aphrodite his wife |
| ARES (son of Zeus and Hera) | MARS (Mavors) | God of offensive war | weapons of war and destruction |
| APHRODITE (daughter of Zeus and Dione), also called Cypris, Cytherea | VENUS | Goddess of love and beauty; fertility | usually attended by her son Eros (Cupid) whose father was Ares |
| ATHENA or Pallas (daughter of Zeus: born from his head) | MINERVA | Goddess of wisdom; defensive war; spinning, weaving, protectress of Athens; arts of peace | owl; olive tree; aegis; helmet, shield, spear |
| HERMES (son of Zeus and Maia) | MERCURY | Messenger of gods; speed, travelers, commerce, thieves; guide of souls of dead to underworld; cunning | winged hat; winged sandals; caduceus (winged wand with entwined serpents) |
| APOLLO or Phoebus (son of Zeus and Leto, or Latona) | | God of sun; prophecy; music; medicine; archery; patron god of young men | lyre; bow and arrow |
| ARTEMIS (twin sister of Apollo) | DIANA | Goddess of hunting; wild animals; moon; childbirth; patron divinity of maidens | bow and arrow; animals, especially hind |

## OTHER IMPORTANT GODS

*HADES*—also called Pluto; Latin name, *Dis, Orcus*. God of the underworld; brother of Zeus. Ruler of the souls of the dead; euphemistically, also giver of the wealth of the earth.

Hades as the abode of the dead (also called *Erebus, Orcus*): When the body has been properly buried, with a coin in the mouth

**339**

for fare, the soul went on a journey, guided by Hermes. There were a number of rivers in the underworld: Acheron, Phlegethon, Styx, Cocytus, Lethe. Properly buried persons who had their fare were rowed across the Styx by the old ferryman Charon. At the entrance to Hades proper stood the monstrous three-headed watchdog of the underworld, Cerberus. Judgment on the soul was pronounced by three judges, Minos, Aeacus, and Rhadamanthus, and the soul was assigned to Elysium (Elysian Fields), the abode of the blessed, or to Tartarus, the place of punishment. The most famous tales of punishment in Hades concern Tantalus, Ixion, Sisyphus, and the Danaids. Famous mortals who journeyed to the underworld and returned are Odysseus, Aeneas, Heracles, Theseus, and Orpheus.

*PERSEPHONE*—also called Kore; Latin name, *Proserpina*. Queen of the underworld; wife of Hades; daughter of Demeter and Zeus. Stolen by Hades while she was picking flowers in Sicily; sought for a long time by her griefstricken mother; ordered restored by Zeus, but since she had eaten some pomegranate seeds while in Hades, she was required to return to Hades several months a year (symbol of birth and death of vegetation in alternating seasons).

*DIONYSUS*—also called Bacchus; Latin name, *Liber*. Son of Zeus and Semele. God of wine. Symbol of birth and death in conception of his alternating disappearance and rebirth. Often worshipped with wild, orgiastic celebrations. Driven insane by Hera, wandered, followed by many creatures, especially Satyrs, Maenads, and Bacchantes.

*FATES*—called *Moerae* by Greeks; *Parcae* by Romans. Three Fates: Clotho, who spins the thread of life; Lachesis, who draws the thread out; Atropos, who cuts it. Supposed to determine the destiny of human beings. Even the great gods could not annul their decisions, though they might delay them.

*NEMESIS*—Divinity, representing the anger of the gods, sent to punish human beings who are excessively proud, insolent, ar-

**340**

rogant. The gods are conceived of as jealous of human beings, ready to punish those who commit the sin of *hybris*, pride, intemperate actions, insolence, arrogance. *Hybris* is usually thought of as stemming from prosperity, or good fortune. After *hybris* affected a person, the belief was that *Ate*, the goddess of blind infatuation, assailed him, driving him into wrong-doing.

*EUMENIDES* (Erinyes, Furies). Three horrible looking women, Allecto, Tisiphone, Megaera, goddesses of vengeance, who punished those who committed serious crimes by pursuing them eternally and driving them insane (force of conscience).

*MUSES.* Nine daughters of Zeus and Mnemosyne (Memory); patron goddesses of literature, fine arts, and science. Each protected a different sphere: Calliope, epic poetry; Clio, history; Euterpe, lyric poetry; Melpomene, tragedy; Terpsichore, dancing; Erato, love poetry; Polyhymnia, sacred poetry; Thalia, comedy; Urania, astronomy. Associated with Pieria (in Thessaly), Mt. Helicon (in Boeotia), and Mt. Parnassus (in Phocis). Closely connected with Apollo; the winged horse, Pegasus, their special favorite.

## MINOR DIVINITIES

*Satyrs.* Woodland creatures partly animal. Lascivious and intemperate; followers of Dionysus.

*Pan.* Latin, *Faunus.* God of shepherds and herdsmen; half-man, half-goat; plays syrinx (Pan's pipes); follower of Dionysus; inspires terror in travellers (panic).

*Nymphs.* Beautiful goddesses presiding over various aspects of nature: ocean (Oceanids); Mediterranean (Nereids, daughters of Nereus), etc.

*Iris.* The rainbow, messenger of gods, especially Hera.

*Nereus.* Old man of the sea; father of Nereids.

*Proteus.* Old man of the sea; keeper of Poseidon's seals; gift of prophecy; capable of changing his shape at will.

*Amphitrite.* Nereid; wife of Poseidon, queen of the sea.

*Triton.* Son of Poseidon and Amphitrite; aids sailors.

*Hebe.* Daughter of Zeus and Hera. Cupbearer of the gods, before being displaced by the Trojan boy, Ganymede.

*Hymen.* God of marriage.

*Thetis.* Sea-divinity. Daughter of Nereus; wife of Peleus, a mortal. Zeus married her to a mortal when he discovered that if he had a son by her, that son would overthrow him. Mother of Achilles.

*Charites.* Latin, Graces. Three goddesses of charm and beauty, gave refinement to life: Euphrosyne (joy), Aglaia (brilliance), Thalia (bloom).

*Asclepius.* Latin, *Aesculapius.* Son of Apollo, transformed from mortal into god; god of medicine.

*Hygeia.* Daughter of Asclepius; goddess of health.

*Eros.* Son of Ares and Aphrodite. Latin, *Cupid.* God of love; carries bow and arrow.

*Dioscuri.* Two sons of Zeus, Castor and Polydeuces (Pollux). Latin, *Gemini.* Gods of athletes and mariners. When Polydeuces died, his immortal brother, Castor, exchanged places with him in Hades on alternate days, and thus they both enjoyed immortality.

*Hecate.* Three-headed goddess of ghosts, sorcery, graveyards, and crossroads.

*Janus.* Italian god; protector of doorways; god of beginnings; two-headed; to the Romans, openings of the doors of his temple symbolized war, closing them peace.

*Lares.* Roman spirits who protected household and its property.

*Penates.* Roman spirits who protected the storeroom containing the food of the household.

*Manes.* Spirits of dead ancestors in Roman religion.

*Genius.* Spirit in Roman religion which protects an individual all his life.

**342**

# ORIGIN OF MEN

I. *Prometheus*. Titan, son of Iapetus; brother of Atlas and Epimetheus. Benefactor and champion of mankind. Created men, and gave them the gift of fire, to advance their civilization. When Zeus in anger deprived them of fire, Prometheus stole it in a hollow reed and restored it to them. Prometheus was punished by Zeus, who had him bound to a rock on Mt. Caucasus, where his liver was eaten daily by the eagle of Zeus. He was finally freed after many centuries by Heracles.

II. *Pandora*. To punish men, Zeus ordered Hephaestus to create the first woman, to plague them. She was given a gift by all the gods, and hence was called Pandora ("all-gifts"). Against the warnings of Prometheus (Forethought), his brother Epimetheus (Hindsight) accepted her as his wife. She brought as her dowry a jar or box filled with evils, which she was told never to open. But out of curiosity she did, and all evils flew out. She closed it, however, when there was only one thing left, Hope.

III. *Deucalion and Pyrrha*. When men became evil, Zeus decided to destroy all mankind, except Deucalion and Pyrrha. They were ordered to build a boat. A flood destroyed all men and women except these two. When their boat landed on Mt. Parnassus, they were instructed to throw stones over their heads: those thrown by Deucalion became men, those by Pyrrha women. Their descendants were Hellen (the first Greek), Aeolus, Dorus, Achaeus, and Ion, the ancestors of the Aeolians, Dorians, Achaeans, and Ionians.

# GLOSSARY

◙

**ACADEMY.** First university in world, founded in Athens by Plato ca. 388/7 B. C.; unbroken existence for ca. 900 years.

**ACHATES.** Trojan: faithful attendant and armor-bearer of Aeneas

**ACHAEA.** Homeric name for Greece: Roman name for province of Greece.

**ACHAEANS.** Early Greek people; Homeric name for Greeks.

**ACHERON.** River (or lake) in Hades.

**ACHILLES.** Greatest Greek warrior in Trojan war; hero of Homer's **"Iliad"**; son of sea-goddess Thetis and Peleus; slayer of Hector; finally killed by being shot in the heel, his only vulnerable spot, by Paris.

**ACROPOLIS.** Hill in Athens which was the religious center of the city; on it were famous temples, such as the Parthenon.

**ADEIMANTUS.** Brother of the Athenian philosopher Plato; one of the speakers in Plato's **"Republic"**.

**ADONIS.** Handsome young Greek hunter of legend loved by Aphrodite; after being killed by a boar, he was permitted to return to earth every year during Spring and Summer; his annual death and resurrection symbolized the cycle of vegetation.

**AEACUS.** Father of Peleus, grandfather of Achilles; after his death he became one of the three judges of Hades; character in **"Frogs"** of Aristophanes.

**AEGEAN CIVILIZATION.** Pre-Greek Bronze Age culture of the Aegean area, ca. 3000-1000 B.C., known through Homeric epics and archaeological discoveries.

**AEGEAN SEA.** Body of water between Hellas and Asia Minor, containing the Cyclades and many other islands.

**AEGEUS.** Legendary King of Athens; father of Theseus; promises Medea asylum in Athens, in Euripides' **"Medea"**.

**AEGIS.** Awe-inspiring protective beastplate worn by Zeus and Athena.

**AEGISTHUS.** Son of Thyestes, cousin of Agamemnon, loved Clyemnestra, wife of Agamemnon, whom they both murdered; after he became king of Mycenae, he was killed by Orestes, Agamemnon's son.

**AENEADAE.** Followers, or descendants of Aeneas: Trojans: Romans.

**AENEAS.** Son of Aphrodite and Anchises; son-in-law of Priam; second in command to Hector in Trojan War; king of the surviving Trojans after the fall of Troy; hero of Vergil's **"Aeneid"**.

**344**

**AENEID.** Epic by the Roman poet Vergil, relating the wanderings and battles of the Trojan hero Aeneas until he founded a city in Italy for the surviving Trojans; greatest nationalistic epic in world literature.

**AEOLIANS.** Branch of the Greek people.

**AEOLUS.** 1. Legendary ancestor of the Aeolians. 2. God of the winds, in Homer's **"Odyssey"** and Vergil's **"Aeneid"**.

**AEROPE.** Faithless wife of Atreus, killed by him; mother of Agamemnon and Menelaus.

**AESCHYLUS.** Athenian tragedian (525-455 B.C.), author of **"Prometheus Bound"** and **"Orestes Trilogy"**.

**AGAMEMNON.** Son of Atreus; husband of Clytemnestra; father of Orestes, Electra, Iphigenia, Chrysothemis; commander-in-chief of the Greek expedition against Troy; on the day of his return to his kingdom Mycenae as a conquering hero, he was murdered by his wife and her lover, Aegisthus.

**AGEMEMNON.** Tragedy by Aeschylus, first play of the **"Orestes Trilogy"**.

**AGATHON.** Athenian tragic poet whose house is the setting of Plato's **"Symposium"**; one of the speakers in this dialogue.

**AGON.** Dramatized debate in Greek Old Comedy.

**AJAX.** 1. Greek warrior at Troy, King of Locrians, son of Oileus; short, but speedy and skilled in archery. 2. Greek warrior at Troy, son of Telamon; cousin of Achilles; distinguished by physical prowess and lack of brains; committed suicide after losing contest with Odysseus over the possession of Achilles' armor.

**ALBA LONGA.** City in Italy founded, according to legend, by Aeneas' son, Ascanius.

**ALCAEUS.** Aristocratic soldier-poet of Lesbos (ca. 600 B.C.); outstanding Greek lyric poet.

**ALCIBIADES.** Brilliant, ambitious, unscrupulous, egoistic young Athenian, disciple of Socrates; inspirer of disastrous Sicilian Expedition during Peloponnesian War; turned traitor to Athens; speaker in Plato's **"Symposium"**.

**ALCINOUS.** King of the mythical Phaeacians, husband of Arete, father of Nausicaa; entertains Odysseus during his wanderings.

**ALCMAN.** Lyric poet of Sparta (ca. 630 B.C.).

**ALCMENA.** Queen of Thebes, wife of Amphitryon; mother of Heracles by Zeus.

**ALEXANDER THE GREAT.** King of Macedon (336-323 B.C.); conqueror of the Persian Empire; founder of Alexandria in Egypt.

**ALEXANDRIANISM.** Artificial, sophisticated, learned, bookish literary style of the Hellenistic Period (323-30 B.C.), involving perfection of form and the theme of romantic love.

**AMATA.** Wife of King Latinus, mother of Lavina in Vergil's **"Aeneid"**; hostile to Aeneas because she favored Turnus as her son-in-law; committed suicide.

**AMAZONS.** Mythical tribe of female warriors living in a matriarchal society.

**AMBROSIA.** Food of the gods.

**AMPHITRYON.** King of Thebes, husband of Alcmena.

**ANACREON.** Outstanding Greek lyric poet (ca. 563-478 B.C.), who wrote on the themes of wine, women, and song.

**ANATOLIA.** Coast of Asia Minor, inhabited by Greeks.

**ANAXAGORAS.** Greek philosopher (5th Cent. B.C.) who held that the cause of motion was Nous (Mind, Reason, God).

**ANAXIMANDER.** Greek philosopher (6th Cent. B.C.) who held that the ultimate material substance of the universe was Infinite (formless matter).

**ANAXIMENES.** Greek philosopher (6th Cent. B.C.) who held that the ultimate material substance of the universe was air.

**ANCHISES.** Trojan prince, father of Aeneas by Venus; accompanied Aeneas on his wanderings, died in Sicily.

**ANDROMACHE.** Beloved wife of the Trojan hero Hector; concubine of Achilles' son, Neoptolemus; discovered later by Aeneas as wife of Hector's brother, Helenus.

**ANNA.** Devoted sister of Dido, Queen of Carthage.

**ANNALS.** Greatest historical work of Tacitus, dealing with the events of A.D. 14-68.

**ANTICLEIA.** Wife of Laertes; mother of Odysseus; died of grief waiting for his return; her soul seen in Hades by Odysseus.

**ANTIGONE.** Greek ideal of filial and sisterly devotion; daughter of Oedipus and Jocasta; accompanied and tended her blind father Oedipus in his wanderings; buried alive by Creon for defying his orders that no one was to give decent burial to her brother Polynices; heroine of Sophocle's tragedy **"Antigone".**

**ANTILOCHUS.** Greek warrior at Troy; son of Nestor; close friend of Achilles.

**ANTINOUS.** Leading suitor of Penelope; slain by Odysseus.

**ANTISTROPHE.** Part of Greek choral lyric, performed by half of chorus.

**ANTONY.** Roman general, follower of Julius Caesar; member of the Second Triumvirate; lover and later husband of Cleopatra; committed suicide after defeat at Battle of Actium (31 B.C.) by Octavian (Augustus).

**ANYTUS.** One of the accusers of Socrates in his trial (399 B.C.).

**APHRODITE.** Greek divinity (Roman counterpart, Venus); goddess of love and beauty; lover of Ares (Mars); mother of Eros (Cupid).

**APOLLO.** Greek divinity (also called Phoebus); god of sun, prophecy, music, medicine, archery.

**APOLOGY.** Work of Plato purporting to be Socrates' speech of defense in his trial (399 B.C.).

**ARCHILOCHUS.** Outstanding Greek elegiac and iambic poet (ca. 650 B.C.).

**ARCHONS.** Nine annual civil executives of Athens.

**ARES.** Greek divinity (Roman counterpart, Mars); god of offensive war.

**ARETE.** Queen of mythical Phaeacians; wife of Alcinous, mother of Nausicaa.

**ARGONAUTS.** Fifty Greek heroes who accompanied Jason in search of the Golden Fleece.

**ARGOS.** Greek city-state in N. E. Peloponnesus; Homeric name for Argolis, Peloponnesus, Greece.

**ARGUS.** 1. 100-eyed monster assigned by Hera to watch Io, beloved of Zeus; slain by Hermes. 2. Old hunting dog of Odysseus.

**ARISTODEMUS.** Disciple of Socrates; one of the characters of Plato's **"Symposium"**.

**ARISTOPHANES.** Athenian (ca. 446-385 B.C.), greatest writer of Greek Old Comedy; author of **"Birds"**, **"Frogs"**, **"Clouds"**, and other comedies.

**ARISTOTLE.** Greek philosopher (384-322 B.C.), pupil of Plato, tutor of Alexander the Great, founder of the Lyceum: author of numerous works, including the **"Poetics"**, **"Politics"**, **Nicomachean Ethics"**, and treatises on logic, science, metaphysics; creator of the syllogism and formal logic.

**ARTAPHERNES.** Persian commander of the expedition against Greece in 490 B.C.

**ARTEMIS.** Greek divinity (Roman counterpart, Diana), twin sister of Apollo; goddess of hunting, moon; patron divinity of maidens.

**ARTEMISIA.** Queen of Halicarnassus; subject of Xerxes, King of Persians; distinguished herself at Battle of Salamis (480 B.C.).

**ASCANIUS.** Also called Iulius; son of Aeneas and Creusa; rescued from Troy by Aeneas; accompanied him in his wanderings; founded Alba Longa in Italy.

**ASTYANAX.** Infant son of Hector and Andromache; sacrificed at tomb of Achilles by the Greeks.

**ATE.** Greek goddess of infatuation who, when men committed the sin of **"hybris"**, blinded them to the consequences of their actions.

**ATHENA.** Greek divinity (Roman counterpart, Minerva); born fully grown, fully armed from Zeus' head; goddess of wisdom, defensive war, household arts; protectress of Athens.

**ATHENS.** Greek city-state in E. central Greece; political center of Attica; first democracy in world; dominated Athenian Empire, 5th Cent. B.C.; cultural and artistic center; after political eclipse, university center of ancient world.

**ATLAS.** Titan; brother of Prometheus; assigned the eternal task of holding the heavens on his shoulders after defeat of Titans by gods.

**ATREUS.** Grandson of Tantalus and son of Pelops; father of Agamemnon and Menelaus; slain by his brother Thyestes.

**ATTICA.** Peninsula in E. central Greece, the political center of which was the city-state of Athens.

**AUGUSTUS.** First Roman emperor (30 B.C.-A.D. 14); grandnephew and adopted son of Julius Caesar.

**AULIS.** Harbor in Boeotia; mustering place of Greek expedition to Troy; here Agamemnon sacrificed his daughter Iphigenia.

**BACCHUS.** See DIONYSUS.

**BIRDS.** Comedy by Aristophanes.

**BOEOTIA.** Greek region in E. Central Hellas, N. W. of Attica; principal city, Thebes.

**BRISEIS.** Beloved war captive of Achilles; dispute with Agamemnon over possession of her led to sulking of Achilles at Troy.

**CADUCEUS.** Wand of Hermes; winged, with two serpents.

**CAESAR.** Roman general, statesman, and author; member of First Triumvirate; conqueror of Gaul; dictator of Rome; assassinated by Roman Senators 44 B.C.; his name became a title of the Roman emperors.

**CALCHAS.** Official soothsayer of the Greek expedition against Troy.

**CALYPSO.** Nymph, daughter of Atlas; kept Odysseus on her island for 7 years.

**CAMILLA.** Warrior-maid, ally of Turnus in Vergil's **"Aeneid"**; slain in battle.

**CARTHAGE.** Powerful Phoenician commercial colony in N. Africa, near modern Tunis; according to legend, found by Dido; destroyed by the Romans after the three Punic Wars (264-146 B.C.).

**CASSANDRA.** Daughter of Priam; prophetess whose predictions were never believed, slain by Clytemnestra after she was brought to Mycenae as Agamemnon's concubine.

**CATHARSIS.** According to Aristotle, the proper effect of tragedy—the purging of the emotions of pity and fear.

**CATULLUS.** Roman lyric poet (ca. 84-54 B.C.), famous for his love poems to Lesbia (Clodia).

**CEBES.** Theban; one of the speakers in Plato's **"Phaedo"**.

**CENTAURS.** Half-man half-horse creatures of mythology.

**CEPHALUS.** Wealthy alien business man of Piraeus whose home is the setting of Plato's **"Republic"**.

**CERBERUS.** Three-headed watch-dog of Hades.

**CERES.** See DEMETER.

**CHARYBDIS.** Mythical whirlpool in Straits of Messina, opposite Scylla.

**CHIMAERA.** Mythical monster, partly lion, goat, dragon, slain by Bellerophon.

**CHOEPHOROE (Libation-Bearers).** Tragedy by Aeschylus; 2nd play of **"Orestes Trilogy"**.

**CHRYSEIS.** Beloved war captive of Agamemnon at Troy; the request for her ransom by her father leads to quarrel between Agamemnon and Achilles.

**CHRYSOTHEMIS.** Weak-willed daughter of Agamemnon and Clytemnestra.

**CHORAL LYRIC.** Greek literary form, for various social and religious functions, sung and danced by a chorus.

**CICERO.** Distinguished Roman lawyer, orator, statesman, writer; assassinated in 43 B.C.

**CIRCE.** Enchantress encountered by Odysseus in his travels, who turned his men into swine and with whom he lived for a year.

**CITY OF GOD.** Defense of Christianity by St. Augustine.

**CLEISTHENES.** Athenian reformer; founder of democracy (508 B.C.).

**348**

**CLOUDS.** Comedy by Aristophanes.

**CLYTEMNESTRA.** Wife of Agamemnon; daughter of Leda; sister of Helen; murdered her husband on his return from Troy; married her lover Aegisthus; killed by her son Orestes.

**COCYTUS.** River of Hades.

**CONSUL.** One of two annual chief-executives of Roman Republic.

**CORCYRA.** Island off W. coast of Greece; ally of Athens in Peloponnesian War.

**CORINTH.** City-state of Greece on Isthmus of Corinth; scene of Euripides' **"Medea"**.

**CREON.** 1. Uncle of Oedipus; later king of Thebes; executes Antigone for burying her brother Polynices against his orders. 2. King of Corinth, slain by Medea's sorcery after he married his daughter to Jason.

**CRETE.** Large island S. of Aegean, S.E. of Hellas; cradle of European culture; home of Idomeneus, Greek ally at Troy.

**CREUSA.** Daughter of Priam, wife of Aeneas, mother of Ascanius; died in the fall of Troy.

**CRITO.** Friend and admirer of Socrates.

**CROESUS.** King of Lydian Empire, conqueror of Greeks of Anatolia; reported by Herodotus to have had a conversation on happiness with Solon; his empire ended by Cyrus, King of Persia; famous for his wealth.

**CRONUS.** (Roman counterpart, Saturn); Titan; seized power of the universe from his father Uranus, and was in turn overthrown by his son Zeus; agricultural divinity.

**CUMAE.** Greek colony on the coast of Italy N. of Naples; in Vergil's **"Aeneid"** the place where the Trojans first landed in Italy, and home of the Sibyl who guides Aeneas to Hades.

**CUPID.** See EROS.

**CYCLADES.** Large group of islands in Aegean Sea serving as communication bridge between Greece and Asia Minor.

**CYCLOPS.** Barbaric, cannibalistic, one-eyed, cave-dwelling giants of legend; appear in Homer's **"Odyssey"**, Vergil's **"Aeneid"**, Theocritus' **"Idyls"**.

**CYPRIS.** Alternate name for Aphrodite.

**CYRUS.** Founder of Persian Empire (550 B.C.); conqueror of Lydian Empire, Assyria, Babylonia, etc.

**DACTYLIC HEXAMETER.** Standard meter of ancient epic poetry; consists of six feet in the verse, either dactyls ($- \smile \smile$) or spondees ($- -$).

**DANAIDS.** 49 daughters of Danaus, King of Argos, who slew their husbands on their marriage night; punished in Hades by being forced to try to fill with water a vessel with holes in it.

**DANAE.** Mother of Perseus by Zeus, who visited her as a shower of gold; cast into sea in a chest with her infant son, but rescued.

**DAPHNIS.** Semi-divine Sicilian shepherd who boasted of his eternal love for a nymph; Aphrodite made him fall in love with someone else, and he died resisting his uncontrollable emotion, mourned by woodland creatures.

**349**

**DARIUS.** King of Persia (521-486 B.C.); suppressed Ionian Revolt; organized 1st expedition against Greece.

**DATIS.** Persian commander of the expedition against Greece in 490 B.C.

**DEIPHOBUS.** Son of Priam and Hecuba; Hector's favorite brother; husband of Helen after death of Paris, treacherously slain by Menelaus with Helen's aid.

**DELIAN LEAGUE.** Confederacy of Greek city-states, organized in 477 B.C., under Athenian leadership, for defense against Persia, with headquarters on the island of Delos; transformed into Athenian Empire in 454 B.C.

**DELOS.** Small island in the Cyclades group; religious center sacred to Apollo; headquarters of the Delian League.

**DELPHI.** Greek city-state in Phocis, on the slopes of Mt. Parnassus; famous as the center of the oracle of Apollo.

**DEMETER.** Greek divinity (Roman counterpart, Ceres); goddess of grain; mother of Persephone.

**DEMOCRITUS.** Greek philosopher (5th Cent. B.C.), co-founder of the atomic theory; the "laughing philosopher."

**DEMOSTHENES.** 1. Athenian general, one of the leaders of the Sicilian Expedition, captured and executed by Sicilians. 2. Athenian orator and statesman (384-322 B.C.), leader of democratic forces in Athens, organized Greek opposition to Philip of Macedon; committed suicide.

**DE RERUM NATURA.** Didactic epic on the physics of Epicurean philosophy by the Roman author Lucretius.

**DEUS EX MACHINA.** Technical device in Greek theater: consists of dummy of a god suspended from metal crane; employed, mostly by Euripides, for unravelling in a miraculous way the unsolved problems of the tragedy.

**DIALECTIC METHOD.** Socrates' manner of teaching through questions and answers, involving exposure of ignorance and elimination of error in judgments through reason.

**DIALECTICS.** The highest study in Plato's educational curriculum for perfecting the true philosopher; it involves absolutely no sense perception and is aimed at attaining the Idea of the Good, the highest form of reality.

**DIANA.** See ARTEMIS.

**DIDO.** Legendary Queen of Carthage; leading character in Vergil's **"Aeneid"**; gives hospitality to the shipwrecked Trojans, becomes Aeneas' lover; commits suicide when he abandons her to go on to Italy to fulfill his destiny.

**DIOMEDES.** Son of Tydeus, King of Argos, outstanding Greek hero in Trojan War, despite his youth; leading character in Homer's **"Iliad"**.

**DIONYSUS.** Greek divinity, also called Bacchus (Roman counterpart, Liber); god of wine; the origins of tragedy and comedy are to be traced back to his worship.

**DIOTIMA.** Prophetess of Mantineia, from whom Socrates, in his speech in Plato's **"Symposium"**, pretends he learned about the nature of love.

**DITHYRAMB.** Greek choral lyric in honor of Dionysus; origin of tragedy.

**DORIANS.** Branch of the Greek people.

**ELECTRA.** Daughter of Agamemnon and Clytemnestra; sister of Orestes; a virile personality who abets the murder of Clytemnestra and her lover Aegisthus by Orestes to avenge the murder of Agamemnon.

**ELECTRA.** Tragedies by Sophocles and Euripides, on same theme as **"Choephoroe"** of Aeschylus.

**ELEGIAC POETRY.** Originally Greek semi-lyric literary form, accompanied by flute, written in couplets of alternating dactylic hexameters and modified dactylic pentameters, and used for such subjects as military themes, banquet songs, political thought, tombstone epitaphs; later used exclusively for love poetry.

**ELPENOR.** Youngest member of Odysseus' crew; dies accidentally on Circe's island; is promised proper burial by Odysseus when he meets his soul in Hades.

**ELYSIAN FIELDS.** Also called Elysium; the place where, in Greek legend, the souls of worthy people lived in eternal happiness; at first located in the far west, later in Hades.

**EMPEDOCLES.** Greek philosopher (5th Cen. B.C.), who espoused the doctrine of the 4 elements (earth, air, fire, water) as the ultimate principles of the universe, and explained change and motion through the forces of attraction and repulsion.

**EPHEBIC OATH.** Oath of devotion to Athens taken by citizens at the age of 18, when they entered compulsory military service.

**EPIC.** Long narrative poem in dignified style on majestic subject, the exploits of a national hero at the beginnings of a people's legendary past.

**EPICUREANISM.** Hellenistic and Roman philosophy, whose aim was to teach personal happiness, peace of mind and tranquillity, through escape from evils, eradication of superstition and fear of gods and death by scientific knowledge; taught avoidance of entangling responsibilities, moderate living, desirability of virtue and justice.

**EPICURUS.** Hellenistic philosopher (342-270 B.C.), founder of Epicureanism.

**EPINICION.** Greek choral lyric commemorating athletic victory; written especially by Pindar.

**EPISODE.** Act of Greek drama.

**EPITHALAMIUM.** Choral lyric performed at marriage.

**EPODE.** Third stanza of Pindaric ode, performed by entire chorus.

**EPOPS.** Hoopoe (lapwing), king of the birds in Aristophanes' **"Birds"**.

**ER.** Mythical character in Plato's **"Republic"**, who was taken for dead in battle, visited Hades, but regained consciousness on his funeral pyre, and related his experiences in the afterlife.

**ERETRIA.** Greek city-state in Euboea, which aided the Ionians against Persia, and was captured and destroyed by the Persians in 490 B.C.

**ERIS.** Greek goddess of discord; she threw in the "apple of discord" at the

**351**

marriage of Peleus and Thetis, which led to the judgment of Paris and the Trojan War.

**EROS.** Greek divinity (Roman counterpart, Cupid); god of love; son of Aphrodite and Ares.

**ETEOCLES.** Son of Oedipus and Jocasta; brother of Polynices and Antigone; he and his brother slew each other in a duel during the siege of Thebes by the Seven against Thebes.

**ETRURIA.** Plain in Italy on the W. coast, north of Latium.

**ETRUSCANS.** People from Asia Minor who settled in the plain of Etruria in Italy ca. 1000 B.C.; conquered and ruled Rome during early Roman kingdom; aid Trojans in Vergil's **"Aeneid"**.

**EUELPIDES.** Athenian adventurer in Aristophanes' **"Birds"**.

**EUMAEUS.** Faithful swineherd of Odyssseus; helps him slay suitors.

**EUMENIDES.** Greek divinities, also called Erinyes, Furies; goddesses of vengeance who eternally pursue criminals and drive them insane.

**EUMENIDES.** Tragedy by Aeschylus, 3rd play of **"Orestes Trilogy"**.

**EURIPIDES.** Athenian writer of tragedy (480-406 B.C.), e.g., **"Trojan Women"**, **"Electra"**, **"Hippolytus"**, **"Medea"**.

**EURYALUS.** Courageous Trojan in Vergil's **"Aeneid"**, slain in ambush with his friend Nisus.

**EURYCLEIA.** Faithful old nurse of Odyseus.

**EURYDICE.** 1. Wife of Creon, King of Thebes; commits suicide after the deaths of Antigone and her son Haemon. 2. Young wife of Orpheus, who died shortly after their marriage; he was permitted to bring her back from Hades, but lost her forever when he looked at her before they reached the upper world.

**EURYLOCHUS.** Leading member of Odysseus' crew, characterized by poor judgment.

**EURYMACHUS.** Prominent suitor of Penelope, slain by Odysseus.

**EURYMEDON.** Athenian general in Sicilian expedition; slain in battle.

**EURYXIMACHUS.** Athenian physician, one of speakers in Plato's **"Symposium"**.

**EVANDER.** Mythical Greek king in Italy, ruling at site of later Rome; aids Trojans in Vergil's **"Aeneid"**; father of Pallas.

**EXODOS.** Part of Greek tragedy following last choral ode.

**FATES.** Also called Moerae, Parcae; divinities who determined irrevocably the destinies of human beings.

**FLAVIAN DYNASTY.** Three Roman emperors (69-96 A.D.), Vespasian and his sons, Titus and Domitian.

**FROGS.** Comedy by Aristophanes.

**FURIES.** See EUMENIDES.

**GALATEA.** Sea-nymph; the Cyclops Polyphemus pined with unrequited love for her.

**GANYMEDE.** Handsome Trojan boy who displaced Hebe as cupbearer of the gods.

**GERMANY.** Historical monograph on geography, peoples, and customs of ancient Germany by the Roman historian Tacitus.

**GLAUCON.** Brother of Athenian philosopher Plato; speaker in the "Republic".

**GOLDEN AGE.** 1. Legendary first period of human existence. 2. Of Athens, Periclean Age, 461-429 B.C. 3. Of Roman literature, 70 B.C.-A.D. 14.

**GOLDEN BOUGH.** Mythical branch which Aeneas must find and pluck before he can visit Hades.

**"GOOD" EMPERORS.** Five Roman emperors (A.D. 96-180), Nerva, Trajan, Hadrian, Antoninus Pius, Marcus Aurelius.

**GORGO.** Character in 15th "Idyl" of Theocritus.

**GORGONS.** Three horrible creatures of mythology; one of them, Medusa, who turned people into stone when they looked at her, was slain by Perseus.

**GREAVES.** Bronze shin-guards, part of soldier's armor in Homer's "Iliad".

**GYLIPPUS.** Spartan general who successfully assisted in the defense of Syracuse against the great Athenian expedition in 413 B.C.

**HADES.** 1. Greek divinity, also called Pluto (Roman counterpart, Dis, Orcus); god of underworld and souls of dead. 2. The abode of the souls of dead, divided into Elysium and Tartarus.

**HAEMON.** Son of Creon, King of Thebes; commits suicide when Creon causes death of his fiancee Antigone.

**HANNIBAL.** Famous Carthaginian general who successfully invaded Italy by crossing the Alps in 2nd Punic War (218-201 B.C.), but was finally defeated.

**HARMODIUS AND ARISTOGEITON.** Two Athenians who killed the tyrant Hipparchus (514 B.C.) and were celebrated in Athens as heroes of Athenian democracy.

**HARPIES.** Half-maiden, half-bird creatures of mythology who attacked banqueters and defiled their food.

**HECATOMB.** Great public sacrifice.

**HECTOR.** Eldest son of Priam and Hecuba; outstanding Trojan hero, who slew Achilles' friend Patroclus, and was in turn killed in a duel with Achilles.

**HECUBA.** Wife of Priam; after fall of Troy she was taken into captivity to Greece.

**HELEN.** Wife of Menelaus; her elopement with Paris to Troy caused the Trojan War; after Paris' death she married his brother Deiphobus; she was captured by Menelaus at Troy, but after reconciliation returned with him to Sparta; reputed the most beautiful woman of her time.

**HELIOS.** Early Greek god of sun; son of Hyperion; the slaying of his sacred cattle by Odysseus' men caused their destruction.

**HELLAS.** 1. Part of kingdom of Achilles in Thessaly. 2. Later, Greek name for peninsula of Greece.

**HELLENISTIC CULTURE.** The civilization of the East after death of Alexander the Great (356-323 B.C.); intermingling of Greek and Oriental culture resulting from Alexander's conquests and policies.

**HELLESPONT.** The Dardanelles, the straits separating Europe from Asia; important strategic waterway and commercial route.

**HELOTS.** The serfs of the Spartans.

**HEMLOCK.** The poison used in executions in Athens; Socrates drank the hemlock.

**HEPHAESTUS.** Greek divinity (Roman counterpart, Vulcan); god of fire, smith of the gods; lame; husband of Aphrodite.

**HERA.** Greek divinity (Roman counterpart, Juno); wife of her brother Zeus; queen of gods; patron divinity of marriage.

**HERACLES.** Roman name, Hercules; son of Zeus and Alcmena; the strongman of Greek mythology, characterized by brains, brawn, gluttony, drunkenness; famous for his twelve labors.

**HERACLITUS.** Greek philosopher (6th-5th Cent. B.C.); doctrines that fire was ultimate material principle of universe, that nothing is static ("All is flux"), and that change is the conflict of opposites; the "weeping philosopher".

**HERMES.** Greek divinity (Roman counterpart, Mercury); messenger of the gods; guides souls to underworld; equipped with winged hat, winged sandals, caduceus.

**HERODOTUS.** Greek historian (ca. 485-425 B.C.); Father of History; author of **"History"** (of the Persian Wars).

**HESTIA.** Greek divinity (Roman counterpart, Vesta); goddess of hearth.

**HIERO.** Tyrant of Syracuse (5th Cent. B.C.); Pindaric ode in his honor.

**HIPPARCHUS.** Tyrant of Athens (528-514 B.C.), son of Peisistratus; slain by Harmodius and Aristogeiton.

**HIPPIAS.** Tyrant of Athens (528-510 B.C.), son of Peisistratus; overthrown and exiled, he turned traitor and assisted the Persians in invading Greece.

**HIPPOLYTE.** Queen of Amazons, captured by Theseus, King of Athens; mother by Theseus of Hippolytus.

**HIPPOLYTUS.** Son of Theseus and Hippolyte; characterized by chastity and love of hunting; unjustly accused by his stepmother Phaedra, who was in love with him, and slain as result of Theseus' hasty curse.

**HIPPOLYTUS.** Tragedy by Euripides.

**HISTORIA.** Herodotus' history of the Persian Wars.

**HISTORIES.** Account of the events from A.D. 68-96 by Roman historian Tacitus.

**HOMER.** Greek epic poet (9th Cent. B.C.), author of **"Iliad"**, and **"Odyssey"**; first extant European author; world's greatest epic poet.

**HOMERIC QUESTION.** Debate started in 1795 by the German scholar F. A. Wolf, involving the authorship of the **"Iliad"** and **"Odyssey"**; for a long time it was held that these epics were not the work of one man but collections of folk tales or that they were written by two different authors; today it is generally accepted that they were composed by one man, Homer, who used earlier traditional material and style.

**HORACE.** Roman lyric poet, satirist, moralist (65-8 B.C.); member of

**354**

literary circle of Maecenas during Augustan Age; author of **"Odes"**, **"Satires"**, and other works.

**HYBRIS.** Sin, in Greek thought, of excessive pride, insolence, arrogance; it was supposed to come about through too much prosperity and to be punished, because of the jealousy of the gods, by Nemesis.

**HYPOKRITES.** Greek word for "actor".

**IAMBIC POETRY.** Greek semi-lyric literary form used for satire.

**ICHOR.** The blood of the gods.

**IDA.** Mountain near Troy.

**IDEALISM.** Philosophic position which regards ideas and concepts perceived by reason as true, and rejects sense perception and material things as invalid sources of truth.

**IDYLS.** Pastoral poetry and mimes of Greek author Theocritus.

**ILIAD.** Epic poem by Homer, having as its central theme wrath of Achilles.

**ILIUM.** Troy; 3 miles from Hellespont; scene of Homer's **"Iliad"**, Euripides' **"Trojan Women"**, Vergil's **"Aeneid"** (Book II).

**IN MEDIAS RES.** The technique of beginning a narrative in the middle of the story; employed by Homer and Vergil.

**IO.** One of the loves of Zeus; turned into heifer by Hera; pursued by 100-eyed Argus; her future is predicted by Prometheus in Aeschylus' **"Prometheus Bound"**.

**IONIA.** Central coast of Asia Minor, inhabited by Greeks.

**IONIANS.** Branch of Greek people.

**IPHIGENIA.** Also called Iphianassa; daughter of Agamemnon and Clytemnestra; sacrificed by Agamemnon at Aulis to obtain favorable winds for the Greek expedition against Troy; according to another version, she was rescued by Artemis and made priestess among the Taurians, from whom she was rescued by her brother Orestes.

**IRIS.** Greek divinity; the rainbow; messenger of Hera.

**ISMENE.** Daughter of Oedipus and Jocasta; sister of Antigone; character in Sophocles' **"Oedipus at Colonus"** and **"Antigone"**.

**ITHACA.** Island off W. central coast of Greece; home of Odysseus.

**IULUS.** See ASCANIUS.

**JANUS.** Roman two-headed divinity; protector of doorways; god of beginnings; the opening of the doors of his temple symbolized war, the closing peace.

**JASON.** Greek adventurer who succeeded in obtaining the Golden Fleece with aid of the sorceress Medea; when he divorced her to marry the young princess of Corinth she murdered the girl, her father, and her own two children by Jason.

**JOCASTA.** Queen of Thebes, wife of Laius and, after his death, of her own son Oedipus; committed suicide when she discovered she was married to her son.

**JULIO-CLAUDIAN DYNASTY.** Five Roman emperors (30 B.C.-A.D. 68), Augustus, Tiberius, Caligula, Claudius, Nero.

**JUNO.** See HERA.

**JUPITER.** See ZEUS.

**JUVENAL.** Greatest Roman writer of satire (ca. A.D. 60-150).

**LACEDAEMONIA (LACONIA).** S.E. part of Peloponnesus, with political center at Sparta; in **"Iliad"** and **"Odyssey"**, kingdom of Menelaus.

**LAERTES.** Aged father of Odysseus.

**LAESTRYGONIANS.** Giant cannibals encountered by Odysseus.

**LAIUS.** King of Thebes, husband of Jocasta, father of Oedipus; killed by Oedipus.

**LAMACHUS.** Athenian general killed by Syracusans in Sicilian Expedition.

**LAOCOÖN.** Trojan priest who warned Trojans not to drag the wooden horse into Troy; killed with his sons by two serpents.

**LARES.** Protecting spirits of Roman household; usually associated with Penates.

**LATINS.** Italic inhabitants of the plain of Latium in Italy.

**LATINUS.** Mythical weak-willed king of the early Latins whose daughter, Lavinia, Aeneas marries.

**LATIUM.** Plain in W. central Italy; in the N. part of Latium was the river Tiber and Rome.

**LAUSUS.** Young son of Etruscan tyrant Mezentius, slain by Aeneas.

**LAVINIA.** Daughter of King Latinus and Queen Amata whose hand Aeneas wins.

**LAVINIUM.** Mythical city in Latium founded by Aeneas and named after his Italian wife Lavinia.

**LEDA.** Queen of Sparta, wife of Tyndareus; visited by Zeus in form of swan; mother of Helen, Clytemnestra, Castor, Pollux.

**LEONIDAS.** Spartan king who died heroically defending the Pass of Thermopylae with 300 Spartans against the Persians in 480 B.C.

**LESBIA.** Pseudonym used by Catullus for his mistress, probably Clodia.

**LESBOS.** Large island off N.W. coast of Asia Minor; home of Alcaeus and Sappho.

**LETHE.** River of forgetfulness in Hades whose water was drunk by souls before reincarnation.

**LETO (LATONA).** Beloved of Zeus; mother of Apollo and Artemis.

**LEUCIPPUS.** Greek philosopher (5th Cent. B.C.); co-founder with Democritus of atomic theory.

**LIBATION.** An offering of wine, poured on the ground, to the gods.

**LIVIA.** Wife of Augustus; first Roman empress; mother of Emperor Tiberius.

**LOXIAS.** Variant name of Apollo.

**LUCRETIUS.** Roman poet (ca. 99-55 B.C.), author of **"De Rerum Natura"**, didactic epic on the physical science of Epicureanism.

**LYCEUM.** School in Athens founded by Aristotle ca. 335 B.C.; center of Peripatetic philosophy.

**LYCON.** One of accusers of Socrates, mentioned in Plato's **"Apology"**.

**LYRIC.** Short poem, set to music, revealing the personal emotion or thought of the author.

**MACEDONIA.** Large kingdom N. of Greece whose rulers Philip II and his son Alexander the Great conquered Greece and the Persian Empire.

**MAECENAS.** Friend of Augustus; literary patron of the outstanding authors of the Augustan Age, e.g. Vergil, Horace.

**MAGNA GRAECIA.** Italian name for S. Italy, populated by numerous Greek city-states.

**MANES.** Spirits of dead ancestors in Roman family religion.

**MARATHON.** Village ca. 26 miles N.E. of Athens where Athenians defeated Persians in 490 B.C.

**MARCUS AURELIUS.** Roman emperor (A.D. 161-190); Stoic philosopher; author of **"Meditations"**.

**MARDONIUS.** Son-in-law of King Darius of Persia; commander of Persian forces in Greece after Battle of Salamis; defeated at Plataea, 479 B.C.

**MARS.** See ARES.

**MATERIALISM.** Philosophic position which bases knowledge of truth on observations through sense-perception, and which regards ideas and concepts as reflection of material things and processes.

**MEDEA.** Sorceress wife of Jason who aided him in obtaining the Golden Fleece; when he divorced her she killed his bride, her father, and her own two children by Jason.

**MEDEA.** Tragedy by Euripides.

**MEDON.** Herald of Odysseus at Ithaca; consorts with Penelope's suitors, but his life is spared by Odysseus.

**MELANTHIUS.** Traitorous goatherd of Odysseus, mutilated and slain by him.

**MELETUS.** One of accusers of Socrates in Plato's **"Apology"**.

**MELOS.** Island in Cyclades group in Aegean sea; besieged, captured and brutally treated by Athens in 416 B.C., during Peloponnesian War.

**MENELAUS.** King of Sparta, brother of Agamemnon, first husband of Helen; after fall of Troy he was reunited with her; prominent character in Homer's **"Iliad"** and **"Odyssey"**.

**MENTOR.** Friend of Odysseus, custodian of his property in Ithaca during his 20-year absence.

**MEROPE.** Queen of Corinth, wife of Polybus; foster-mother of Oedipus.

**MERCURY.** See HERMES.

**MEZENTIUS.** Exiled Etruscan tyrant; father of Lausus; ally of Turnus in Vergil's **"Aeneid"**; slain by Aeneas.

**MILETUS.** Greek city-state on coast of Ionia; birthplace of world philosophy; destroyed by Persians, 494 B.C.

**MILTIADES.** Athenian statesman and general; strategist of Athenian victory over Persians at Marathon, 490 B.C.

**MINERVA.** See ATHENA.

**MINOS.** Powerful king of Crete; son of Zeus and Europa; labyrinth built for him by Daedalus; became one of judges of Hades.

**MUSES.** 9 daughters of Zeus and Mnemosyne; patron goddesses of literature, fine arts, science, each protecting different sphere.

**MYCENAE.** Kingdom of Agamemnon in N.E. Peloponnesus.

**357**

**MYRMIDONS.** Brutal, obedient soldiers of Achilles.

**MYTILENE.** Greek city-state on Island of Lesbos; home of Sappho and Alcaeus; revolted from Athenian Empire, 427 B.C.

**NAUSICAA.** Young princess of Scheria; daughter of Alcinous and Arete; offers hospitality to shipwrecked Odysseus and guides him to her father's palace.

**NECTAR.** Drink of the gods.

**NEMESIS.** 1. In Homer, public indignation against those who break unwritten clan laws. 2. Later, divinity sent by gods to pursue and punish those guilty of sin of hybris.

**NEOPTOLEMUS.** Cruel son of Achilles; slayer of Priam, Astyanax, Polyxena; Andromache, Hector's wife, became his concubine.

**NEPTUNE.** See POSEIDON.

**NERO.** Roman emperor (A.D. 54-68), last of Julio-Claudian Dynasty; cruel, egoistic; believed to have caused great fire at Rome; first persecutor of Christians; orders suicide of Seneca.

**NESTOR.** Aged king of Pylus; Greek hero in Trojan War; counsels harmony and compromise, talkative, reminisces about his youth; visited by Odysseus' son Telemachus.

**NICIAS.** Athenian general of Sicilian Expedition; captured and executed by Syracusans, 413 B.C.

**NICOMACHEAN ETHICS.** Work of Aristotle; probably edited by his son, Nicomachus.

**NISUS.** Courageous Trojan in Vergil's **"Aeneid"**; slain in ambush with his friend Euryalus.

**NYMPHS.** Beautiful minor goddesses associated with various aspects of nature.

**OCEANUS.** Titan, son of Uranus and Ge; river supposed to encircle earth; neutral in conflict between Titans and gods; advises Prometheus to submit to Zeus in **"Prometheus Bound"**.

**ODES.** Lyric poems of Roman author Horace.

**ODYSSEUS.** Also called Ulysses; king of Ithaca; husband of Penelope; father of Telemachus; leading Greek warrior in Trojan War; hero of Homer's **"Odyssey"**.

**ODYSSEY.** Epic poem by Homer, having as its central theme the wanderings and homecoming of Odysseus.

**OEDIPUS AT COLONUS.** Tragedy by Sophocles.

**OEDIPUS REX.** Tragedy by Sophocles.

**OGYGIA.** Mediterranean island, home of nymph Calypso, with whom Odysseus stayed 7 years.

**OLIGARCHY.** Government by the few.

**OLYMPIA.** Greek city-state in W. central Peloponnesus; site of the Olympic Games.

**OLYMPUS.** Mountain in N.E. Thessaly, highest in Greece; supposed home of the Olympian gods.

**ORCHESTRA.** Circular "dancing place" of Greek theater where all the action takes place.

**ORESTEIA.** Tragic trilogy by Aeschylus, consisting of **"Agamemnon"**, **"Libation-Bearers"**, **"Eumenides"**; only extant trilogy.

**ORESTES.** Son of Agamemnon and Clytemnestra; brought up in Phocis after his father's murder; later, abetted by his sister Electra, kills Clytemnestra and her lover Aegisthus; driven insane by Eumenides, but finally acquitted.

**ORGANON.** Aristotle's 6 treatises on logic.

**ORPHEUS.** Mythical poet, whose wife Euridyce was killed shortly after their marriage; because of the charm of his music he was permitted to bring her back from Hades, but lost her forever when he looked at her before they reached the upper world.

**PALINURUS.** Aeneas' pilot who was lost overboard; he is promised proper burial when Aeneas meets his soul in Hades.

**PALLADIUM.** Small image of Athena supposed to protect Troy; stolen from Troy by Odysseus and Diomedes during Trojan War.

**PALLAS.** 1. Variant name of Athena. 2. Young son of King Evander in Vergil's **"Aeneid"**; slain by Turnus.

**PAN.** Greek divinity (Latin counterpart, Faunus); god of shepherds and herdsmen; half-man, half-goat.

**PANDORA.** First woman, according to Greek legend; brought box of evils with her to earth as dowry.

**PARABASIS.** Part of Greek Old Comedy; address of chorus to audience giving poet's views.

**PARIS.** Trojan prince; son of Priam; awards golden apple to Aphrodite; elopes with Helen of Troy; lacks sense of responsibility; kills Achilles.

**PARMENIDES.** Greek philosopher (6th Cent. B.C.); Father of Idealism; denied material world and sense-perception as true; truth only in eternal, static ideas perceived by reason.

**PARNASSUS.** Mountain in central Hellas, in Phocis; associated with Apollo and the Muses.

**PARODOS.** 1. Passageway through which chorus enters orchestra in Greek theater. 2. Entrance dance of chorus in Greek drama.

**PARTHENON.** Famous temple of Athena on Acropolis in Athens; part of it used as treasury of Athenian Empire.

**PASTORAL POETRY.** Also called Bucolic; lyric poem dealing with lives and loves of shepherds; created by Theocritus.

**PATROCLUS.** Closest friend of Achilles at Troy; his death at hands of Hector caused Achilles to return to battle.

**PAUSANIAS.** One of speakers in Plato's **"Symposium"**.

**PEGASUS.** Winged horse of Muses; used by Bellerophon when he slew the Chimaera.

**PEISISTRATUS.** 1. Son of Nestor, King of Pylus; accompanies Telemachus to Sparta, in Homer's **"Odyssey"**. 2. Tyrant of Athens (560-528 B.C.).

**PELASGIANS.** Name of primitive inhabitants of Greece.

**359**

**PELEUS.** Greek hero, husband of sea-goddess Thetis; father of Achilles.

**PELOPONNESIAN LEAGUE.** Confederacy of most of free city-states of Peloponnesus under Spartan hegemony (ca. 500-370 B.C.).

**PELOPONNESIAN WAR.** Disastrous struggle between Athens and Sparta and their allies (431-404 B.C.), resulting in defeat of Athens; the events of 431-411 B.C. are described by the Greek historian Thucydides.

**PELOPONNESUS.** Southern Hellas.

**PELOPS.** Son of Tantalus; father of Atreus and Thyestes; killed and served as food to the gods by Tantalus; restored to life, later won Hippodamia as his bride by defeating her father Oenomaus in a chariot race.

**PENATES.** Spirits of Roman religion supposed to protect food storehouse.

**PENELOPE.** Odysseus' faithful wife, mother of Telemachus; postpones choice of one of her numerous suitors as second husband; reunited with Odysseus after his 20-year absence.

**PERICLES.** Athenian statesman, founder of Athenian Empire, leader during Golden Age of Athens (461-429 B.C.); died of plague early in Peloponnesian War.

**PERIPATETICS.** Aristotle's followers; name due to fact that Aristotle taught his students while walking around courtyard of the Lyceum.

**PERSEPHONE.** Greek divinity (Roman counterpart, Proserpina); daughter of Demeter; queen of Hades.

**PERSEUS.** Son of Zeus and Danae; cast into sea as infant with his mother, but rescued; later, killed Gorgon, Medusa, rescued and married Andromeda.

**PERSIAN WAR.** Struggle between Persians and Greeks, 492-479 B.C., resulting in defeat of Persia; described by Greek historian Herodotus.

**PHAEACIANS.** Mythical people ruled by King Alcinous; Odysseus hospitably entertained by them on his travels.

**PHAEDO.** Work of Plato, containing a description of Socrates' last hours and his discussion of immortality.

**PHAEDRA.** Daughter of Minos, King of Crete; wife of Theseus; falls in love with her stepson Hippolytus, and commits suicide when he rejects her love; falsely accuses him of making advances to her.

**PHAEDRUS.** One of speakers in Plato's "Symposium".

**PHIDIPPIDES.** Young horse-loving son of Strepsiades in Aristophanes' "Clouds".

**PHILIP II.** King of Macedon, father of Alexander the Great, conqueror of the Greeks (360-338 B.C.).

**PHILIPPIDES.** Professional runner sent from Athens to Sparta to request aid in the battle against the Persians at Marathon (490 B.C.).

**PHILOETIUS.** Faithful herdsman of Odysseus; aids him in slaying suitors.

**PHOCIS.** Central region of Hellas, N. of Gulf of Corinth; principal city, Delphi on Mt. Parnassus.

**PHOENICIANS.** Famous sea-faring people from coast of Palestine, from whom Greeks learned alphabet; Carthage, a Phoenician colony.

**PHOENIX.** Aged foster-father of Achilles; accompanies Odysseus and Ajax on embassy to Achilles to induce him to return to battle.

**PIETAS.** Sense of duty to state, gods, head of household, inculcated in Romans as part of character training.

**PINDAR.** Greatest Greek choral lyric poet (ca. 522-443 B.C.); famous for "epinicia", odes commemorating athletic victories.

**PINDARIC ODE.** Choral lyric poem containing units of 3 stanzas, strophe, antistrophe, epode.

**PIRAEUS.** Seaport of Athens.

**PISTHETAERUS.** Athenian adventurer in Aristophanes' "Birds".

**PLATAEA.** Greek city-state in Boeotia, where combined Greek armies defeated Persians under Mardonius in 479 B.C.; ally of Athens in Peloponnesian War; destroyed by Sparta, 427 B.C.

**PLATO.** Greek philosopher (428-347 B.C.); pupil of Socrates; founder of Academy in Athens; created dialogue form of philosophic exposition; basic principle, theory of ideas; author of "Apology", "Phaedo", "Symposium", "Republic", and many other works.

**POETICS.** Work of Aristotle.

**POLEMARCHUS.** Son of Cephalus whose house is setting in Plato's "Republic"; one of speakers in this dialogue.

**POLIS.** Greek name for autonomous city-state of Hellenic world (ca. 800-300 B.C.).

**POLYBUS.** King of Corinth; foster-father of Oedipus.

**POLYNICES.** Son of Oedipus and Jocasta; when expelled by his brother Eteocles from Thebes he organized the expedition of the Seven against Thebes; killed in duel with Eteocles; burial denied to his body by King Creon; his sister Antigone, defying Creon's order, buries him, and is ordered put to death.

**POLYPHEMUS.** One of the giant cannibalistic Cyclopes; his one eye was burned out by Odysseus, after Polyphemus devoured some of his men in his cave; pined with unrequited love for the nymph Galatea.

**POLYXENA.** Daughter of Priam and Hecuba; sacrificed, after fall of Troy, at Achilles' grave by his son Neoptolemus.

**POMPEY.** Roman general; conqueror of eastern part of Roman Empire; member of 1st Triumvirate; son-in-law of Julius Caesar; killed in Egypt after defeat in Battle of Pharsalus (48 B.C.) at hands of Caesar.

**POSEIDON.** Greek divinity (Roman counterpart, Neptune); god of sea; weapon, trident.

**POTIDAEA.** Greek city-state in N. Greece; subject of Athenian Empire; intervention of Corinth and Sparta in revolt of Potidaea one of immediate causes of Peloponnesian War.

**PRAXINOE.** Character in 15th "Idyl" of Theocritus.

**PRIAM.** Aged King of Troy, husband of Hecuba; father of 62 children, notably Hector, Paris, Cassandra; killed in fall of Troy by Neoptolemus, Achilles' son.

**PRINCIPATE.** Constitutional designation of Roman Empire established by

Augustus; within framework of "Restored Republic" the emperor ("**princeps**") held enormous extraordinary powers; lasted 27 B.C.-A.D. 284.

**PROLOGUE.** First act of Greek drama; part that precedes entrance of chorus.

**PROMETHEUS BOUND.** Tragedy by Aeschylus.

**PROSCENIUM.** Façade of skene building of Greek theater, scenery of play, usually represents front of palace or temple.

**PROSERPINA.** See PERSEPHONE.

**PROTAGORAS.** Famous Greek Sophist (5th Cent. B.C.); most important idea, "Man is the measure of all things".

**PUNIC WARS.** Three wars between Rome and Carthage (264-146 B.C.), resulting each time in the defeat of Carthage, and finally its complete destruction.

**PYLADES.** Son of King Strophius of Phocis; best friend of Orestes, whom he aids in killing Clytemnestra and Aegisthus; also aids Orestes in rescuing his sister Iphigenia; marries Electra.

**PYLUS.** Kingdom of Nestor in S.W. Peloponnesus.

**PYTHAGORAS.** Greek philosopher (6th Cent. B.C.); belief in number abstractions as ultimate principle of universe, knowledge of truth through mathematics, reincarnation of souls.

**QUIRINUS.** Name of Romulus after his deification.

**REPUBLIC.** Work of Plato dealing with absolute justice, the ideal state, and educational curriculum for developing philosopher-kings.

**RHEA SILVIA.** Also called Ilia; mother of Romulus and Remus by Mars.

**ROME.** City in N. Latium in Italy on River Tiber; according to legend, founded by Romulus, 753 B.C.; conqueror of Italy; capital of Roman Empire.

**ROMULUS.** Twin brother of Remus; son of Rhea Silvia by Mars; according to legend, the twins were cast into Tiber River in box, but were saved and nursed by a she-wolf; legendary founder and first king of Rome.

**RUTULIANS.** People of Turnus, opponents of Trojans in Vergil's **"Aeneid"**.

**SABINE FARM.** Estate in Sabine Mts. given to Roman poet Horace by his patron Maecenas.

**SAPPHO.** Outstanding Greek lyric poet (ca. 590 B.C.); world's greatest woman poet.

**SARDIS.** Capital of Lydian Empire.

**SATIRES.** Poetic works of the Roman authors Horace and Juvenal.

**SATYR PLAY.** Last play of tetralogy in Greek dramatic performance, somewhat lighter than tragedies and dealing with Dionysus.

**SATYRS.** Greek minor divinities; partly animal; woodland creatures; followers of Dionysus.

**SCYLLA.** Female monster on rock opposite Charybdis; destroyed mariners as they sailed through Straits of Messina.

**SCHERIA.** Mythical Mediterranean island, home of the Phaeacians, who entertained Odysseus on his travels.

**SEJANUS.** Relative of Roman Emperor Tiberius; prefect of Praetorian

Guard; left in Rome as vice-emperor when Tiberius retired to Capri; intrigued to succeed Tiberius, who ordered him executed.

**SENECA.** Tutor and minister of Roman Emperor Nero; Stoic philosopher; author of moral works and tragedies; ordered to commit suicide by Nero because of suspected complicity in conspiracy against him.

**SIBYL.** Deiphobe, prophetess of Cumae in Italy; predicts Aeneas' future, and guides him through Hades.

**SICILIAN EXPEDITION.** Grandiose, but utterly unsuccessful, attempt of Athens to conquer Sicily, 415-413 B.C.; described by historian Thucydides.

**SICILY.** Large island S.W. of Italy, inhabited by Greeks; unsuccessful attempt of Athens to conquer it (415-413 B.C.); becomes Roman province 241 B.C.

**SILVER AGE.** Of Roman literature, A.D. 14-180.

**SIMAETHA.** Love-sick girl in 2nd "Idyl" of Theocritus.

**SIMMIAS.** One of speakers in Plato's **"Phaedo".**

**SIMONIDES.** Outstanding Greek lyric poet (556-467 B.C.), famous for epitaphs in elegiac meter.

**SINON.** Greek spy who convinced the Trojans to drag wooden horse into Troy, in Vergil's **"Aeneid".**

**SIRENS.** Two mermaids who lure sailors to destruction on rocks by their singing.

**SISYPHUS.** Punished in Hades by being compelled eternally, but unsuccessfully, to push a rock to the top of a hill.

**SKENE.** Building in front of orchestra in Greek theater, serving as dressing room for actors.

**SOCRATES.** Athenian philosopher (469-399 B.C.); Father of Ethics; founder of inductive reasoning; used dialectic method, teaching and learning through questions and answers; teacher of Plato; executed by Athenians on charges of unorthodoxy and corrupting youth.

**SOCRATIC PROBLEM.** Since Socrates wrote nothing, and his thinking is known largely through the works of Plato and Xenophon, what is the pure essence of Socrates' teaching as distinguished from that of his pupils, especially Plato?

**SOLON.** Athenian aristocrat (ca. 640-559 B.C.), statesman, reformer, elegiac poet; one of the 7 wise men of Greece; in Herodotus' **"History"** he is said to have visited Croesus and to have had a discussion on happiness with him.

**SOPHIST.** Private teachers of Greek world, 5th Cent. B.C., who exacted high fees, and taught how to be successful in political, social, and economic life through public speaking, clever methods of arguing; opposed traditional Greek morality and religion, absolute standards of conduct; espoused concepts of relativity in ethics, individual self-interest as paramount, justice as the enforced will of the stronger ("might makes right").

**SOPHOCLES.** Athenian writer of tragedy (ca. 497-405 B.C.); author of **"Oedipus Rex", "Oedipus at Colonus", "Antigone", "Electra",** and many other plays.

**SPARTA.** Greek city-state in S.E. Peloponnesus, political center of Lacedaemonia (Laconia); head of Peloponnesian League (ca. 500-370 B.C.); defeated Athens in Peloponnesian War; highly militarized, authoritarian society.

**SPHINX.** Mythical winged creature, part woman, part lion; plagued city of Thebes, killing all who could not answer her riddle; when Oedipus answered it she disappeared.

**ST. AUGUSTINE.** Christian writer (354-430 A.D.), author of *City of God* and *Confessions,* and many other works.

**STASIMON.** Choral ode in Greek drama.

**STOICISM.** Hellenistic and Roman philosophy, founded by Zeno (ca. 330-260 B.C.), but developed and modified over 5 centuries; taught personal happiness, inner calm and contentment through belief in predestination, living in harmony with pre-arranged universe, suppression of all emotion, accepting all that happens as good, acquiescing in one's place in society and doing one's duty diligently.

**STREPSIADES.** Old Athenian gentleman, principal character in **"Clouds"** of Aristophanes.

**STYX.** Principal river of Hades over which souls were ferried by Charon.

**SYCHAEUS.** Husband of Queen Dido of Carthage; murdered by her brother Pygmalion.

**SYLLOGISM.** Invented by Aristotle; logical formula employing deductive reasoning from universal to particular; pattern: major premiss, minor premiss, conclusion.

**SYMPOSIUM.** Work of Plato on subject of love.

**SYRACUSE.** Greek city-state on S.E. coast of Sicily.

**TACITUS.** Roman historian (ca. 55-120 A.D.), author of **"Annals"**, **"Histories"**, **"Germany"**, and other works.

**TALTHYBIUS.** Herald of the Greeks at Troy.

**TANTALUS.** Son of Zeus; favorite of gods; punished in Hades for crimes, especially serving flesh of his son Pelops to the gods, by being tantalized, for he could not drink though standing in water or reach fruit over his head.

**TARTARUS.** Lowest part of Hades where incurable sinners were eternally punished.

**TEIRESIAS.** Blind soothsayer of Thebes; character in Homer's **"Odyssey"**, Sophocles' **"Oedipus Rex"** and **"Antigone"**.

**TELEMACHUS.** Young son of Odysseus and Penelope; in Homer's **"Odyssey"**, goes in search of his father, and helps him slay his mother's suitors.

**TELEOLOGY.** Philosophic view, especially held by Aristotle, that everything has a rational purpose and develops and moves to an end, that all things evolve from lower to higher forms up to the ultimate end, God.

**TETRALOGY.** Group of four plays in Greek tragedy consisting of trilogy and satyr play.

**THALES.** Greek philosopher (6th Cent. B.C.); Father of Philosophy; belief in water as ultimate material principle of universe.

**THEATRON.** Part of Greek theater where audience sat, on sloping hollowed-out hillside.

**THEBES.** Principal city-state of Boeotia.

**THEMISTOCLES.** Athenian statesman and general; strategist of Battle of Salamis (480 B.C.); founder of Athenian navy; was later exiled from Athens, and turned traitor.

**THEOCRITUS.** Hellenistic writer (ca. 270 B.C.); Father of Pastoral Poetry; author of "Idyls"; greatest poet of Alexandrian period.

**THEORY OF IDEAS.** Plato's basic view that true reality is the super-sensory world of abstract ideas perceived only by reason; ideas have an independent existence outside the mind and constitute unchanging, eternal truth; concrete things are copies of ideas and yield only relative truth (opinion).

**THERMOPYLAE.** Narrow pass heroically defended against the Persians in 480 B.C. by Leonidas and 300 Spartans in a delaying action.

**THERSITES.** Rank-and-file Greek soldier at Troy; first spokesman of common people; ridiculed in Homer's **"Iliad"**, Plato's **"Republic"**.

**THESEUS.** Legendary king of Athens, son of Aegeus; slayer of Procrustes and the Minotaur; defeated Amazons and captured their queen, Hippolyte, by whom he had a son, Hippolytus; caused Hippolytus' death by hastily cursing him when he was falsely accused by his wife Phaedra; welcomes Oedipus to Attica.

**THESPIS.** Athenian (ca. 535 B.C.); Father of Drama; created first actor.

**THESSALY.** Northern Hellas.

**THETIS.** Sea-goddess, wife of Peleus; mother of Achilles.

**THYESTES.** Son of Pelops; brother of Atreus; killed Atreus for feeding his children's flesh to him, and was in turn killed by Atreus' son Agamemnon.

**THRASYMACHUS.** Sophist; one of the speakers in Plato's **"Republic"**.

**THUCYDIDES.** Greek historian (ca. 460-400 B.C.), author of **"History of Peloponnesian War"**.

**TIBER.** River in N. Latium in Italy on which Rome is situated.

**TIBERIUS.** Stepson of Augustus; 2nd Roman emperor (A.D. 14-37).

**TITANS.** Huge offspring of Ge and Uranus, early Greek nature divinities of great strength, personifying earthquakes, volcanic eruptions; important Titans were Oceanus, Cronus, Prometheus, Atlas; ruled universe until overthrown by Olympian gods.

**TRAJAN.** Roman emperor (A.D. 98-117); conqueror, enlarged Roman Empire to its greatest extent.

**TRIDENT.** Three-pronged weapon of Poseidon.

**TROJAN HORSE.** Wooden horse devised by Odysseus, filled with picked Greek soldiers, and left outside Troy; the Trojans were induced to drag it into Troy; during the night the Greeks inside were released and captured the city.

**TROJAN WOMEN.** Tragedy by Euripides.

**TURNUS.** Chief of the Rutulians; principal enemy of Aeneas in Italy, in Vergil's **"Aeneid"**; slain in duel with Aeneas.

**TYRANT.** Unconstitutional rulers who overthrew aristocrats in Greek city-states (6th Cent. B.C.) with support of coalition of non-aristocratic classes.

**TYRTAEUS.** Elegiac poet of Sparta (ca. 650 B.C.), wrote martial songs.

**ULYSSES.** See ODYSSEUS.

**VENUS.** See APHRODITE.

**VERGIL.** Outstanding Roman author of Augustan Age (70-19 B.C.): member of literary circle of Maecenas; author of epic **"Aeneid"**, and other works.

**VESPASIAN.** Roman emperor (A.D. 69-79); founder of Flavian Dynasty; Jerusalem destroyed in his reign.

**VESTA.** See HESTIA.

**VULCAN.** See HEPHAESTUS.

**XANTHIAS.** Slave of Dionysus in Aristophanes' **"Frogs"**.

**XENOPHANES.** Greek philosopher (6th Cent. B.C.); belief in Oneness as ultimately reality of universe, pantheistic god.

**XERXES.** King of Persia, son of King Darius; led unsuccessful Persian invasion of Greece in 480 B.C.

**ZENO.** 1. Greek philosopher (5th Cent. B.C.); belief in static universe. 2. Hellenistic philosopher (ca. 330-260 B.C.), founder of Stoicism.

**ZEUS.** Greek divinity (Roman counterpart, Jupiter); son of Cronus; husband of his sister Hera (Juno); king of Olympian gods; of sky, heavenly phenomena, hospitality; weapon, thunderbolt; protective armor, aegis.

# BIBLIOGRAPHY

### CHAPTER I

Alsop, J. W. *From the Silent Earth: a Report of the Greek Bronze Age.* New York: Harper & Row, 1964.

Ludwig, E. *Schliemann: the Story of a Gold-seeker.* Boston: Little, Brown, 1931.

Nilsson, M. P. *The Minoan-Mycenaean Religion and its Survival in Greek Religion.* 2nd Ed. Lund: Gleerup, 1950.

Poole, Lynn and Gray. *One Passion, Two Lives: the Story of Heinrich and Sophia Schliemann.* New York: Crowell, 1966.

Taylor, L. W. *The Mycenaeans.* London: Thames & Hudson, 1964.

Vermeule, E. *Greece in the Bronze Age.* Chicago: University of Chicago Press, 1964.

Webster, T. B. L. *From Mycenae to Homer,* 2nd Ed. London: Methuen, 1964.

### CHAPTER II

Bassett, S. E. *The Poetry of Homer.* Berkeley: University of California Press, 1938.

Beye, C. R. *The Iliad, the Odyssey, and the Epic Tradition.* Garden City: Doubleday, 1966.

Bowra, C. M. *Tradition and Design in the Iliad.* Oxford: Clarendon Press, 1930.

Clarke, H. W. *The Art of the Odyssey.* Englewood Cliffs: Prentice-Hall, 1967.

Finley, M. I. *The World of Odysseus.* 2nd Ed. Harmondsworth: Penguin, 1962.

Kirk, G. S. *Homer and the Epic.* New York: Cambridge University Press, 1965.

Knight, W. F. J. *Many-Sided Homer.* New York: Barnes & Noble, 1969.

**367**

Owen, E. T. *The Story of the Iliad*. New York: Oxford University Press, 1947.

Reinhold, M. *Barron's Simplified Approach to Homer: The Iliad*. Woodbury: Barron, 1967.

Reinhold, M. *Barron's Simplified Approach to Homer: The Odyssey*. Woodbury: Barron, 1967.

Scott, J. A. *Homer and his Influence*. Boston: Marshall Jones, 1925.

Scott, J. A. *The Unity of Homer*. Berkeley: University of California Press, 1921.

Wace, A. J. B., and Stubbings, F. H. *Companion to Homer*. London: Macmillan, 1962.

Whitman, S. H. *Homer and the Heroic Tradition*. Cambridge, Mass.: Harvard University Press, 1958.

Woodhouse, W. J. *The Composition of Homer's Odyssey*. Oxford: Clarendon Press, 1930.

Young, A. M. *Troy and Her Legend*. Pittsburgh: University of Pittsburgh Press, 1948.

### CHAPTER III

Andrewes, A. *The Greek Tyrants*. London: Hutcheson, 1956.

Fowler, W. W. *The City-State of the Greeks and Roman*. London: Macmillan, 1893.

Glotz, G. *The Greek City and its Institutions*. London: Routledge & Kegan Paul, 1965.

Halliday, W. R. *The Growth of the City State*. London: Hodder & Stoughton, 1923.

Starr, C. G. *The Origins of Greek Civilization*. New York: Knopf, 1961.

Ure, P. N. *The Origin of Tyranny*. New York: Russell & Russell, 1962.

### CHAPTER IV

Bowra, C. M. *Greek Lyric Poetry from Alcman to Simonides*. 2nd Ed. Oxford: Clarendon Press, 1961.

Bowra, C. M. *Pindar*. Oxford: Clarendon Press, 1964.

Davison, J. A. *From Archilochus to Pindar*. New York: St. Martin's, 1968.

Norwood, G. *Pindar*. Berkeley: University of California Press, 1945.

Robinson, D. M. *Sappho and her Influence*. Boston: Marshall Jones, 1924.

Weigall, A. *Sappho of Lesbos; her Life and Times*. New York: Stokes, 1932.

## CHAPTER V

Agard, W. R. *The Greek Mind.* Princeton: Van Nostrand, 1957.

Agard, W. R. *What Democracy Meant to the Greeks.* Chapel Hill: University of North Carolina Press, 1942.

Ferguson, W. S. *Greek Imperialism.* Boston: Houghton, Mifflin, 1913.

Flacelière, R. *Daily Life in Greece at the Time of Pericles.* London: Weidenfeld & Nicolson, 1965.

Forrest, W. G. *The Emergence of Greek Democracy.* London: Weidenfeld & Nicolson, 1966.

Glover, T. R. *Democracy in the Ancient World.* New York: Cooper Square, 1966.

Jones, A. H. M. *Athenian Democracy.* Oxford: Blackwell, 1957.

Jones, A. H. M. *Sparta.* Oxford: Blackwell & Mott, 1967.

Laistner, M. L. W. *A History of the Greek World from 479 to 323 B.C.* 3rd Ed. New York: Macmillan, 1957.

Pohlenz, M. *Freedom in Greek Life and Thought. The History of an Ideal.* New York: Humanities Press, 1966.

Webster, T. B. L. *Everyday Life in Classical Athens.* London: Batsford, 1969.

Zimmern, A. E. *The Greek Commonwealth: Politics and Economics in Fifth-Century Athens.* 5th Ed. Oxford: Clarendon Press, 1931.

## CHAPTER VI

Arnott, P. D. *An Introduction to the Greek Theatre.* London: Macmillan, 1959.

Bieber, M. *The History of the Greek and Roman Theater.* 2nd Ed. Princeton: Princeton University Press, 1961.

Flickinger, R. C. *The Greek Theater and its Drama.* 4th Ed. Chicago: University of Chicago Press, 1936.

Haigh, A. E. *The Tragic Drama of the Greeks.* Oxford: Clarendon Press, 1938.

Harsh, P. W. *A Handbook of Classical Drama.* Stanford: Stanford University Press, 1944.

Hathorn, R. Y. *The Handbook of Classical Drama.* New York: Crowell, 1967.

Kitto, H. D. F. *Greek Tragedy: a Literary Study.* 3rd Ed. New York: Barnes & Noble, 1951.

Lucas, D. W. *The Greek Tragic Poets: their Contribution to Western Life and Thought.* 2nd Ed. London: Cohen & Wist, 1959.

Norwood, G. *Greek Tragedy.* 2nd Ed. London: Methuen, 1928.

**369**

Pickard-Cambridge, A. W. *The Theatre of Dionysus in Athens.* Oxford: Clarendon Press, 1946.

Reinhold, M. *Classical Drama; Greek and Roman.* Woodbury: Barron, 1959.

Webster, T. B. L. *Greek Theatre Production.* London: Methuen, 1956.

## CHAPTER VII

Golden, L. *In Praise of Prometheus. Humanism and Rationalism in Aeschylean Thought.* Chapel Hill: University of North Carolina Press, 1966.

Murray, G. *Aeschylus, the Creator of Tragedy.* Oxford: Clarendon Press, 1940.

Podlecki, J. *The Political Background of Aeschylean Tragedy.* Ann Arbor: University of Michigan Press, 1966.

Sheppard, J. T. *Aeschylus and Sophocles: their Work and Influence.* 2nd Ed. New York: Longmans Green, 1946.

Smyth, H. W. *Aeschylean Tragedy.* Berkeley: University of California Press, 1924.

## CHAPTER VIII

Adams, S. M. *Sophocles, the Playwright.* Toronto: Universty of Toronto Press, 1957.

Bowra, C. M. *Sophoclean Tragedy.* Oxford: Clarendon Press, 1965.

Cameron, A. *The Identity of Oedipus the King.* New York: New York University Press, 1968.

Kitto, H. D. F. *Sophocles: Dramatist and Philosopher.* London: Oxford University Press, 1958.

Knox, B. M. W. *The Heroic Temper: Studies in Sophoclean Tragedy.* Berkeley: University of California Press, 1964.

Knox, B. M. W. *Oedipus at Thebes.* New Haven: Yale University Press, 1957.

Letters, F. J. H. *The Life and Work of Sophocles.* London: Sheed & Ward, 1953.

Sheppard, J. T. *Aeschylus and Sophocles: their Work and Influence.* 2nd Ed. New York: Longmans Green, 1946.

Waldock, C. H. *Sophocles, the Dramatist.* Cambridge: Cambridge University Press, 1966.

Webster, T. B. L. *An Introduction to Sophocles.* 2nd Ed. London: Methuen, 1969.

## CHAPTER IX

Bates, W. N. *Euripides: a Student of Human Nature.* Philadelphia: University of Pennsylvania Press, 1930.

Conacher, D. J. *Euripidean Drama. Myth, Theme and Structure.* Toronto: Toronto University Press, 1967.

Greenwood. L. H. G. *Aspects of Euripidean Tragedy.* Cambridge: Cambridge University Press, 1953.

Grube, G. M. A. *The Drama of Euripides.* 2nd Ed. London: Methuen, 1961.

Lucas, F. L. *Euripides and his Influence.* Boston: Marshall Jones, 1923.

Norwood, G. *Essays in Euripidean Drama.* Berkeley: University of California Press, 1954.

Murray, G. *Euripides and his Age. New Ed.* Oxford: Oxford University Press, 1946.

Segal, E. W. *Euripides: a Collection of Critical Essays.* Englewood Cliffs: Prentice-Hall, 1968.

Webster, T. B. L. *The Tragedies of Euripides.* London: Methuen, 1967.

## CHAPTER X

Lever, K. *The Art of Greek Comedy.* London: Methuen, 1956.

Lord, L. E. *Aristophanes: his Plays and Influence.* Boston: Marshall Jones, 1925.

Murray, G. *Aristophanes: a Study.* New York: Oxford University Press, 1933.

Norwood, G. *Greek Comedy.* London: Methuen, 1931.

Whitman, C. H. *Aristophanes and the Comic Hero.* Cambridge, Mass.: Harvard University Press, 1964.

## CHAPTER XI

Bury, J. B. *The Ancient Greek Historians.* New York: Macmillan, 1909.

Glover, T. R. *Herodotus.* Berkeley: University of California Press, 1924.

Immerwahr, H. R. *Form and Thought in Herodotus.* Cleveland: Western Reserve University Press, 1966.

Myres, J. L. *Herodotus, Father of History.* Oxford: Clarendon Press, 1953.

De Sélincourt, A. *The World of Herodotus.* Boston: Little, Brown, 1962.

## CHAPTER XII

Adcock, F. E. *Thucydides and his History*. Cambridge: Cambridge University Press, 1963.

Bury, J. B. *The Ancient Greek Historians*. New York: Macmillan, 1909.

Finley, J. H., Jr., *Thucydides*. Cambridge, Mass.: Harvard University Press, 1942.

Henderson, B. W. *The Great War between Athens and Sparta*. London: Macmillan, 1927.

Romilly, J. de. *Thycidides and Athenian Imperialism*. Oxford: Blackwell, 1963.

## CHAPTER XIII

Adams, C. D. *Demosthenes and his Influence*. New York: Longmans Green, 1927.

Baldry, H. C. *The Unity of Mankind in Greek Thought*. Cambridge: Cambridge University Press, 1965.

Ehrenberg, V. *Alexander and the Greeks*. Oxford: Blackwell, 1938.

Glover, T. R. *From Pericles to Philip*. 4th Ed. London: Methuen, 1926.

Jones, A. H. M. *The Athens of Demosthenes*. Cambridge: Cambridge University Press, 1952.

Laistner, M. L. W. *A History of the Greek World from 479-323 B.C.* 3rd Ed. New York: Macmillan, 1957.

Milns, R. D. *Alexander the Great*. London: Hale, 1968.

Snyder, J. W. *Alexander the Great*. New York: Twayne, 1966.

Tarn, W. W. *Alexander the Great*. 2 Vols. Cambridge: Cambridge University Press, 1948.

Wilcken, U. *Alexander the Great*. New York: Norton, 1967.

## CHAPTER XIV

## PRE-SOCRATIC PHILOSOPHERS

Bailey, C. *The Greek Atomists and Epicurus*. Oxford: Clarendon Press, 1928.

Burnet, J. *Early Greek Philosophy*. 4th Ed. London: Black, 1963.

Freeman, K. *The Pre-Socratic Philosophers*. Oxford: Blackwell, 1946.

Fuller, B. A. G. *History of Greek Philosophy*. 3rd Ed. New York: Holt, 1965.

Guthrie, W. K. C. *The Greek Philosophers*. New York: Harper & Row, 1960.

Kirk, G. S., and Raven, J. E. *The Presocratic Philosophers.* 2nd Ed. Cambridge: Cambridge University Press. 1964.

Thomson, G. *Studies in Ancient Greek Society, II: The First Philosophers.* London: Lawrence & Wishart, 1955.

Untersteiner, M. *The Sophists.* Oxford: Blackwell, 1954.

## SOCRATES

Chroust, A. H. *Socrates, Man and Myth.* London: Routledge & Kegan Paul, 1957.

Gulley, N. *The Philosophy of Socrates.* London: Macmillan, 1968.

Strauss, L. *Socrates and Aristophanes.* New York: Basic Books, 1966.

Taylor, A. E. *Socrates.* Garden City: Doubleday, 1953.

Winspear, A. D., and Silverberg, T. *Who Was Socrates?* 2nd Ed. New York: Russell & Russell, 1960.

## PLATO

Barker, E. *Greek Political Theory: Plato and his Predecessors.* Rev. Ed. London: Methuen, 1960.

Barker, E. *The Political Thought of Plato and Aristotle.* New York: Russell & Russell, 1959.

Brumbaugh, R. S. *Plato for the Modern Age.* New York: Crowell-Collier, 1962.

Crossman, R. H. S. *Plato To-Day.* Rev. Ed. London: Allen & Unwin, 1959.

Gouldner, A. W. *Enter Plato. Classical Greece and the Origins of Social Theory.* New York: Basic Books, 1965.

Grube, G. M. A. *Plato's Thought.* Boston: Beacon Hill, 1958.

Havelock, E. A. *Preface to Plato.* Cambridge, Mass.: Harvard University Press, 1963.

Lodge, R. C. *The Philosophy of Plato.* London: Humanities Press, 1956.

Randall, J. H., Jr. *Plato: Dramatist of the Life of Reason.* New York: Columbia University Press, 1969.

Shorey, P. *Platonism, Ancient and Modern.* Berkeley: University of California Press, 1938.

Shorey, P. *What Plato Said.* Chicago: Chicago University Press, 1933.

Taylor, A. E. *Plato, the Man and his Work.* 7th Ed. London: Methuen, 1963.

Taylor, A. E. *Platonism and its Influence.* Boston: Marshall Jones, 1924.

**373**

Winspear, A. D. *The Genesis of Plato's Thought*. 2nd Ed. New York: Dryden, 1956.

## CHAPTER XV

Allan, D. J. *The Philosophy of Aristotle*. Oxford: Clarendon Press, 1952.

Barker E. *The Political Thought of Plato and Aristotle*. New York: Russell & Russell, 1959.

Barker, E. *The Politics of Aristotle*. New York: Oxford University Press, 1952.

Butcher, S. H. *Aristotle's Theory of Poetry and Fine Art*. 4th Ed. London: Macmillan, 1923.

Cooper, L. *Aristotle on the Art of Poetry*. Boston: Ginn, 1913.

Grene, M. *A Portrait of Aristotle*. Chicago: University of Chicago Press, 1963.

Golden, L., and Hardison, O. B. *Aristotle's Poetics*. Englewood Cliffs: Prentice-Hall, 1968.

Jones, H. J. F. *On Aristotle and Greek Tragedy*. New York: Oxford University Press, 1962.

Lloyd, G. E. R. *Aristotle. The Growth and Structure of his Thought*. London: Cambridge University Press, 1968.

Mure, G. R. G. *Aristotle*. New York: Oxford University Press, 1964.

Owen, A. S. *Aristotle on the Art of Poetry*. Oxford: Clarendon Press, 1931.

Potts, L. J. *Aristotle on the Art of Fiction*. London: Cambridge University Press, 1953.

Ross, W. D. *Aristotle*. Rev. Ed. New York: Barnes & Noble, 1964.

Randall, J. H. *Aristotle*. New York: Columbia University Press, 1960.

## CHAPTER XVI

Bury, J. B., *et al. The Hellenistic Age*. 2nd Ed. Cambridge: Cambridge University Press, 1923.

Cary, M. *A History of the Greek World from 323 to 146 B.C.* Rev. Ed. New York: Barnes & Noble, 1963.

De Witt, N. W. *Epicurus and his Philosophy*. Minneapolis: University of Minnesota Press, 1954.

Edelstein, L. *The Meaning of Stoicism*. Cambridge, Mass.: Harvard University Press, 1966.

Farrington, B. *The Faith of Epicurus*. London: Weidenfeld & Nichololson, 1967.

Hadas, M. *Hellenistic Culture*. New York: Columbia University Press, 1959.

Hicks, R. R. *Stoic and Epicurean*. New York: Scribner's, 1910.

Panichas, G. A. *Epicurus*. New York: Twayne, 1967.

Tarn, W. W., and Griffith, G. T. *Hellenistic Civilization*. 3rd. Ed. London: Arnold, 1952.

Rist, John. *Stoic Philosophy*. New York: Cambridge University Press, 1970.

CHAPTER XVII

Boren, H. *The Roman Republic*. Princeton: Van Nostrand, 1965.

Frank T. *Life and Literature in the Roman Republic*. New Ed. Berkeley: University of California Press, 1956.

Marsh, F. B. *A History of the Roman World from 146 to 30 B.C.* 3rd Ed. London: Methuen, 1963.

Scullard, H. H. *A History of the Roman World from 753 to 146 B.C.* 3rd Ed. London: Methuen, 1961.

Starr, C. G., Jr. *The Emergence of Rome as Ruler of the Western World*. Ithaca: Cornell University Press, 1950.

CHAPTER XVIII

Dudley, D. R. editor. *Lucretius*. London: Routledge & Kegan Paul, 1965.

Hadzsits, G. D. *Lucretius and his Influence*. New York: Longmans, Green, 1935.

Santayana, G. *Three Philosophical Poets*. Cambridge, Mass.: Harvard University Press, 1910.

Sikes, E. E. *Lucretius, Poet and Philosopher*. Cambridge: Cambridge University Press, 1936.

Winspear, A. D. *Lucretius and Scientific Thought*. Montreal: Harvest House, 1963.

CHAPTER XIX

Frank, T. *Catullus and Horace: Two Poets in their Environment*. New York: Holt, 1928.

Harrington, K. P. *Catullus and his Influence*. Boston: Marshall Jones, 1923.

Quinn, K. *The Catullan Revolution*. Carlton: Melbourne University Press, 1959.

Wheeler, A. L. *Catullus and the Traditions of Ancient Poetry*. Berkeley: University of California Press, 1934.

CHAPTER XX

Bowersock, G. W. *Augustus and the Greek World.* New York: Oxford University Press, 1966.

Buchan, J. *Augustus.* Boston: Houghton, Mifflin, 1937.

Earl, D. C. *The Age of Augustus.* New York: Crown, 1968.

Holmes, T. R. *The Architect of the Roman Empire, 27 B.C.-A.D. 14.* Oxford: Clarendon Press, 1931.

Marsh. F. B. *The Founding of the Roman Empire.* 2nd Ed. London: Oxford University Press, 1927.

Newman, J. K. *Augustus and the New Poetry.* Bruxelles-Berchem: Latomus, 1967.

Rowell, H. T. *Rome in the Augustan Age.* Norman: University of Oklahoma Press, 1962.

Syme, R. *The Roman Revolution.* New York: Oxford University Press, 1960.


CHAPTER XXI

Bowra, C. M. *From Virgil to Milton.* London: Macmillan, 1945.

Camps, W. A. *An Introduction to Virgil's Aeneid.* Oxford: Oxford University Press, 1969.

Commager, S., editor. *Vergil: a Collection of Critical Essays.* Englewood Cliffs: Prentice-Hall, 1966.

Dudley, D. R., editor. *Virgil.* London: Routledge & Kegan Paul, 1969.

Frank, R. *Vergil, a Biography.* New York: Holt, 1922.

Glover, T. R. *Virgil.* 6th Ed. London: Arnold, 1930.

Knight, W. F. J. *Roman Vergil.* Harmondsworth: Penguin, 1966.

Letters, F. J. H. *Vergil.* New York: Sheed & Ward, 1946.

Mackail, J. W. *Virgil and his Meaning to the World of To-day.* Boston: Marshall Jones, 1922.

Otis, B. *Virgil, a Study in Civilized Poetry.* Oxford: Clarendon Press, 1962.

Poschl, V. *The Art of Vergil.* Ann Arbor: University of Michigan Press, 1962.

Putnam, M. C. J. *The Poetry of the Aeneid.* Cambridge, Mass.: Harvard University Press, 1966.

Quinn, K. *Virgil's 'Aeneid': a Critical Description.* London: Routledge & Kegan Paul, 1968.

Williams, R. D. *Virgil.* Oxford: Clarendon Press, 1967.

**376**

CHAPTER XXII

Commager, S. *The Odes of Horace*. New Haven: Yale University Press, 1962.

Fraenkel, E. *Horace*. New York: Oxford University Press, 1966.

Frank, T. *Catullus and Horace: Two Poets in their Environment*. New York: Holt, 1928.

Perret, J. *Horace*. New York: New York University Press, 1964.

Rudd, N. *The Satires of Horace*. Cambridge: Cambridge University Press, 1966.

Sedgwick, H. D. *Horace: A Biography*. Cambridge, Mass.: Harvard University Press, 1947.

Showerman, G. *Horace and his Influence*. Boston: Marshall Jones, 1922.

Wilkinson, L. P. *Horace and his Lyric Poetry*. 2nd Ed. New York: Cambridge University Press, 1951.


CHAPTER XXIII

Charlesworth, M. P. *The Roman Empire*. New York: Oxford University Press, 1951.

Parker, H. M. D. *A History of the Roman World from A.D. 138-337*. 2nd Ed. London: Methuen, 1958.

Salmon, E. T. *A History of the Roman World from 30 B.C. to A.D 138*. 5th Ed. London: Methuen, 1966.

Starr, C. G. *Civilization and the Caesars: The Intellectual Revolution in the Roman Empire*. Ithaca: Cornell University Press, 1954.

Waddy, L. *Pax Romana and World Peace*. New York: Norton, 1951.


CHAPTER XXIV

Duff, J. W. *Roman Satire: its Outlook on Social Life*. Berkeley: University of California Press, 1936.

Highet, G. *Juvenal the Satirist*. Oxford: Clarendon Press, 1954.


CHAPTER XXV

Dudley, D. R. *The World of Tacitus*. London: Secker & Warburg, 1969.

Laistner, M. L. W. *The Greater Roman Historians*. Berkeley: University of California Press, 1947.

Mendell, C. W. *Tacitus: the Man and his Work*. New Haven: Yale University Press, 1957.

Syme, R. *Tacitus.* 2 Vols. Oxford: Clarendon Press, 1958.
Walker, B. *The Annals of Tacitus. A Study in the Writing of History.* 2nd Ed. Manchester: Manchester University Press, 1960.

## CHAPTER XXVI

Barrow, R. H. *Introduction to St. Augustine, The City of God.* London: Faber & Faber, 1950.
Battenhouse, R., editor. *A Companion to the Study of St. Augustine.* Oxford: Oxford University Press, 1955.
Brown, P. R. L. *Augustine of Hippo.* Berkeley: University of California Press, 1967.
Deane, H. A. *The Political and Social Ideas of St. Augustine.* New York: Columbia University Press, 1963.
Portalié, E. *A Guide to the Thought of St. Augustine.* Chicago: Regnery, 1960.

## MYTHOLOGY

Aken, A. R. van. *The Encyclopedia of Mythology.* Englewood Cliffs: Prentice-Hall, 1965.
Gayley, G. M. *The Classic Myths in English Literature and in Art.* New Ed. New York: Ginn, 1911.
Grant, M. *Myths of the Greeks and Romans.* New York: New American Library, 1962.
Guerber, H. A. *The Myths of Greece and Rome.* Rev Ed. New York: American, 1938.
Hamilton, E. *Mythology.* New York: New American Library, 1940.
Howe, G., and Harrer, G. *A Handbook of Classical Mythology.* New York: Crofts, 1929.
*Larousse Encyclopedia of Mythology.* London: Hamlyn, 1959.
Rose, H. J. *A Handbook of Greek Mythology.* New York: Dutton, 1928.
Rose, H. J. *Gods and Heroes of the Greeks.* London: Methuen, 1957.
Tripp, E. *Crowell's Handbook of Classical Mythology.* New York: Crowell, 1970.

# GENERAL

# BIBLIOGRAPHY

## GREEK AND ROMAN HISTORY AND SOCIETY

Blunt, A. W. F. *The Ancient World and its Legacy to Us*. Oxford: Clarendon Press, 1928.

Cary, M., and Haarhoff, T. J. *Life and Thought in the Greek and Roman World*. New York: Barnes & Noble, 1959.

Grant, M. *Ancient History*. New York: Harper & Row, 1965.

Roebuck, C. A. *The World of Ancient Times*. New York: Scribner, 1966.

Starr, C. G. *A History of the Ancient World*. New York: Oxford University Press, 1965.

## GREEK HISTORY

Barr, S. *The Will of Zeus. A History of Greece from the Origins of Hellenic Culture to the Death of Alexander*. Philadelphia: Lippincott, 1961.

Botsford, G. W., and Robinson, C. A., Jr. *Hellenic History*. 5th Ed., rev. by D. Kagan. New York: Macmillan, 1968.

Burn. A. R. *The Warring States of Greece*. London: Thames and Hudson, 1962.

Bury, J. B. *A History of Greece to the Death of Alexander the Great*. 3rd Ed. rev. by R. Meiggs. New York: Macmillan, 1952.

Cook, R. M. *The Greeks Until Alexander*. London: Thames & Hudson, 1962.

Hammond, N. G. L. *A History of Greece to 322 B.C.* 2nd Ed. Oxford: Clarendon Press, 1967.

Smith, M. *The Ancient Greeks*. Ithaca: Cornell University Press, 1960.

## ROMAN HISTORY

Barr, S. *The Mask of Jove. A History of Graeco-Roman Civilization from the Death of Alexander to the Death of Constantine.* Philadelphia: Lippincott, 1966.

Boak, A. E. R. *A History of Rome to 565 A.D.* 5th Ed. rev. by W. G. Sinnigen. New York: Macmillan, 1965.

Bourne, F. C. *A History of the Romans.* Boston: Heath, 1966.

Cary, M. *A History of Rome down to the Reign of Constantine.* New Ed. London: Macmillan, 1954.

Fowler, W. W. *Rome.* 2nd Ed. rev. by M. P. Charlesworth. London: Oxford University Press, 1947.

Frank, T. *Roman Imperialism.* New York: Macmillan, 1914.

## GREEK CIVILIZATION

Agard, W. R. *The Greek Mind.* Princeton: Van Nostrand, 1957.

Andrewes, A. *The Greeks.* London: Hutchinson, 1967.

Arnott, P. D. *An Introduction to the Greek World.* London: Macmillan, 1967.

Bowra, C. M. *The Greek Experience.* Cleveland: World, 1958.

Burns, C. D. *Greek Ideals: A Study of Social Life.* 2nd Ed. London: Bell, 1919.

Chamoux, F. *The Civilization of Greece.* New York: Simon and Schuster, 1965.

Couch, H. N. *Classical Civilzation: Greece.* 2nd Ed. New York: Prentice-Hall, 1951.

Dickinson, G. L. *The Greek View of Life.* 7th Ed. Garden City: Doubleday, 1936.

Dodds, E. R. *The Greeks and the Irrational.* Berkeley: University of California Press, 1951.

Finley, M. I. *The Ancient Greeks: An Introduction to their Life and Thought.* London: Chatto & Windus, 1963.

Grant, M., and Pottinger, D. *The Greeks.* New York: Nelson, 1958.

Greene, W. C. *The Achievement of Greece.* Cambridge, Mass.: Harvard University Press, 1923.

Hadas, M. *The Greek Ideal and its Survival.* New York: Harper & Row, 1960.

Hamilton, E. *The Greek Way to Western Civilization.* New York: Norton, 1942.

Kitto, H. D. F. *The Greeks.* Harmondsworth: Penguin, 1951.

Livingstone, R. W. *The Greek Genius and its Meaning to Us.* 2nd Ed. Oxford: Clarendon Press, 1915.

Livingstone, R. W. *Greek Ideals and Modern Life.* Oxford: Clarendon Press, 1935.

Lloyd-Jones, H. *et al. The Greeks.* London: Watts, 1962.

Petrie, A. *An Introduction to Greek History, Antiquities and Literature.* 2nd Ed. London: Oxford University Press, 1962.

Starr, C. G. *The Origins of Greek Civilization.* New York: Knopf, 1961.

Van Hook, L. *Greek Life and Thought.* Rev. Ed. New York: Columbia University Press, 1930.

## ROMAN CIVILIZATION

Balsdon, J. P. V. D., editor. *The Romans.* London: Watts, 1965.

Barrow, R. H. *The Romans.* Harmondsworth: Penguin, 1949.

Dudley, D. R. *The Civilization of Rome.* New York: New American Library, 1960.

Geer, R. M. *Classical Civilization: Rome.* 2nd Ed. New York: Prentice-Hall, 1950.

Grant, M. *The World of Rome.* London: Weidenfeld, 1960.

Hamilton, E. *The Roman Way to Western Civilization.* New York: New American Library, 1957.

Lewis, N., and Reinhold, M. *Roman Civilization.* 2 Vols. 2nd Ed. New York: Harper & Row, 1966.

MacKendrick, P. *The Roman Mind at Work.* Princeton: Van Nostrand, 1958.

Mattingly, H. *Roman Imperial Civilization.* London: Arnold, 1957.

Petrie, A. *An Introduction to Roman History, Literature and Antiquities.* 3rd Ed. New York: Oxford University Press, 1963.

## GREEK AND ROMAN LITERATURE

Feder, L. *Crowell's Handbook of Classical Literature.* New York: Crowell, 1964.

Higginbotham, J. *Greek and Latin Literature. A Comparative Study.* London: Methuen, 1969.

## GREEK LITERATURE

Bowra, C. M. *Ancient Greek Literature.* New York: Oxford University Press, 1960.

Bowra, C. M. *Landmarks in Greek Literature.* London: Weidenfeld & Nicolson, 1966.

Flacelière, R. *A Literary History of Greece.* Chicago: Aldine, 1964.

Hadas, M. *A History of Greek Literature*. New York: Columbia University Press, 1950.

Lesky, A. *A History of Greek Literature*. New York: Crowell, 1966.

Rose, H. J. *A Handbook of Greek Literature*. London: Methuen, 1964.

## ROMAN LITERATURE

Bieler, L. *History of Roman Literature*. London: Macmillan, 1966.

Copley, F. *Latin Literature*. Ann Arbor: University of Michigan Press, 1969.

Duff, J. W. *The Literary History of Rome. From the Origins to the Close of the Golden Age*. 3rd Ed. by A. M. Duff. New York: Barnes & Noble, 1963.

Duff, J. W. *A Literary History of Rome in the Silver Age from Tiberius to Hadrian*. Rev. Ed. by A. M. Duff. New York: Barnes & Noble, 1960.

Grant, M. *Latin Literature*. New Ed. Harmondsworth: Penguin, 1958.

Hadas, M. *A History of Latin Literature*. New York: Columbia University Press, 1952.

Rose, H. J. *A Handbook of Latin Literature*. 5th Ed. London: Methuen, 1966.

## GREEK AND ROMAN RELIGION

Altheim, F. *A History of Roman Religion*. London: Methuen, 1938.

Bailey. C. *Phases in the Religion of Ancient Rome*. Berkeley: University of California Press, 1932.

Carter, J. B. *The Religious Life of Ancient Rome*. Boston: Houghton, Mifflin, 1911.

Cumont, F. *After Life in Roman Paganism*. New Haven: Yale, 1923.

Cumont, F. *Oriental Religions in Roman Paganism*. Chicago: Open Court, 1911.

Fowler, W. W. *The Religious Experience of the Roman People*. London: Macmillan, 1922.

Grant, F. C. *Ancient Roman Religion*. New York: Liberal Arts, 1957.

Murray, G. *Five Stages of Greek Religion*. 3rd Ed. Boston: Houghton, Mifflin, 1952.

Nilsson, M. P. *A History of Greek Religion*. 2nd Ed. Oxford: Clarendon Press, 1949.

Rose, H. J. *Ancient Greek Religion*. London: Hutchinson, 1950.

Rose, H. J. *Ancient Roman Religion*. London: Hutchinson, 1948.

## GREEK AND ROMAN POLITICAL LIFE

Abbott, F. F. *Roman Politics*. Boston: Marshall Jones, 1923.

Abbott, F. F. *Society and Politics in Ancient Rome*. New York: Scribner, 1909.

Adcock, F. E. *Roman Political Ideas and Practice*. Ann Arbor: University of Michigan Press, 1959.

Greenidge, A. H. J. *A Handbook of Greek Constitutional History*. London: Macmillan, 1896.

Greenidge, A. H. J. *Roman Public Life*. London: Macmillan, 1901.

Homo, L. P. *Roman Political Institutions from City to State*. New York: Knopf, 1929.

Stevenson, G. H. *Roman Provincial Administration*. Oxford: Blackwell, 1939.

## GREEK AND ROMAN PRIVATE LIFE

Carcopino, J. *Daily Life in Ancient Rome: the People and the City at the Height of the Empire*. New Haven: Yale, 1940.

Cowell, F. R. *Everyday Life in Ancient Rome*. 2nd Ed. London: Batsford, 1962.

Fowler, W. W. *Social Life at Rome in the Age of Cicero*. New York: Macmillan, 1909.

Gulick, C. B. *The Life of the Ancient Greeks*. New York: Appleton, 1902.

Johnston, M. *Roman Life*. Chicago: Scott Foresman, 1957.

McDaniel, W. B. *Roman Private Life and its Survivals*. Boston: Marshall Jones, 1924.

Robinson, C. E. *Everyday Life in Ancient Greece*. Oxford: Clarendon Press, 1933.

Webster, T. B. L. *Everyday Life in Classical Athens*. London: Batsford, 1969.

# INDEX